Materi

Beyond Romantic Bodies,

Romantic Reconfigurations:
Studies in Literature and Culture 1780–1850

Series Editors:
Professor Tim Fulford, De Montfort University
Professor Alan Vardy, Hunter College and the Graduate Center, CUNY

As befits a series published in the city of Roscoe and Rushton, a city that linked Britain to the transatlantic trade in cotton, in sugar, and in people, *Romantic Reconfigurations* reconfigures the literary and cultural geographies and histories of Romanticism. Topics featured include, but are by no means confined to, provincial and labouring-class writing, diasporic and colonial writing, natural history and other scientific discourse, journalism, popular culture, music and theatre, landscape and nature, cosmopolitanism and travel, poetics and form.

Material Transgressions

Beyond Romantic Bodies, Genders, Things

Edited by
Kate Singer, Ashley Cross, and Suzanne L. Barnett

LIVERPOOL UNIVERSITY PRESS

First published 2020 by
Liverpool University Press
4 Cambridge Street
Liverpool
L69 7ZU

This paperback edition published 2023

British Library Cataloguing-in-Publication data
A British Library CIP record is available

ISBN 978-1-78962-177-8 cased
ISBN 978-1-80207-836-7 paperback

Typeset by Carnegie Book Production, Lancaster
Printed and bound by CPI Group (UK) Ltd, Croydon CR0 4YY

Contents

Figures

Contributors

Suzanne L. Barnett is the author of *Romantic Paganism: The Politics of Ecstasy in the Shelley Circle* (Palgrave Macmillan, 2018) as well as essays in the collections *Frankenstein and Its Classics: The Modern Prometheus from Antiquity to Science Fiction* (Bloomsbury Academic, 2018), *Keats's Negative Capability: New Origins and Afterlives* (Liverpool University Press, 2019), and the *Oxford Handbook of Romantic Prose* (Oxford University Press, 2021). Her articles have also appeared in *Essays in Romanticism*, the *Keats-Shelley Journal*, *Romantic Circles*, the *Keats Letters Project*, and *PMLA*. She is an associate editor of *Romantic Circles Reviews & Receptions* and the co-editor of an ongoing series of digital editions of William Godwin's Juvenile Library texts for *Romantic Circles*.

Ashley Cross is Professor of English at Manhattan College in the Bronx. Her monograph, *Mary Robinson and the Genesis of Romanticism: Literary Dialogues and Debts, 1784–1821*, was published by Routledge in 2017. Her articles on the Shelleys, Mary Robinson, Coleridge, Aphra Behn, Robert Southey, Anna Seward, and Charlotte Dacre have been published in *ELH, Women's Writing, Studies in Romanticism, European Romantic Review, Rylands Library Bulletin, Wordsworth Circle, MLA Approaches to Teaching,* Thomson/Gale's *British Writers Supplement*, and Beth Lau's *Fellow Romantics: Male and Female Romantic Writers in Dialogue*. She is currently working on a monograph tentatively titled *Love Matter(s), 1789–1832*.

Emily J. Dolive is a postdoctoral fellow at Baylor University in Waco, Texas. She received her M.A. in Literature from the University of New Hampshire and her Ph.D. from the University of North Carolina at Greensboro. Her dissertation and book project examine how women poets navigated and reshaped the literary marketplace during the French Revolution and Napoleonic Wars. This work reveals the intersections of war, gender, and prosody. Currently, she is writing an article on war elegies by Mary Robinson, Felicia Hemans, and Jane Alice Sargant.

Holly Gallagher is a Lecturer of Science Writing at the University of Georgia. She recently defended her Ph.D. dissertation, 'Why Always Cleopatra: Gender, Affect, and National Identity in Nineteenth-Century Spaces of Art', and completed a Women's Studies Graduate Certificate at the University of Georgia. In her dissertation, she looks at images of Cleopatra as case studies to show how art spaces in nineteenth-century literary works are places where shared perceptions of art often involve lessons of emotional expression and affective response. She has also worked in curation for the Modern and Contemporary Art Department at the Baltimore Museum of Art.

Michael Gamer is Professor of English and Comparative Literature at the University of Pennsylvania and British Academy Global Professor at Queen Mary University, London. He is author of *Romanticism, Self-Canonization, and the Business of Poetry* (Cambridge University Press, 2017) and *Romanticism and the Gothic: Genre, Reception, and Canon Formation* (Cambridge University Press, 2000). As part of the Multigraph Collective, he also helped write *Interacting with Print: Modes of Reading in the Age of Print Saturation, 1700–1900* (University of Chicago Press, 2018). He is currently at work on an edition of the works of Ann Radcliffe and a monograph, the working title of which is *Romantic Melodrama: Feeling in Search of Form*.

Jillian Heydt-Stevenson is Associate Professor of English at the University of Colorado, Boulder and has published on narrative theory, fashion, cosmopolitanism, ruins, landscape architecture, visual culture, travel narratives, gender, and literature and film. Heydt-Stevenson is the author of *Austen's Unbecoming Conjunctions: Subversive Laughter, Embodied History* (Palgrave, 2005); she co-edited *Recognizing the Romantic Novel: New Histories of British Fiction, 1780–1830* (with Charlotte Sussman; Liverpool University Press, 2008); and she is associate editor of Wordsworth's *Last Poems: 1821–1850* (with Jared Curtis; Cornell University Press, 1999). She recently completed *Radiant Matters: Connecting Things in 18th- and 19th-Century French and British Literature* and is currently writing a book-length study tentatively entitled *Palmyra and London: Cultural Interactions between the East and the West, 1753–1853*.

Sonia Hofkosh is Associate Professor of English at Tufts University, where she teaches courses in British Romanticism, feminist science fiction, feminist theory, and material and visual culture. The author of *Sexual Politics and the Romantic Author* (Cambridge University Press, 1998) and co-editor, with Alan Richardson, of *Romanticism, Race, and Imperial Culture, 1780–1834* (Indiana University Press, 1996), she has published on various topics, including women's magazines, Jane Austen, Anna Barbauld's poetics of the everyday, and early photography. She recently edited the *Romantic Circles Praxis* volume, 'Mary Wollstonecraft Even Now' and is working on a book about artifactuality in Romantic formulations of the subject.

Harriet Kramer Linkin is Emerita Distinguished Professor of English at New Mexico State University. She has published widely on Romantic-era writers (particularly William Blake and Mary Tighe) and is the editor of *The Collected Letters of Mary Blachford Tighe* (Lehigh University Press, 2020), the first edition of *Mary Tighe's Verses Transcribed for H.T.* (*Romantic Circles*, 2014), the first edition of *Mary Tighe's Selena: A Scholarly Edition* (Ashgate, 2012), the first scholarly edition of *The Collected Poems and Journals of Mary Tighe* (University Press of Kentucky, 2005) and the co-editor (with Stephen C. Behrendt) of two collections on Romantic women poets: *Romanticism and Women Poets: Opening the Doors of Reception* (University Press of Kentucky, 1999) and *Approaches to Teaching Women Poets of the British Romantic Period* (MLA, 1997).

Mark Lounibos is Associate Professor of English at Finlandia University in Michigan's Upper Peninsula. He has published work on the intersection of political and religious dissent in both early and second-generation British Romanticism and has recently contributed to the new digital edition of *The Cambridge Guide to the Eighteenth-Century Novel 1660–1820*. As a professor at a small teaching college, he also works on the relationship between class and contemporary undergraduate composition pedagogy. His current literary studies research focuses on ecological thought, particularly new materialist questions, in both the British Jacobin and anti-Jacobin novel.

Mark Lussier is Professor of English and Senior Sustainability Scholar at Arizona State University. His publications include *Romantic Dynamics: The Poetics of Physicality* (Palgrave Macmillan, 1999), *Romanticism and Buddhism* (*Romantic Circles Praxis Series*, 2006) *Engaged Romanticism: Romanticism as Praxis* (Cambridge Scholars Publishing, 2008), and *Romantic Dharma: The Emergence of Buddhism into Nineteenth-Century Europe* (Palgrave Macmillan, 2011). His essays have appeared in numerous collections and journals, including *Arts Quarterly, Blake 2.0, Blake: An Illustrated Quarterly, Interrogating*

Orientalism, *Ecological Theory*, *Italian Culture*, *Literature Compass*, *Literature and Religion*, *Nineteenth-Century Contexts*, *Palgrave Advances: William Blake Studies*, *Romanticism and the City*, *Romanticism on the Net*, *Studies in Romanticism*, *Visible Language*, *Women's Studies*, and *The Wordsworth Circle*. During his tenure at ASU, he has won numerous teaching awards, including special recognition from the ASU Parents Professor of the Year program and the Distinguished Faculty Teaching Award from the College of Liberal Arts and Sciences.

Katrina O'Loughlin is Lecturer in English (Romantic and Nineteenth-Century Literature) at the University of Brunel London and, prior to that, an Australian Discovery Early Career Research (DECRA) Fellow at the University of Western Australia (2015–18). She has published on eighteenth- and nineteenth-century women writers; travel, encounter, and exchange; and the history of emotion, including *Women, Writing, and Travel in the Eighteenth Century* (Cambridge University Press, 2018). Research for this chapter, 'Affect in the Margins: Marking Readers in the Elegiac Sonnets', was supported by the Australian Research Council (DE150101612: 'A republic of feeling').

Donelle Ruwe, Professor and Chair of English, Northern Arizona University, is the author of *British Children's Poetry in the Romantic Era: Verse, Riddle, and Rhyme* (Palgrave Macmillan, 2014), the editor of a collection of essays, *Culturing the Child 1660–1830* (Scarecrow, 2005), and co-editor of *Children, Childhood, and Musical Theater* (Routledge, 2020). She has published numerous scholarly articles on children's literature, Romantic poetics, and women writers in journals such as *Writing Women*, *Eighteenth-Century Life*, *The Lion and the Unicorn*, *The English Journal*, *Children's Literature*, and *Nineteenth-Century Contexts*. Ruwe is co-president of the 18th- and 19th-Century British Women Writers Association and has received numerous awards for her poetry, including the Camber Press Prize for her chapbook *Another Message You Miss the Point of*.

David Sigler is Associate Professor of English, University of Calgary, and the author of *Sexual Enjoyment in British Romanticism* (McGill-Queen's University Press, 2015), co-editor of *Lacan and Romanticism* (SUNY Press, 2019), and editor of *British Women and War, 1660–1835* (Routledge, 2019), a volume in the Routledge History of Feminism series. His work on British Romanticism has appeared in journals such as *Rhizomes*, *Litteraria Pragensia*, and *Women's Writing*, and in edited collections such as *Jane Austen and Comedy* (Bucknell University Press, 2019) and *Keats's Negative Capability: New Origins and Afterlives* (Liverpool University Press, 2019).

Kate Singer is Associate Professor of English and Chair of the Critical Social Thought program at Mount Holyoke College and author of *Romantic Vacancy: The Poetics of Gender, Affect, and Radical Speculation* (SUNY Press, 2019). She has published essays on Percy Shelley, Maria Jane Jewsbury, Letitia Landon, and Mary Robinson in *Studies in Romanticism*, *European Romantic Review*, *Romantic Circles*, *Pedagogy*, and *Literature Compass*. She has also had essays appear in *Jane Austen and Sciences of the Mind* (Routledge, 2017), *Romanticism and Speculative Realism* (Bloomsbury, 2019), with another in *Romantic Automata: Exhibits, Figures, and Organisms* (Bucknell University Press, 2020). She co-edits the Pedagogies section of *Romantic Circles*, including the journal *Romantic Pedagogy Commons*. She is currently working on a project exploring Romanticism, critical theory, tropes of shapeshifting, and notions of ontological change.

Mary Beth Tegan is Professor of English at Saint Xavier University and specializes in nineteenth-century British literature and women's narrative. Publishing most recently in *The Eighteenth Century: Theory and Interpretation*, *Women's Writing*, and *Persuasions*, Tegan writes on female novelists' management of literary affect. She is currently working on a monograph titled *Vanity's Heirs: Popular Romance and the Reproduction of Women Writers*, which pursues questions raised by the persistent links between vanity, imitation, and popular romance reading made in literary reviews and conduct literature of the late eighteenth and nineteenth centuries.

Chris Washington is Assistant Professor of English at Francis Marion University. The University of Toronto Press published his monograph, *Romantic Revelations: Visions of Post-Apocalyptic Hope and Life in the Anthropocene*, in September 2019. With Anne McCarthy he is co-editor of the collection *Romanticism and Speculative Realism* (Bloomsbury, 2019). He has published essays in *Romantic Circles Praxis*, *The Keats-Shelley Journal*, *Essays in Romanticism*, *European Romantic Review*, *Romantic Circles Pedagogy Commons*, and *Literature Compass*. He is also the editor of the forthcoming volume of essays, *Teaching Romanticism in the Anthropocene* for *Romantic Circles Pedagogy Commons*. He is currently working on a monograph, *#OccupyRomanticism: Revolutionary Climate Protest from Then to Now* and, with Kate Singer, another book, *Intersex Intertexts*.

Introduction

Living in a New Material World

Kate Singer, Ashley Cross, and Suzanne L. Barnett

In one of the most materially destructive scenes within Romantic texts, *Frankenstein*'s Victor thinks 'with a sensation of madness on [his] promise of creating another like' the first creature and, 'trembling with passion, tore to pieces the thing on which [he] was engaged' (III.3 par. 4).[1] Despite his patient collection of the materials necessary to build the female creature, when he contemplates her potential budding subjectivity, Victor tears her apart before she ever achieves subject status. The intense violence of this scene, its viscerality, seems to imply that Victor, knowingly or not, destroys a living being. Here, Victor refuses to see his own materiality—or his interconnectedness with the various forms of matter around him—and this denial reproduces its own lacuna as he tears the female creature to bits. Set amid the rich material flux of the tides, trade winds, and coastal ecology of the Orkney islands, however, this moment of decomposition perversely reveals the rampant and fluid materialities already circulating through the text. When the female creature is released from her feminine body into the capacious sea, she becomes once again a 'thing' of vibrant matter. Shelley both acknowledges and sets aside the cultural constructions of the new creature as female and sexually dangerous when she highlights the interplay of matter: Victor's hands, his trembling and fainting body, the torn parts of the new creature, the sepulchral earth, the landscape, the seascape, and all the clouds in the sky. As these materials intermix, Shelley subtly introduces us to a new materiality—the dynamic interplay among substance, form, and

[1] Mary Shelley, *Frankenstein; or, the Modern Prometheus*, 3 vols. (London: Lackington, Hughes, Harding, Mavor, and Jones, 1818; Henry Colburn and Richard Bentley, 1831), A *Romantic Circles* Electronic Edition, ed. Stuart Curran, 2009, at https://www.rc.umd.edu/editions/frankenstein.

affect—that challenges the stable matter underwriting Enlightenment ideas of the subject, gender, and the body. Such transgressive materiality, more ubiquitous in Romantic texts than we have previously realized, informs this collection and offers the possibility to redraw genders, bodies, things, and texts outside cultural narratives that would insist on their static categorization as discrete bodies with reified identities, as either subjects or objects.

We offer this reading as complement to and as entanglement with interpretations furnished by poststructuralists and new historicists who view the destruction of the female creature as a masculine, ideological antagonism toward the independent feminine subject—or even the imagination of her very possibility. Victor's fantasy of the female creature's sexual life, in those readings, manifests a well-known eighteenth-century ideological narrative about gender: that woman, if she were to become a 'thinking and reasoning' being, would destroy humanity with her perverse knowledge and her impassioned desires. At this crucial moment, Shelley does not simply show that women are the victims of men's imaginings, a narrative that would replay the cultural turn's critique of ideologies that shape gender, bodies, and women's writing; nor does she rehearse the vexed materiality of the female body. Rather, the material disruption that occurs when Victor reanimates the female creature as 'thing'—matter—ironically exacts another level of violence and destroys the cultural narrative itself.

The female creature's 'thing-power' does threaten humanity but not through her voracious desire to propagate her own species, as Victor imagines.[2] Her destruction ensures the male creature cannot reproduce heteronormatively and guarantees his existential and ontological loneliness, simultaneously aborting Victor's courtship narrative as well. The abrupt end of these heteronormative narratives catapults the creature and Victor into the territory of posthuman ambiguity and decenters humanity as the only bodies and subjects that matter. Where the cultural critique can only leave behind a wake of destructive options—Victor either has to destroy the female creature or she comes into being as a duly feminine subject—the new materialist reading steps out of these binary options of human/nonhuman, male/female, subject/object to offer a more fluid ontology of being that underlies the more rigid social scripts. Neither subject nor object, the female creature's vibrant matter elicits a confluence of agential materialities that Victor's anthropocentric, first-person perspective elides: Victor's and the creature's affects, the body parts dead and alive, the scientific apparatus, the rugged rocks, and the movement and sounds of the ocean waves, to list only a few.[3]

[2] Jane Bennett, *Vibrant Matter: A Political Ecology of Things* (Durham, NC: Duke University Press, 2010), p. 22.

[3] Bennett calls 'the federation of actants' that make up an assemblage a 'creature that the concept of moral responsibility fits only loosely and to which the charge of blame will

In the moments directly following the female creature's violent dismembering, we see an incipient sense of this new materiality in Victor's relationship to the sea. Each moment Victor interacts with the sea—immediately after the female creature's destruction, after the creature departs, and after Victor throws the body parts overboard—he lets the sea's motion wash over him, moving out of himself. Gazing at the sea, he 'felt the silence, although [he] was hardly conscious of its extreme profundity', and he absorbs the sea's stillness (III.3 par. 6). Victor's intra-connectedness manifests as a desire 'to pass [his] life on that barren rock'; while he actually becomes entangled with the landscape, he mistakenly imagines himself in isolation and the sea as 'an insuperable barrier between [him] and [his] fellow-creatures' (III.3 par. 20). But Victor's separation from these fellow-creatures exists only if he returns to the cultural narratives that drove him to destroy the female creature in the first place, narratives that create an 'insuperable barrier' between human and nonhuman. By contrast, the sea's 'agreeable sensations' offer an alternative. When Victor turns away from the sea, he feels 'like he belonged to a race of human beings' (III.3 par. 20) and thus fully reasserts the Enlightenment narrative of Eurocentric male dominance that will destroy both him and the creature in volume III. At the end of the novel, however, the creature registers his possibility as new materiality when he plans his own death on the 'funeral pile'. As he is 'lost in distance and darkness', his being and our perspective of him merge with the vast arctic matter, 'lost amidst the waves' (III.3 par. 17) that surround him.

When we unearth such matter(s) in these familiar scenes, we can reread in this novel (and in many other Romantic texts) the transgressive materiality already moving—and in fact never really buried—through their own dynamic parts. As our reading of *Frankenstein* suggests, Shelley and other Romantic writers not only pursue ideology critique but also explore alternative understandings of materiality as fluid, unstable, and affective, understandings that move beyond concepts that fix gendered bodies and intellectual capacities, whether human or textual.[4] Such materialities we define as transgressive, in the sense that they move beyond prescribed limits, stepping across or removing a distance between, breaking, violating, infringing, contravening, trespassing, exceeding those boundaries never really created but already intra-mingling their own dynamic parts. 'Passing beyond some limit', as the *OED* terms it, a transgression deftly dissolves perceived boundaries between bodies or between the notions of ideas and things. Romantic texts are particularly expressive of

not quite stick' (p. 28). We could read the creature's body as an assemblage of parts, but more expansively the creature instigates an assemblage with all the other forms and fields of matter around him.

[4] Take as representative contemporary examples of such fixity the works of Jean-Jacques Rousseau, Edmund Burke, Johann Kaspar Lavatar, and Hannah More.

this traversal of boundaries: the Romantic fragment poem, the tendency for authors such as Charlotte Smith and William Wordsworth to reissue, revise, and repackage their projects, and the fluid conversations between text and image, page and stage, textuality and orality that have been so well documented by Blakeans, scholars of balladry, and others. Yet another transgression occurs within texts whose materiality alters as they off-gas affects that promise (or threaten) to change the very materiality of the bodies that read, carry, and feel them. When bodies morph, so does the notion of binary sex and gender that has traditionally adhered to those bodies, and this morphing exposes models beyond a two-sex system. In this volume, the idea of transgression serves as a flexible and capacious discursive and material movement that braids together fluid forms of affect, embodiment, and textual materialities.

Even Mary Wollstonecraft, arguably the mother of Romantic gender critique, both interrogates how Enlightenment language and discourse operate on gendered subjects and explores these shifting bodies. From her metaphors of pollution in *A Vindication of the Rights of Woman* (1792) to her consideration of women as animals, she poses radical notions of the unsex'd, non-gendered, flexible body that move beyond her much-cited critique of binary gender performances. When Samuel Taylor Coleridge depicts the 'delicious surges' of the titular instrument in 'The Eolian Harp' (1796), he describes the transmission of affect as vibrations and particles moving through the air, through the harp strings, and along the heart-strings of 'this subject Lute'. Charlotte Smith's *Elegiac Sonnets* (1784) may be the most powerful example of a textual body that changes over time, as Smith adds to and alters its successive editions and their affects into an undulating, sea-borne entity that pervades her speakers, her landscapes, and her readers. In Smith's volume, we can see something endemic to other writers: that her language has its own materiality, a tributary to other forms and movements that are not divided from objects and bodies. Such examples suggest that these and other Romantic writers experiment seriously with dominant metaphysical, ontological, and epistemological understandings of their time that saw matter as fixed, experiments that dramatically expand our current historicist and linguistic approaches to genders and bodies.

Prescient intimations of new materialist models, particularly as they circulate around gender, appear as early as Jerome McGann's *The Poetics of Sensibility* (1996), though McGann does not label them as such. He describes Coleridge's 'The Eolian Harp', for example, 'as a non-conscious tool for revealing the vital correspondences that pour through the material world', emphasizing how the poet moves beyond Hartleyan materialism to conceptualize 'the corporeality of thought' as 'emotion'.[5] As McGann later comments

[5] Jerome McGann, *The Poetics of Sensibility: A Revolution in Literary Style* (Oxford: Oxford University Press, 1996), p. 21.

on Asia's revelation in *Prometheus Unbound* (1820), Percy Shelley depicts the hydrogen cycle, love, life, and the coming of dawn as 'the energetic translation of all of these terms into and out of each other' in ways that seem to us to veer toward Jane Bennett's confabulation of 'energy as matter' (McGann, p. 134; Bennett, p. 20). Ashley Cross extends this discussion of Coleridge to Mary Robinson's dialogue with him, a shared poetics that 'represent[s] a poetry of intense, sympathetic, and spontaneous responsiveness to nature and to the other'. Robinson's fluid corporeality becomes amplified through one of her most ardent interlocutors, Charlotte Dacre, who, as Cross explains, 'is intent on disrupting the opposition between body and spirit'.[6] Adriana Craciun has also shown how Dacre's demon lovers and revenants reveal 'the radical potential of all *bodies*, not just selves, to lose cohesion, organization, and even materiality as it is usually understood (as a naturally occurring, fixed state), and to perform material transformations'.[7]

Recent work on Romanticism and affect theory has likewise touched on new materialities that cross mind and world, especially Mary Favret's discussion of climate as a figure for poetic mood (and vice versa) that draws from Kevis Goodman's formulation of the georgic as a mode that crosses words and things.[8] As Favret writes, poetry can become a figure for affect, 'a global system of exchange … moving over local and national borders', a system of shifting materiality that 'no one individual could perceive' (p. 131). While Favret and Goodman work through new developments in media and in climate that disperse affects, Marjorie Levinson has resurrected Spinoza's unique form of embodied affect through the aegis of Wordsworth.[9] In her reading of 'A slumber did my spirit seal', Lucy's body affects and is affected by the other bodies around it even as it literally becomes the 'rocks and stones and trees' at the poem's end, fusing human and nonhuman into an affective and embodied ecology of transmission, change, and response.[10] This sense of fluidity and interoperability

[6] Ashley Cross, *Mary Robinson and the Genesis of Romanticism: Literary Dialogues and Debts, 1784–1821* (New York: Routledge, 2017), pp. 37, 202.

[7] Adrian Craciun, *Fatal Women of Romanticism* (Cambridge: Cambridge University Press, 2003), p. 118.

[8] See Mary Favret, *War at a Distance: Romanticism and the Making of Modern Wartime* (Princeton, NJ: Princeton University Press, 2009), especially pp. 131–42; Kevis Goodman, *Georgic Modernity and British Romanticism: Poetry and the Mediation of History* (Cambridge: Cambridge University Press, 2004), p. 11.

[9] Marjorie Levinson, 'A Motion and A Spirit: Romancing Spinoza', *Studies in Romanticism*, 46: 4 (Winter 2007), pp. 367–408.

[10] Other important works on Romanticism and affect that, in various ways, touch upon embodiment and subjectivity include Thomas Pfau's *Romantic Moods: Paranoia, Trauma, and Melancholy, 1790–1840* (Baltimore, MD: Johns Hopkins University Press, 2005); Richard Sha and Joel Faflak's *Romanticism and the Emotions* (Cambridge: Cambridge University Press, 2014); Steven Goldsmith's *Blake's Agitation: Criticism and the Emotions*

of matter coalesces in Kate Singer's essay on Charlotte Smith's new materialism, where particulate, fluid materiality of oceanic waves, coastal winds, and poetic voice confabulate a nonhuman affect that moves in and among bodies.[11]

Romantic deconstructionists (such as those collected in *Material Events* and *Romantic Materialities*) have attended to the matter of the world outside (or alongside) the human subject. They reconsider Paul de Man's notions of materiality not as material referents but as a more ineffable force, or 'materiality without matter', as Jacques Derrida terms it.[12] This volume pursues the deconstructionist move from the subject to the materiality of language and also tangles with speculative realist approaches in order to think about other forms of nonhuman or posthuman materiality not subjugated to human exceptionalism. Romanticists moving well past the subject consider the objective world as they grapple with speculative realism, object-oriented ontology (OOO), and their implications for ecology and the Anthropocene, including Mary Jacobus's *Romantic Things*, Evan Gottlieb's *Romantic Realities: Speculative Realism and British Romanticism*, Chris Washington's *Romantic Revelations: Visions of Post-Apocalyptic Life and Hope in the Anthropocene*, and Washington's and Anne C. McCarthy's *Romanticism and Speculative Realism*.[13] Such readings attend to objects long overlooked due to our obsession with Romantic subjectivity. For example, Gottlieb's chapter on Keats recognizes new materiality in the undigested puddings and creams of Porphyro's banquet in Keats's 'The Eve of St. Agnes'. Gottlieb sees them as vibrantly undigested objects 'unassimilated to purely human devices and desires' (p. 205). Even earlier, Sara Guyer's and Celeste Langan's introduction to *Romantic Materialities* emphasizes thing theory, and their volume grapples with materiality and ideality, with things as

(Baltimore, MD: Johns Hopkins University Press, 2013); Miranda Burgess, 'On Being Moved: Sympathy, Mobility, and Narrative Form', *Poetics Today*, 32: 2 (2011), pp. 289–321.

[11] Kate Singer, 'Limpid Waves and Good Vibrations: Charlotte Smith's New Materialist Affect', *Essays in Romanticism*, 23: 2 (2016), p. 92; and *Romantic Vacancy: The Poetics of Gender, Affect, and Radical Speculation* (Albany, NY: SUNY Press, 2019).

[12] Jacques Derrida, 'Typewriter Ribbon', in *Material Events: Paul de Man and the Afterlife of Theory*, eds. Tom Cohen, Barbara Cohen, J. Hillis Miller, and Andrzej Warminski (Minneapolis: University of Minnesota Press, 2000), p. 350.

[13] Adam Potkay, 'Wordsworth and the Ethics of Things', *PMLA*, 123: 2 (March 2008), pp. 390–404; K. Boehm, ed., *Bodies and Things in Nineteenth-Century Literature and Culture* (New York: Palgrave, 2012); Mary Jacobus, *Romantic Things: A Tree, a Rock, a Cloud* (Chicago, IL: University of Chicago Press, 2012); Sara Guyer and Celeste Langan, eds., *Romantic Materialities*, *Romantic Circles* Praxis Series (February 2015), at https://romantic-circles.org/praxis/materialities/index.html; Evan Gottlieb, *Romantic Realities: Speculative Realism and British Romanticism* (Edinburgh: Edinburgh University Press, 2016); Chris Washington, *Romantic Revelations: Visions of Post-Apocalyptic Life and Hope in the Anthropocene* (Toronto: University of Toronto Press, 2019); and Chris Washington and Anne C. McCarthy, *Romanticism and Speculative Realism* (London: Bloomsbury, 2019).

they are and things as they might be. Nonetheless, some of these materialist approaches retain a split between subject and object, material and language, thing and human. As Rebekah Sheldon has recently argued, even new materialists such as Bennett and Karen Barad often retain discrete objects as the point of analysis rather than understanding them in material flux within a series of human and nonhuman agential relations.[14] The essays in this volume seek to redress such distinctions. Romanticism's special attention to notions of change within nature, politics, industry, and language, these essays show, make it especially fertile ground to transgress notions of the discrete object and formulate something more choratic, fluid, and playful.

Other scholars have taken strides to understand how Romantic-era writers see the world not as a series of objects, not as an exchange between human and nonhuman, subject and object, but as a web of affects, material threads, and texts. Sonia Hofkosh and Michael Gamer have repeatedly drawn our attention to texts as revisionary things, Hofkosh to the text's somatic touch and Gamer to the near-neurotic Romantic tendency of authors to repackage their editions, which themselves become things in flux.[15] Amanda Jo Goldstein has detailed a Lucretian materiality inherent in much Romantic-era writing and in a science that begins to trace the swerves of atomic matter and opens us to the quantum rhythms and physics that Mark Lussier and Arkady Plotnitsky have located in Percy Shelley's works. As Lussier reminds us, Romantic-era understandings of physics, chemistry, biology, and rhythm attain a syncretic, philosophical complexity and fluidity.[16]

Building on such syncretic understandings, *Material Transgressions* thinks outside of Romantic and theoretical ideologies that reiterate notions of sexed bodies, embodied subjectivities, isolated things, or stable texts. The essays in this collection examine how Romantic writers rethink materiality, especially the subject–object relationship, in order to challenge the tenets of the Enlightenment and the culture of sensibility that privileged the hegemony of the speaking and feeling lyric subject. In doing so, they reimagine the gendered thinking and materialities that defined women and men as being at the mercy of biologically sexed bodies, discrete texts, or mind/body binaries. The writers addressed by

[14] Rebekah Sheldon, 'Form/Matter/Chora: Object-Oriented Ontology and Feminist New Materialism', in *The Nonhuman Turn*, ed. Richard Grusin (Minneapolis: University of Minnesota Press, 2015), pp. 193–222.

[15] Sonia Hofkosh, 'What Wordsworth Touched', in *Romantic Materialities*; Michael Gamer, *Romanticism, Self-Canonization, and the Business of Poetry* (Cambridge: Cambridge University Press, 2017).

[16] Amanda Jo Goldstein, *Sweet Science: Romantic Materialism and the New Logics of Life* (Chicago: University of Chicago Press, 2017); Mark Lussier, *Romantic Dynamics: The Poetics of Physicality* (Basingstoke: Macmillan, 2000); Arkady Plotnitsky, 'All Shapes of Light: The Quantum Mechanical Shelley,' in *Shelley: Poet and Legislator of the World*, eds. Betty Bennett and Stuart Curran (Baltimore: Johns Hopkins University Press, 1995), pp. 263–74.

this collection engage with other important concerns of British Romanticism—including genres, nature, material culture, textuality, and performance—in order to undo supposedly invariable matter, and representations of it, that limited their writing, agency, knowledge, and even being. The processes these texts enact—assemblages, ghost dances, pack mentality, reiterative writing, shapeshifting, multi-voiced choric oralities—redefine restrictive structures in order to craft alternative modes of being in the world. These materialist transgressions help us to reimagine how materiality can be understood both in the Romantic period and now. Such dynamism not only reveals a new materialist imaginary for Romanticism but also unveils textualities, affects, figurations, and linguistic movements that alter new materialism's often strictly ontological approach. Texts and figures, when put into motion by Romantic authors, become exceptionally flexible and adroit in reshaping materialities as we know them.

Towards a Romantic Materiality

Material Transgressions seeks to shift focus from cultural materialism—which sees matter as static, stable ground—to materiality, which traces movement, relations, and changeability. Although Romanticism has sometimes been aligned with idealism (given its philosophical associations with Immanuel Kant, Friedrich Schlegel, and Friedrich Hegel and its identification with the Wordsworth circle), it has also been associated with the materialism of Coleridge and Percy Shelley, who were influenced by David Hartley and David Hume in their early years but later sought less mechanistic and determinative philosophies. There is also a long record of materialist approaches to Romantic literature, from more narrowly-defined Marxist analyses like those of E.P. Thompson and Franco Morretti to older historicism like that of Carl Woodring and David Erdman, to the historical materialism that has come to dominate Romantic Studies following the early work of Raymond Williams, Levinson, McGann, and Marilyn Butler. The task of historical materialist Romanticism, to borrow Ellen Rooney's words on feminist materialism, has been 'to retrieve it from the linguistic idealism' of late twentieth-century critical discourse and to account for the material and historical circumstances that shaped texts and authors.[17] William Keach, for example, has attended carefully to the materiality of Romantic language, tracing how the 'arbitrary signs' so important to the linguistic turn not only remained physically grounded, but also had concrete effects shaped by gender, sexuality, class, and race.[18] Foucauldian readings of the Gothic, including Diane Hoeveler's

[17] Ellen Rooney, 'What Can the Matter Be?' *American Literary History*, 8: 4 (Winter, 1996), pp. 745–58, 748.

[18] William Keach, *Arbitrary Power: Romanticism, Language, Politics* (Princeton, NJ: Princeton University Press, 2004).

work, have foregrounded sexuality and gender as a matrix of power that reveals the tyranny over women and their bodies. Marjorie Levinson's brand of new historicism posited a 'deconstructive materialism' that could uncover a text's historically repressed content, whereas Clifford Siskin's analysis of the cultural production of Romantic discourse in *The Historicity of Romantic Discourse* finds an 'epistemic Romanticism that tends to swallow everything in its path' into a general cultural category constituted by the self-disciplining Romantic subject.[19] Scholars interested in the history of science, including Sharon Ruston and Tim Fulford, have tried to flesh out questions of materiality by attending to Romantic investments in physics, chemistry, geology, botany, and biology.[20] Romanticists have also sought to elaborate other forms of social engagement with notions of sociability, coterie publics, and developing forms of print and media culture.[21] Building a diverse and complex historical understanding of the Romantic period, such scholarship has provided powerful and increasingly subtle forms of historicized ideology critique.

[19] Marjorie Levinson, *Wordsworth's Great Period Poems* (Cambridge: Cambridge University Press, 1986); Clifford Siskin, *The Historicity of Romantic Discourse* (Oxford: Oxford University Press, 1988); Jon Klancher, 'English Romanticism and Cultural Production', in *The New Historicism*, ed. H. Aram Veeser (New York: Routledge, 1989, 2013), pp. 77–88, 81.

[20] See also Sharon Ruston, *Creating Romanticism: Case Studies in the Literature, Science, and Medicine of the 1790s* (New York: Palgrave, 2013); Tim Fulford, Debbie Lee, and Peter J. Kitson, *Literature, Science, and Exploration in the Romantic Era: Bodies of Knowledge* (Cambridge: Cambridge University Press, 2007); Alan Richardson, *British Romanticism and the Science of the Mind* (Cambridge: Cambridge University Press, 2001); Robert E. Mitchell, *Bioart and the Vitality of Media* (Seattle: University of Washington Press, 2010); Richard Sha, 'Toward a Physiology of the Romantic Imagination', *Configurations*, 17: 3 (Fall 2009), pp. 197–226. See also Janina Wellmann, *The Form of Becoming: Embryology and the Epistemology of Rhythm, 1760–1830* (Brooklyn, NY: Zone Books, 2017).

[21] See Jeffrey N. Cox, *Poetry and Politics in the Cockney School: Shelley, Keats, Hunt, and Their Circle* (Cambridge: Cambridge University Press, 1998); Clara Tuite and Gillian Russell, eds., *Romantic Sociability: Social Networks and Literary Culture in Britain, 1770–1840* (Cambridge: Cambridge University Press, 2006); Tim Fulford, *Romantic Poetry and Literary Coteries: The Dialect of the Tribe* (New York: Palgrave, 2015); Paul Magnuson, *Reading Public Romanticism* (Princeton, NJ: Princeton University Press, 1998); Jon Mee, *Conversable Worlds: Literature, Contention, and Community, 1762 to 1830* (Oxford: Oxford University Press, 2013); Andrew Burkett, *Romantic Mediations* (Albany, NY: SUNY Press, 2016); Celeste Langan, 'Telopathos: Medium Cool Romanticism', *Romanticism on the Net*, 41–2 (2006), at https://www.erudit.org/en/journals/ron/2006-n41–42-ron1276/013154ar/ and 'Understanding Media in 1805: Audiovisual Hallucination in "The Lay of the Last Minstrel"', *Studies in Romanticism*, 40: 1 (Spring 2001), pp. 49–70; Langan and Maureen N. McLane, 'The Medium of Romantic Poetry', in *Cambridge Companion to British Romantic Poetry*, eds. James Chandler and Maureen McLane (New York: Cambridge University Press, 2008), pp. 239–62; and Yohei Igarashi, *The Connected Condition: Romanticism and the Dream of Communication* (Palo Alto, CA: Stanford University Press, 2019).

For Romantic scholars interested in gender and sexuality, the gendered body has often been the starting point for such ideology critique. As with feminist materialist work more generally, such accounts have primarily focused on the material and historical realities that determine and construct ideologies of gender or examine the impact of those realities on sexed bodies. Often, however, in historicist analysis, the sexed body has remained an unquestioned term, a material ground that implicitly privileges nature over history. The essential work of recovering women writers and their texts itself has its own materialist agenda of unearthing the female corpus, as a long-standing metonym of the female authorial body. Even when writers have created cross-dressing characters, written under gender-swapped pseudonyms, or in other ways emphasized the performance of gender, the sexed body remains a privileged referent. To cite just one example, no matter how much Mary Robinson saw her authorial identity as performance, those textual performances were read, and continue to be read, against her sexed and sexualized, disabled body, despite—and often at the expense of—her attention to other matter(s).[22] If the performativity of gender dissociates gender and sex, it often, and perhaps inevitably, establishes such performance against bodily materiality and privileges linguistic construction as a means to overcome or reinflect that corporeality.

The valuable *Cambridge Companion to Women's Writing in the Romantic Period* (2015) provides a useful, recent example of feminist work in Romanticism that seeks to move beyond the act of recovery to equality and accuracy of representation through a 'thick description' of women's writing.[23] It registers the current temperature of scholarly work on women writers, which resides for the most part within a historicist matrix, and, even as it offers a wealth of critical knowledge on women's writing in the Romantic period, implicitly points to a need to think about materialism in new ways. These important essays, on the one hand, emphasize women writers' efforts to mediate eighteenth-century gender codes that formed their writing and their lives as authors; as Devoney Looser states in her preface, the essays focus on 'how gender shaped writing and reception' and seek to uncover 'the reach and implication of these gendered patterns in literary history'.[24] On the other hand, however, as much as the volume traces constructions of and interventions into gender ideology, through its affirmation of the 'women writers' designation, the volume privileges the female body as the marker of difference, even when gender is

[22] Kate Singer, 'Mary Robinson and the Idiot's Guide to Sensibility and Oblivion', *Literature Compass*, 12: 12 (December 2015), pp. 667–74.

[23] The term is Clifford Geertz's in *The Interpretation of Cultures* (New York: Basic Books, 1973).

[24] Devoney Looser, 'Preface', in *Cambridge Companion to Women's Writing in the Romantic Period*, ed. Devoney Looser (Cambridge: Cambridge University Press, 2015), pp. xiii–xviii, xvii, xvii.

read as performative. The binary remains in place, although with variations on either side, and more radical revisions of sexed bodies become, unintentionally, sidelined. To put this bluntly, the fight for the 'rights of woman'—for women's status as equal subjects—continues (and, of course, needs to continue) in new form. In such a framework, women writers (indeed, all writers who resist gender categories), then, have two primary options: either to reinforce or challenge the gender ideologies that shape their sexed bodies, to become subjects or to be objects.

Material Transgressions moves beyond potential (in)stabilities of gender toward the capacious dynamism of matter itself, thus moving away from previous investigations that have taken the materiality of sexual difference as the starting point for analysis. Indeed, this study revisits all these old materialisms, with their determinative understandings of history, matter, and temporality, in an attempt to think with more flexibility about how matter instead continually shapes, moves, and flows. Such a notion of materiality morphs history and temporality, too, in wonkier ways than we have previously felt or thought. What happens when the sexed body itself becomes part of a larger configuration of bodies, things, texts, and affects, not the primary marker of sexed identity? How might we rethink women's writing and Romantic writing more generally if we see humans as a material part of a material world, a world of texts, things, bodies, affects, that are all fluctuating and mobile? How, that is, did Romantic writers challenge the very ideas of materiality that underwrote the ideologies of discrete, sexed bodies and texts? To ask such questions is neither to undermine the brilliant feminist and historicist work that has been done (and without which this project could not have materialized); nor is it to argue that gender and sex are irrelevant. Instead, the essays in this collection not only continue to push beyond binaries of gender, but they also attempt to explode them through attention to other matter(s). While challenging gender binaries was more crucial for women writers of the period, these questions were also pursued by male writers interested in destabilizing gender and the material ground of the sexed body, as the inclusion of male authors in this volume attests.

Nor does a focus on such concerns require us to think ahistorically. Historical and cultural changes in the Romantic period, especially changes in thinking about gender and sexuality, print culture, and science, created a perfect storm for explorations of materiality and embodiment. Concepts of sexual embodiment were in flux at the end of the eighteenth century, as scientific views shifted from a single-sex anatomical model to a two-sex model, at the same time as sexual desire was being unhinged from sexed bodies.[25]

[25] On the history of sexuality in the eighteenth and early nineteenth centuries, see especially the work of Katherine Binhammer, 'The Sex Panic of the 1790s', *Journal of the*

However, the ideological power of the two-sex model often occluded these shiftings and solidified sexual difference, codifying a binary, biological dimorphism as the foundation of both embodiment and materiality. For much of the last decade of the twentieth century and the start of the twenty-first, Romantic studies replicated this binarism in pursuing masculine and feminine Romanticisms, following the argument of Anne K. Mellor's *Romanticism & Gender* (1993). Romantic scholarship, as we discuss in more detail below, has shifted away in recent years from its focus on the historically-constructed subject to think more transgressively about sexual embodiment: Emma Donaghue on Sapphic friendships; Adriana Craciun on the radical danger of the sexualized body; Susan Lanser on the sexuality of history and the Sapphic's formative role in modernity; Andrew Elfenbein on the homoerotics of Romantic Genius; Richard Sha on the sexual perversity of Romantic aesthetics; Jacqueline Labbe on Charlotte Smith's performativity and on women writers' de-gendering of landscape; Claudia Johnson on equivocal beings; Susan Wolfson on the borderlines of gender; and Judith Pascoe on Mary Robinson's (and William Wordsworth's) performative subjectivity.[26] As scholarship on the history of sexuality has begun to show, the Romantic period inhabits a liminal space that afforded a multiplicity of possible sexualities, from heteronormative domesticity to homosexual Sapphic and sodomitic love to other non-procreative modes, like masturbation and Sadean

History of Sexuality, 6: 3 (1996), pp. 409–34; Anna Clark, *Desire: A History of European Sexuality* (New York: Routledge, 2008); Susan Lanser, *The Sexuality of History: Modernity and the Sapphic, 1565–1830* (Chicago, IL: University of Chicago Press, 2014); Thomas Laqueur, *Making Sex* (Cambridge, MA: Harvard University Press, 1990); Roy Porter, *Flesh in the Age of Reason* (New York: W.W. Norton, 2003); Randolph Trumbach, 'The Transformation of Sodomy from the Renaissance to the Modern World and Its General Sexual Consequences', *Signs*, 37: 4 (2012), pp. 832–48, and *Sex and the Gender Revolution* (Chicago, IL: University of Chicago Press, 1998), vols. 1 and 2; *Sexual Knowledge, Sexual Science: The History of Attitudes to Sexuality*, eds. Roy Porter and Mikulas Teich (Cambridge: Cambridge University Press, 1994); Londa Schiebinger, *Nature's Body: Gender and the Making of Modern Science* (Boston, MA: Beacon, 1993).

[26] Adriana Craciun, *Fatal Women of Romanticism*; Emma Donoghue, *Passions Between Women* (New York: Harper Perennial, 1996); Andrew Elfenbein, *Romantic Genius: The Prehistory of a Homosexual Role* (New York: Columbia University Press, 1999); Claudia Johnson, *Equivocal Beings: Politics, Gender, and Sentimentality in the 1790s* (Chicago, IL: University of Chicago Press, 1995); Jacqueline Labbe, *Charlotte Smith: Romanticism, Poetry, and the Culture of Gender* (Manchester: Manchester University Press, 2003) and *Romantic Visualities: Landscape, Gender, and Romanticism* (New York: Palgrave Macmillan, 1998); Susan Lanser, *The Sexuality of History*; Judith Pascoe, *Romantic Theatricality: Gender, Poetry, and Spectatorship* (Ithaca, NY: Cornell University Press, 1997); Richard C. Sha, *Perverse Romanticism: Aesthetics and Sexuality in Britain, 1750–1832* (Baltimore, MD: Johns Hopkins University Press, 2009); Susan Wolfson, *Borderlines: The Shiftings of Gender in British Romanticism* (Palo Alto, CA: Stanford University Press, 2006).

domination.[27] Even Jane Austen, once a figure of affective individualism, has been reconceived in terms of her erotic affect, thanks to Jillian Heydt-Stevenson's work.[28] Greater understanding of sexuality as natural, not sinful, made way for experimentation and attention to sexual enjoyment, as David Sigler has shown.[29] And the proliferation of new sexual identities meant a multiplicity of significations separate from sexed bodies that destabilized fixed notions of identity and embodiment, even as it produced a 'sex panic' and increased policing of those identities and bodies.[30]

The explosion of print culture in the Romantic era also challenged notions of embodiment. Even as notions of Romantic genius were being solidified, authorial identity became a complex entanglement, well beyond an individual writer, including authors, readers, publishers, printers, shippers, booksellers, circulating libraries, and other outlets, as well as new media and new technologies, genres, forms, affects, and, finally, temporalities.[31] Textual embodiments by their very nature are at once material objects and loci of performative subjectivities, physical and virtual. As book history has shown us, books function as texts, objects, cultural transactions, and experiences.[32] They were places for authors to inscribe their subject status and to feel its loss as authors became commodities through their books. But even as books became increasingly

[27] See Adriana Craciun, 'Romantic Poetry, Sexuality, and Gender', in *Cambridge Companion to British Romantic Poetry*, eds. James Chandler and Maureen N. McLane (Cambridge: Cambridge University Press, 2008), pp. 155–77; and Jillian Heydt-Stevenson, 'Sexualities', in *Cambridge Companion to Women's Writing in the Romantic Period*, ed. Devoney Looser (Cambridge: Cambridge University Press, 2015), pp. 198–212.

[28] Jillian Heydt-Stevenson, *Austen's Unbecoming Conjunctions: Subversive Laughter, Embodied History* (New York: Palgrave, 2005).

[29] David Sigler, *Sexual Enjoyment in British Romanticism: Gender and Psychoanalysis, 1753–1835* (Montreal: McGill-Queen's University Press, 2015).

[30] Suzanne L. Barnett, *Romantic Paganism: The Politics of Ecstasy in the Shelley Circle* (New York: Palgrave, 2018).

[31] This model begins with historian Robert Darnton's description of a 'communication circuit' in 'What is the History of Books?' *Daedelus*, 111: 3 (1982), pp. 65–83. See also Leslie Howsam, *Old Books and New Histories: An Orientation to Studies in Book and Print Culture* (Toronto: University of Toronto Press, 2006); *The Cambridge Companion to the History of the Book*, ed. Leslie Howsam (Cambridge: Cambridge University Press, 2014); *An Introduction to Book History*, eds. David Finkelstein and Alistair McCleery (New York: Routledge, 2005, 2013); *The Broadview Introduction to Book History*, eds. Michelle Levy and Tom Mole (Peterborough, ON: Broadview Press, 2017); Michelle Levy, 'Do Women Have a Book History?' *SiR*, 53: 3 (Fall 2014), pp. 297–317; Andrew Piper, *Dreaming in Books: The Making of the Bibliographic Imagination in the Romantic Age* (Chicago, IL: Chicago University Press, 2009); Jon Klancher, 'Configuring Romanticism and Print History', *European Romantic Review*, 23: 3 (June 2012), pp. 373–9.

[32] Leslie Howsam, 'The Study of Book History', in *The Cambridge Companion to the History of the Book*, pp. 1–13.

commodified as things to be bought and sold, they exhibited agency in their own right. In *The Reading Nation in the Romantic Period* (2004), William St Clair has given us a way of thinking about physical books as both a body and a not-body, the physical book taking on multiple lives in its dissemination through people, institutions, and their afterlives.[33] One has only to think, again, of Smith's morphing sonnet sequence or of the conflation of Shelley's novel and her creature, from her own introduction to its many afterlives. These texts offered places to revise, remake, and sustain posthuman modes of being.

Textual embodiments have often been allegorized as sexed bodies, but their cascading shapes can give us even broader notions of material forms and movements.[34] Writing—in whatever form—has allowed writers to escape the materiality of their sexed bodies and simultaneously to assert their difference, to dematerialize and rematerialize gender and bodies. Textual embodiments in the Romantic period were uniquely transgressive, shaping changes in the marketplace that increased book production, commodified literary culture, and enabled women writers entrance into the public sphere on a large scale.[35] This enhanced print culture increased women's mobility and their ability to create communities and to become 'mothers of the nation'.[36] In the Romantic period, writers were, all at once, buying books and writing them, not simply to become consuming subjects and authors of commodities but also creators of new genres, forms, and intra-textual relationships in tandem and against other writers.[37] New media like the newspapers and the annuals offered writers volatile forms and forums to explore and explode their sexed experiences.

Texts and bodies are, of course, on a more basic level, matter. A series of Romantic-era scientific discoveries and paradigm shifts also provided the foundations

[33] William St Clair, *The Reading Nation in the Romantic Period* (Cambridge: Cambridge University Press, 2004).

[34] Recall the twentieth-century concern about whether a text is sexed: what kind of body is a text? What kind of text is a body? As one example, see Toril Moi, *Sexual/Textual Politics* (New York: Methuen & Co., 1985; reprinted by Routledge, 2002).

[35] The print explosion between 1775–1800 increased book production from 3,000 titles to 8,000 titles per year, and women writers published around 2,584 volumes of poetry alone between 1780 and 1830. See Michelle Levy, 'Women and Print Culture, 1750–1830', in *The History of British Women's Writing: 1750–1830*, ed. Jacqueline Labbe (New York: Palgrave Macmillan, 2010), p. 31; and Adriana Craciun, 'Romantic Poetry, Sexuality, and Gender', p. 161.

[36] Anne K. Mellor, *Mothers of the Nation: Women's Political Writing in England, 1780–1830* (Indianapolis: Indiana University Press, 2002).

[37] Daniela Garofalo, *Women, Love, and Commodity Culture* (Basingstoke: Ashgate, 2012); Beth Kowaleski-Wallace, *Consuming Subjects: Women, Shopping, and Business in the Eighteenth-Century* (New York: Columbia University Press, 1997); Laura Mandell, *Misogynist Economies: The Business of Literature in Eighteenth-Century Britain* (Lexington: University of Kentucky Press, 1999).

for multiple, overlapping understandings of dynamic materiality. While influences such as Newtonian mechanism, Humean skepticism, Kantian idealism, and Cartesian dualism were still circulating, other influential scientific and philosophical texts offered the material as something more fluid, interconnected, and entangled. Despite John Locke's and Hume's contentions that bodily sensations, through reflection, give rise to subjectivity, both philosophers engender a body whose fluctuating bundles of sensation, bodily movement, and states of consciousness belie a marked skepticism about fixity. Advances in chemistry, physics, and brain science, particularly under the aegis of sensibility's emphasis on the web of nerves, begin with mechanistic and repetitive notions of Hartleyan vibration or chemical affinity, but soon build what Lussier calls 'dynamic' science.[38] Both chemistry and physics adopted new understandings of matter, such as affinity and 'force', which, as Richard Sha writes, were affective and material. Humphry Davy and John Abernathy posited a vital electric fluid that moved through all things, while materialists such as William Lawrence argued that the body's and brain's material organizations were responsible for its fluxes.[39] Davy and Erasmus Darwin saw a scientific world where chemical and biological mechanisms attend to, and create, changes in form.[40] The embodied brain became an important site of contention about the quality and quantity of the mind's conscious executive control over the body's physiological actions and reactions, as early models of brain science posited a cognitive unconscious that operated through autonomic brain functions.[41] Such questions naturally extended to discussions of politics, and Lawrence's model of unsupervised materiality, for example, became popularly identified with the radical overthrow of the government by a mass uprising from below. Not only the brain but landscapes too could unearth shifting layers of sediments for both creative and political purposes. As Kevis Goodman has noted in her treatment of Charlotte Smith, *Beachy Head* raises questions about the shifting layers of sediments being uncovered and discussed at the time.[42] Such dynamism reveals how notions of bodies, affects, and their textual manifestations develop a wide variety of materialities that might be set together, not as a grand unified field theory, but as a set of responses to and openings onto differential forms of matter that anticipate the similarly varied propositions of new materiality.

[38] G.J. Barker-Benfield, *The Culture of Sensibility: Sex and Society in Eighteenth-Century Britain* (Chicago, IL: University of Chicago Press, 1992); and Lussier, *Romantic Dynamics*.
[39] Mitchell, *Bioart and the Vitality of Media*; Sharon Ruston, *Shelley and Vitality* (London: Palgrave Macmillan, 2005); Richard C. Sha, 'The Motion Behind Romantic Emotion: Toward a Chemistry and Physics of Feeling', in *Romanticism and the Emotions*, eds. Joel Faflak and Richard C. Sha (Cambridge: Cambridge University Press, 2014), pp. 19–47.
[40] See Anne K. Mellor's discussion of both scientists in *Mary Shelley: Her Life, Her Fiction, Her Monsters* (New York: Routledge, 2009), pp. 89–114; and Ruston, *Shelley and Vitality*.
[41] Richardson, *British Romanticism and the Science of the Mind*.
[42] Kevis Goodman, 'Conjectures on Beachy Head: Charlotte Smith's Geological Poetics and the Ground of the Present', *ELH*, 81: 3 (Fall 2014), pp. 983–1006.

New Materialism as Romantic Methodology

A fundamental argument of this collection is that new materialism may provide the most helpful theoretical model and praxis for considering a dynamic materiality in Romantic-era texts. New materialism seeks to explain a world—things as they are—that is rapidly changing. While the idea of a 'changing world' is both inherently subjective and nothing new (as Heraclitus would have reminded us almost 2,500 years ago, everything flows), the Romantic era corresponds with the Anthropocene, the geologic age in which we too live, an age of mass extinctions, climate change, Deep Time, space exploration, and technological advancements on a truly epic scale. As Victor Frankenstein himself notes, quoting Percy Shelley's 'Mutability' as he crosses the 'sea of ice', 'man's yesterday may ne'er be like his morrow, / Nought may endure but mutability' (II.2. par. 3). Such attention to the material world means that we must stop putting ourselves at the Copernican center of the universe, always acting and shaping nature, and understand, as Stacy Alaimo claims, 'the anthropocene subject as immersed and enmeshed in a world' that acts as much upon and through us.[43] Like the writers of the Romantic era, we are material creatures living in an emphatically material world and seeking new ways to explain that materiality as it continuously takes new forms within and without us.

New materialism actually resembles pre-Socratic materialism, sharing some characteristics with philosophers like Heraclitus and Thales, ancient and neoplatonic writers like Lucretius and Plotinus, and the foundational tenets of Buddhism. However mechanistic, some Enlightenment philosophers, including Julien Offray de La Mettrie, Pierre Jean Georges Cabanis, Étienne Bonnot de Condillac, Joseph Priestley, and David Hartley—all figures familiar to many Romantic-era writers—probe in complicated ways the materiality of the eighteenth century. Nor is 'new materialism', strictly speaking, singular—the plural, 'materialisms', more accurately captures its variety of approaches and critical apparatuses apparatuses, including the vital materialism of Bennett, the activist materialism of Dimitris Papadopoulos, or the material feminisms of Alaimo and Susan Hekman, to name just a few. What all of these old–new materialisms have in common, however, is a resistance to the ways in which some historicism since the 1980s has treated matter: not its critique of a historical contextualizing of event, subject, and thing, so much as its assumption of materiality as a stabilizing ground for social construction, the matter of history, and, especially, gendered identities affixed to sexed bodies.[44] Acknowledging

[43] Stacy Alaimo, *Exposed: Environmental Politics and Pleasures in Posthuman Times* (Minneapolis: University of Minnesota Press, 2016), p. 157.

[44] New materialism pushes against feminisms focused on social and historical constructions of gender, against Marxist-historical claims for the social constraints of economic and

new discoveries in science, particularly within quantum physics, biology, chemistry, and the earth sciences, as Diana Coole and Samantha Frost detail in their introduction to *New Materialisms*, new materialists emphasize how matter is renewed not as static substance but as emergent and fluid.[45] In its simplest iteration, matter, always in movement, is a presence that pervades all things (or the 'everlasting universe of things', as Percy Shelley terms it in 'Mont Blanc'). Yet matter, as Pheng Cheah writes, is not always substance but also force. Bennett, too, in her popular *Vibrant Matter*, seeks a form of materiality that is both energy and matter.[46] One can hear intimations of Coleridge's interspersed breaths and Robinson's bustling urban landscape, a materiality that moves away from the more systematic mechanism of Locke and Priestley toward something more protean. Bennett's notion of 'impersonal affect' also provides an understanding of materiality that is both unintentional and agential. Drawing on both Lucretius and Spinoza, she describes, with special attention to the nonhuman, how bodies move and are moved by each other thanks to 'the capacity of any body for activity and responsiveness' (p. xii). Bennett's affect is not a separate, vital force but rather something that allows her to 'equate affect with materiality' (p. xiii).

Teresa Brennan, another seminal theorist whose notions of affect become equated with moving matter, attends specifically to the transmission of affect.[47] For Brennan, affective transfer occurs via 'entrainment', the movement of pheromones and hormones as well as vibrations of rhythm and even images from body to body, sometimes even creating an atmosphere of materiality that shifts and alters the bodies that enter it. Brian Massumi's notion of affect as intensity shares this sense of a field of material movement that occurs before we are conscious of it, an unsettled agitation only later categorized as clear 'emotions' once they are codified by perception or conceptualized through language as anger, fear, or love.[48] Massumi especially opens up the virtuality of material affect, where a pool of possible affect is available until a selection process captures it as an emotion, a physiological and a conceptual state. These theorists together provide different models for understanding matter as moving

social class, and, especially pertinent to Romantic studies, against the fundamental divide between subject and object typified by critics like Earl Wasserman, Harold Bloom, and M.H. Abrams, and continued in feminist criticism seeking to reveal women as subjects, not objects, such as the work of Stuart Curran, Margaret Homans, and Anne K. Mellor.

[45] Diana Coole and Samantha Frost, *New Materialisms: Ontology, Agency, and Politics* (Durham, NC: Duke University Press, 2010).

[46] Pheng Cheah, 'Non-Dialectical Materialism', in *New Materialisms*, pp. 70–91; and Bennett, *Vibrant Matter*.

[47] Teresa Brennan, *The Transmission of Affect* (Ithaca, NY: Cornell University Press, 2004).

[48] Brian Massumi, *Parables for the Virtual: Movement, Affect, Sensation* (Durham, NC: Duke University Press, 2002).

imperceptibly, and they formulate affect as material sharing or transmission in ways that often undermine discrete bodies and, as this volume affirms, Enlightenment notions of embodiment. Hartley's, Priestley's, and Davy's ways of thinking about 'vibrunticles' and 'phlogiston' as a material, active spirit of the universe and vital fluid similarly paved the way for a material transgressiveness that Romantic literature enacts.

New materialists and affect theorists generally posit such particulate materiality, whether traveling or inter-affecting, as a form of endemic relationality among and within matter, whatever its form. Bennett's understanding of 'things' provides a stark contrast to object-oriented ontologists, such as Tim Morton, who polemicize objects as withdrawn from our understanding of them and occurring in the material world before they relate to other objects. For Bennett, instead, matter is always in an assemblage with other pieces or forms of matter, whether in the electrical grid of the United States or through the various food cycles of humans, animals, landfills, or in a classroom of readers. Such a confederation of things in relation can be compared to Karen Barad's influential notion of entanglement.[49] Drawing on her background in quantum physics, Barad reinterprets the Heisenberg–Bohr debates to show that matter can be both particles and waves not due to an observer's different views of them but because different apparatuses create matter differently. Her notion of 'intra-action' suggests that matter's ontologies, especially subjects and objects, do not exist prior to a particular apparatus that cuts them into subjects and objects; it is an act that occurs iteratively every time we see or understand matter into being. Barad uses touch as an example of entanglement wherein matters—things, bodies, texts—always touch and are touched, often crossing human–nonhuman boundaries.[50] This occurs when we touch texts with our eyes, our pens, our cursors, and perform our sometimes tetchy, continuous editing.[51]

Romantic writers were already exploring such ideas, intervening into ideologies and methodologies that sought to delimit and compartmentalize material bodies from the affective and intra-active relations that entangled them. We can see these texts playing with the intra-active relations among bodies that speak to a fluid materiality, and they pointedly do this through language that both bridges those bodies and is itself a body. Thus, another intervention that this volume seeks to make is to read writers whose linguistic play is also material play, writers who experiment with the materiality of texts and language itself

[49] Karen Barad, *Meeting the Universe Halfway: Quantum Physics and the Entanglement of Matter and Meaning* (Durham, NC: Duke University Press, 2007).

[50] Barad, 'On Touching—The Inhuman That Therefore I Am', *differences*, 23: 3 (2012), pp. 206–23.

[51] In their introduction to *Romantic Materialities*, Langan and Guyer refer to Sonia Hofkosh's coinage of the phrase 'tandem touching' to describe this phenomenon.

as other forms that matter. While Bennett and Sheldon encourage scholars to read with keen eyes for the allegedly hidden materialities lurking in representations, figures, forms, and pages, they are not ultimately interested in language's participation in a new materialist ontology. This volume attempts to provide a literary methodology capable of reading texts and language as materialities mixing with those of the world and, above all, altering the matters they do not mimetically represent. As Coleridge expounds to William Godwin in a letter of 22 September 1800, we 'would endeavour to destroy the old antithesis of *Words & Things*, elevating, as it were, words into Things, & living Things too'.[52]

The Matter of the Essays

The collected essays offer a diversity of approaches to exploring the instabilities of materiality through language, themselves creating an assemblage whose relations will, we hope, produce their own agential forces. To help identify, if not delineate, three different configurations of materiality, we have divided this book into three sections. Although the first section deals more specifically with textualities, the second with things, and the third with bodies, all three sections, in different ways, combine inquiries into how texts, bodies, and things circulate affect through new matrices of materiality that explode gender binaries.

The essays on textual embodiments begin the volume because they take on the Romantic fascination with and propensity for the manipulation of sentence, page, genre, book, and even the corpus as bodies that are ever-changing. While we still think of a book as physical material—perhaps the most stable form of text—that once printed is a static, historical object, the essays in this collection attempt to destabilize this idea from the very start, exploring linguistic and textual experimentation as new materiality. This first section examines how Romantic authors resisted the reification of their texts (and authorial selves) as commodified and sexed objects by exploiting their performative, virtual, malleable, and fluid materiality to create spooling textual editions, texts that morph, and texts that allegorize the unstable human body. Books and words become vibrant, shapeshifting things with the power to move, touch, and affect others and themselves.

Authors such as William Blake, Mary Tighe, Coleridge, Smith, and Felicia Hemans attend to the text as a body that is always growing and transfiguring in ways that imbricate readers into their nonhuman vortices. If the late eighteenth-century increase in book production was in part an effort to stabilize authorship and identity through a material, manipulable thing, the

[52] *The Collected Letters of Samuel Taylor Coleridge*, ed. Earl Leslie Griggs, 6 vols. (Oxford: Clarendon, 1956–71), I: pp. 625–6.

book itself functioning like a discrete body, this emphasis did not mean the end of manuscript culture, as Harriet Kramer Linkin argues in 'The Destabilizing Materiality of the Autograph for Blake, Coleridge, and Tighe'. Manuscript culture enabled these writers to 'produce a new materiality through autographic printed texts that preserve their idiolectic voices and unique, fluctuating signatures, countering the potential ontological restrictiveness of a commercially published book' (p. 32), as Linkin's examples of Blake's anti-creation myth, Coleridge's recursive iterations, and Tighe's private printings of *Psyche* (1805) illustrate. When Michael Gamer and Katrina O'Loughlin analyze the marginalia in copies of Smith's *Elegiac Sonnets* in 'Affect in the Margins: Marking Readers in the *Elegiac Sonnets*', they reveal how Smith's printed page offered another means to challenge the material restrictions of authorship and to circulate affect in new ways that blurred the lines between persona and poet, between author and reader, and between book-writer and book-owner. Recovering the traces readers left behind in their copies of Smith's volume, from the first edition to the fifth, Gamer and O'Loughlin highlight the affective force of Romantic readers on the materiality of the book. In 'Remapping the Printed Page in Women's Post-Waterloo Poetry', Emily J. Dolive also explores the movement of printed pages as a means to counter ideologies of femininity that delimited women's participation in war activities. Felicia Hemans and Jane Alice Sargant manipulate text and genre, specifically the wartime elegy and the ballad, 'instigat[ing] and support[ing] the fluid movement between and beyond genders' (p. 87). In their texts, Dolive argues, 'print moves and mingles with different materials to resist stable constructions of femininity, war, and the book itself' (p. 87).

The disruptive and fluid forms created by such textual embodiments produced and circulated new affects that had their own materiality, in turn shaping and disrupting the possibilities for gendered bodies. Like Sargant and Hemans, Anna Jameson chooses a genre—in this case the diary—that enacts and literalizes its own instability through its textual maneuvers. Holly Gallagher suggests in 'Vibrant Art on the Grand Tour in Anna Jameson's *Diary of an Ennuyée*' that Jameson's text creates a poetic vision that 'synthesize[s] this material world she moves in' (p. 107), a bricolage of visual and verbal texts, affective experience, and emotional response that emphasizes the vibrant things that shaped the Grand Tour and the diarist's reciprocal relationship with the objects, landscapes, and art she experiences.

'Transgressive Things', the collection's second section, pivots from the shapeshifting fluctuations of Romantic-era textuality to consider the play of things, objects, and the materials that populate them. While phenomenological things have so often been read in productive dialectic relationships to thinking, language, negativity, and imaginative futurity in Romantic scholarship, these essays speak to the animation, responsiveness, and the itinerancy of things that transgress subject–object distinctions. For many women writers, the objectification of non-normative subjects is based on their denigrated gender, race, or class, and the vibrancy of things dissolves those subjectivities. In 'Hester Stanhope, "*Un être à part*": Material Transgression and Belonging in the East', Jillian Heydt-Stevenson maps Stanhope's itinerant subjectivities as English woman, Turk, Bedouin man, warrior, politician, sibyl, and archeologist and documents the volatile, interwoven ways Stanhope experienced transgressive materiality. If Stanhope's flagrant cross-dressing, which mingled human and nonhuman materials (clothing, antiquities), undermines the idea of woman at the mercy of a biologically-sexed body, her appropriation of a colossal statue on the first archeological expedition in Syria exemplifies her 'scandalous' interactions with her environment, as she transgresses gendered spheres of battle, travel, and sex to forge 'an experience that radically imbricates her with the material world' (p. 130) and 'actualize[s] her dynamic potential' (p. 128). Mary Beth Tegan's '"The Redundancy of Copious Nothings": Fictional Offspring, Or, the Reproductions of Female Vanity' offers an alternative narrative to one in which women's novels become excessive, disruptive, 'copious nothings' that transitively undermine the status of the writer and make her object-like, her imagination merely a fecund vanity. Reading Burney's novels and Wollstonecraft's reviews of them, Tegan argues that the passion of vanity did not simply offer emotion to denigrate women's fiction but also supplied a proactive affect that blurs the borders of excessive objects and human subjects.

Both Mark Lounibos and Sonia Hofkosh give further credence to the nonhuman agencies of objects whose presence, as Lounibos writes, signals the 'acute sensitivity to the profound shifts in human and nonhuman relationships being driven by early industrial capitalism and the accompanying representational reassignments of material agents' (p. 174). His investigation into the Jacobin novel in 'Revolutionary Objects in Elizabeth Inchbald's *Nature and Art*' considers how quotidian objects such as fiddles, wigs, sheep, and umbrellas figure as what Bennett calls 'conative actants' (p. 122). These vibrant materials serve in this Jacobin novel to critique the denial of nonhuman agency, a tenet that has been used to exploit working-class laborers as objects of commodity culture. In 'Dancing with Ghosts in "Isabella; or, The Pot of Basil"', Hofkosh similarly observes thing-power in John Keats's poem by drawing our attention to the everyday relationships (and slippages), 'the dissonant connections' (Bennett, p. 4), between subject and object as Isabella's tears grow the basil plant that holds her dead lover's head. Hofkosh terms this dynamic, intimate transaction between person and thing a 'ghost dance' that raises issues about commodity fetishism as well as the relations between reader and text, returning us to the text itself as a transgression into the not-quite-human. Such relations might, she suggests, potentially disrupt normative models of human–nonhuman relations and offer other, more radical possibilities for practices of being in the world. In 'It's the End of the World as We Know It and I Feel Queer: Mary Shelley, Queer Affect, and Shapeshifting Through *The Last Man*', Kate Singer locates queer ways of being when she reads Mary Shelley's novel as a 'post-apocalyptic survival guide ... that offers a theory and a praxis for how to change materially after disaster' (p. 214). Showing how Shelley convenes affect as a means of shapeshifting bodies from nonhuman to human and back again, Singer argues that the material affects in *The Last Man* 'offer a theory of change that reshapes what we know about and how we might enact revolution' (p. 214) in the posthuman post-reality of the post-apocalypse.

Transgressive materialities circulate through various media and kinds of bodies, undermining the anthropomorphic primacy of the human and the rigidity of heteronormative gender identities. Thus, the final section, 'Materialities Sexual and Animal', attends to differences—especially sexual and animal—in a range of authors and texts (including novels, fiction for children, critical nonfiction, and poetry) that transverse both humans and objects and challenge how we define and categorize human bodies and civilizations. Such reconsiderations of categories and phenotypes variegate matter without privileging certain forms, shapes, or bodies and produce new posthuman entanglements. David Sigler's 'John Barnet and the Materiality of Desire in James Hogg's *Justified Sinner*' reflects on Hogg's treatment of desire as a material force that has dangerous consequences for both sexual and racial politics. Sigler analyzes the conversation between Reverend Wringhim and his servant, John Barnet, about the paternity of Wringhim's alleged natural son in *The Private Memoirs and Confessions of a Justified Sinner* (1824). These hinky exchanges raise the question of 'how ... the signifier tie[s] the subject through desire to new forms of materiality' (p. 250), thus negotiating the gap between the materiality of desire and of bodies that finds later expression in Lacan. Chris Washington's 'Werewolf Wollstonecraft: *homo homini lupus*, or, Romantic Beast Wars' enlarges the materialities moving among families to those within the state as he considers the figure of the werewolf in Rousseau and Wollstonecraft. Because werewolves, like women, fall outside the law of *homo homini lupus* that underwrites any law, any sovereignty, he argues, 'woman' as outlaw can reconfigure human society from the outside, as Wollstonecraft's novel, *Maria: or, The Wrongs of Woman* (1798) theorizes. This conflation of women and werewolves as outlaw allows for the rejection of marriage in favor of the pack, a structure that undoes binary gender through 'covenants of loving care for each member of the pack by each member' (p. 259), a form of Baradian entanglement that reconfigures materialities as they flow through familial and political organizations.

In addition to thinking about the materialities of bodies, families, and desire, Donelle Ruwe pushes us to consider the materiality of the imagination in '*Phantasmion*, or the Confessions of a Female Opium Eater'. She argues that Sara Coleridge, the daughter of an opium addict and an addict herself, was both an astute critic of her father's theories of the relationship between the body and the imagination and an author who celebrates a vision of opium-induced imagination as a powerful and inherently transgressive bodily faculty. While Coleridge's own body becomes a permeable vessel for opium, which facilitates the repetitive forays of an imagination that can infect others as well as pass her addiction to her children, *Phantasmion* (1837) explores a fluid materiality through the figure of the involute and human-to-insect metamorphoses. The protagonist's ingestion of vapors and fluids leads to new personal discoveries, forms of knowledge, and emotional entrainment while his actual bodily transformations lead to radical cross-species forms of empathy. Finally, in 'Voices against the Universe: Material Transgressions in the Blakean Multiverse', Mark Lussier considers the voices of women in William Blake's illuminated prophecies— particularly Oothoon's largely unheeded voice in *Visions of the Daughters of Albion* (1793)—to uncover a feminine, semiotic alternative to the relentless monological language of the symbolic employed by Blake's male characters, an alternative that suggests a 'gritty courage of everyday life' (p. 318). Lussier argues that the experimental interplay of Blake's words and images 'becom[e] the very material conditions for an affective textuality designed to establish a field of force within which numerous forms of consciousness collide' (p. 321).

Together, the essays of this collection and the dynamic materiality they put into play invite readers to enter a new Romantic world in which the fluid matter of bodies, texts, things, and affects can unmake and remake the human. Instead of being borne away by the waves, *Material Transgressions* enfolds us within them and finds posthumans already in relation to all the matter of the Romantic universe, thunderously circulating under new spacetimes.

Bibliography

Alaimo, Stacy. *Exposed: Environmental Politics and Pleasures in Posthuman Times.* Minneapolis: University of Minnesota Press, 2016.

Barad, Karen. *Meeting the Universe Halfway: Quantum Physics and the Entanglement of Matter and Meaning.* Durham, NC: Duke University Press, 2007.

——. 'On Touching—The Inhuman That Therefore I Am'. *differences*, 23: 3 (2012), pp. 206–23.

Barker-Benfield, G.J. *The Culture of Sensibility: Sex and Society in Eighteenth-Century Britain.* Chicago, IL: University of Chicago Press, 1992.

Barnett, Suzanne L. *Romantic Paganism: The Politics of Ecstasy in the Shelley Circle.* New York: Palgrave, 2018.

Bennett, Jane. *Vibrant Matter: A Political Ecology of Things.* Durham, NC: Duke University Press, 2010.

Binhammer, Katherine. 'The Sex Panic of the 1790s'. *Journal of the History of Sexuality*, 6: 3 (1996), pp. 409–34.

Boehm, K., ed. *Bodies and Things in Nineteenth-Century Literature and Culture.* New York: Palgrave, 2012.

Brennan, Teresa. *The Transmission of Affect.* Ithaca, NY: Cornell University Press, 2004.

Burgess, Miranda. 'On Being Moved: Sympathy, Mobility, and Narrative Form'. *Poetics Today*, 32: 2 (2011), pp. 289–321.

Burkett, Andrew. *Romantic Mediations.* Albany, NY: SUNY Press, 2016.

Cheah, Pheng. 'Non-Dialectical Materialism'. In *New Materialisms*, eds. Diana Coole and Samantha Frost, pp. 70–91.

Clark, Anna. *Desire: A History of European Sexuality.* New York: Routledge, 2008.

Coleridge, Samuel Taylor. *The Collected Letters of Samuel Taylor Coleridge*, ed. Earl Leslie Griggs, 6 vols. Oxford: Clarendon, 1956–71.

Coole, Diana and Samantha Frost, eds. *New Materialisms: Ontology, Agency, and Politics.* Durham, NC: Duke University Press, 2010.

Cox, Jeffrey N. *Poetry and Politics in the Cockney School: Shelley, Keats, Hunt, and Their Circle.* Cambridge: Cambridge University Press, 1998.

Craciun, Adriana. *Fatal Women of Romanticism.* Cambridge: Cambridge University Press, 2003.

——. 'Romantic Poetry, Sexuality, and Gender'. In *Cambridge Companion to British Romantic Poetry*, eds. James Chandler and Maureen N. McLane. Cambridge: Cambridge University Press, 2008, pp. 155–77.

Cross, Ashley. *Mary Robinson and the Genesis of Romanticism: Literary Dialogues and Debts, 1784–1821.* New York: Routledge, 2017.

Darnton, Robert. 'What is the History of Books?' *Daedelus*, 111: 3 (1982), pp. 65–83.

Derrida, Jacques. 'Typewriter Ribbon'. In *Material Events: Paul de Man and the Afterlife of Theory*, eds. Tom Cohen, Barbara Cohen, J. Hillis Miller, and Andrzej Warminski. Minneapolis: University of Minnesota Press, 2000, pp. 277–360.

Donoghue, Emma. *Passions Between Women.* New York: Harper Perennial, 1996.

Elfenbein, Andrew. *Romantic Genius: The Prehistory of a Homosexual Role.* New York: Columbia University Press, 1999.

Faflak, Joel and Richard Sha, eds. *Romanticism and the Emotions.* Cambridge: Cambridge University Press, 2014.

Favret, Mary. *War at a Distance: Romanticism and the Making of Modern Wartime.* Princeton, NJ: Princeton University Press, 2009.

Finkelstein, David and Alistair McCleery, eds. *An Introduction to Book History.* New York: Routledge, 2005, 2013.

Fulford, Tim. R*omantic Poetry and Literary Coteries: The Dialect of the Tribe.* New York: Palgrave, 2015.

Fulford, Tim, Debbie Lee, and Peter J. Kitson. *Literature, Science, and Exploration in the Romantic Era: Bodies of Knowledge.* Cambridge: Cambridge University Press, 2007.

Gamer, Michael. *Romanticism, Self-Canonization, and the Business of Poetry.* Cambridge: Cambridge University Press, 2017.

Garofalo, Daniela. *Women, Love, and Commodity Culture*. Basingstoke: Ashgate, 2012.

Geertz, Clifford. *The Interpretation of Cultures*. New York: Basic Books, 1973.

Goldsmith, Steven. *Blake's Agitation: Criticism and the Emotions*. Baltimore, MD: Johns Hopkins University Press, 2013.

Goldstein, Amanda Jo. *Sweet Science: Romantic Materialism and the New Logics of Life*. Chicago: University of Chicago Press, 2017.

Goodman, Kevis. 'Conjectures on Beachy Head: Charlotte Smith's Geological Poetics and the Ground of the Present'. *ELH*, 81: 3 (Fall 2014), pp. 983–1006.

——. *Georgic Modernity and British Romanticism: Poetry and the Mediation of History*. Cambridge: Cambridge University Press, 2004.

Gottlieb, Evan. *Romantic Realities: Speculative Realism and British Romanticism*. Edinburgh: Edinburgh University Press, 2016.

Guyer, Sara and Celeste Langan, eds. *Romantic Materialities. Romantic Circles* Praxis Series (February 2015), at https://romantic-circles.org/praxis/materialities/index.html.

Heydt-Stevenson, Jillian. *Austen's Unbecoming Conjunctions: Subversive Laughter, Embodied History*. New York: Palgrave, 2005.

——. 'Sexualities'. In *Cambridge Companion to Women's Writing in the Romantic Period*, ed. Devoney Looser. Cambridge: Cambridge University Press, 2015, pp. 198–212.

Hofkosh, Sonia. 'What Wordsworth Touched'. In *Romantic Materialities*, eds. Sara Guyer and Celeste Langan. *Romantic Circles* Praxis Series (February 2015), at https://romantic-circles.org/praxis/materialities/praxis.materialities.2015.hofkosh.html.

Howsam, Leslie. *Old Books and New Histories: An Orientation to Studies in Book and Print Culture*. Toronto: University of Toronto Press, 2006.

——. 'The Study of Book History'. In *The Cambridge Companion to the History of the Book*. Cambridge: Cambridge University Press, 2014, pp. 1–13.

Igarashi, Yohei. *The Connected Condition: Romanticism and the Dream of Communication*. Palo Alto, CA: Stanford University Press, 2019.

Jacobus, Mary. *Romantic Things: A Tree, a Rock, a Cloud*. Chicago, IL: University of Chicago Press, 2012.

Johnson, Claudia. *Equivocal Beings: Politics, Gender, and Sentimentality in the 1790s*. Chicago, IL: University of Chicago Press, 1995.

Keach, William. *Arbitrary Power: Romanticism, Language, Politics*. Princeton, NJ: Princeton University Press, 2004.

Klancher, Jon. 'Configuring Romanticism and Print History'. *ERR*, 23: 3 (June 2012), pp. 373–9.

——. 'English Romanticism and Cultural Production'. In *The New Historicism*, ed. H. Aram Veeser. New York: Routledge, 1989, 2013, pp. 77–88.

Kowaleski-Wallace, Beth. *Consuming Subjects: Women, Shopping, and Business in the Eighteenth-Century*. New York: Columbia University Press, 1997.

Labbe, Jacqueline. *Charlotte Smith: Romanticism, Poetry, and the Culture of Gender.* Manchester: Manchester University Press, 2003.

——. *Romantic Visualities: Landscape, Gender, and Romanticism.* New York: Palgrave Macmillan, 1998.

Langan, Celeste. 'Telopathos: Medium Cool Romanticism'. *Romanticism on the Net,* 41–2 (2006), at https://www.erudit.org/en/journals/ron/2006-n41–42-ron1276/013154ar/.

——. 'Understanding Media in 1805: Audiovisual Hallucination in "The Lay of the Last Minstrel"'. *Studies in Romanticism,* 40: 1 (Spring 2001), pp. 49–70.

Langan, Celeste and Maureen N. McLane. 'The Medium of Romantic Poetry'. In *Cambridge Companion to British Romantic Poetry,* eds. James Chandler and Maureen McLane. Cambridge: Cambridge University Press, 2008, pp. 239–62.

Lanser, Suasan. *The Sexuality of History: Modernity and the Sapphic, 1565–1830.* Chicago, IL: University of Chicago Press, 2014.

Laqueur, Thomas. *Making Sex.* Cambridge, MA: Harvard University Press, 1990.

Levinson, Marjorie. 'A Motion and A Spirit: Romancing Spinoza'. *Studies in Romanticism,* 46: 4 (Winter 2007), pp. 367–408.

——. *Wordsworth's Great Period Poems.* Cambridge: Cambridge University Press, 1986.

Levy, Michelle. 'Do Women Have a Book History?' *Studies in Romanticism,* 53: 3 (Fall 2014), pp. 297–317.

——. 'Women and Print Culture, 1750–1830'. In *The History of British Women's Writing: 1750–1830,* ed. Jacqueline Labbe. New York: Palgrave Macmillan, 2010, pp. 29–45.

Levy, Michelle and Thomas Mole. *The Broadview Introduction to Book History.* Peterborough, ON: Broadview Press, 2017.

Looser, Devoney. 'Preface'. In *Cambridge Companion to Women's Writing in the Romantic Period,* ed. Devoney Looser. Cambridge: Cambridge University Press, 2015, pp. xiii–xviii.

Lussier, Mark. *Romantic Dynamics: The Poetics of Physicality.* Basingstoke: Macmillan, 2000.

McGann, Jerome. *The Poetics of Sensibility: A Revolution in Literary Style.* Oxford: Oxford University Press, 1996.

Magnuson, Paul. *Reading Public Romanticism.* Princeton, NJ: Princeton University Press, 1998.

Mandell, Laura. *Misogynist Economies: The Business of Literature in Eighteenth-Century Britain.* Lexington: University of Kentucky Press, 1999.

Massumi, Brian. *Parables for the Virtual: Movement, Affect, Sensation.* Durham, NC: Duke University Press, 2002.

Mee, Jon. *Conversable Worlds: Literature, Contention, and Community, 1762 to 1830.* Oxford: Oxford University Press, 2013.

Mellor, Anne K. *Mary Shelley: Her Life, Her Fiction, Her Monsters.* New York: Routledge, 2009.

——. *Mothers of the Nation: Women's Political Writing in England, 1780–1830.* Indianapolis: Indiana University Press, 2002.

——. *Romanticism and Gender.* New York: Routledge, 1993.

Mitchell, Robert E. *Bioart and the Vitality of Media.* Seattle: University of Washington Press, 2010.

Moi, Toril. *Sexual/Textual Politics.* New York: Methuen & Co., 1985; reprinted by Routledge, 2002.

Pascoe, Judith. *Romantic Theatricality: Gender, Poetry, and Spectatorship.* Ithaca, NY: Cornell University Press, 1997.

Pfau, Thomas. *Romantic Moods: Paranoia, Trauma, and Melancholy, 1790–1840.* Baltimore, MD: Johns Hopkins University Press, 2005.

Piper, Andrew. *Dreaming in Books: The Making of the Bibliographic Imagination in the Romantic Age.* Chicago, IL: Chicago University Press, 2009.

Plotnitsky, Arkady. 'All Shapes of Light: The Quantum Mechanical Shelley'. In *Shelley: Poet and Legislator of the World,* eds. Betty Bennett and Stuart Curran. Baltimore: Johns Hopkins University Press, 1995, pp. 263–74.

Porter, Roy. *Flesh in the Age of Reason.* New York: W.W. Norton, 2003.

Porter, Roy and Mikulas Teich. *Sexual Knowledge, Sexual Science: The History of Attitudes to Sexuality.* Cambridge: Cambridge University Press, 1994.

Potkay, Adam. 'Wordsworth and the Ethics of Things'. *PMLA,* 123: 2 (March 2008), pp. 390–404.

Richardson, Alan. *British Romanticism and the Science of the Mind.* Cambridge: Cambridge University Press, 2001.

Rooney, Ellen. 'What Can the Matter Be?' *American Literary History,* 8: 4 (Winter 1996), pp. 745–58.

Ruston, Sharon. *Creating Romanticism: Case Studies in the Literature, Science, and Medicine of the 1790s.* New York: Palgrave, 2013.

——. *Shelley and Vitality.* London: Palgrave Macmillan, 2005.

St Clair, William. *The Reading Nation in the Romantic Period.* Cambridge: Cambridge University Press, 2004.

Schiebinger, Londa. *Nature's Body: Gender and the Making of Modern Science.* Boston, MA: Beacon, 1993.

Sha, Richard C. *Perverse Romanticism: Aesthetics and Sexuality in Britain, 1750–1832.* Baltimore, MD: Johns Hopkins University Press, 2009.

——. 'Toward a Physiology of the Romantic Imagination'. *Configurations,* 17: 3 (Fall 2009), pp. 197–226.

Sheldon, Rebekah. 'Form/Matter/Chora: Object-Oriented Ontology and Feminist New Materialism'. In *The Nonhuman Turn,* ed. Richard Grusin. Minneapolis: University of Minnesota Press, 2015, pp. 193–222.

Sigler, David. *Sexual Enjoyment in British Romanticism: Gender and Psychoanalysis, 1753–1835.* Montreal: McGill-Queen's University Press, 2015.

Singer, Kate. 'Limpid Waves and Good Vibrations: Charlotte Smith's New Materialist Affect'. *Essays in Romanticism,* 23: 2 (2016), pp. 175–92.

——. 'Mary Robinson and the Idiot's Guide to Sensibility and Oblivion'. *Literature Compass,* 12: 12 (December 2015), pp. 667–74.

——. *Romantic Vacancy: The Poetics of Gender, Affect, and Radical Speculation.* Albany, NY: SUNY Press, 2019.

Siskin, Clifford. *The Historicity of Romantic Discourse.* Oxford: Oxford University Press, 1988.

Trumbach, Randolph. *Sex and the Gender Revolution,* vols. 1 and 2. Chicago, IL: University of Chicago Press, 1998.

——. 'The Transformation of Sodomy from the Renaissance to the Modern World and Its General Sexual Consequences'. *Signs,* 37: 4 (2012), pp. 832–48.

Tuite, Clara and Gillian Russell, eds. *Romantic Sociability: Social Networks and Literary Culture in Britain, 1770–1840.* Cambridge: Cambridge University Press, 2006.

Washington, Chris. *Romantic Revelations: Visions of Post-Apocalyptic Life and Hope in the Anthropocene.* Toronto: University of Toronto Press, 2019.

Washington, Chris and Anne C. McCarthy. *Romanticism and Speculative Realism.* London: Bloomsbury, 2019.

Wellmann, Janina. *The Form of Becoming: Embryology and the Epistemology of Rhythm, 1760–1830.* Brooklyn, NY: Zone Books, 2017.

Wolfson, Susan. *Borderlines: The Shiftings of Gender in British Romanticism.* Stanford, CA: Stanford University Press, 2006.

Part One

Textual Embodiments

Chapter One

The Destabilizing Materiality of the Autograph for Blake, Coleridge, and Tighe

Harriet Kramer Linkin

Print historians point to the final quarter of the eighteenth century as a period that saw an explosion in the amount of printed materials produced by the English book trade: according to James Raven's analysis of the printed items recorded in the *English Short Title Catalogue*, while the total number of titles rose from 2,000 to 3,000 between 1750 and 1775, that number leapt from 3,000 to 8,000 between 1775 and 1800.[1] This quadrupling of numbers from 1750 to 1800 lends statistical support to what Harold Love aptly terms 'the ambiguous triumph of print' over scribal culture by the end of the century and evidences the increasing consolidation of literary production in the form of commercially published books.[2] Even so, many writers and readers continued to engage in a flourishing manuscript culture, sharing autographic work through drafts, letters, journals, albums, commonplace books, handmade books, salons, and coteries. Although Love observes that scribal publication after 1800 'has been regarded as aberrant, or was the consequence of constraint rather than choice' (p. 288), he importantly documents its continuation. Raven similarly cautions against seeing the trajectory of the book trade up to 1850 as one of steady development in which print culture replaces manuscript culture but suggests instead that its 'history should include consideration of contradictions and resistances as well as compliance and development' ('Book Trades', p. 4). Others, such

[1] See James Raven, *The Business of Books: Booksellers and the English Book Trade 1450–1850* (New Haven, CT: Yale University Press, 2007), p. 8. Also see Raven's earlier essay, 'The Book Trades', in *Books and their Readers in Eighteenth-Century England: New Essays*, ed. Isabel Rivers (London and New York: Leicester University Press, 2001), pp. 2–3.

[2] Harold Love, *The Culture and Commerce of Texts* (Oxford: Clarendon, 1993), p. 284.

as Donald Reiman, George Justice, Michelle Levy, and Betty Schellenberg, even position scribal and print publication in the early nineteenth century as complementary forms, rather than competing technologies, 'locking in battle in a Darwinian struggle to the death'.[3] Building on the idea of scribal and print productions as complementary forms, this essay will look at three Romantic-era writers—William Blake, Samuel Taylor Coleridge, and Mary Tighe—who integrate print and manuscript technologies. I suggest these writers produce a new materiality through autographic printed texts that preserve their idiolectic voices and unique, fluctuating signatures, countering the potential ontological restrictiveness of a commercially published book that structurally reproduces identical copies of the same work. They offer paradigmatic examples of the ways some Romantic-era authors deploy scribal practices in print media to inscribe individuality and personality, effectively autographing the print copies of their works to transform them from uniform products into objects embodying vital processes, enacting the restless modulations Percy Bysshe Shelley delineates in 'Mutability', the motile surface John Keats describes in 'Ode on a Grecian Urn', or the kaleidoscopic subjectivity William Wordsworth builds by revisiting spots of time, through the fluidity of material variation. Blake creates the process of illuminated printing, which enables him to make each copy of his texts a unique graphic object, most expansively in *Songs of Innocence and of Experience*. Coleridge habitually revises his printed texts and destabilizes each version to re-engage the immediacy of poetic vision through a vocalized experience, perhaps most dramatically in the many iterations of 'The Rime of the Ancient Mariner'. Tighe initially rejects print publication for the affective palpability of scribal publication but then inscribes privately printed copies of *Psyche; or, the Legend of Love* to specific members of her coterie, a dedicatory process that her coterie continues after Tighe dies by inscribing manuscript versions of the poems that appear in her posthumously published *Psyche, with Other Poems* in their commonplace books. All three explore the implications of being bound in bookish or human form in their poems even as they use the materiality of their autographic texts to reconfigure a print publication system that might otherwise lock them or their texts into fixed identities or commodities. Blending print and scribal practices and technologies, they seek to maintain autonomy over the creation and distribution of their art and therein provide alternate models

[3] George Justice, 'Introduction', in *Women's Writing and the Circulation of Ideas*, eds. George Justice and Nathan Tinker (Cambridge: Cambridge University Press, 2002), p. 10. Also see Donald Reiman, *The Study of Modern Manuscripts: Public, Confidential, and Private* (Baltimore, MD: Johns Hopkins University Press, 1993); Michelle Levy, *Family Authorship and Romantic Print Culture* (Basingstoke: Palgrave Macmillan, 2008); and Betty A. Schellenberg, *Literary Coteries and the Making of Modern Print Culture* (Cambridge: Cambridge University Press, 2016).

of materialization in an age that witnesses the ascendancy of commercial printing. If, as David Thorburn and Henry Jenkins argue, 'older media may develop new functions ... as the emerging technology begins to occupy the cultural space of its ancestors', Blake, Coleridge, and Tighe deliberately disrupt the potential erasures effected by commercial print through the destabilizing materiality of their hand-imprinted signatures.[4]

William Blake and Illuminated Printing

Blake's *Songs of Innocence and of Experience* (1794) and its constituent volumes *Songs of Innocence* (1789) and *Songs of Experience* (1794) may provide the most spectacular examples of a text that refuses the ontological status of a fixed work: a book that never takes the same manifested form twice, either through the sequencing or inclusion of its lyrics or the coloring and content of its illustrations, a book comprised of poems and images that repeatedly question what it means for humans to contain their fluid wildness within socially circumscribed roles or structures. Although the texts of the individual poems never vary, the narrative, aesthetics, and affect of each of the three books' collected poems changes with every iteration so that there is, as Andrew Lincoln puts it, 'no definitive text of the *Songs*', only 'particular arrangements of the poems': twenty-five unique copies of *Songs of Innocence*, four unique copies of *Songs of Experience*, and twenty-five unique copies of *Songs of Innocence and of Experience*, culminating in fifty versions of *Innocence* and twenty-nine versions of *Experience*.[5] For Paul Mann, even to name an iteration of the *Songs* a 'copy' is a misnomer, 'because the production-aesthetic is anti-mimetic at every turn: the

[4] See David Thornburn's and Henry Jenkins's 'Introduction' to *Rethinking Media Change: The Aesthetics of Transition* (Cambridge, MA: MIT Press, 2004), p. 2. Much recent work on materiality in Romantic poetry focuses on the ways authors seek to transmit sound, sight, and affect through print media, as in Celeste Langan's and Maureen McClane's discussion of orality in *The Lyrical Ballads* in 'The Medium of Romantic Poetry' (*The Cambridge Companion to British Romantic Poetry*, eds. James Chandler and Maureen N. McClane [Cambridge: Cambridge University Press, 2008], pp. 239–62); Andrew Burkett's attention to Blake's visuality in 'Blake's Moving Images' (*Romantic Mediations: Media Theory and British Romanticism* [Albany, NY: SUNY Press, 2016], pp. 75–114); or Kate Singer's reading of Charlotte Smith's affective sensibility in 'Limpid Waves and Good Vibrations: Charlotte Smith's New Materialist Affect' (*Essays in Romanticism*, 23: 2 [2016], pp. 175–92). This essay positions scribal practice as an intervention in the binding representation of sound, sight, and affect in print.

[5] Andrew Lincoln, 'Introduction', in *William Blake: Songs of Innocence and of Experience* (Princeton, NJ: The William Blake Trust/Princeton University Press, 1991), pp. 9, 18. Estimation of the number of copies Blake produced of the *Songs* varies from source to source. I cite the most recent numbers available from *The William Blake Archive*, eds. Morris Eaves, Robert Essick, and Joseph Vicsomi, at www.blakearchive.org.

books are not copies *of* anything, there is no "original" behind them'.[6] Blake's invention of the technique of illuminated printing—engraving word and image on a single plate—made it feasible for him to handle every stage of production, from inception to execution to distribution: he would write, illustrate, engrave, ink, print, hand-color, bind, and sell autographic texts that 'look more like illuminated manuscripts than printed books' (Lincoln, p. 15). Like a manuscript, every single printed copy is marked by the differentiating presence of his hand.[7]

While the coloring, background, and borders change significantly in each iteration, *Songs of Innocence* always opens with two juxtaposed images that depict the initialization and outcome of the composition process that the opening lyric delineates: a frontispiece that visualizes a moment of inspiration as a piper-shepherd gazes at a child hovering above him, and a title-page that pictures a moment of instruction as a girl and boy read or look at a book positioned on a maternal figure's lap. The 'Introduction' that follows these images offers a lyric analysis of what happens between the moment of inspiration and the moment of instruction by mapping the mediating stages that bring books into being and showing the impact and consequences of those stages on the creator, the creation, and the receiver as an artist hones spontaneous sensory experience into the formalized, mechanically reproducible format of a written poem. Blake mirrors the free-form origins of artistic creation syntactically in the first four lines through a brilliant use of dangling modifiers that make the attribution of agency impossible:

> Piping down the valleys wild
> Piping songs of pleasant glee
> On a cloud I saw a child.
> And he laughing said to me.
>
> Pipe a song about a Lamb;
> So I piped with merry chear.

[6] Paul Mann, 'Apocalypse and Recuperation: Blake and the Maw of Commerce', *ELH*, 52: 1 (Spring 1985), p. 13. For essential discussions of Blake's production aesthetic and printing techniques, see Robert Essick's *William Blake, Printmaker* (Princeton, NJ: Princeton University Press, 1980); Morris Eaves's *The Counter-Arts Conspiracy: Art and Industry in the Age of Blake* (Ithaca, NY: Cornell University Press, 1992); and Joseph Viscomi's *Blake and the Idea of a Book* (Princeton, NJ: Princeton University Press, 1993). John Jones offers a helpful overview of 'Blake's Production Methods' in *Palgrave Advances in William Blake Studies*, ed. Nicholas Williams (New York: Palgrave Macmillan, 2006), pp. 25–41. For a detailed analysis of the way these material approaches to Blake's production methods intersect with network and media theory, see Andrew Burkett, *Romantic Mediations: Media Theory and British Romanticism* (Albany: SUNY Press, 2016).

[7] I do not want to omit reference to Catherine Blake, who engaged in many of these processes.

Piper pipe that song again—
So I piped, he wept to hear.[8]

In the 'valleys wild' of the first stanza, the rules of grammar (and the laws of gravity) do not yet apply. The piping simply occurs, unattached to a particular individual, potentially the speaker, potentially the child—either of whom might be on a cloud, either of whom might be wild—until the second stanza, when the child's speech acts begin to create definitions: he commands the speaker to 'pipe' in line five and then names the speaker a 'piper' in line seven after the speaker performs that identifying action with full grammatical agency: 'I piped'. And, thus, the poem commences unfolding the series of steps that transform the raw matter of improvisation into the materialized form of books, indicating what each step does to the work and its audience.

Each phase of the progression that turns the piped melody into an engraved poem reveals an increase in referential and interpretive specificity coincident with a decrease in spontaneity and musicality as the piper shifts from piping to singing to writing:

Drop thy pipe thy happy pipe
Sing thy songs of happy chear,
So I sung the same again
While he wept with joy to hear

Piper sit thee down and write
In a book that all may read—
So he vanish'd from my sight.
And I pluck'd a hollow reed.

And I made a rural pen,
And I stain'd the water clear,
And I wrote my happy songs
Every child may joy to hear. (lines 9–20, E 7)

Consistently termed a 'song', the object the piper produces modulates from a tune expressing an emotion (pleasant glee) into a tune about a specific subject (a lamb), then a song with words but no piping, and finally an inscribed poem whose words can be read and heard but whose original melody is transformed into the metered rhythm of recitation. At every point of the

[8] William Blake, 'Introduction', in *The Complete Poetry and Prose of William Blake*, ed. David V. Erdman (Berkeley & Los Angeles: University of California Press, 1982), lines 1–8, p. 7.

song's metamorphosis, 'Introduction' reflects the impact of the change on the piper's relationship with his immediate and future audience and his audience's immediate and projected response. As the song gains specificity, it elicits an increasingly defined and directed response from its immediate audience—the child—who simply laughs while the pleasant tune plays, but who weeps to hear the song about the lamb (notably its repetition, which locks it into a controlled pattern), and who weeps with joy after hearing the lyrics that instantiate a more directed experience of the melody. Both child and melody disappear when the piper writes his 'happy songs' so that he can only imagine how future children 'may joy to hear' them. Paradoxically, while the movement from piping to singing to writing provides greater direction for and from the writer, print, in separating the writer from the audience, provides greater verbal and oral interpretive possibilities for readers. Just before the child vanishes, he points to the virtues of print in providing the potential of a greater audience for books over performances: 'all may read' (line 14). But the 'Introduction' to *Songs of Innocence* illuminates the problem of commercial publishing for the writer: the immediacy of the artist's voice is lost as the writer becomes an incorporated identity. The piper loses direct contact with his audience, who can no longer hear his voice. Books acquire an autonomous existence that separates the creator from the creation as well as the audience, a division Blake depicts in the two juxtaposed plates that precede the 'Introduction': the piper and child gazing at one another versus the two children gazing at the book.

How can Blake reinsert his voice or authorial presence? Through individual vocalizing, reintroducing his autograph through the non-uniform reproduction of illuminated printing. Because every copy of every Blake book presents a new performance, Blake resists the stasis of mechanistic reproduction through the variations he inscribes via illuminated printing. In *Songs*, those variations occur foremost through the extraordinary palette of colors Blake uses to differentiate the designs of each iteration over a period of thirty-eight years, which range from the soft pastels of *SI* copy I to the rich, intensely vibrant shades of *SIE* copy Z.[9] Equally if not more significant are the dizzying array of sequences Blake arranges for the individual lyrics in each collection, which not only transform the overall narrative structure of the *Songs* in all but six versions (*SIE* copies U, W–Z, AA) but also establish altering interpretive contexts for each poem in the sequence. Beyond the major permutations Blake introduces through color and sequence are the many local variations that make each hand-colored print unique: trees and streams and clouds and birds appear or disappear; the sun rises or sets or casts a powerful red light through skies that sometimes become hills; rainbows, moons, and stars come and go; suns

[9] See G.E. Bentley Jr., *Blake Books* (Oxford: Clarendon Press, 1977), for a comprehensive overview of Blake's use of color.

and moons turn into hats or haloes and back again; sometimes the children are dressed or dangle grapes, and sometimes they are tellingly without either. Faces look happy or sad or curious or confrontational (the piper in the frontispieces to *Experience*); sometimes they gaze at one another and sometimes away (Eve looking up at Adam or down at the ground in the frontispieces to the combined *Songs*). The matter that makes up the material of Blake's graphic universe fluctuates from one manifestation to the next.

Often Blake displays the autographic fluidity of illuminated printing through shifting representations of human bodies, particularly in poems that question what it means to be embodied. Perhaps the most famous example occurs in 'The Little Black Boy', whose speaker contemplates his racialized body from several perspectives, declaring 'I am black, but O! my soul is white; / White as an angel is the English child: / But I am black as if bereav'd of light' (lines 2–4, E 9) and anticipating a future 'When I from black and he from white cloud free, / And round the tent of God like lambs we joy: / Ill shade him from the heat' (lines 23–5, E 9). The fifty designs that envision that future scenario depict the speaker in shades that range from white and pink to brown and black, each shade inviting a different reading of what the speaker (or viewer) imagines or understands the future to encompass and what kind of 'body' the speaker might inhabit. Similarly, the fifty designs for 'The Little Boy Found' show the boy being led through the fen by an adult figure who alternately manifests as Jesus or his mother; sometimes the adult and child have haloes; sometimes the boy wears a hat; sometimes a red moon appears behind the adult's head. These various configurations suggest multiple conclusions to the lost child's experience: is he being brought to his mother by Jesus, or has he been reunited with her, and is this happening on earth or in heaven? Like the twenty-nine varying expressions on the faces of Blake's many-colored tigers, which controvert the dreaded 'fearful symmetry' of 'The Tyger' as effectively as Blake's sly eye-rhyme, each autographic iteration of the *Songs* pushes against stasis and uniformity through a material mutability Blake makes possible via illuminated printing.

Blake's invention of illuminated printing merges print technologies with manuscript practices to produce a new medial materiality that enables him to resist what his philosophy identifies as the consolidation or stultification of vibrant animated energies into the diminished forms of static bodies and books. In *The Marriage of Heaven and Hell,* Blake's speaker describes the derogating process of printing houses that reduce the wild matter of dragons, vipers, eagles, and lions into 'unnam'd forms' that become the mild 'forms of books' to be 'arranged in libraries' (E 40). In *The Book of Urizen,* Blake first articulates his larger myth of the fall into creation, where the limitless energies of unbound eternal beings are confined within human bodies because Urizen writes a book that creates 'a solid without fluctuation' (4: 11, E 71).

In *Jerusalem,* Los attempts to revert Urizen's bookish consolidations through art, 'Striving with Systems to deliver Individuals from those Systems' (11: 5, E 154). With *Songs,* Blake introduces the means to deliver individuals from those systems: via the autographic medium of illuminated printing, which enables him to embody variation and flux, to enact the transgressive materiality that Oothoon champions in *Visions of the Daughters of Albion* when she sees the Marygold as nymph and flower (1: 6–7, E 46) or that the speaker of 'The Fly' wants to query when he asks 'Am not I / A fly like thee? / Or art not thou / A man like me?' (*SIE* lines 5–8, E 23). Even as Blake's words interrogate the stolidity of a single materialized reality, his autographic illuminations make manifest a vibrant, ever-changing multiverse.

Samuel Taylor Coleridge and the Endless Cycle of Revision

While Blake creates books that destabilize the fixities of mechanical reproduction so that each copy embodies an autographic iteration, Coleridge produces poems that resist the stasis of completion: because they exist as nominal fragments, like 'Kubla Khan' or 'Christabel', or mutate through a continuous cycle of revision, like 'The Rime of the Ancient Mariner', they manifest as vital processes or ongoing conversations rather than finished products or summative statements. Unlike the verbal texts engraved in Blake's *Songs*, the words in Coleridge's verses appear to be in a constant state of flux. When Jack Stillinger estimated the multiple versions Coleridge produced of his seven most famous poems between 1796 and 1834, he counted sixteen independently authoritative printed and manuscript versions of 'The Eolian Harp', twelve versions of 'This Lime-Tree Bower My Prison', ten versions of 'Frost at Midnight', eighteen versions of 'The Rime of the Ancient Mariner', five versions of 'Kubla Khan', eighteen versions of 'Christabel', and fifteen versions of 'Dejection: An Ode'.[10] In some instances, Coleridge only changes a line or two; at other times, he makes large-scale transformations and interventions by adding, deleting, or reworking entire sections of poems, as with 'The Eolian Harp', 'This Lime-Tree Bower My Prison', and 'Frost at Midnight', or by composing the marginal glosses for 'The Rime of the Ancient Mariner' and the Ramsgate copy of 'Christabel'.[11] Each revision, no

[10] Jack Stillinger, *Coleridge and Textual Instability: The Multiple Versions of the Major Poems* (New York: Oxford University Press, 1994), pp. 26–99. For other significant discussions of Coleridge's revisionary habits see Zachary Leader's chapter on 'Coleridge's Revisionary Complexity' in *Revision and Romantic Authorship* (Oxford: Clarendon Press, 1996), pp. 121–63; Ve-Yin Tee's *Coleridge, Revision, and Romanticism* (New York: Continuum, 2009); and Tim Fulford's *Romantic Poetry and Literary Coteries: The Dialect of the Tribe* (New York: Palgrave Macmillan, 2015), pp. 23–97.

[11] S.T. Coleridge, *Christabel, &c.*, 2nd ed. (London: John Murray, 1816), RHT 19th-173,

matter how minor or major, demonstrates an intentionality that alters the meaning, structure, style, and, ultimately, the ontological status of the poem, as there is no definitive set of sequenced words named by the poem's title. Coleridge even calls attention to the intentional impermanence of his texts through direct addresses to readers that either invoke the poems' hypoplastic development, as in his prefaces to 'Christabel' and 'Kubla Khan', or highlight their transitioning status, via notes or extensive errata lists that change the texts 'right before the readers' eyes' (Stillinger, p. 109). In tandem with these formal print mechanisms that destabilize his texts from one commercial publication to the next, Coleridge transforms individual presentation copies with handwritten emendations that suborn commercial uniformity through personal inscription, as in a rare description of Geraldine's bosom: 'It was dark and rough as the Sea Wolf's hide'.[12] Thus in the dramatic example *Sibylline Leaves* affords, Coleridge not only presents one of the eighteen versions of 'Rime' and offers an errata list in the prefatory pages that contains a new stanza for 'The Eolian Harp' (the famous 'one life passage'), which he expects his reader to insert 177 pages later, but he also inscribes at least thirty presentation copies with insertions, corrections, comments, and annotations that vary from copy to copy.[13]

The textual instability produced by this plenitude of printed versions, annotated printed versions, and manuscript versions provides the means by which Coleridge escapes textual containment, wriggling from the grasp of definitive form as elusively as Blake: each version of a Coleridge poem operates as the next in an ongoing series of working drafts that resist reification and closure by re-envisioning moments of inspiration in new materializations. While Blake inscribes a materially differentiated voice through the autographic variability of illuminated printing, Coleridge continually reanimates moments of imaginative experience by rewriting and glossing them, or he resumes a one-sided dialogue with absent interlocutors by returning to his conversation poems. If the poet in 'Kubla Khan' expresses frustration at his inability to recall a vision of a damsel with a dulcimer and what he could accomplish through visionary recollection—'Could I revive within me / Her symphony and song, / To such a deep delight 'twould win me, / That with music loud and long, / I would build that dome in air'—Coleridge revives a portion of the vision

Princeton University Library, Princeton. The title-page inscription reads 'with MSS corrections and additions by the Author. 25 Novr 1824 Ramsgate'.

[12] This line appears in a copy of the 1816 *Christabel* edition at Harvard and a copy of the 1828 *Poetical Works* at the Fitzwilliam Museum (Stillinger, p. 201).

[13] See J.C.C. Mays, ed., *The Poetical Works*, 3 vols., *The Collected Works of Samuel Taylor Coleridge*, eds. H.J. Jackson and George Whalley, vol. 16 (Princeton, NJ: Princeton University Press, 2001), I: p. 1335 for discussion of the thirty presentation copies of *Sibylline Leaves* (London: Rest Fenner, 1817).

each time he revisits the poem.[14] Similarly, when Coleridge tries to assuage his feelings of isolation and alienation by building emotional connections to his son in 'Frost at Midnight', to Charles Lamb in 'This Lime-Tree Bower My Prison', or to Sara Hutchinson in 'Dejection: An Ode', he recreates the possibility of enacting union with his interlocutors and readers through verse in each version.[15] Revision, emendation, commentary, and even fragmentation mean that Coleridge is never locked into a single, completed iteration, so that textual instability sustains a vocalized textual vitality, as in the never-ending story of 'Christabel'.

The poem that receives Coleridge's steadiest revisionary attention, 'The Rime of the Ancient Mariner', may most fully articulate what he seeks to accomplish through the destabilizing materiality of his multiple versions, by insisting on the importance of process over product; of identity located and reformulated in a recursive act of telling rather than a static, consistent declaration; and of human connection made through a specific, directed, individualized aurality. In the many versions of the 'Rime' that Coleridge prepares—and that his mariner fictively recites to the selected listeners who repeat and interpret his tale—Coleridge suggests that the best way individuals can know themselves or explain themselves to others is by remembering and relating the narrative that constructs their selfhood. The mariner can only answer the question 'what manner of man art thou?' by telling his story, which cannot be contained in a summative term or a single recitation because the telling always leads to the Sisyphean question 'what manner of man art thou?'[16] As Susan Eilenberg puts it, his 'relation to his tale is tautological, at once totally arbitrary and totally determined. The Mariner tells his tale to explain that he is the man who tells the tale in order to explain what manner of man he is'.[17] When the 'Rime' begins, the mariner appears as an 'It' who becomes an 'I' with a unique personal

[14] S.T. Coleridge, 'Kubla Khan', in *Christabel: Kubla Khan, A Vision; The Pains of Sleep* (London: John Murray, 1816), lines 42–6.

[15] Tim Fulford underscores the potential pragmatism of Coleridge's revisionary strategies, as he refashions his verses for new audiences. See Fulford, *The Late Poetry of the Lake Poets: Romanticism Revised* (Cambridge: University of Cambridge Press, 2013).

[16] S.T. Coleridge, 'The Rime of the Ancient Mariner', *Sibylline Leaves*, line 581. This is not to say that critical discussion of the poem has not provided a series of persuasive terms to denote the mariner's historical experience (as a slaver or explorer or victim of yellow fever), or his psychological condition (repetition compulsion or post-traumatic stress disorder). Damien Walford Davies offers a comprehensive overview of the many approaches critics have taken to naming the mariner's condition in his thoroughly persuasive claim that the mariner suffers from PTSD; see 'Diagnosing "The Rime of the Ancient Mariner": Shipwreck, Historicism, Traumatology', *Studies in Romanticism*, 55: 4 (Winter 2016), pp. 503–35.

[17] Susan Eilenberg, *Strange Power of Speech: Wordsworth, Coleridge, and Literary Possession* (New York: Oxford University Press, 1992), p. 33.

identity through his performative framing of the experiences that shape him, and it is through that frame-building performance that he materializes into some 'manner of man' for his auditor (hermit, minstrel, wedding guest, glossist, reader) as well as himself. The poem asserts that the mariner's manner cannot be categorized by a word or phrase but must be rebuilt via an explanatory history each time the mariner faces the agonizing question 'what manner of man art thou?' because his 'I' is shaped by actions that separate him from the 'we' of his fellow mariners and cannot be neatly summarized by or attributed to conventional codes. He is the mariner who first differentiates himself as an 'I' by shooting the albatross and then by drinking his own blood to speak, acts that signal a consciousness literally at odds with the corporate identity of the other two hundred men. The isolation he experiences precedes the soul-wrenching agony he expresses after the other mariners die—'Alone, alone, all, all alone, / Alone on a wide wide sea! / And never a saint took pity on / My soul in agony' (lines 236–9)—and wrenches his frame when the hermit asks 'what manner of man art thou?': 'Forthwith this frame of mine was wrenched / With a woeful agony, / Which forced me to begin my tale; / And then it left me free' (lines 582–5). Freedom from 'it'—the agony, the tale—momentarily occurs in the process of relating his history and rebuilding the frame of his identity but always returns him to his manifestation as an 'it': 'It is an ancient mariner'. 'It' leaves the mariner free to become an 'it' again and start his tale anew, to begin constructing an image of his human embodiment for his next listener through the words he speaks.

Coleridge not only mirrors the circularity of the mariner's experience through his writing process but also signals the significance of the parallel when he rededicates an epigram he wrote for Henry James Pye to himself, 'To the author of the Ancient Mariner': 'Your Poem must *eternal* be, / Dear Sir!—It cannot fail: / For tis incomprehensible / And without head or tail'.[18] When Coleridge introduces this epigram in the *Biographia Literaria,* he offers an anecdote that further emphasizes the uroboric circularity of the 'Rime' and its recursive process of self-discovery by claiming that an amateur poet wanted to meet him but feared he had offended Coleridge by writing a 'severe epigram on my *ancient mariner.* ... [I] begged to hear it recited: when, to my no less surprise than amusement, it proved to be one I had myself some time before written and inserted in the Morning Post' (*BL* 1: p. 28). As John Beer observes, both the anecdote and epigram make manifest the theory of narrative poetics Coleridge voices in a 7 March 1815 letter to Joseph Cottle: 'The common end of all *narrative*, nay of *all* Poems, is to convert a *series* into a *Whole*: to make

[18] S.T. Coleridge, *Biographia Literaria*, 2 vols. (London: Rest Fenner, 1817), 1: p. 28. Coleridge first published these lines 'To Mr. Pye on his carmen seculare' in *The Morning Post* (24 January 1800).

those events, which in real or imagined History move on in a *strait* line, assume to our Understandings a *circular* motion—the snake with it's Tail in it's [*sic*] Mouth'.[19] Like the mariner, whose straight line of reported events effects an infinite loop that returns him to his beginning, Coleridge's habitual mode of rewriting enacts the circular motion that keeps the snake's tail in its mouth. But there is an important difference between the mariner's recursive experience and Coleridge's revisionary versing: while the mariner appears to be stuck in a compulsive repetition that continually rebuilds and rimes his storied identity as the 'ancient mariner', Coleridge creates a new version each time he revises or re-engages one of his poems, returning from the dead-end of completion to inscribe an alternating autographic entity. Thus what Coleridge ultimately accomplishes through his revisionary process is a material embodiment of the active, fluid process of imagination he repeatedly maps in 'The Eolian Harp', where he poses a question that provides a crucial counterpoint to the hermit's: 'And what if all of animated nature / Be but organic harps diversely framed, / That tremble into thought, as o'er them sweeps / Plastic and vast, one intellectual breeze, / At once the Soul of each, and God of all?'[20] For Coleridge, poems and bodies are diverse frames that can only materialize or be known through recursive acts of writing or speech. Although the 'Harp''s interpellated 'beloved woman! … Meek daughter in the family of Christ!' (lines 50–3) might prefer Coleridge to declare categorically 'what manner of man' he is, Coleridge resists being locked into a definitive frame or form through fragmentation and revision, using each iteration and emendation to materialize the fluid 'shapings of the unregenerate mind' (line 55).

Mary Tighe and Coterie Publication

Like Blake and Coleridge, and most Romantic-era poets, Tighe shared manuscripts of her work with a select group of friends and family members, presenting them with dozens of elegantly penned autograph copies, sometimes illustrated with watercolor tailpieces, and often embellished with fine calligraphy, each one graphologically incarnating her poetic persona for her reader.[21] But unlike Tighe, Blake and Coleridge experienced the economic necessity of pursuing commercial publication and resisted commodification and textual

[19] John Beer, 'Romantic Apocalypses', *Romanticism and Millenarianism*, ed. Tim Fulford (New York: Palgrave Macmillan, 2002), p. 66, citing *The Collected Letters of Samuel Taylor Coleridge*, ed. E.L. Griggs, 6 vols. (Oxford: Oxford University Press, 1956–71), 4: p. 545.

[20] Mays I: p. 234, lines 44–8.

[21] See my 'Mary Tighe and the Coterie of British Women Poets' in *The History of Women's Writing, 1750–1830*, ed. Jacqueline Labbe (London: Palgrave, 2010), pp. 301–20 and Amy Prendergast, *Literary Salons Across Britain and Ireland in the Long Eighteenth Century* (New York: Palgrave Macmillan, 2015), pp. 169–73.

uniformity by blending scribal practices with print technologies to manifest the idiolectic vitality of their voices and visions. Tighe could afford the luxury of choosing whether or not to make her work available to the public and elected to circulate it exclusively within her literary coterie. Though she had the opportunity to publish a version of the volume that would eventually become the posthumous edition of *Psyche, with Other Poems* (1811), she declined, opting instead to print a private edition of *Psyche; or, The Legend of Love* (1805), which she distributed to the members of her coterie. With that typeset private edition of *Psyche,* Tighe effectively adapted print technologies to further scribal practice, imbuing the printed copies with the affective materiality of her manuscripts through autographic inscriptions. Tighe completed *Psyche* in 1802 and began sending manuscript copies to friends, who urged her to consider preparing an edition for the public. She expressed delight with their personal approbation but insisted she never wanted to become a public author, as she indicates in a letter to Joseph Cooper Walker on 16 August 1803:

> I hope my vanity of authorship may never conquer the repugnance I now feel to stand forth to the public & say Hear me, but I will not deny that I feel nothing more delightful to self love than to be listen'd to with a smile, nor is that pleasure in any degree lessen'd by a consciousness that I should place the smile to the account of partiality.[22]

In a postscript to the manuscript copy she prepared for Lady Eleanor Butler and Sarah Ponsonby she asserts the same, that she writes 'only for the more interested eye of friendship':

> The author who dismisses to the public the darling object of his solitary cares, must be prepar'd to consider with indifference the various reception it may there meet with; But from those who write only for the more interested eye of friendship no such indifference can be expected—I must therefore be forgiven the egotism which makes me anxious to recommend to <u>my</u> readers the tale with which I now present them.[23]

By underlining '<u>my</u> readers', Tighe underscores the close connection she sustains with her audience, real readers in contrast with the implied readers Blake's child conjures for the piper or the idealized auditors Coleridge tries to reach in his conversation poems. While Blake continually interjects his voice

[22] Letter to Joseph Cooper Walker, MS 1461/5/43–44, Trinity College Library, Dublin.

[23] 'Psyche. or The Legend of Love. 1803', MS 22985B, National Library of Wales, Aberystwyth. A lightly edited version of this postscript becomes the preface for the 1805 print edition of *Psyche.*

through the autographic variation of illuminated printing, and Coleridge keeps his texts in process through revision and fragmentation, Tighe rejects the commodifying impact of commercial production and sustains a personal materialized identity through coterie publication.

When Tighe decides against publishing a commercial edition of *Psyche* with other poems, she expresses her concern with becoming a commodified subject whose identity or value would be determined by the impersonal gaze of indifferent, objectifying reviewers rather than 'the interested eye of friendship'. On 24 December 1804 she tells Walker '[I] had almost been persuaded to expose to the mercy of the reviewers, Edinburg butchers & all, my poor little Psyche & a volume of smaller poems … . I have however resolv'd upon printing a few copies of Psyche only, which I confess I have great pleasure already in distributing in idea' (TCD MS 1461/7/193–4). She had John Carpenter print fifty typescript copies of *Psyche*, which she distributed to friends and family, dedicating and dating them with personal inscriptions and autographs that not only materialized the connectedness expressed in the preface (the manuscript postscript) but also individualized each copy as a unique embodiment of a specific relationship: 'To Sarah Tighe from her affectionate niece M Tighe', 'To Camilla Blachford from her grateful and affectionate M Tighe. London, July 1805', 'To Robert Bligh from his affectionate cousin M Tighe. Brompton, Aug 1805', 'To William Parnell from his obligest friend M Tighe. July 1805', 'To Catherine Stewart, from her affectionate & obliged friend M Tighe. London, July 25 1805', or 'To the Rev. J. Kearney D.D. Provost of T:C:D: from his obliged & obedient servant M Tighe. Dec 7 1805'.[24] As Paula Feldman notes, these signatures counter the seeming anonymity of the edition, which does not name Tighe as the author in typescript on the title page.[25] But what Tighe accomplishes by omitting a print attribution is bypassing the culturally-required corporate identity that would position her on the title page as 'Mrs. Henry Tighe' rather than the personalized 'M Tighe' who writes for her interested friends. She not only maintains her individualized personal identity as M Tighe, niece, or cousin, or friend, but she also transforms these otherwise uniform printed books back into scribal copies for each reader.

For Tighe the materialization or manifestation of personhood as resistance to commodification comprises a major issue in the poem itself, which, like Coleridge's 'Rime', focuses on the ongoing process of constructing identity and, like Blake's 'Introduction' to the *Songs of Innocence,* speaks to the importance of immediacy and presence. In Tighe's radical revision of the Cupid and Psyche

[24] Averill Buchanan lists these inscriptions (and another thirteen) in *Mary Blachford Tighe: The Irish Psyche* (Newcastle upon Tyne: Cambridge Scholars Publishing, 2011), pp. 211–12.
[25] Paula Feldman, 'Women Poets and Anonymity in the Romantic Era', *New Literary History*, 33: 2 (Spring 2002), pp. 279–80.

myth, Psyche is an objectified beauty who transgresses when she disobeys a prohibition against looking and knowing but refuses to accept the consequences of her transgression by actively seeking restoration. The poem transforms the myth into a *bildungsroman* that features Psyche encountering a series of moral and psychological dilemmas that she must resolve before she can 'see' Cupid again, who accompanies her on the quest disguised as a knight. All of the encounters introduce Psyche to female figures who model different ways of gazing and knowing. If the query that awakens Blake's Oothoon is 'Art thou a flower! Art thou a nymph!' (1: 6, E 46), and if the question that haunts the 'Rime' is 'what manner of man art thou?', then the question that shapes Tighe's *Psyche* is 'what manner of woman will you be?' As the narrative traces the developmental experiences Psyche undergoes while her sense of her self and her place in the world evolve, Tighe conflates and contrasts Psyche's transforming habitus with her own position as a poet who declares her right to look and to be inspired by her muse, interrupting the narrative with autographic interjections that directly address her real readers: 'Oh, you for whom I write! whose hearts can melt / At the soft thrilling voice whose power you prove, / You know what charm, unutterably felt, / Attends the unexpected voice of Love: / … You best can tell the rapture Psyche feels / When Love's ambrosial lip the vows of Hymen seals' (1.451–9). These irruptions disrupt narrative time and space to assert authorial presence and story as vocalizing process, as when Tighe invokes the muse—'Oh, Muse divine! thee only I implore, / Shed on my soul thy sweet inspiring beams' (1.502–3) or 'Oh, daring muse! wilt thou indeed essay / To paint the wonders which that lamp could shew?' (2.190–1)—and expresses the pleasure she takes in witnessing the very tale she is writing:

> Delightful visions of my lonely hours!
> Charm of my life, and solace of my care!
> Oh! would the muse but lend proportioned powers,
> And give me language, equal to declare
> The wonders which she bids my fancy share,
> When rapt in her to other worlds I fly,
> ******
> My Psyche's wanderings then she loves to trace,
> Unrols the glowing canvass to my sight;
> Her chaste calm eye, her soft attractive grace,
> The lightning of her heavenly smile so bright,
> All yield me strange and unconceived delight:
> Even now entranced her journey I pursue,
> And gaze enraptured on her matchless knight;
> Visions of love, pure, innocent and true!
> Oh! may your graceful forms for ever bless my view! (5.1–36)

The delight this voice expresses in vocalizing vision as poetic process makes the poem's conclusion all the more devastating, as Psyche settles into a static, apotheosized identity—Cupid's bride and Venus's daughter-in-law—and Tighe bemoans her own return to a non-visionary reality, no longer in the process of becoming, but having been, and thus in a state of inertia: 'Dreams of Delight farewell! ... / The page remains—but can the page restore / The vanished bowers which Fancy taught to bloom? / Ah no! ... / Consigned to dark oblivion's silent tomb / The visionary scenes no more I see, / Fast from the fading lines the vivid colours flee!' (6.532–40).

In the final stanza of *Psyche,* Tighe suggestively links the end of visionary processes with the institutionalization of the individual in a gendered framework, addressing the very dilemma that drives Blake and Coleridge to reiterate their voices and visions through autographic materiality. Although Tighe did not directly pursue the strategies Blake and Coleridge deployed to transform the potential uniformity of their commercial publications, the private edition of *Psyche* took on a rhizomic life of its own as friends and strangers alike borrowed copies, made their own manuscript copies, and shared those copies with others who made their own manuscript copies of the manuscript copies. Thus, Tighe's one foray into print technology exemplified and perpetuated the scribal practices of coterie publication, rematerializing each print copy of *Psyche* as a graphological manuscript to be shared with friends. Calls to publish *Psyche* appeared in multiple print venues, but Tighe remained committed to manuscript culture as a coterie poet to the end of her days, sending autograph copies of work to friends, inscribing lyrics in others' albums, periodically hosting a salon, and letting friends copy pieces from her beautifully transcribed two-volume manuscript collection, *Verses Transcribed for H.T.*[26] Tighe likely enjoyed some of the fame she acquired as 'the Author of Psyche', as she indicates in a negative comment in September 1806 that 'one of the miseries of authorship' entailed being solicited for subscriptions: 'Certainly one of the miseries of authorship is the necessity of receiving the detestable performances which every stupid writer thinks it is honoring you to communicate – This vile nonsense was sent to the Author of Psyche with a demand of a guinea subscription'.[27] Proud to be known as the author of *Psyche* and other poems, she sought to establish, voice, and materialize the terms of her authorial identity through the vitalizing, fluid, affective interactions of manuscript culture.

[26] For examples of these calls, see my 'Mary Tighe: A Portrait of the Artist for the Twenty-First Century', in *A Companion to Irish Literature*, ed. Julia M. Wright, 2 vols. (West Sussex: Wiley-Blackwell, 2010), 1: pp. 292–3. See my online edition of Tighe's *Verses Transcribed for H.T.* (1805), *Romantic Circles* (2015), at https://romantic-circles.org/editions/tighe_verses.

[27] The 'vile nonsense' was H. Byrne's *The Chaplet of Fame* (Dublin: John Jones, 1806), mentioned in Tighe's 'Critical Reviews', MS 4804, National Library of Ireland, Dublin.

A year after Tighe died, her husband Henry Tighe and brother John Blachford edited and published the 1811 *Psyche, with Other Poems* by 'the Late Mrs. Henry Tighe' with Longman and company, which embalmed Tighe and her poetry in the very format she rejected. If they felt guilty about going against Tighe's expressed wishes, a prefatory address to the reader sought to justify the publication of her poems as more than a 'monument of private regret' for a gifted writer who died prematurely, but a 'duty in surviving friends no longer to withhold from the public such precious relics'; given their aesthetic, scholarly, and moral excellence, 'her friends ... thought themselves justified in displaying them to the world' (pp. iii–iv). In addition to a re-edited version of 'Psyche', the volume included thirty-nine of the approximately 150 lyrics Tighe is known to have composed between 1788 and 1809, which, the preface discreetly notes, were 'not originally intended or pointed out by herself for publication' (p. v). Although Tighe did not select lyrics to accompany *Psyche* for the volume she considered publishing in 1804, she did transcribe 121 of her poems in the carefully arranged volumes of *Verses Transcribed for H.T.*, whose sequences delineate Tighe's emergence, development, and journey as a poet writing for her coterie, from her initial dedication to the muse on the banks of 'The Vartree' to the final sonnet's response to a sonnet from Lady Dacre.[28] As Buchanan observes, Henry Tighe modelled sections of the 1811 edition on *Verses* (pp. 123–4), but the posthumous edition ultimately refashioned the Tighe who self-identified as a coterie poet producing autographic manuscripts and private printings for her friends into a commercial commodity sometimes fetishized as a beautiful dead poetess.[29]

Intriguingly, the women who loved Tighe sought to re-embody her in more fluid forms by continuing the scribal practices of their coteries. Her mother, Theodosia Blachford, assembled an alternate anthology of her work in 1811, *Mary, a Series of Reflections During Twenty Years*, which used a hybrid format of typescript and manuscript to offer a chronological overview of Tighe's lyric productions that emphasized her spiritual journey and mental states from 1789 to 1809.[30] Another private edition like the 1805 *Psyche*, the

[28] See the introduction to *Verses* for discussion of how Tighe stages her journey as a coterie poet.

[29] See Samantha Matthews, *Poetical Remains: Poets' Graves, Bodies, and Books in the Nineteenth Century* (Oxford: Oxford University Press, 2004), pp. 77–89 and my 'Mary Tighe and Literary History: The Making of a Critical Reputation', *Literature Compass*, 7: 7 (2010), pp. 564–76.

[30] Mary Tighe, *Mary, a Series of Reflections During Twenty Years* ([n.p.], 1811). Only two of the twenty copies are known to exist (at the National Library of Ireland and the Houghton Library at Harvard). Both contain inscriptions in Theodosia Blachford's hand. See Buchanan (pp. 130–1) and Paula Feldman and Brian Cooney, *The Collected Poetry of Mary Tighe* (Baltimore, MD: Johns Hopkins University Press, 2016), pp. 22–4.

twenty copies of *Mary* were hand inscribed with the caveat 'Not to be given away, nor lent nor shown to any but a very partial friend', implicitly echoing Tighe's introduction to *Psyche*; and the copies contained a printed statement that 'Many of these reflections were written in very early youth, and may be inaccurate; but are not the less valuable for whom *alone* this Selection is intended'. Blachford included thirty poems: seventeen that did not appear in the 1811 *Psyche, with Other Poems* as well as thirteen that did.[31] Because Henry Tighe sold the copyright for *Psyche, with Other Poems* to Longman in July 1811, the thirteen poems reprinted from the posthumous edition are hand transcribed in *Mary*, returning those poems from commercial print to manuscript and restoring the 'late Mrs. Henry Tighe' to her intimate friends as 'Mary'. An inscription in the Houghton Library copy notes, 'I have only had a very few copies of this selection printed privately by a friend to be given only to her most partial & serious friends'.[32] Those partial and serious friends continued the project of reclaiming Tighe as a coterie poet through additional manuscript compilations, such as E.I. Fox's album of twenty 'Poems by Mrs. H. Tighe. Including Twelve Poems not published with Psyche'.[33] Fox's album tellingly opens with Tighe's 'A Faithful Friend is the Medicine of Life', focuses on friendship poems, and closes with a heartfelt tribute 'To the Memory of Mrs. Henry Tighe' that names her twice as 'Linda', Tighe's coterie name.[34] Similarly, Tighe's cousin and sister-in-law Caroline Hamilton created multiple mini-anthologies of Tighe's poems in her many diaries and commonplace books, such as MS 42,118, which transcribes four Tighe poems in a cluster of nineteen family lyrics that focus on familial landscapes in Wicklow and Kilkenny.[35] These alternate anthologies, manuscripts, and commonplace books effectively destabilize and rematerialize the body her male representatives encrypted in *Psyche, with Other Poems* by re-embodying Tighe graphologically in their own idiolectic hands and therein carried on Tighe's ethos as a coterie poet committed to scribal practices.

[31] *Mary* includes four additional poems not by Tighe, handwritten notes, an allegorical explanation of *Psyche*, and an extract from a review of *Psyche*; the Houghton copy also includes a description of one of Tighe's dreams.

[32] EC8. T4484 811M, Houghton Library, Harvard University, Cambridge. See Buchanan (p. 203).

[33] E.I. Fox, 'Poems by Mrs. H. Tighe. Including Twelve Poems not published with Psyche', undated MS book, Belfast Public Library, Belfast. Fox provides alternate titles to twelve lyrics (eight from *Verses* and four from *Psyche*) and minor word variations in fifteen.

[34] Fox footnotes the first reference as follows: 'Her own poetic appellation see her poem on the Vartree' (n.p.).

[35] Caroline Hamilton, MS 42,118, National Library of Ireland, Dublin. Hamilton includes lyrics by Tighe, William Tighe, herself, and her husband Charles Hamilton.

Conclusion

Even as print culture began to establish standard formats for the publication of books in the Romantic era, Blake, Coleridge, and Tighe used scribal practices to contest or expand the boundaries and limitations of commercial publication. Each one found a material means to insert variation, vision, and voice in the work they presented to their readers: Blake diversified every iteration of his handmade books through his technique of illuminated printing; Coleridge unsettled the textual authority and finitude of any single version of his poems through revision, fragmentation, and annotation; and Tighe resisted the impersonality and commodification of commercial print culture by circulating her work in manuscripts and privately printed editions. All three found ways to destabilize the potential fixity of print by vocalizing the ongoing processes of their imaginations through a transgressive autographic materiality. In doing so they enact a basic tenet of Romanticism in material form, making immanent the fluctuating subjectivity of human perception. And in doing so they create an ironic dilemma for scholars of Romanticism, whose efforts to preserve their writings in the form of editions inevitably reproduce the conditions and containments they seek to transgress through the insistent vitality of their idiosyncratic autographs. The history of Blake's textual legacy may provide the most extreme example of the difficulties posed to the scholars who sought to make his work available to the world, initially printing his poetry without any images (and struggling to translate his handwritten words and punctuation into typographic symbols), then providing a few facsimile renditions of his illuminated books, and finally offering a plenitude of those books through the multiple iterations visible at the *William Blake Archive*.[36] Similarly, the dilemma of selecting one version of a Coleridge poem to represent his work remains a constant issue in Coleridge studies, which some editors have tried to resolve by printing parallel texts that display early and late versions of select poems on the facing pages of their editions.[37] Although there is less of a history of textual criticism for Tighe,

[36] See Sarah Haggarty and Jon Mee, *William Blake—Songs of Innocence and of Experience: A Reader's Guide to Essential Criticism* (New York: Palgrave Macmillan, 2013) or Roger Whitson and Jason Whittaker, *William Blake and the Digital Humanities: Collaboration, Participation, and Social Media* (London: Routledge, 2013) for overviews of Blake's publication history and the impact of the *William Blake Archive*.

[37] John Beer prints the 1798 and 1828 versions of 'The Rime' in S.T. Coleridge, *Poems*, rev. ed. (London: Dent, 1999). Duncan Wu prints parallel texts for eight poems in *Romanticism: An Anthology*, 4th ed. (West Sussex: Wiley-Blackwell, 2012), pp. 620–703. Martin Wallen prints three versions of the 'Rime' on each page of his *Coleridge's Ancient Mariner: An Experimental Edition of Texts and Revisions 1798–1828* (Barrytown, NY: Station Hill, 1993). Mays offers a two-volume edition of Coleridge's poems: while the first offers a

the discovery of more and more autograph copies of her poems and the variations in those copies significantly complicates the task of presenting her work to twenty-first century readers.[38] When Blake, Coleridge, and Tighe contest our efforts to contain them by generating autographic texts that blend scribal practices with print technology, they enact the very legacy of Romanticism, materializing what William Wordsworth called 'the evermore about to be', the animating force of Romantic imagination.[39]

Bibliography

Beer, John. 'Romantic Apocalypses'. In *Romanticism and Millenarianism*, ed. Tim Fulford. New York: Palgrave Macmillan, 2002, pp. 53–69.

——, ed. *S.T. Coleridge: Poems*, rev. ed. London: Dent, 1999.

Bentley, G.E., Jr. *Blake Books*. Oxford: Clarendon Press, 1977.

Blake, William. *The Complete Poetry and Prose of William Blake*, ed. David V. Erdman. Berkeley and Los Angeles: University of California Press, 1982.

Buchanan, Averill. *Mary Blachford Tighe: The Irish Psyche*. Newcastle upon Tyne: Cambridge Scholars Publishing, 2011.

Burkett, Andrew. *Romantic Mediations: Media Theory and British Romanticism*. Albany, NY: SUNY Press, 2016.

Byrne, H. *The Chaplet of Fame*. Dublin: John Jones, 1806.

Coleridge, S.T. *Biographia Literaria*, 2 vols. London: Rest Fenner, 1817.

——. *Christabel, & c.*, 2nd ed. London: John Murray, 1816. RHT 19th-173, Princeton University Library, Princeton.

——. *Christabel: Kubla Khan, A Vision; The Pains of Sleep*. London: John Murray, 1816.

——. *The Collected Letters of Samuel Taylor Coleridge*, ed. E.L. Griggs, 6 vols. Oxford: Oxford University Press, 1956–71.

——. *Sibylline Leaves*. London: Rest Fenner, 1817.

——. 'To Mr. Pye on his carmen seculare'. *The Morning Post* (24 January 1800).

Davies, Damien Walford. 'Diagnosing "The Rime of the Ancient Mariner": Shipwreck, Historicism, Traumatology'. *Studies in Romanticism*, 55: 4 (Winter 2016), pp. 503–35.

Eaves, Morris. *The Counter-Arts Conspiracy: Art and Industry in the Age of Blake*. Ithaca, NY: Cornell University Press, 1992.

Eaves, Morris, Robert Essick, and Joseph Viscomi, eds. *The William Blake Archive* (1996), at http://www.blakearchive.org.

'Reading Text' that contains a single version of each poem, the second volume presents a 'Variorum Text' of all the known versions of a poem in a chronological sequence that records all the variants.

[38] As Feldman and Cooney acknowledge in their discussion of textual principles, 'Sometimes discretion was required' (p. xvii).

[39] William Wordsworth, *The Prelude* (London: Moxon, 1850), 6: p. 542.

Eilenberg, Susan. *Strange Power of Speech: Wordsworth, Coleridge, and Literary Possession*. New York: Oxford University Press, 1992.

Essick, Robert. *William Blake Printmaker*. Princeton, NJ: Princeton University Press, 1980.

Feldman, Paula. 'Women Poets and Anonymity in the Romantic Era'. *New Literary History*, 33: 2 (Spring 2002), pp. 279–89.

Feldman, Paula and Brian Cooney, eds. *The Collected Poetry of Mary Tighe*. Baltimore, MD: Johns Hopkins University Press, 2016.

Fox, E.I. 'Poems by Mrs. H. Tighe. Including Twelve Poems not published with Psyche'. Undated MS book, Belfast Public Library, Belfast.

Fulford, Tim. *The Late Poetry of the Lake Poets: Romanticism Revised*. Cambridge: University of Cambridge Press, 2013.

——. *Romantic Poetry and Literary Coteries: The Dialect of the Tribe*. New York: Palgrave Macmillan, 2015.

Haggarty, Sarah and Jon Mee. *William Blake—Songs of Innocence and of Experience: A Reader's Guide to Essential Criticism*. New York: Palgrave Macmillan, 2013.

Hamilton, Caroline. Album. MS 42,118, National Library of Ireland, Dublin.

Jones, John H. 'Blake's Production Methods'. In *Palgrave Advances in William Blake Studies*, ed. Nicholas M. Williams. Basingstoke: Palgrave Macmillan, 2006, pp. 25–41.

Justice, George. 'Introduction'. In *Women's Writing and the Circulation of Ideas*, eds. George Justice and Nathan Tinker. Cambridge: Cambridge University Press, 2002, pp. 1–16.

Langan, Celeste and Maureen McClane. 'The Medium of Romantic Poetry'. In *The Cambridge Companion to British Romantic Poetry*, eds. James Chandler and Maureen N. McClane. Cambridge: Cambridge University Press, 2008, pp. 239–62.

Leader, Zachary. *Revision and Romantic Authorship*. Oxford: Clarendon Press, 1996.

Levy, Michelle. *Family Authorship and Romantic Print Culture*. Basingstoke: Palgrave Macmillan, 2008.

Lincoln, Andrew. 'Introduction'. In *William Blake: Songs of Innocence and of Experience*. Princeton, NJ: The William Blake Trust/Princeton University Press, 1991, pp. 9–24.

Linkin, Harriet Kramer. 'Mary Tighe and the Coterie of British Women Poets'. In *The History of Women's Writing, 1750–1830*, ed. Jacqueline Labbe. London: Palgrave, 2010, pp. 301–20.

——. 'Mary Tighe and Literary History: The Making of a Critical Reputation'. *Literature Compass*, 7: 7 (2010), pp. 564–76.

——. 'Mary Tighe: A Portrait of the Artist for the Twenty-First Century'. In *A Companion to Irish Literature*, ed. Julia M. Wright, 2 vols. West Sussex: Wiley-Blackwell, 2010, 1: pp. 292–309.

Love, Harold. *The Culture and Commerce of Texts*. Oxford: Clarendon, 1993.

Mann, Paul. 'Apocalypse and Recuperation: Blake and the Maw of Commerce'. *ELH*, 52: 1 (Spring 1985), pp. 1–32.

Matthews, Samantha. *Poetical Remains: Poets' Graves, Bodies, and Books in the Nineteenth Century*. Oxford: Oxford University Press, 2004.

Mays, J.C.C., ed. *The Poetical Works*, 3 vols. *The Collected Works of Samuel Taylor Coleridge*, eds. H.J. Jackson and George Whalley, vol. 16. Princeton, NJ: Princeton University Press, 2001.

Prendergast, Amy. *Literary Salons Across Britain and Ireland in the Long Eighteenth Century*. New York: Palgrave Macmillan, 2015.

Raven, James. 'The Book Trades'. In *Books and their Readers in Eighteenth-Century England: New Essays*, ed. Isabel Rivers. London and New York: Leicester University Press, 2001, pp. 1–34.

———. *The Business of Books: Booksellers and the English Book Trade 1450–1850*. New Haven, CT: Yale University Press, 2007.

Reiman, Donald. *The Study of Modern Manuscripts: Public, Confidential, and Private*. Baltimore, MD: Johns Hopkins University Press, 1993.

Schellenberg, Betty A. *Literary Coteries and the Making of Modern Print Culture*. Cambridge: Cambridge University Press, 2016.

Singer, Kate. 'Limpid Waves and Good Vibrations: Charlotte Smith's New Materialist Affect'. *Essays in Romanticism*, 23: 2. (2016), pp. 175–92.

Stillinger, Jack. *Coleridge and Textual Instability: The Multiple Versions of the Major Poems*. New York: Oxford University Press, 1994.

Tee, Ve-Yin. *Coleridge, Revision, and Romanticism*. New York: Continuum, 2009.

Thorburn, David and Henry Jenkins, eds. *Rethinking Media Change: The Aesthetics of Transition*. Cambridge, MA: MIT Press, 2004.

Tighe, Mary. *The Collected Poetry of Mary Tighe*, eds. Paula Feldman and Brian Cooney. Baltimore, MD: Johns Hopkins University Press, 2016.

———. 'Critical Reviews'. MS 4804, National Library of Ireland, Dublin.

———. Letters to Joseph Cooper Walker. MS 1461, Trinity College Library, Dublin.

———. *Mary, a Series of Reflections During Twenty Years*. N.P., 1811. EC8. T4484 811M, Houghton Library, Harvard University, Cambridge.

———. 'Psyche. or The Legend of Love. 1803'. MS 22985B, National Library of Wales, Aberystwyth.

———. *Verses Transcribed for H.T.* (1805), ed. Harriet Kramer Linkin. *Romantic Circles* (2015), at https://romantic-circles.org/editions/tighe_verses.

Viscomi, Joseph. *Blake and the Idea of the Book*. Princeton, NJ: Princeton University Press, 1993.

Wallen, Martin. *Coleridge's Ancient Mariner: An Experimental Edition of Texts and Revisions, 1798–1828*. Barrytown, NY: Station Hill, 1993.

Whitson, Roger and Jason Whittaker. *William Blake and the Digital Humanities: Collaboration, Participation, and Social Media*. London: Routledge, 2013.

Wordsworth, William. *The Prelude*. London: Moxon, 1850.

Wu, Duncan. *Romanticism: An Anthology*, 4th ed. West Sussex: Wiley-Blackwell, 2012.

Chapter Two

Affect in the Margins

Marking Readers in the *Elegiac Sonnets*

Michael Gamer and Katrina O'Loughlin

The marks left by readers in their personal copies of Charlotte Smith's *Elegiac Sonnets* provide mesmerizing traces of how manuscript engages print and readers engage writers in the Romantic period. This is particularly true of Smith's readers, who left numerous and more extensive marginalia than readers of other poets of these same years. Read across multiple editions, the marginalia left in Smith's volumes challenge us to reconsider how readers used books—and how books might use their readers—in soliciting and forging affective relationships through print. It also foregrounds how Smith's careful recollecting and reframing of her own poetry in printed editions might license readers in turn to change how they responded to her verse. This Smith's readers also did consistently, and in ways that grew more involved and complex as the collection grew: additional references, updates and corrections to the printed text, and commentary of various kinds mark the margins of Smith's printed work. What moved readers in this way from one mode of annotation to several? What might the form and content of these marks tell us about readers' material and emotional engagements with the poetry? And, most curiously, why did Smith's readers respond in writing more often and with greater urgency than the readers of other late eighteenth-century sonneteers, particularly as the *Elegiac Sonnets* grew? Tracing these various annotations, from the most conventional to the most transgressive, heightens our historical sense of the dynamism of Smith's publishing practice and illuminates the sentimental and aesthetic bonds she formed with readers through various editions. However, there is also something more radical at work here in the marked margins: a blurring of lines between persona and poet, between author and reader, and between book-writer and book-owner.

Given the limited attention that has been paid to marginalia outside of book history, an important part of the work of this essay is descriptive and qualitative: to share the most interesting reader copies of *Elegiac Sonnets*; to ask what they can tell us about Smith's poetry and career that might otherwise remain invisible; and to insist in a very immediate way on the presence and significance of marginalia in Romantic-era writing. But there is a quantitative case to be made as well, one that requires examining dozens of reader copies of *Elegiac Sonnets* and contemporaneous volumes published by William Lisle Bowles, Mary Robinson, and Anna Seward. Existing copies of these latter collections, we show, partially resemble Smith's in the kinds of marks that readers have left behind in them. But what is missing in these latter copies is a similar intensity and frequency of response. Smith seems to have elicited reader commentary at once more involved, more sustained, and more interventionist in nature. Equally suggestive is when and where such responses occur. If we are to judge from their annotations, the most engaging versions of *Elegiac Sonnets* for readers were not those final, authoritative editions favored by modern editors. Instead, what attracted reader commentary were Smith's earlier editions, particularly the third (1786) and fifth (1789), each of which differed radically from its predecessors. These were not just new printings but transformations, providing new prefaces and poems and re-ordered contents. That these transformations have remained largely unnoticed by scholars stems, we suspect, from a general critical preference for first and last versions and the more satisfying tales of origins and final states that come with them.

In the case of *Elegiac Sonnets*, modern editors of Smith's poetry typically have tried to deliver both first and last simultaneously. Today, readers of *Elegiac Sonnets* usually encounter the final versions and ordering of the poems—volume one as it was published in 1792 and volume two as it was published in 1800, after Smith had parted with the copyright—even as they are asked to dwell at length on the story of their inception. A narrative of triumph in adversity, the details of Smith's struggle to sell the collection make clear just how *ad hoc* and desperate she was at the beginning of her career. With her husband Benjamin imprisoned for debt, Smith approached James Dodsley and Charles Dilly with the manuscript of *Elegiac Sonnets* in the early months of 1784 in hopes of raising funds to support herself and her children. Neither publisher chose to purchase; almost as an afterthought, Dodsley offered to print the manuscript at his own expense and take any profits in the unlikely event it proved popular. To these rebuffs Smith responded with characteristic shrewdness. Declining both offers, she enlisted the support of William Hayley, whose popularity as a poet was at its peak and who allowed the volume to be dedicated to him. Returning to Dodsley with a powerful patron and an endorsed product, Smith elected not to sell *Elegiac Sonnets* outright but rather to gamble on its success, printing on speculation and retaining the right to all royalties. As it sold and resold in ever-expanding forms, the volume's sustained popularity allowed Smith in later years to rewrite these early negotiations as a tale of vindication, the continued success of her ever-expanding collection its own testimony of triumph.[1]

Given the collection's popularity and compelling narrative of origin, it is not that surprising that a portion of Smith's readers responded in the margins of their copies of *Elegiac Sonnets*: where it was known, the story of the imperiled but enterprising woman writer may have provoked specific forms of identification between Smith and sympathetic readers who supported her financially through the purchase of her books. But the conspicuous annotation over the *series* of editions—where readers responded more often and with greater range and intensity than readers of other popular sonnet collections—gives rise to the more difficult (and central) questions of this essay. How precisely did Smith invite readers to imagine their role within the collection? What in the printed text solicited those extra marks in the margins, inviting a different form of intimacy between writer and reader? Why do the tenor of these responses change as *Elegiac Sonnets* grew? And how might the marginalia, by transgressing the apparently 'fixed' form of the book, necessarily challenge our understanding of the affective bonds between readers and writers in this period?

I. Marks

> When we handle books sensitively, observing them closely so as to learn as much as we can from them, we discover a thousand little mysteries .... In and around, beneath and across them we may find traces ... that could teach us a lot if we could make them out.
>
> —Roger E. Stoddard, *Marks in Books* (1985)[2]

> Readers' marks are better at providing examples ... than general rules; but if we cast our net widely they can reveal both large-scale patterns of use and extraordinary encounters of individuals and their books.
>
> —William Sherman, *Used Books* (2012)[3]

[1] See 'Charlotte Smith', *Public Characters of 1800–1801* (London: R. Phillips, 1801), pp. 43–64, 51; and Samuel Egerton Brydges, Esq., 'Memoir of Charlotte Smith', *Censura Literaria*, 10 vols. (London: Longman, 1805–9), 4: pp. 69–84.

[2] Roger Stoddard, *Marks in Books, Illustrated and Explained* (Cambridge, MA: Harvard University Press, 1985), p. 1; qtd. in William Sherman, *Used Books: Marking Readers in Renaissance England* (Philadelphia: University of Pennsylvania Press, 2012), p. xi.

[3] Sherman, *Used Books*, p. xvi.

Readers have left traces of their presence in books as long as there has been reading. At least since Roger Stoddard's foundational *Marks in Books* (quoted above), literary anthropologists and cultural historians have asked what might be gleaned from the 'thousand little mysteries' a well-read book presents. William Sherman's *Used Books* (also quoted above) provides a similar, though more cautious, account. 'Renaissance readers', he notes, 'tended to be more systematic and less psychologically revealing than post-Romantic readers'. Canvassing books of the early modern period, Sherman finds most reader marks—though with wonderful exceptions—to be of the note-taking variety: either the work of students or else incidental lists and memoranda 'with no obvious connection with the text they accompanied'.[4] Today many would consider such marks vandalism, but the eighteenth and nineteenth centuries were more forgiving. When paper was costly, any white space was a siren call, whether for practical uses like practicing penmanship or more generative activities like list-making, original composition, or graffiti. Friends lending books to Samuel Coleridge expected him to comment in them as he read and sometimes even requested that he do so.[5] Within the realm of fiction, Catherine Earnshaw of *Wuthering Heights* stands as a kind of fantasy of an engaged if undutiful reader emerging from the material traces she has left in her books:

> It was a Testament, in lean type, and smelling dreadfully musty: a fly-leaf bore the inscription—'Catherine Earnshaw, her book', and a date some quarter of a century back. I shut it, and took up another, and another, till I had examined all. Catherine's library was select, and its state of dilapidation proved it to have been well used; though not altogether for a legitimate purpose: scarcely one chapter had escaped a pen-and-ink commentary ... covering every morsel of blank that the printer had left. Some were detached sentences; other parts took the form of a regular diary, scrawled in an unformed childish hand. At the top of an extra page (quite a treasure, probably, when first lighted on) I was greatly amused to behold an excellent caricature of my friend Joseph,—rudely, yet powerfully sketched. An immediate interest kindled within me for the unknown Catherine, and I began forth-with to decipher her faded hieroglyphics.[6]

Through Lockwood's narration, Brontë compiles a digest of Romantic reading while dramatizing precisely the kind of 'extraordinary encounter' referred to

4 Sherman, *Used Books*, p. xiii.

5 H.J. Jackson, *Marginalia: Readers Writing in Books* (New Haven, CT and London: Yale University Press, 2001), p. 7.

6 [Emily Brontë], *Wuthering Heights* (New York: Harper, 1848), p. 18; qtd. in Jackson, *Marginalia*, p. 20.

by Sherman. The scene dramatizes the seductive promise of marginalia, what it means to discover another reader reading. Catherine's numerous marginalia do more than supply Lockwood with a telling glimpse into her mind; they reorient the books themselves so that the volumes are no longer about their respective authors but rather about a reader who has dared to inscribe herself directly into their pages. Leafing through her library, Lockwood assesses not just Catherine's general engagement with books but also her attitudes toward religion, ownership, and authority. What is most striking about the passage is how quickly Catherine's status changes from reader to author; arrested by her voice, Lockwood shifts almost immediately from reading the text in his hand to reading Catherine's commentary. He takes 'up another, and another, till I had examined all'.

Whether out of embarrassment or because the reasons for his curiosity seem to him natural, he provides no explanation for his compulsive literary voyeurism. His response suggests, however, that Catherine's various marginalia tantalize because of their powers of evocation and promise of intimacy. Through them we discover a person in the past again made present and—as Lockwood discovers later that night—a person deceased come again to life. We meet Catherine, furthermore, in her moments of private reading, and we are led to assume that her responses will prove more unguarded, and thus more genuine, than they would be in a public persona (a powerful narrative strategy in a book where we, as readers, are invited to piece together characters and relationships from historical and psychological fragments). The excitement of such an encounter provides Lockwood with an opportunity to flirt with more general theories of character formation and reflective writing, as Catherine's 'pen-and-ink commentary' yields to 'a regular diary, scrawled in an unformed childish hand'. In his presentation, reading and commentary lead to reflective composition: those who write in the margins of books inevitably become writers themselves, as relationships between author and reader, reader and text, blur in the fluid movement of material affect.

As this scene of reading in *Wuthering Heights* suggests, the marks in the margins of Catherine Earnshaw's books effectively reframe 'the book' in startling ways. The book in the hands of Catherine becomes no longer attached—no longer 'Testament'—to its original author (now merely the figure who has furnished the 'lean type'). Instead, the book is rematerialized by its reader in manuscript and in the margins until it is effectively reauthored, becoming 'Catherine Earnshaw, her book'. No longer anonymous, Catherine-the-reader has become an author to another reader, another subject to be read in and across the text. Considered in this way, the scene becomes emblematic of the transgressive potential of marginalia, where a reader (Catherine) not only becomes a writer but also effectively transforms her own reader (Lockwood) into another writer (the narrator of the scene) as well. If this testifies to just how generally accepted the ties between marginalia and selfhood had become by the end of the Romantic period, it also reveals how marginalia potentially destabilized identity and the fixity of the book.

Asking 'What was the place of the writing reader' in the Romantic period, Heather Jackson has argued for marginalia as a constitutive, distinctively proprietorial feature of its culture. '[M]ost if not all readers were writing readers on occasion', she notes: 'Writing in books was a recognized privilege of ownership [and] most forms of note-taking were not merely tolerated but valued'.[7] As her term 'note-taking' suggests, the vast majority of Jackson's writing readers were students and professionals annotating reference works.[8] Our project here is at once more narrow and more literary, consisting of volumes of sonnets published in the late eighteenth century by Bowles, Robinson, Seward, and Smith. The following table shows markings in copies of fifteen different editions published by the four poets between 1784 (the first edition of Smith's *Elegiac Sonnets*) and 1800 (the sixth edition of Bowles's *Sonnets*). To build meaningful comparisons, we have limited our survey to editions of *Elegiac Sonnets* and to competing sonnet collections published in the same years.

These figures are compiled from 152 volumes held by fifty libraries in North America and the United Kingdom and comprise the majority of known volumes held by public institutions.[9] As with any collection of data, ours poses some of the usual concerns. Among these is a dependence on rare book librarians, who several times generously relayed their findings to save us the costs of travel. Their sense of what constitutes 'marks' and 'marginalia' inevitably differs from our own. Then there is the potential arbitrariness of distinctions among marks—what should signify, and in what quantity? As anyone familiar with marginalia knows, readers' marks vary widely. In order to capture something of the nature of Smith's contemporaneous readers' relationships to her works, our tabulations limit themselves to marks that appear roughly contemporary and that respond to the text at hand—as with these pages from a copy of the third edition of Bowles's *Sonnets* (1794) held by McMaster University (see Fig. 1).

[7] H.J. Jackson, *Romantic Readers: The Evidence of Marginalia* (New Haven, CT: Yale University Press, 2005), p. 58.

[8] Jackson, *Romantic Readers*, pp. 60–120.

[9] Barbican House, Beinecke, Blickling Hall, Bodleian, Boston Athenaeum, Brighton Hove, British Library, Cadbury, University of California Davis, Cambridge, Jesus College Cambridge, Chawton House, the Clark, Colorado, Cornell, Duke, the Folger, Harvard, Huntington, Illinois, Indiana, Jerwood, John Rylands, Kansas, Kentucky, Leeds, Lewis-Walpole, Library Company, Library of Congress, McMaster, Michigan, Missouri at Kansas City, National Library of Scotland, National Library of Wales, Newberry, New York Public Library, New York University, North Carolina, Ohio State, Otago, New College Oxford, University of Pennsylvania, Princeton, Stanford, Texas, Toronto, Virginia, Washington State, and Winchester College. Without the help of those who examined books on our behalf, this work would have not been possible.

Table

Author/Edition	No marking	Signature only	Light marking	Moderate markings	Heavy markings
Bowles, William					
Fourteen Sonnets (1789)	2				
1789 2nd edition	6		2		
1794 3rd	5	2	2	1	
1796 4th	8				
1798 5th	5	1	1		1
1800 6th	4	2	3	1	
% Totals (46 examined)	65.21% (30)	10.87% (5)	17.39% (8)	4.35% (2)	2.17% (1)
Robinson, Mary					
Sappho and Phaon (1796)	6	3	2		
% Totals (11 examined)	54.54% (6)	27.27% (3)	18.18% (2)	0% (0)	0% (0)
Seward, Anna					
Original Sonnets (1799)	2		1		
1799 2nd edition	12	2	5		1
% Totals (23 examined)	60.87% (14)	8.70% (2)	26.09% (6)	0% (0)	4.35% (1)
Smith, Charlotte					
Elegiac Sonnets (1784)	2		2	2	1
1784 2nd edition	4		1		
1786 3rd	8	5	2	2	3
1786 4th	1		2		4
1789 5th	16	2			3
1790 (Dublin)	3			1	1
% Totals (65 examined)	52.31% (34)	10.77% (7)	10.77% (7)	7.69% (5)	18.46% (12)

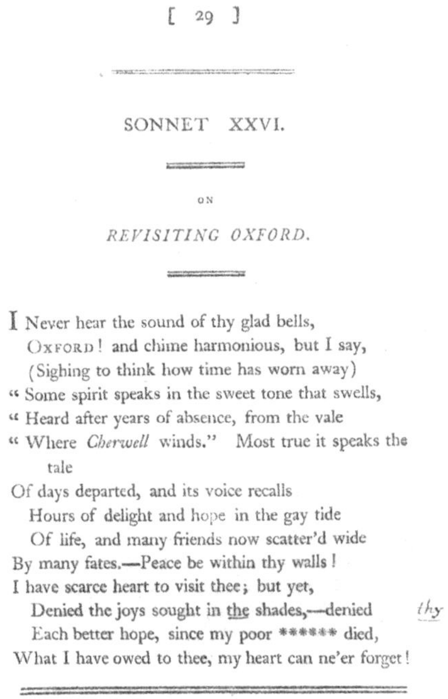

[29]

SONNET XXVI.

ON

REVISITING OXFORD.

I Never hear the sound of thy glad bells,
OXFORD! and chime harmonious, but I say,
(Sighing to think how time has worn away)
" Some spirit speaks in the sweet tone that swells,
" Heard after years of absence, from the vale
" Where *Cherwell* winds." Most true it speaks the tale
Of days departed, and its voice recalls
Hours of delight and hope in the gay tide
Of life, and many friends now scatter'd wide
By many fates.—Peace be within thy walls!
I have scarce heart to visit thee; but yet,
Denied the joys sought in the shades,—denied thy
Each better hope, since my poor ****** died,
What I have owed to thee, my heart can ne'er forget!

Figure 1: Two marked pages of William Lisle Bowles, *Sonnets, and Other Poems*, 3rd ed. (Bath, 1794). Images courtesy of the William Ready Division of Archives and Research Collections, McMaster University Library.

These comprise two of the five marked pages in this copy; all have been annotated by the same reader. On the left-hand page, 'the' has been changed to 'thy' in the twelfth line. The two annotations on the right-hand page are taken from a list of errata provided at the end of the volume, the reader having transcribed the correct lines on the bottom of the page and tagged the appropriate lines in the margin. As these comprise the most extensive annotations in a copy where few pages are marked at all, we have classified it under the 'light marking' category. A typical example might boast a few markings and annotations and perhaps a signature. Those with more frequent marking and lengthier responses we have called either 'moderate' or 'heavy', depending on the number and intensity of the marginalia. Under the 'heavy' category, we also include copies where readers have tipped in additional poems, illustrations, clippings, and other material. In each case, these 'thickened' copies also feature frequent markings and reflective, even critical, commentary.

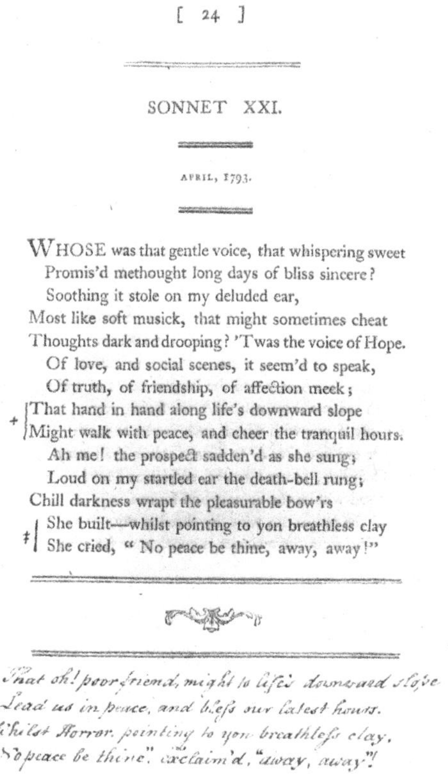

[24]

SONNET XXI.

APRIL, 1793.

WHOSE was that gentle voice, that whispering sweet
  Promis'd methought long days of bliss sincere?
  Soothing it stole on my deluded ear,
Most like soft musick, that might sometimes cheat
Thoughts dark and drooping? 'Twas the voice of Hope.
  Of love, and social scenes, it seem'd to speak,
  Of truth, of friendship, of affection meek;
+ That hand in hand along life's downward slope
  Might walk with peace, and cheer the tranquil hours.
  Ah me! the prospect sadden'd as she sung;
  Loud on my startled ear the death-bell rung;
Chill darkness wrapt the pleasurable bow'rs
‡ She built—whilst pointing to yon breathless clay
  She cried, "No peace be thine, away, away!"

+ That oh! poor friend, might to life's downward slope
  Lead us in peace, and bless our latest hours.
‡ Whilst Horror, pointing to yon breathless clay,
  "No peace be thine", exclaim'd, "away, away"!

What the data does not immediately communicate is the relative paucity of commentary across the volumes. Modern studies of book use and marginalia had led us, however mistakenly, to expect a greater level of reader engagement, although Sherman notes fewer marginalia in early modern literary texts than in those of political and religious controversy.[10] Nevertheless, we were surprised. What recent projects like *Book Traces* have found in plenty of mid-nineteenth-century books does not appear to extend to sonnet collections half a century earlier.[11] Equally interesting is the scarcity of what we have

[10] Sherman, *Used Books*, p. xiii. Here, see also Jackson, *Marginalia*, p. 300, who describes annotation as 'in retreat' by 1830, and Andrew Stauffer, 'An Image in Lava: Annotation, Sentiment, and the Traces of Nineteenth-Century Reading', *PMLA*, 134: 1 (January 2019), pp. 81–98.

[11] See Stauffer, 'An Image in Lava' and *Book Traces* (www.booktraces.org), a crowd-sourcing project that has described nineteenth-century marginalia as 'virtually ubiquitous'.

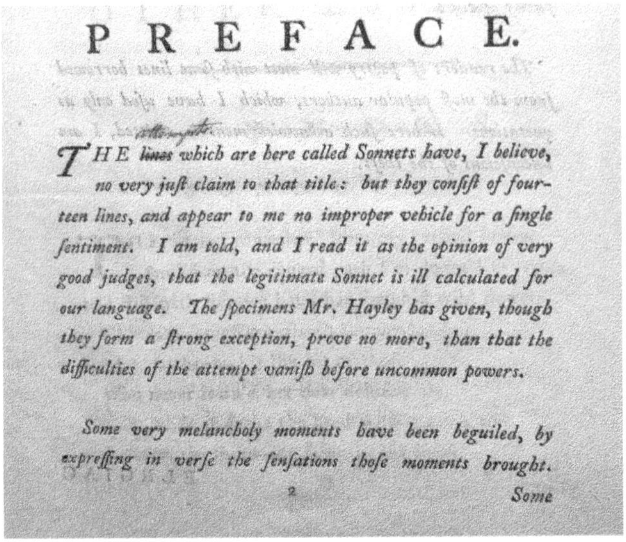

PREFACE.

THE lines which are here called Sonnets have, I believe, no very juſt claim to that title: but they conſiſt of fourteen lines, and appear to me no improper vehicle for a ſingle ſentiment. I am told, and I read it as the opinion of very good judges, that the legitimate Sonnet is ill calculated for our language. The ſpecimens Mr. Hayley has given, though they form a ſtrong exception, prove no more, than that the difficulties of the attempt vaniſh before uncommon powers.

Some very melancholy moments have been beguiled, by expreſſing in verſe the ſenſations thoſe moments brought.

2 Some

Figure 2: Two marked pages of Charlotte Smith, *Elegiac Sonnets*, 1st ed. (London, 1784). Copy held by the British Library.

called, for lack of a better term, 'moderate' engagement, like those readers who might mark favorite poems and provide periodic commentary. Evidently, readers of late eighteenth-century sonnet collections respond either at length and with enthusiasm, or barely at all.

Still, for the purposes of this essay, the percentage of copies of *Elegiac Sonnets* with heavy markings (18.46%) is genuinely suggestive and far higher than that of examined copies of Robinson (0%), Bowles (2.17%), or Seward (4.35%). Even allowing for accidents of data collection and categorization, contemporary readers appear many times more likely to mark heavily their copies of *Elegiac Sonnets* than other sonnet sequences. Their responses, moreover, intensify as Smith's collection grows. Annotations to the first two editions of *Elegiac Sonnets* are nearly always corrections, corroborating revisions Smith made to her preface and to individual poems after the first edition. Even here, however, there is a notable exception: in the Stainforth copy held by the British Library, a reader has made changes that, while still fairly straightforward, exceed those typical of early editions of Smith (see Fig. 2).

On the left-hand page, in the first line of the preface, the reader has corrected 'lines' to 'attempts', a change that finds no place in any edition of *Elegiac Sonnets*. On the right, the reader has corrected line 109 of 'The Origin of Flattery' to 'Thy dulcet spirit meets the letter'd mind'. Contrast this line to its three published versions:

1st ed.: 'Thy pleasing spirit for the letter'd mind'.
2nd ed.: 'Thy dulcet spirit for the letter'd mind'.

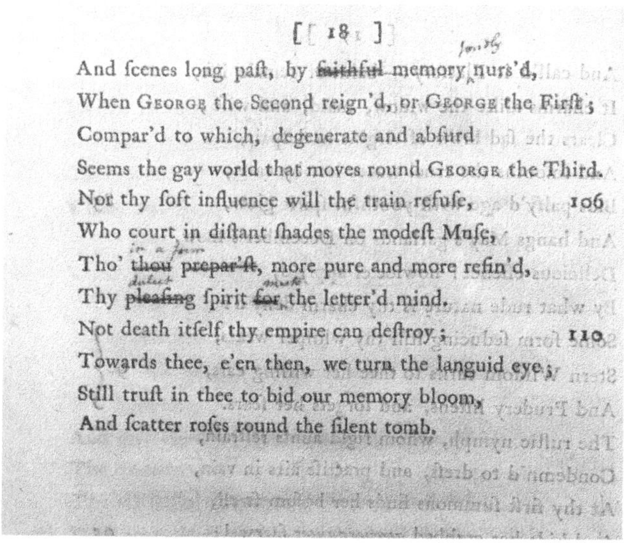

[18]

And ſcenes long paſt, by faithful memory nurs'd,
When George the Second reign'd, or George the Firſt;
Compar'd to which, degenerate and abſurd
Seems the gay world that moves round George the Third.
Nor thy ſoft influence will the train refuſe,
Who court in diſtant ſhades the modeſt Muſe,
Tho' thou prepar'ſt, more pure and more refin'd,
Thy pleaſing ſpirit for the letter'd mind.
Not death itſelf thy empire can deſtroy;
Towards thee, e'en then, we turn the languid eye;
Still truſt in thee to bid our memory bloom,
And ſcatter roſes round the ſilent tomb.

5th ed. and later: 'Thy soothing spirit meets the letter'd mind'.[12]

Here, 'meets' is suggestive, since it indicates that the correction likely was made after the publication of the fifth edition of *Elegiac Sonnets* in 1789. As the corrections are in the same hand and appear to be made at the same time, one would expect the line to be corrected to conform to the 1789 version; instead, it corresponds to no existing version of the text but makes an independent, original configuration of two different published versions. Given the assiduity with which the reader has annotated and extra-illustrated the volume, it is difficult to dismiss the change as merely a failure of collation. Although minor, this annotation is nevertheless an intervention, a proposed improvement to a line Smith herself could not seem to nail down. In this light, 'meets' takes on a further metaphorical significance, since the reader has transgressed, however slightly, into the realm of original composition, effectively 'meeting' the author on her own ground.

Part of what is in play here is authority, of both writer and reader: observing a line take three different forms over as many editions becomes an invitation—at least to one active reader—to tinker. What we wish to note alongside this point is the degree to which authors can promote or discourage such tinkering, particularly through the paratexts of their collections. Looking to the prefatorial materials of *Elegiac Sonnets*, for example, we find them marked by a brevity that creates an inviting space for readers. Smith's original dedication characterizes the

[12] 'The Origin of Flattery' does not appear in the third and fourth editions of *Elegiac Sonnets*.

poems as 'simple effusions', a representation echoed in her preface, where she calls them 'Lines' and (in the second edition) 'little Poems' with 'no just claim to the title' of sonnet. Significantly, however, Smith slyly casts her refusal of the sonnet not as a personal shortcoming but as a failure of the form itself in English:

> I am told, and I read it as the opinion of very good judges, that the legitimate Sonnet is ill calculated for our language. The specimens Mr. Hayley has given, though they form a strong exception, prove no more, than that the difficulties of the attempt vanish before uncommon powers.[13]

In their reticence and quiet authority, these lines are tonally of a piece with Smith's representation of the sonnets themselves. Within them, however, are couched a vein of critique and the germ of an argument for innovation on the part of poet and perhaps readers (the looked-for intervention of 'uncommon powers'), which becomes even stronger in the preface Smith supplies to her third edition:

> The reception given by the Public, as well as my particular Friends, to the two first Editions of these small Poems, has induced me to add to the present such other Sonnets as I have written since … . A few of those last written, I have attempted on the Italian model; with what success I know not, but I am persuaded that to the generality of readers those which are less regular will be more pleasing.[14]

Projecting neither overreaching confidence nor timorous modesty, the new preface recasts Smith's earlier statements into more contentious (though still decorous) form. The 'Lines' and 'little Poems' of the first two editions are now become 'Sonnets', and 'the opinion of very good judges, that the legitimate Sonnet is ill calculated for our language' has become her own view expressed in her own voice—the beginnings of a manifesto on poetic form. Not only has the Petrarchan model moved from being 'legitimate' to merely 'Italian', but also Smith now anticipates that the pleasure readers take from 'less regular' sonnets will stem less from her facility in that form than from the superiority of the form itself.

Smith's paratextual revisions for her third edition are more suggestive than argumentative. Through them she projects a kind of openness also modeled

[13] Charlotte Smith, *Elegiac Sonnets, and Other Essays* (London: Dodsley, 1784), p. vii.

[14] Charlotte Smith, *Elegiac Sonnets*, 3rd ed. (London: Dodsley, Gardner, and Bew, 1786), p. v. Further references to this edition will be cited parenthetically in the text by page number (for prose) or line number (for poetry).

by the poetry itself. Throughout her career Smith was encouraging rather than prescriptive about matters of form. Experimental and fond of feedback, her strategy was to project in her poems and prefatory materials an understated elegance that she associated with gentility and taste, and other sonnet writers quickly followed suit. Publishing his own *Fourteen Sonnets* in 1789, William Lisle Bowles duplicated Smith's approach by including the briefest of prefaces. When reviewers noted similarities to *Elegiac Sonnets*, he added a second paragraph claiming many of the poems to have been 'written prior to Mrs. Smyth's Publication' and 'from his own Feelings'.[15] Bowles's rewritten preface thus duplicates the terms by which Smith presented her sonnets—as products of genuine feeling inspired by local landscapes—even as it declares its independence from her. Seven years later, Samuel Coleridge affixed to his pamphlet *Sonnets from Various Authors* a critical preface on the sonnet, detailing its history and arguing that sonnets should cultivate loneliness, bring together moral sentiment and natural landscape, and use 'whatever [rhyme scheme] rapid expression ... will permit'.[16] Written primarily as a defense of Bowles, Coleridge's guidelines also hearken to Smith, whom he invokes at the opening of his essay. The short collection of sonnets he includes models precisely the kind of engagement Smith seems to have encouraged from the earliest editions of *Elegiac Sonnets*, a fluid relationship between readers and writers that transforms the apparent materiality of the book.

II. Changing Frames

Smith's involvement in provoking response in her readers is as fascinating as it is difficult to assess. Occurring both in the paratexts of *Elegiac Sonnets* and in the poems themselves, the eliciting of interactive responses from readers is most visible in the poems that frame the collection. Smith's opening sonnet, for example, is justifiably famous, presenting poetic sensibility as both a blessing and a curse—and hence as the reason for, and problem posed by, the volume:

> The partial Muse, has from my earliest hours
>   Smiled on the rugged path I'm doom'd to tread,
> And still with sportive hand has snatch'd wild flowers,
>   To weave fantastic garlands for my head:
> But far, far happier is the lot of those
>   Who never learn'd her dear delusive art,

[15] William Lisle Bowles, *Sonnets, Written Chiefly upon Picturesque Spots, during a Tour* (Bath: R. Crutwell, 1789), p. 7.

[16] Samuel Coleridge, [*Sonnets from Various Authors*] (London, 1796), p. ii.

Which while it decks the head with many a rose,
  Reserves the thorn, to fester in the heart.[17]

At one level, her opening octet presents a dilemma afflicting the speaker alone: the same 'partial Muse' that has inspired Smith's poetry has also bestowed the curse of feeling so deeply as to turn sorrow into a perpetual state. Were the speaker not treading on her 'doomed … path', the 'dear delusive art' of poetry might prove an unmixed blessing, but within a life punctuated by sorrow, inspired sensitivity translates grief into feeling even more fully:

For still she bids soft Pity's melting eye
  Stream o'er the ills she knows not to remove,
Points every pang, and deepens every sigh
  Of mourning friendship, or unhappy love.
Ah! then, how dear the Muse's favors cost,
  If those paint sorrow best —— who feel it most! (9–14)

Here, 'soft Pity's melting eye' enfolds swelling tears with the acts of perceiving and reading, so that the eye functions as a sign of feeling (a mark of sorrow) and as an organ of transmission (an emotional conduit between the poet and the world, and between the poet and her reader). Accompanied by a note directing readers to Alexander Pope's *Eloisa to Abelard*, the italics of the final line signal other sources for Smith's sorrows as well. Whether belonging to Smith's speaker or her reader, 'soft Pity's melting eye' comes suitably chaperoned by both Smith herself and by poetic tradition recognizable to—and inhabitable by—her readers. Sentimental readers identifying with Smith's doomed poet-wanderer can do so, therefore, secure in the knowledge that they are in good literary company. At the very least, the nod to Pope invites readers to consider the dual nature of Smith's grief by signaling its dual origins, which are both experiential (personal) and aesthetic (impersonal). It reminds readers that she, too, is a reader like them.

These same dynamics work in the closing sonnet to Smith's first edition, which opens by first invoking, and then rejecting, lyric and pastoral traditions:

Blest is yon shepherd, on the turf reclined,
  Who on the varied clouds which float above
Lies idly gazing—while his vacant mind
  Pours out some tale antique of rural love!

[17] Charlotte Smith, *Elegiac Sonnets and Other Essays* (London: Dodsley, 1784), p. 1, lines 1–8. Subsequent quotations from this edition will be cited parenthetically in the text by line number.

Ah! he has never felt the pangs that move
  Th' indignant spirit, when with selfish pride,
  Friends, on whose faith the trusting heart rely'd,
Unkindly shun th' imploring eye of woe!
  The ills they ought to soothe, with taunts deride,
And laugh at tears themselves have forced to flow. (1–10)

By the terms of Smith's opening sonnet—that the best poets most keenly feel the emotions they paint—the reclining shepherd is, of course, not a real poet at all. A mere repeater of antique tales, he unthinkingly 'pours out' his songs with a 'vacant mind'. As if to echo this formal orthodoxy, Smith opens conventionally in the rhyme scheme (a-b-a-b) of a Shakespearean sonnet, thus giving her conventional poet a conventional quatrain. With the 'Ah!' of the fifth line, however, she breaks this formal pattern, suggesting that real feeling, particularly sorrow, requires not just a freer rhyme scheme (a-c-c-d-c-d) but also at least two additional lines in which to overflow—though the final quatrain could easily be considered of a piece with the six lines preceding it:

Nor his rude bosom those fine feelings melt,
  Children of Sentiment and Knowledge born,
Thro' whom each shaft with cruel force is felt,
  Empoison'd by deceit—or barb'd with scorn. (11–14)

Closing Smith's first published collection, 'Blest is yon shepherd' nicely recalls the terms of 'Sonnet I'. Reprising the governing image of the feeling eye, the poem contrasts the male shepherd's 'idl[e] gazing' with the 'imploring eye of woe' of her female speaker. Genuine feeling is thus trenchantly—even polemically—gendered female. Compelling poetry, Smith argues, can never come from the 'antique' conventionality of a 'vacant mind'. Instead, a poet-reader must engage and transform these materials, however painfully, via genuine feeling, hard-won experience, and the work of 'paint' or pen.

'Blest is yon Shepherd' does not so much reject poetic tradition as argue for its provisionality and insufficiency, so the poet's life and feelings stand alongside poetry as additional, driving forces of her art. In saying this, we are hardly the first commentators to note the play between literary biography and tradition in Smith's poetry.[18] Our point, in fact, is that this dialogue between the personal and the poetic was grasped by her earliest readers, who found the tension between them as fascinating as have modern commentators, all of which testifies to the open, interactive, and personalized tenor

[18] See especially Jacqueline M. Labbe, *Charlotte Smith: Romanticism, Poetry, and the Culture of Gender* (Manchester and New York: Manchester University Press, 2003), pp. 1–3.

of Smith's poem-making. Taking up her opening sonnet, two of Smith's most perceptive readers, Stuart Curran and Daniel Robinson, have argued cogently that Smith's most apparently personal lines engage deeply—and often subversively—with formal convention.[19] For Curran, the interest lies in Smith's reversal of gender roles, her appropriation of Petrarch's wandering, unrequited lover to delineate a very different set of sorrows. For Robinson, the crux is Smith's deep knowledge of elegy and sonnet traditions, which enables her to mix Shakespearean form with Petrarchan themes and to transform Petrarch's laurel in lines 3–4 into the mad 'garlands' of Ophelia and Lear. Beyond the gesture to Pope's *Eloisa*, there are its preceding three 'elegiac' quatrains, which formally and thematically echo the final stanzas of Thomas Gray's *Elegy Written in a Country Churchyard* (1751). Finally, there are Smith's stark innovations and reversals, another means by which she engages readers' affective responses. Her opening lines, for instance, may evoke the speaker of Petrarch's *Canzonetti*, but they identify no 'Laura', no forsaken object of love. Her deliberate refusal of an elegiac *cause* allows Smith to evade many of the conventional balms of eighteenth-century poetry, whether the consolations of religion, family, or art.[20] For contemporaries like Anna Seward, Smith's practices amounted to a double horror, where everything of merit in the *Elegiac Sonnets* was plagiarized from august literary forebears only to be anchored in a poet's life that provided few details.[21] For Smith, this deep play between art and private life was precisely the point.

We rehearse these earlier readings here to redirect them by asking what kinds of spaces—conceptual and material—are created through this intense play between the personal and the poetic, between feeling and form. How might poems that present lived experience as underwriting the poet's art, in turn license readers to become not just fans, but even writers themselves? How did Smith's continuous remaking of the *Elegiac Sonnets* create opportunities for readers to inscribe themselves into the collection, to blur boundaries between writer and reader, book-writer and book-owner, and exceed the boundedness of the book? We would like to suggest that Smith's formal innovations

[19] See Stuart Curran, 'Introduction', *The Poems of Charlotte Smith* (Oxford: Oxford University Press, 1993), pp. xv–xvi; and Daniel Robinson, '*Elegiac Sonnets*: Charlotte Smith's Formal Paradoxy', *Papers on Language and Literature*, 39: 2 (Spring 2003), pp. 186–90, 204–11. See also Jacqueline Labbe, 'The Hybrid Poems of Smith and Wordsworth: Questions and Disputes', *European Romantic Review*, 20: 2 (April 2009), pp. 219–26; and Curran, 'Romantic Elegiac Hybridity,' in *The Oxford Handbook of The Elegy*, ed. Karen Weisman (Oxford: Oxford University Press, 2010), pp. 238–50.

[20] For this point we are indebted to the work of D. Robinson; see '*Elegiac Sonnets*', p. 217.

[21] See *Letters of Anna Seward*, 6 vols. (Edinburgh: Constable; London: Longman, 1811), 1: pp. 162–3, 2: pp. 161–6, and 2: p. 223. In addition, see Seward to Walter Scott, 20 June 1803, NLS MSS 865, fols. 25–8.

supplement the characteristic openness of her prefatory materials, encouraging contemporary readers to respond to her work as a first step to creating their own. The very ordering and arrangement of each edition contributes to these conditions of possibility for reader response. Like Lockwood, the reader is drawn into the volume.

While Smith's choice of opening poem never altered over the many editions of *Elegiac Sonnets*, her choice of concluding poem changed as her reputation grew and her relations with her readers shifted. Closing the first edition of *Elegiac Sonnets*, 'Blest is yon shepherd' had insisted on Smith's mastery of literary tradition even as it affirmed her opening sonnet's claims to lived experience and genuine feeling. When a new edition was called for, however, Smith chose to rearrange the poems in order to foreground the movement between literary form and lived experience. Her second edition thus ends with the sonnets written in the voice of Werther, closing with him directing Charlotte where to bury him 'and sigh for the unhappy suicide':

> And sometimes, when the sun with parting rays
> Gilds the long grass that hides my silent bed,
> The tear shall tremble in my CHARLOTTE's eyes;
> Dear precious drops! they shall embalm the dead.
> Yes! CHARLOTTE o'er the mournful spot shall weep,
> Where her poor WERTER and his sorrows sleep.[22]

At first glance, Smith's choice to end her second edition with these lines would seem a turn toward the literary, complete with its requisite features of persona, fictional source, and a hyperbolic typography. But two factors reintroduce the personal and amplify the tension. First, Werther's imagined suicide calls our attention back to earlier sonnets written in Smith's own voice expressing similar desires. Second, the doubleness of 'CHARLOTTE' in the poem at once refers to Werther's Charlotte and knowingly invokes Charlotte Smith the poet as well.[23] Most stunning of all, though, is the reversal achieved by this pun. Even as one Charlotte speaks the poem in the voice of Werther, another Charlotte sits weeping by the grave of that speaker. This amounts, in effect, to one Charlotte weeping over another, or Smith weeping over her own tomb, so that both the literary and the biographical arc of the collection come to a single point. As a poetic effect

[22] *Elegiac Sonnets and Other Essays*, 2nd ed. (Chichester: Denet Jacques, 1784), p. 26, lines 8–14.

[23] Here, see Kathryn Pratt, 'Charlotte Smith's Melancholia on the Page and Stage', *Studies in English Literature, 1500–1900*, 41: 3 (Summer, 2001), p. 570, and Jacqueline Labbe, 'Introduction', in *The Works of Charlotte Smith, Volume 14*, ed. Jacqueline Labbe, General Editor Stuart Curran, 14 vols. (London: Pickering & Chatto, 2007), 14: p. 5.

it is extraordinary, but no less powerful is the mechanism by which it materializes in her own (self)production.

Planning her third edition a year later, Smith again altered her collection, removing the 'Other Poems' and introducing twenty new sonnets. These were not merely appended to the second edition. Instead, several were introduced to complete earlier mini-cycles, including the Werther poems, which were moved within the collection to its newly-formed center. The effect was to create a distinctly two-part sequence. The first half largely preserves the earlier editions, focusing on Smith's wandering and despairing speaker who, rejecting suicide, nevertheless imagines her own grave while speaking in the voice of Werther. While repeating the gestures of the earlier sonnets, the remaining poems broaden in scope and intensity. Cyclical in nature, the movement of these later poems is also decidedly centrifugal, encompassing a widening group of allegiances: from sympathetic auditors, familiar landscapes, and intimate friends to genteel patrons, poetic forebears, and entire aesthetic traditions. As the sonnets progress, these personal and literary affiliations are increasingly, even pointedly, tied to Smith the author rather than to her speaker.

These figures firmly connect the author of *Elegiac Sonnets* to a world at once personal, literary-historical, and social. The biographical ties arguably begin to be established as early as the 'Sonnet X: To Mrs. G.', which closes with the hope that their long-standing friendship will continue. The third edition's widening literary map, meanwhile, could be said to begin in earnest either with sonnets XIII–XVII, adapted from Petrarch and Metastasio, or even earlier with Smith's pointed quoting of other poets. Wherever one discovers the origin, the emerging map portrays the author and person, 'Charlotte Smith', as a markedly different being than her speaker, vibrantly connected rather than isolated. Whether through allusion, quotation, or direct address, her final sixteen sonnets (XXI–XXXVI) declare affiliations with the Earl of Egremont, William Hayley, Lady Abergavenny, Goethe, Thomas Otway, James Thomson, William Collins, a 'Miss C—', William Hayley again, and an unnamed 'Friend'. Looking across the collection as a whole, these declared allegiances form a marked counterpoint to the cyclical loneliness of the poems. The speaker of *Elegiac Sonnets* may continue to wander in isolation, but the poems themselves chart a very different course for its well-connected author, one emphasizing the breadth of her connections, both living and artistic, and the depth of those affective ties within and across the book.

Nowhere is this gap more profoundly exploited than in 'Sonnet XXXVI', which closes the collection:

> Should the lone Wanderer, fainting on his way,
> Rest for a moment of the sultry hours,

And tho' his path thro' thorns and roughness lay,
  Pluck the wild rose, or woodbines gadding flowers:
Weaving gay wreaths, beneath some sheltering tree,
  The sense of sorrow, he awhile may lose;
So have I sought thy flowers, fair Poesy!
  So charm'd my way, with Friendship and the Muse.[24]

These lines form a counterpart to those opening the collection, repeating dominant tropes of roses, thorns, wreaths, and the flowers of Poesy as sources of momentary solace from the ills of the world. At the same time, however, these repeated figures in 'Sonnet XXXVI' show just how much has changed. Where 'Sonnet I' figured Smith's speaker as a lone wanderer, here that wanderer is decidedly *not* the speaker of the poem. Whether this is the poet Smith looking back on the tribulations of her speaker or, more likely, on some other man or woman of sensibility doomed to tread the same path, the opening octet of 'Sonnet XXXVI' places its speaker in a better place, however temporary. Smith's closing sestet might imagine a renewal of trials and darker days ahead, but the contrasts established between her first and final sonnet—and the gulf it imagines between the comparative lots of the speaker of *Elegiac Sonnets* and its author, whose way has been 'charm'd ... with Friendship and the Muse'—are impossible to ignore.

This evolving distance between speaker and author creates a space not just for narrative but also for readers to interpolate themselves, since Smith's closing sonnet presents her own progression as brought about by the pleasures of reading—and writing—poetry. However much 'Sonnet I' posited poetic gifts as both a blessing and a curse, 'Sonnet XXXVI' presents these same gifts as having, like friendship, the power to 'charm' one's way and form one's artistry. As such, the poem provides an apt ending to the collection by presenting its author as at least partially transformed by the process of composing and sharing verse with a sympathetic coterie. The implication is that Smith's readers—at least those readers fully sharing her sensibilities—will have undergone a similar transformation. In a poetic collection underwritten by sympathetic exchange, such a claim doubles as an invitation to purchasers, whom Smith invites not just to immerse themselves in her sonnets but also to compose and share their own. Readers strongly identifying with the poems are presented with the possibility of transforming themselves not into the forlorn speaker of *Elegiac Sonnets* but into writers themselves. That this occurs with the closing poem of the collection is hardly accidental. Where one poet's writing ends, others' might begin, creating—through shared affect—a book where readers and writers might occupy a common ground and where the

[24] Charlotte Smith, *Elegiac Sonnets*, 3rd ed. (London: Dodsley, 1786), p. 37, lines 1–8.

discrete categories of 'reader' and 'writer' give way to relations at once more interactive and more egalitarian.

But how did Smith's most sympathetic readers actually respond? To turn from the marks readers left in the first two editions of *Elegiac Sonnets* to those left in the next three is to be struck by their noticeable change in emphasis. With the usual corrections and attributions come more emphatic responses to specific passages. In copies of the third edition held by Winchester College and Indiana University, for example, readers have systematically noted Smith's various allusions, supplying sources and commentary as they go. Smith's note to line eight of 'Sonnet XII'—in which she states 'This line is not my own, but I know not where to look for it'—draws ample commentary: several readers supply Edward Young's name, and two add the phrases 'gloomy habits' and 'mournful temper'.[25] Whether these are merely verbal echoes or more pointed observations on the effects of elegiac reading is an open question. More striking to us is the tone of Smith's note, which invites readers to respond—and many did.

Other readers of the third, fourth, and fifth editions show an interest in formal issues. In a copy held by Cornell University, for instance, a reader has tracked Smith's knowledge of Horace, noting points of possible influence and in two instances supplying the original Latin.[26] Other copies note Petrarchan references, marking pertinent lines in Smith's preface, indexing her efforts in that form, and even supplying the original Italian. One reader notes various experimental rhyme schemes with both satisfaction and dismay, while another inserts Petrarchan sonnets by other English poets to create a kind of anthology. Here, the Jesus College copy at Cambridge University provides the richest example of this thread of response. Having identified Smith's Petrarchan sonnets in the margins of the preface, the reader supplies a headnote above each of these poems, noting whether 'she rhymes perfectly after Petrarch' and reminding readers that Petrarch's is 'the true Italian sonnet'.[27] Surveying the range of responses to Smith's third and fourth

[25] The Winchester College Library copy bestows either '+' or 'x' marks on twenty of Smith's sonnets and notes references to Edward Young at p. 41; the Indiana University copy (PR3688 S4 E3 1786) possesses a similar note here as well as many other marks and marginalia that, while erased by a later reader, are still sometimes decipherable using digital manipulation technologies. Our thanks to Isabel Planton for providing enhanced images to 'Sonnet XII', 'Sonnet XIII: From Petrarch', 'Sonnet XVI: From Petrarch', 'Sonnet XVIII: To the Earl of Egremont', 'Sonnet XIX: To Mr. Hayley', 'Sonnet XXI: Supposed to be Written by Werther', and 'Sonnet XXIII: By the Same'.

[26] See Cornell Library shelf mark Petrarch PR3688.S4 E5 1786a, a copy signed by Smith. The Latin transcriptions occur on p. 13.

[27] These comments occur in the Jesus College edition (call number G.7.8[1]) on pp. v, 30, and 34.

editions, then, we find less a shift from one kind of marking to another than widening and deepening engagement. Readers still make corrections, but only as a small part of a broader array of responses that include attribution, selection, annotation, critical commentary, anthologization, illustration, and original composition. These 'thickening' activities, as we show in the final section, do not simply mimic the activities of the late eighteenth-century newspapers and periodicals from which they draw. They amount to a form of book-making in and of itself.

III. Tipping Points

> Here, we consider the practice of 'thickening' by pasting or 'tipping in' prints, autograph letters, printed pages, maps, original art, or other materials into published books. To describe these processes simply as 'adding' misses the point …. [T]he practice is both dialogic and self-reflexive: formally, thickened books consciously reflect on augmentation as a form of interacting with the printed text. As a radical form of annotation, interleaving and extra-illustration function in ways akin to an individual reader's marginalia: inserted materials variously reiterate, elucidate, emend, recast, argue with, and critique.
>
> —The Multigraph Collective, 'Thickening' (2018)[28]

Late eighteenth-century book ownership came with pleasures largely unknown to modern readers, the most obvious of which was the customization of books. Having paid for their copy, purchasers of *Elegiac Sonnets* would need to consider, among other things, several questions regarding binding: yes or no; lavish or plain; standalone or with other publications? They might even extend these questions to other forms of accessorizing, such as the addition of the author's portrait and other illustrations or the incorporation of associated matter such as reviews, laudatory poems, or other commentary. Given the Romantic book's status as a luxury item, we might find a pertinent analogy in how we personalize modern consumer technology: our pleasure in choosing not just the specs of a new laptop but also its cover and other peripherals. Yet, as the epigraph on 'thickening' books notes, eighteenth-century readers customized books in ways that went far beyond merely adding to them. Their

[28] The Multigraph Collective, *Interacting with Print: Elements of Reading in the Era of Print Saturation* (Chicago, IL: University of Chicago Press, 2018), pp. 288–9. For a broader survey of the uses to which nineteenth-century readers put books, see Leah Price, *How to Do Things with Books in Victorian England* (Princeton, NJ and Oxford: Princeton University Press, 2012).

textual, visual, and bibliographic alterations represent a different form of intervention: they 'reiterate, elucidate, emend, recast, argue with, and critique', materially re-forming the book itself.

Readers performed all of these interventions more often and with greater intensity with *Elegiac Sonnets* than other late eighteenth-century sonnet collections. Extant copies show readers engaging enthusiastically with Smith as commentators, if not book-makers, in their own right. Of the several terms available to describe how readers customize or add to books—grangerization, extra-illustration, scrap-booking—'thickening' most accurately describes how readers of *Elegiac Sonnets* made their copies their own. Of the sixty-four copies of *Elegiac Sonnets* we have examined, at least five have been thickened; by contrast, our canvassing of eighty-eight copies of Bowles, Robinson, and Seward has discovered only one such volume, and that copy boasts only a single illustration and scant marginalia.[29] Of the copies of Smith, three of these are fifth editions. A Harvard copy tips in an author's portrait from the *European Magazine* and carries ample annotations and observations, probably by a Miss Addington; another held by the British Library has tipped in a print of the Three Graces and indexed the other illustrations in the volume. The best known, however, is the copy held by the British Library and featured on the Eighteenth-Century Collections Online (ECCO) database, which contains two tipped-in illustrations facing the title and half-title pages. Trimmed and folded to fit the volume, the first depicts a woman, sumptuously dressed in an elaborately trimmed dress and a hat with large feathers, sitting under a tree contemplating the moon, which shines on a river below her. Below the illustration are four lines of poetry, only two of which are readable, though they are of a piece with the image's rich drapery and landscape: 'Ah then that I to thy soft scenes might go / Poor wretched wanderer in this vale of Woe'. The second is a portrait of Smith, also luxuriously dressed (see Fig. 3).

Neither ECCO nor the British Library note that the copy is extra-illustrated, although the additions add a sumptuousness not present in the original volume. Presenting Smith in a turban, lace veil, and elaborately trimmed jacket of what is likely velvet, the portrait was originally published by J. Robins & Co. in 1819, based on an earlier image of Smith published in 1799 by Vernor & Hood[30] (see Fig. 4).

[29] This is a copy of the sixth edition of Bowles' *Sonnets, and Other Poems* (Bath: Crutwell; and London: Dilly, 1798) held by the University of North Carolina Library, call number PR4161.B4 A6 1798. It carries a single added illustration and marginalia on pp. 166–9.

[30] Our thanks to Stephen Behrendt for identifying these images. See also his invaluable 'Following Charlotte Smith's *Elegiac Sonnets* through the Press', in *Entree au Schrift und Bild: Titelblatt und Frontispiz im England der Neuzeit*, eds. Werner Busch, Hubertus Fischer, and Joachim Möller (Berlin: Lit Verlag, 2008), pp. 250–74.

Figure 3: Tipped-in author's portrait in the British Library copy of *Elegiac Sonnets*, 5th ed. (1789).

Although featuring a similar style of gown and headwear, the earlier image is far more austere, presenting Smith in a gesture of thought and without the later portrait's sumptuous attire. Composition, line, and tone all lack the energy and contrast of the second image. The differences between original and revised portraits nicely capture how the owner of the British Library copy sought to thicken the volume: the second image amplifies the first by layering on new, sensuous materials.

Still, the most extraordinary copy of *Elegiac Sonnets* is a signed fourth edition held by the Folger Shakespeare Library in Washington DC.[31] There, a reader (the hand suggests a woman) has annotated and interleaved the volume, nearly doubling its size. Strikingly, she also adds new opening and closing poems to the volume, effectively reframing Smith's collection (see Fig. 5).

Beyond these framing poems are several notes and annotations, and—more radically—full transcriptions of a dozen poems: four by Egerton Brydges, one

[31] The copy is call number M.b.4. As its manuscript additions are unpaginated, we describe their placement in the body of this essay rather than in the notes.

Figure 4: 'Mrs Charlotte Smith', published by Vernor & Hood, 1799.
Image courtesy of Stephen Behrendt.

by John Milton, one praising Smith from the *General Evening Post*, two in translation by Petrarch, Shakespeare's 'Let not the marriage of true minds', a poem entitled 'Printed after Shakespear's Play of Anthony & Cleopatra Abridged for the Stage' by Edward Capell, and a 'Sonnet, by Miss P.Y. when Lame, Addressed to her Canary Bird'. Some are transcribed into the volume's endpapers; the majority are written on blank leaves and inserted at specific

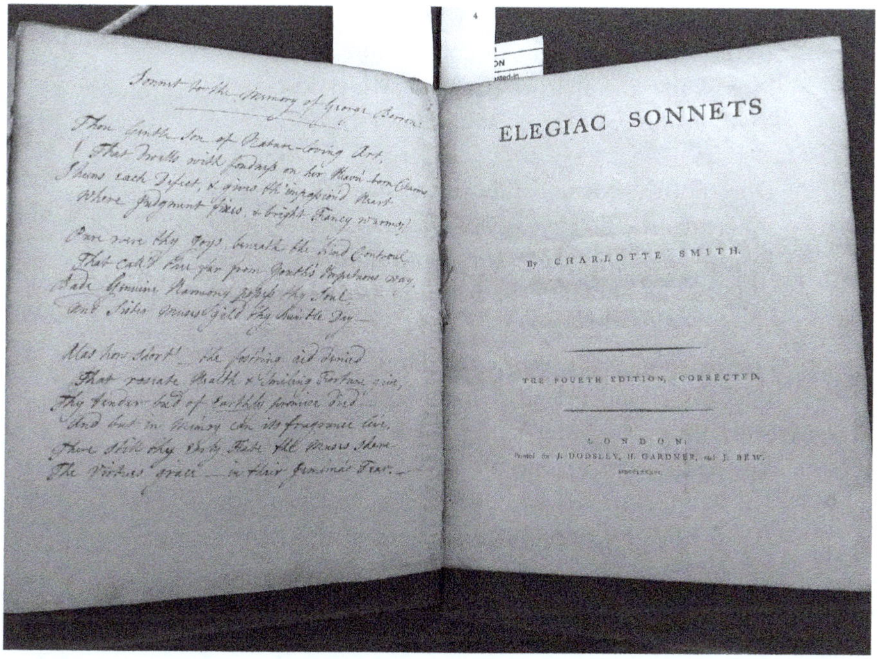

Figure 5: 'Sonnet to the Memory of George Barron', from Folger Library copy of *Elegiac Sonnets.*

moments in Smith's text to create dialogues with particular poems. Taken as a whole, these additions partake of both the scrap-book and the anthology, but with a difference: those interleaved within Smith's collection reply, often pointedly, to the poems they face. In at least one case—the homage to Smith, transcribed from the *General Evening Post* and placed just after Smith's closing poem—the reader has altered its eighth line to accord more closely with her beliefs.

Remarkable as they are, these interventions are nothing compared to those performed by the original poems tipped into the volume. All of these in some way respond to, correct, and even rewrite specific sonnets by Smith. It is as if, having found the already published poems inadequate to her needs, the reader has finally yielded to original composition to give her response to Smith its fullest expression. Many of these poems are first-rate; some even show a refreshing, nearly humorous, awareness of self. The sonnet facing Smith's 'Sonnet II', for example, carries the title, 'The foregoing Sonnet Altered—as thought the truest expression of the Sentiment, tho' worse poetry'. It is an intervention at once laudatory and critical, a homage that is both remonstration and celebration. These twin tendencies are nicely captured in her opening sonnet, which faces Smith's opening poem:

'If those paint Sorrow best who feel it most', —
   Yet sure, Who paint in colours soft as thine,
Must know the sharper stings of Mis'ry lost
   As in the converse of some Pow'r Divine!

Does not the Muse, while she to Fancy's eye
   Recalls the flow'ry Scenes that bloom no more,
Ev'n in the falling tear, the rising sigh,
   Does she not then the Sense of Joy restore?

She bids that Sense Immortal Hope disclose; —
Like some kind Friend that mingling in our woes,
Steals from the bitter current as it flows:
But if the Syren's Song no Ray impart,
No Balm to soothe while she deplores the smart, —
'Tis a False Friend,—& tear her from thy heart.*

At the end of the sonnet an asterix points the reader to a note on the reverse of the leaf:

> *Agreeable to the Sentiment of the foregoing Sonnet is that expressed by Melisander in Thomson's Play of Agamemnon —— vis —
>
> — But chief the Muses lent their softening aid,
> At their Enchanting Voice my Sorrows fled,
> Or learn'd to please—while thro' my troubled breast
> They rous'd the Soul of Harmony anew. ——
>
> Certainly these are two great Dangers which must attend the dwelling & expatiating on Afflictions when such complainings bring with them no Alleviation—One, that of Arraigning the Justice or the Goodness of the Supreme Being, the Other, that of Seeking Relief at any rate, in such things as may be displeasing to him, as well as derogatory to us in our present condition.

Poem, annotation, and note together typify the reader's means and ends in her dialogue with Smith's book. Having read *Elegiac Sonnets* through to its completion, the reader takes the argument of Smith's final 'Sonnet XXXVI'—which had praised the consolations of Poetry—and applies it to her opening poem. Surely, she suggests, so skilled an artist must find some comfort in the favors of the Muse and the divine works of nature; one so intimate with the works of Collins, Gray, Pope, and Thomson must know the appropriate passage from *Agamemnon*. And if none of this suffices, surely there is some solace to be found in the Divine.

Such arguments come into play repeatedly over the course of the Folger volume, which consistently engages with Smith's mood as well as with more technical aspects of the poetry. Even more striking for the purposes of this essay, however, is the ease of the dialogue, the reader's familiarity of response and address with Smith. Inserted after Smith's fifth sonnet, for example, is another original 'Sonnet, On Perusing Mrs. C. Smith's 5th & 6th', which asks directly what ills Smith could have borne to be so unhappy before it moves to remonstrations:

> Can no soft Interval of Peace be found?
> No taste of other's Joy suspend thy grief? —
> Then may Celestial Pity ease thy wound!
> 'Till Time shall bring thy only-wish'd relief; (5–8)

Any reader who has commented on the writing of a colleague, friend, or student will recognize the Folger reader's use of the familiar 'you' form—'thy' is repeated three times in four lines—above. Here, however, 'thy' signifies an intimacy with Smith that transgresses the primacy of the work and the authorial subject, occurring along lines that mirror and intervene in Smith's own art. Bound between Smith's fifth and sixth sonnets, the reader's response imposes itself between poems of despair and of death even as it remonstrates with the poet on both subjects. And in a fine piece of intertextual writing, the reader-turned-poet has even adapted the closing metaphor of Smith's 'Sonnet XII: Written on the Sea Shore' to close her own poem: 'Ah me! as richest treasures first subside, / So have I known them Sink beneath the whelming tide'. Such moments of interwriting mimic Smith's own habits of allusion even as their critical dialogue materially reticulates the text.

To peruse the Folger copy is to encounter a text at once intensely personal yet adapting the majority of its practices from printed publications. These include not just volumes like Smith's but also periodicals, which regularly published homages to Smith in the 1780s. The Folger copy marks the kinship between book thickening and commercial book-making while capturing another key aspect of Smith's verse: its capacity to cultivate reader sympathy and identification, and, through that shared sympathy, to create a space for devoted readers to become annotators, critics, and even poets themselves. Within this essay, the copy presents a kind of limit test, showing how radically readers might transform themselves by transforming a book. Especially striking is the resemblance between the reader's original compositions and the wealth of published homages inspired by *Elegiac Sonnets*, such as 'Advice to Mrs. Smith' printed in the *European Magazine* in August of 1786:

> Ah never let thy lyre superior dwell
> On themes thy better judgment must disdain!
> It ill befits, that verse like thine should tell
> Of Petrarch's love, or Werter's frantic pain!
> Let not or foreign taste, or tales enchain
> The genuine freedom of thy flowing line,
> Nor the dark dreams of Suicide obtain
> Deceitful lustre from such tones as thine;
> But still to nature and to virtue given,
> Thy heavenly talent dedicate to heaven![32]

Urging Smith to avoid 'foreign taste[s]' and 'the dark dreams of Suicide' and to dedicate her talent to 'heaven', the poem epitomizes the combination of praise and personal concern that *Elegiac Sonnets* inspired as its reputation grew.

To capture the remarkable discursivity prompted by Smith's mode and materials, we would like to close with a final copy of *Elegiac Sonnets*, in this case a fifth edition purchased by another young fan, the nineteen-year-old William Wordsworth, while in his first year at St. John's College, Cambridge. Smith had chosen to publish her expanded fifth edition in 1789 by subscription, reintroducing the 'Other Poems' of her first two editions and adding five illustrations, twelve new sonnets, and the 'Ode to Despair' from *Emmeline*. Currently housed in the Jerwood Center at Dove Cottage, the volume is especially prized because it contains three signatures by Wordsworth. The first two appear on the inside cover, the former reading 'Wm Wordsworth St. Johns' and the latter being a much later gift inscription to Dora Wordsworth. The third is most interesting of all. Wishing to see his name among the list of subscribers, Wordsworth inscribed his name, the name of a friend, their college affiliation, and the date at the end of that list. He also transcribed two additional sonnets by Smith at the beginning of the volume (see Fig. 6).

Though hardly the same as inscribing a book one has written, Wordsworth's inscriptions carry with them what we hope will be a now familiar combination of intimacy and self-assertion so often present in the marks of readers. Beyond these, the Jerwood copy beautifully captures how other factors—book purchase and ownership—could impact a reader's relationship with an admired author. Part of Wordsworth's affective response, after all, is predicated by his having purchased the book as a young man, a condition that moved him to present the volume to Dora three decades later. Still more is suggested by the autograph in the subscription list, which prompts him to declare himself, in some small way, a co-producer and sponsor of the book. Given this powerful

[32] Anonymous, 'Advice to Mrs. Smith: A Sonnet', *European Magazine*, 10 (August 1786), p. 127.

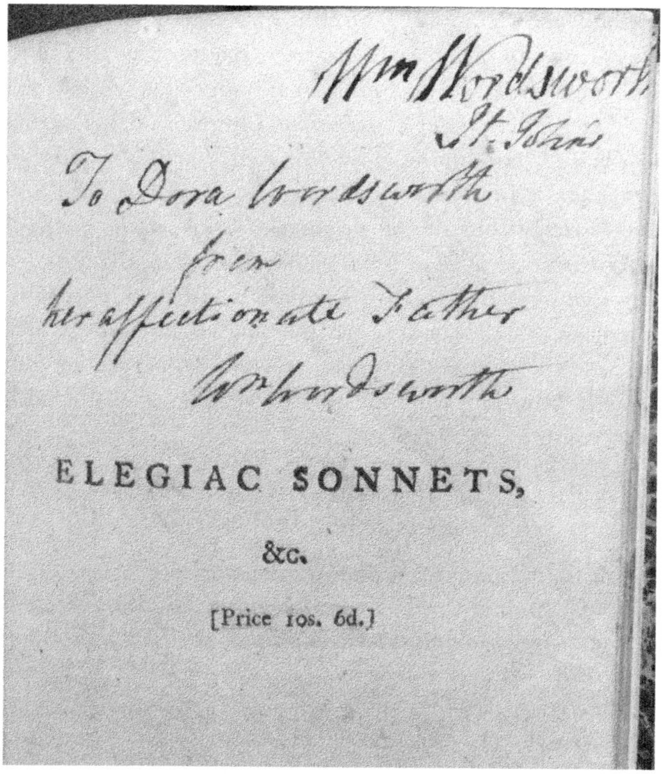

Figure 6:
Two pages
from the
Jerwood Center
copy of
Elegiac Sonnets
(1789).

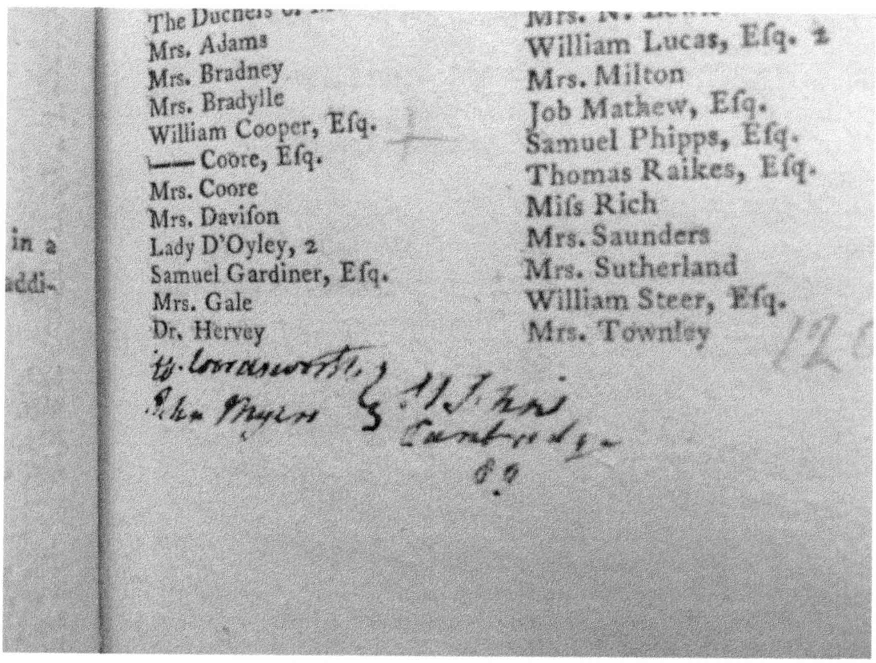

assemblage of emotions and affiliations marked in the volume, it is perhaps not surprising that two years later, on his way to France, Wordsworth felt emboldened to call on Smith unannounced. (Wordsworth, in a letter to his brother Richard, later congratulated himself on his daring; Smith, in a letter to a friend, good-humoredly regretted that the surprise visit by a young fan has made it impossible for her to visit her that day.)[33] Wordsworth's visit—not expected, but not unwelcome—seems, in fact, a logical conclusion and materialization of the *Elegiac Sonnets*'s affective dynamic, which invites readers into first sympathetic, then annotative, and then more writerly and proprietary responses. Small wonder then that the young Wordsworth, enjoying the new auspices of literary sponsorship toward a poet he sought to emulate, found himself, after long wait, at her doorstep, letter of introduction—and perhaps even volume—in hand.

Bibliography

'Advice to Mrs. Smith: A Sonnet'. *European Magazine*, 10 (August 1786), p. 127.

Behrendt, Stephen. 'Following Charlotte Smith's *Elegiac Sonnets* through the Press'. In *Entree au Schrift und Bild: Titelblatt und Frontispiz im England der Neuzeit*, eds. Werner Busch, Hubertus Fischer, and Joachim Möller. Berlin: Lit Verlag, 2008, pp. 250–74.

Bowles, William Lisle. *Sonnets, and Other Poems*. Bath: Crutwell; London: Dilly, 1798.

——. *Sonnets, Written Chiefly upon Picturesque Spots, during a Tour*. Bath: R. Crutwell, 1789.

[Brontë, Emily]. *Wuthering Heights*. New York: Harper, 1848.

Brydges, Samuel Egerton, Esq. 'Memoir of Charlotte Smith'. In *Censura Literaria*, 10 vols. London: Longman, 1805–9, vol. 4, pp. 69–84.

'Charlotte Smith'. In *Public Characters of 1800–1801*. London: R. Phillips, 1801, pp. 43–64.

Coleridge, Samuel. [*Sonnets from Various Authors*]. London, 1796.

Curran, Stuart. 'Introduction'. In *The Poems of Charlotte Smith*. Oxford: Oxford University Press, 1993, pp. xv–xvi.

——. 'Romantic Elegiac Hybridity'. In *The Oxford Handbook of The Elegy*, ed. Karen Weisman. Oxford: Oxford University Press, 2010, pp. 238–50.

Jackson, H.J. *Marginalia: Readers Writing in Books*. New Haven, CT and London: Yale University Press, 2001.

[33] See *The Letters of William and Dorothy Wordsworth: The Early Years, 1797–1805*, ed. Ernest de Selincourt, rev. Chester Shaver (Oxford: Clarendon Press, 1967), 1: p. 68; and *The Collected Letters of Charlotte Smith*, ed. Judith Phillips Stanton (Bloomington: Indiana University Press, 2003), p. 38.

——. *Romantic Readers: The Evidence of Marginalia*. New Haven, CT: Yale University Press, 2005.

Labbe, Jacqueline M. *Charlotte Smith: Romanticism, Poetry, and the Culture of Gender*. Manchester and New York: Manchester University Press, 2003.

——. 'The Hybrid Poems of Smith and Wordsworth: Questions and Disputes'. *European Romantic Review*, 20: 2 (April 2009), pp. 219–26.

——. 'Introduction'. In *The Works of Charlotte Smith, Volume 14*, ed. Jacqueline Labbe. General Editor Stuart Curran, 14 vols. London: Pickering & Chatto, 2007, pp. i–xxiii.

The Multigraph Collective. *Interacting with Print: Elements of Reading in the Era of Print Saturation*. Chicago, IL: University of Chicago Press, 2018.

Pratt, Kathryn. 'Charlotte Smith's Melancholia on the Page and Stage'. *Studies in English Literature, 1500–1900*, 41: 3 (Summer, 2001), pp. 563–81.

Price, Leah. *How to Do Things with Books in Victorian England*. Princeton, NJ and Oxford: Princeton University Press, 2012.

Robinson, Daniel. '*Elegiac Sonnets*: Charlotte Smith's Formal Paradoxy'. *Papers on Language and Literature*, 39: 2 (Spring 2003), pp. 185–220.

Seward, Anna. Letter to Walter Scott, 20 June 1803. NLS MSS 865. Fols. 25–28.

——. *Letters of Anna Seward*, 6 vols. Edinburgh: Constable; London: Longman, 1811.

Sherman, William. *Used Books: Marking Readers in Renaissance England*. Philadelphia: University of Pennsylvania Press, 2012.

Smith, Charlotte. *The Collected Letters of Charlotte Smith*, ed. Judith Phillips Stanton. Bloomington, IN: Indiana University Press, 2003.

——. *Elegiac Sonnets and Other Essays*. London: Dodsley, 1784. Second Edition: Chichester: Printed by Dennett Jaques and sold by Dodsley, Gardner, Baldwin, and Bew, London, 1784. Third edition: London: Dodsley, Gardner, and Bew, 1786. Fifth edition: London: T. Cadell, 1789.

Stauffer, Andrew. 'An Image in Lava: Annotation, Sentiment, and the Traces of Nineteenth-Century Reading'. *PMLA*, 134: 1 (January 2019), pp. 81–98.

——, ed. *Book Traces*. NINES and University of Virginia, at http://www.booktraces.org/.

Stoddard, Roger. *Marks in Books, Illustrated and Explained*. Cambridge, MA: Harvard University Press, 1985.

Wordsworth, William and Dorothy Wordsworth. *The Letters of William and Dorothy Wordsworth: The Early Years, 1797–1805*, ed. Ernest de Selincourt, rev. Chester Shaver. Oxford: Clarendon Press, 1967.

Chapter Three

Remapping the Printed Page in Women's Post-Waterloo Poetry

Emily J. Dolive

In the extensive, sometimes neglected catalogue of war memoirs and songs that permeated Romantic print culture—fueled at once by military officials and the average Joe or Jane—one finds surprising moments of fissured materiality. Not only are bodies broken in war, but notions of stable gender roles, heroism, and print are questioned in such texts. Take for example the following anecdote from the family of the prolific yet critically overlooked poet Jane Alice Sargant. Her more famous military brother Sir Harry Smith writes the following about the aftermath of the Battle of Waterloo in his *Autobiography:*

> In gathering the dead bodies, [my brother Charles] saw among the dead of our soldiers the body of a French officer of delicate mould and appearance. On examining it, he found it was that of a delicate, young, and handsome female. My story ends here, but such is the fact. What were the circumstances of devotion, passion, or patriotism which led to such heroism is, and ever will be, to me a mystery. Love, depend upon it.[1]

The expected material realities of war outline this excerpt, particularly the repeated 'dead bodies' divided between enemy and victor as well as a promise that soldiers' 'heroism' will be proclaimed by others or perhaps make its way into print. However, the repeated adjective 'delicate' destabilizes the known matter of war and war writing. Even before this 'delicate' soldier is confirmed

[1] Sir Harry Smith, *The Autobiography of Lieutenant-General Sir Harry Smith, Baronet of Aliwal on the Sutlej G.C.B. Edited with the addition of some supplemental chapters by G.C. Moore Smith, M.A. In two volumes.* (London: John Murray, 1901), p. 279.

female, the body is considered distinct, as women were often expected to be physically and in writing.[2] Her body's presence then defamiliarizes the battlefield scene and ruptures the attempt at 'gathering' together a corpus of the dead both physically and textually. Requiring a physical 'exam', her distinct 'body' dematerializes into 'mould' and ultimately into 'it'.[3] These terms attempt to dissolve material and gender distinction, to understand or control the 'mystery' of this body. But the material fissure is brief. Smith soon pushes past the unstable body to return to the more familiar, and gendered, materials of 'heroism' and 'Love' that honor, and in turn rematerialize, the body as 'female'. Still, the 'mystery' of her body and her 'heroism' strangely and suddenly rupture the format of this war text. Smith slips into clipped sentences and, in the manuscript, repeated long dashes instead of commas, as the paragraph and chapter end abruptly with this anecdote of the female soldier and a brief mention of commanding generals.[4] The following chapter is devoted to Smith's wife's account of Waterloo, all instances that highlight the instability of war texts when distinct bodies and genders are mixed. While the curious battlefield anecdote may have been a juicy detail suddenly remembered in a largely unorganized memoir, when Smith 'ends here' abruptly without returning to his military exploits and personal reflections of Waterloo, he rests readers' eyes on unstable bodies and texts. Although the disruptive body is soon left behind and the disrupted text is restored in later chapters, Smith inadvertently introduces a material transmission amongst these unstable things—body, heroism, and text—that poets in the immediate aftermath of war, including his sister Jane Alice Sargant, make dynamic enough to present alternative modes of being and modes of print. Sargant and her contemporary Felicia Hemans guide readers' eyes with maps of various materials, including war, gender, and the text itself, which are constantly being mixed and moved on the page.

[2] Adriana Craciun finds 'the nineteenth-century domestication of essential sexual difference' to be entrenched in literary and social spheres. 'Romantic Poetry, Sexuality, Gender', in *The Cambridge Companion to British Romantic Poetry*, eds. James Chandler and Maureen N. McLane (Cambridge: Cambridge University Press, 2008), p. 159. See also Stephen Behrendt, *British Women Poets and the Romantic Writing Community* (Baltimore, MD: Johns Hopkins University Press, 2009), p. 40; and Susan Wolfson, *Borderlines: The Shiftings of Gender in British Romanticism* (Palo Alto, CA: Stanford University Press, 2006), p. 15.

[3] Terms like 'it' and 'things' denote 'dull matter' as opposed to 'vibrant life'. See Jane Bennett, *Vibrant Matter: A Political Ecology of Things* (Durham, NC: Duke University Press, 2010), p. vii. For a related discussion of cross-dressing women during war, see Dianne Dugaw, *Women and Popular Balladry, 1650–1850* (Chicago, IL: University of Chicago Press, 1996).

[4] *Autobiography of Sir Harry Smith*. MS Add. 7036. Cambridge University Library, Cambridge.

Throughout this study, I find that genre and body are destabilized and made mobile in these texts, which allows gender to become fluid and at times nonbinary, by which I mean the expected attributes of male and female merge or disappear altogether. Genre—here used to denote different poetic structures even within a single text—instigates and supports the fluid movement between and beyond genders, which helps poets posit that gender is an erroneous prerequisite for wartime participation.

This essay looks at moments when print moves and mingles with different materials to resist stable constructions of femininity, war, and the book itself. Specifically, manipulations of the printed page seem to intensify during the brief post-Waterloo period in Britain when poetry was at its zenith and, simultaneously, a 'reactionary backlash sought to reinforce hierarchies' both domestic and sexual, according to Adriana Craciun (pp. 161, 155). The popularity of annuals, single-author poetry volumes, and literary periodicals suggests an established conception that polite, recognized poetry must undergo some round of printed life. Because this apparent authority of print so often reinforced post-war gender distinctions—such as 'naturally writ[ing] in different styles' and 'knitting needles' for women instead of political debate or activity—poets like Hemans and Sargant sought alternative constructions of the material page.[5] In their hands, the printed page became fluid, merging once-separate genres, voices, and genders before readers' eyes through linguistic and structural play. As I examine in detail below, Hemans pairs two war poems together on the printed page—one for a male and one for a female soldier—in order to forge a new moving material reality of war and war writing from the dematerializing 'mould' and 'form' of each body.[6] Readers' gazes become fluidly material as Hemans and Sargant move them sharply across opposing genres, distinct voices, and nonhuman nature. Momentarily, the sense of separation on the printed page—enhanced by letters individually cut and set and single poems adrift on an otherwise empty page—is overcome through pointed intertextuality.[7] The separation these texts attempt to overcome represents women's theoretical separation from war and literary discourse, which Hemans and Sargant bridge when they manipulate and mix the language, gendered bodies, and heroic or natural materials of war elegies and ballads. These manipulations, much like what Anthony John Harding calls

[5] Review of Felicia Hemans's *The Restoration of the Works of Art to Italy* and *The Sceptic* in the *British Review*, 15 (January 1820), p. 299 and review of Anna Barbauld's *Eighteen Hundred and Eleven* in the *Quarterly Review*, 16 (June 1812), pp. 309–10.

[6] Kate Singer also argues in part that as the ocean 'intermingles' with and dissolves human bodies broken by war, a movement beyond humanity begins. See 'Limpid Waves and Good Vibrations: Charlotte Smith's New Materialist Affect', *Essays in Romanticism*, 23: 2 (2016), p. 191.

[7] Warren Chappell and Robert Bringhurst, *A Short History of the Printed Word*, 2nd ed. (Vancouver: Hartley and Marks Publishers Inc., 1999), pp. 8, 183–8.

'pressure points', are subtle attempts to bend and break traditional boundaries of gender and genre so that those materials might blend into a new materiality that moves beyond the traditionally understood material realities of war and gender, as seen in Sir Harry Smith's *Autobiography* and countless war verses from the period.[8] Thus women's wartime participation, Hemans and Sargant posit, is not precipitated by recognized matters of war or gender roles but by moments when bodies of page and person merge and recreate one another. In other words, as readers mentally assemble the map of bodies, repeated language, and nonhuman materials on the page, a materiality is created that is both intertextual and nonbinary. In fact, as this study claims, women poets' manipulations of language and structure on the printed page subtly undermine the post-war importance of gendered place and voice, asserting instead a continual fluctuation of being and of writing during war. Material manipulation of the printed page, which was consistently filled with war songs and memoirs in this period, forces readers to think beyond gender and close the great gap between 'distant violence' and readers' supposedly stable society.[9]

To enable readers to interact closely with new, unstable notions of war and gender and print, Hemans and Sargant manipulated the materials of genre, or the expected properties in print, in the popular Field of Battle poem and the wartime elegy. In wartime periodicals, countless Field of Battle poems, often a subgenre of ballads, used female characters as catalysts for imagined, even grotesque excursions to the battlefield.[10] Often, as in Mary Robinson's 'Llwhen and Gwyneth' and Scoto-Britanus's 'Thomas and Kitty', readers follow a woman in pursuit of her beloved soldier until she finds him dead, attempts to staunch his wounds, and subsequently dies on the battlefield herself.[11] As Mary Favret explains, in contrast to the absent bodies of male soldiers in war poetry, women's bodies were the primary mode for visualizing the pain and destruction of war, in part to keep masculinity and by extension patriotism inviolate.[12] Interestingly, the visible, destroyed women were exposed without any memorial apparatus such

[8] Anthony John Harding, 'Felicia Hemans and the Effacement of Woman', in *Romantic Women Writers, Voices, and Countervoices,* eds. Paula L. Feldman and Theresa M. Kelley (Hanover, NH: University Press of New England, 1995), pp. 138–40.

[9] Mary Favret, *War at a Distance: Romanticism and the Making of Modern Wartime* (Princeton, NJ: Princeton University Press, 2010), pp. 13–15.

[10] Simon Bainbridge, *British Poetry and the Revolutionary and Napoleonic Wars* (Oxford: Oxford University Press, 2003), pp. 24–31.

[11] Mary Robinson, 'Llwhen and Gwyneth, written in the year 1782', in *The Poetical Works of the late Mrs. Mary Robinson*, volume II (London: Richard Philips, 1806), pp. 22–9. Scoto-Britanus, 'Thomas and Kitty', *The Courier* (22 January 1796). Reprinted in *British War Poetry in the Age of Romanticism: 1793–1815*, ed. Betty T. Bennett (New York: Garland Publishing, 1976), p. 170.

[12] Mary Favret, 'Coming Home: The Public Spaces of Romantic War', *Studies in Romanticism*, 33: 4 (Winter 1994), pp. 539–48.

as the banners, trumpets, and fame sung or written that often honored their absent male counterparts in panegyric songs or elegies, a distinction Hemans's and Sargant's material mixtures on the page expose. Through pointed interplay between language and generic structures, bodies do not simply shift from female to male but, however briefly, defy both gender and expected generic qualities. Thus, readers' expectations of popular wartime poetry—the fixed materialities of gender and war that were still tightly mapped onto genres like the Field of Battle poem, ballad, and elegy—were quietly disrupted.

In the wartime elegy, another popular form Hemans and Sargant manipulate, dead bodies and even the repercussions of so many lost lives are typically whisked away with consolations like glory, dust, and fame. Brandy Ryan reminds us that 'War and elegy emerge as masculine forces that act upon, or provide obstacles for, women'. Although prominent and feminine in Field of Battle poems and many ballads, women are less visible in the formal war elegy during the Romantic period.[13] While attribution is not always certain, none of the titular elegies in Betty T. Bennett's *British War Poetry in the Age of Romanticism* anthology are identifiably written by women, and they certainly do not elegize women during war with the same materials and language men receive. Only briefly does Matho's 'An Elegy on War' describe a mourning 'wife' and 'The cries of widows' among sustained visions of gory battle (lines 26, 42). More common are elegies or dirges like those for Lord Nelson that utilize a rhetorical question and answer structure—a structure adapted by both Hemans and Sargant—to question 'Saw ye … / The troops arrang'd' and to assert 'A Nation's grief bedew'd his grave' (lines 1–2, 9).[14] On the page this question and answer structure—including quotation marks, question marks, and sometimes silent responses—helps to materialize voice. Post-Waterloo poets dramatize silent responses by women in particular by moving readers' eyes across disparate materials such as battlefield relics, dead bodies, and nonhuman nature, which then speak in unison so that traditional notions of voice are disrupted. Still, as seen even in these brief excerpts, men's bodies and women's voices were missing from popular elegies. Reacting to this absence, Hemans and Sargant seize the opportunity to dissolve and recast expected silences or material differences through textual movement of bodies, genre, and language.

[13] Brandy Ryan, '"Echo and Reply": The Elegies of Felicia Hemans, Letitia Landon, and Elizabeth Barrett', *Victorian Poetry*, 46: 3 (Fall 2008), p. 251. See also Melissa F. Zeiger's *Beyond Consolation: Death, Sexuality, and the Changing Shapes of Elegy* (Cornell, NY: Cornell University Press, 1997), pp. 10–11. Zeiger finds that in elegies women are 'noted only as absences' as opposed to the monuments, memories, and deeds that fill up male elegies.

[14] Matho, 'An Elegy on War', *The Protestant Dissenter's Magazine*, III (1796), pp. 32–33; Anonymous, 'Dirge on the Death of Lord Nelson', *The Morning Chronicle* (8 November 1805); John Mayne, 'Nelson—A Dirge', *The Gentleman's Magazine*, LXXIV (September 1812). All three reprinted in Bennett, pp. 183, 350, 446.

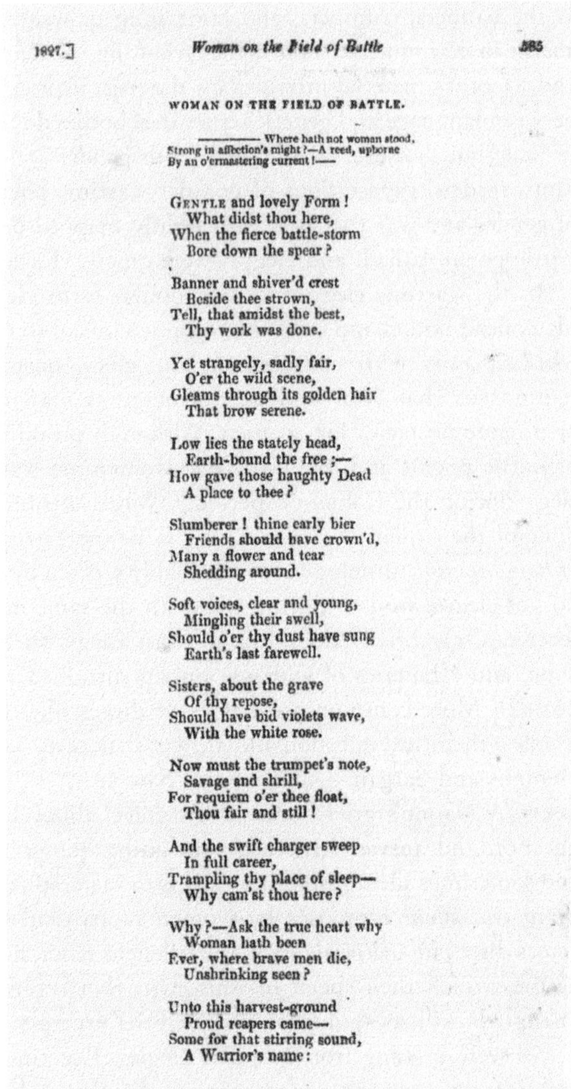

1827.] *Woman on the Field of Battle* 585

WOMAN ON THE FIELD OF BATTLE.

——— Where hath not woman stood,
Strong in affection's might?—A reed, upborne
By an o'ermastering current!—

GENTLE and lovely Form!
What didst thou here,
When the fierce battle-storm
Bore down the spear?

Banner and shiver'd crest
Beside thee strown,
Tell, that amidst the best,
Thy work was done.

Yet strangely, sadly fair,
O'er the wild scene,
Gleams through its golden hair
That brow serene.

Low lies the stately head,
Earth-bound the free;—
How gave those haughty Dead
A place to thee?

Slumberer! thine early bier
Friends should have crown'd,
Many a flower and tear
Shedding around.

Soft voices, clear and young,
Mingling their swell,
Should o'er thy dust have sung
Earth's last farewell.

Sisters, about the grave
Of thy repose,
Should have bid violets wave,
With the white rose.

Now must the trumpet's note,
Savage and shrill,
For requiem o'er thee float,
Thou fair and still!

And the swift charger sweep
In full career,
Trampling thy place of sleep—
Why cam'st thou here?

Why?—Ask the true heart why
Woman hath been
Ever, where brave men die,
Unshrinking seen?

Unto this harvest-ground
Proud reapers came—
Some for that stirring sound,
A Warrior's name:

Figures 7a and 7b: The two poems as they appear in *Blackwood's Magazine* in November 1827.

Hemans uses the literary stage of *Blackwood's Magazine* to create material movement between pages that, standing alone, house distinct genres and gendered bodies. 'Woman on the Field of Battle' and 'To the Memory of Lord Charles Murray' each employ familiar, gendered scenes from war literature strikingly reminiscent of Sir Harry Smith's *Autobiography*. In the first, a golden-haired woman is found dead among male soldiers on the battlefield, which causes the speaker to debate her military motivation and prowess. The latter poem is a familiar elegy for an aristocratic battle commander who was killed abroad and, as the subtitle reveals, 'died in the Cause, and lamented

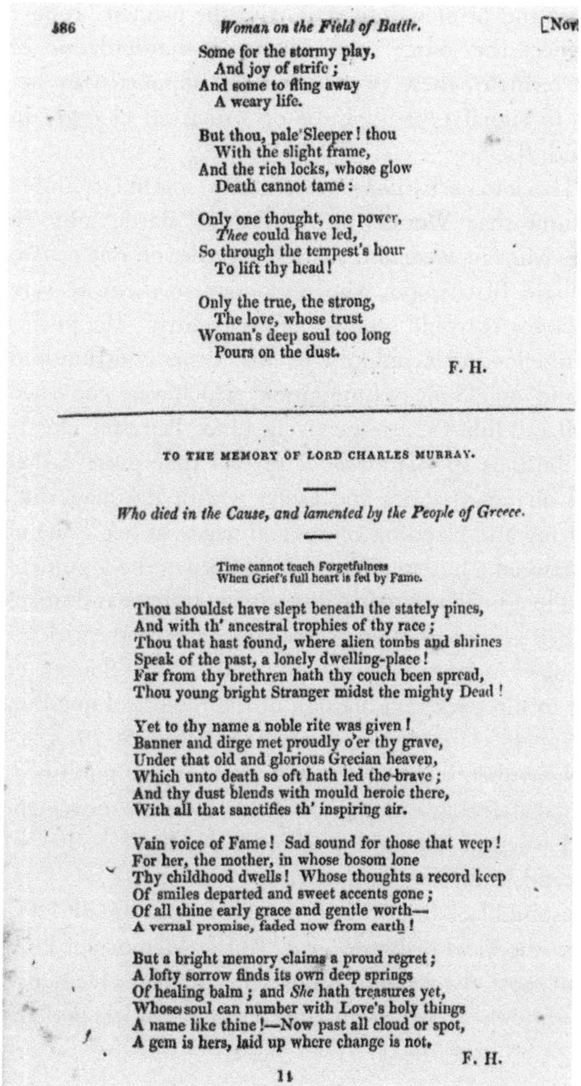

486 *Woman on the Field of Battle.* [Nov.

Some for the stormy play,
And joy of strife;
And some to fling away
A weary life.

But thou, pale Sleeper! thou
With the slight frame,
And the rich locks, whose glow
Death cannot tame:

Only one thought, one power,
Thee could have led,
So through the tempest's hour
To lift thy head!

Only the true, the strong,
The love, whose trust
Woman's deep soul too long
Pours on the dust.

F. H.

TO THE MEMORY OF LORD CHARLES MURRAY.

Who died in the Cause, and lamented by the People of Greece.

Time cannot teach Forgetfulness
When Grief's full heart is fed by Fame.

Thou shouldst have slept beneath the stately pines,
And with th' ancestral trophies of thy race;
Thou that hast found, where alien tombs and shrines
Speak of the past, a lonely dwelling-place!
Far from thy brethren hath thy couch been spread,
Thou young bright Stranger midst the mighty Dead!

Yet to thy name a noble rite was given!
Banner and dirge met proudly o'er thy grave,
Under that old and glorious Grecian heaven,
Which unto death so oft hath led the brave;
And thy dust blends with mould heroic there,
With all that sanctifies th' inspiring air.

Vain voice of Fame! Sad sound for those that weep!
For her, the mother, in whose bosom lone
Thy childhood dwells! Whose thoughts a record keep
Of smiles departed and sweet accents gone;
Of all thine early grace and gentle worth—
A vernal promise, faded now from earth!

But a bright memory claims a proud regret;
A lofty sorrow finds its own deep springs
Of healing balm; and *She* hath treasures yet,
Whose soul can number with Love's holy things
A name like thine!—Now past all cloud or spot,
A gem is hers, laid up where change is not.

F. H.

11

by the People of Greece'.[15] Such surface summaries invite a view of Hemans's conventional approaches to war: male honors and misplaced females. However, Hemans mixes gendered bodies, battle accoutrements, and silent responses through material manipulations like repeated language and placing opposing genres on the same page in order to offer readers an alternative view of wartime

[15] All quotes from these two poems are taken from *Felicia Hemans: Selected Poems, Letters, and Reception Materials*, ed. Susan J. Wolfson (Princeton, NJ: Princeton University Press, 2000), pp. 455–7.

participation. Though editors and printers intervene, and the printed product may or may not exactly reflect the source copy, Hemans's manipulation of the page is documented in terms of these two poems and supported by her regular use of underlining to signal typographical or structural changes in manuscripts (see Figs. 7a and 7b).[16]

Because they were printed back to back in *Blackwood's Magazine* in November 1827, it is reasonable to assume that 'Woman on the Field of Battle' and 'To the Memory of Lord Charles Murray' were also written together on one or two sheets of paper sent to William Blackwood, who responded to them as 'very elegant pieces' and wished Hemans would send in longer poems.[17] The poems came as a pair and were printed as such, unlike Hemans's other contributions such as 'The Homes of England' and 'Song of Emigration', which were published singly in *Blackwood's* in April and July 1827, respectively. Linda Peterson, closely examining Hemans's contributions to *Blackwood's*, reveals that these earlier poems of 1827 commented on news stories and essays within the magazine. Already Hemans is destabilizing and blending genres and pages, as her 'Song of Emigration' uses dialogue between a husband and wife to deepen the argument for surplus population found in a previous article. Hemans manifests and mixes voice on the printed page when key words from each character echo the article's language, such as 'pastures new' to farm in exchange for the 'first' 'flowers' of 'home', encouraging readers to flip back in a revision of the rhetorical question and answer structure common to wartime elegies or dirges (lines 5, 29, 47).[18] Thus, I contend that, by November, when the paired poems were published, Hemans had honed her textual attention and manipulations to create movement between pages, genres, and wartime ideals that allowed gendered bodies to transgress and briefly transcend traditional boundaries.

On the periodical page a solid black line and the repeated signature of 'F.H.' scarcely separate 'Woman on the Field of Battle' and 'To the Memory of Lord Charles Murray'. Familiar to most *Blackwood's* readers by late 1827, Hemans's signatures on the page help unite these two poems and for some readers perhaps

[16] Felicia Hemans, *The Siege of Valencia*, 1823. MS Eng 1227. Houghton Library, Harvard University.

[17] Blackwood Archives, National Library of Scotland. MS 30310, ff. 282–83. Excerpts reprinted in *Felicia Hemans*, ed. Wolfson, p. 457, n. 1.

[18] Linda Peterson, 'Nineteenth-Century Women Poets and Periodical Spaces: Letitia Landon and Felicia Hemans', *Victorian Periodicals Review*, 49: 3 (Fall 2016), pp. 396–414. Peterson examines Hemans's and Landon's periodical contributions from this period to suggest that periodicals were spaces for women poets in particular to practice different personas and try out a range of topics for audiences before commencing large-scale poems and collections that would more firmly solidify their authorial identity or reputation. See the inspiration for Hemans's dialogue in 'The Surplus Population of the United Kingdom', *Blackwood's Edinburgh Magazine*, 21: 124 (April 1827), pp. 379–91.

reveal the author's identity.[19] The intertextual stage is set to continue guiding readers' eyes between the two poems, so that the poems briefly merge the seemingly separate materials of battlefield, genre, and gendered bodies. Hemans unites the contrasting pages and the bodies of the misplaced woman and the soldier's funeral with the same language typically fitted to male elegy, like 'trumpet', 'name', and 'dust' (29, 44, 60). She thus temporarily overcomes the scarcely visible status of women in war elegies by inserting and mixing pieces of other genres, voices, and heroic material. By destabilizing the material text in this way, Hemans can further disrupt the expected materialities of gender and war.

Shared language between 'Woman on the Field of Battle' and 'To the Memory of Lord Charles Murray' helps link seemingly opposite, gendered material realities of war together physically and symbolically. While the unnamed woman is simply a 'lovely form' next to the repeated term 'name' in Lord Murray's titular elegy, their lives and appearance are in fact quite similar (lines 1, 7, 23). Both came 'early' to virtue and to death and are described as 'young' and 'gentle' (17, 21, 1, 6, 17). Lord Murray is 'bright' and 'A gem' (6, 19, 24) whereas the unnamed woman comparably 'Gleams', looks 'golden', and 'glow[s]' (11, 51). Repeated instances of brightness begin to obscure both 'form' and 'name', dematerializing and mixing gendered bodies. Like the yoking device of the repeated 'F.H.', Hemans wavers between naming and unnaming, making and unmaking, as she maps out these material mixtures. Because brightness and gleaming can also correspond to the trope of inspired or transcendent bards, Hemans further disrupts the common construction of sexual female bodies and intellectual male minds.[20] In fact, the woman warrior's 'form' that mixes with light and 'Gleams' suggests agency and movement—as opposed to Murray's contained 'gem' and stable name—which encourages the additional diffusion of war things, genres, and genders on the page. Male or female, Hemans gives the warriors matching adjectives to overlap their distinct texts and bodies and thus resists separate, stable notions of war and war writing.

The gleam across the battlefield and across the page that overlaps these two texts and bodies supports the movement of other battlefield matter to dissolve the erroneous elegiac distinction between the two warriors. As if embodying the active light that 'Gleams' from her body, the woman is the only one who is expressly proven to have fought, 'amidst the best, / Thy *work* was done!' (lines 7–8, emphasis added). Any 'work' in Lord Murray's elegy is taken for

[19] In the other 1827 *Blackwood's* poems noted above, Hemans retains her 'F.H.' signature, which establishes identity and authority. See Paula Feldman, 'Women Poets and Anonymity in the Romantic Era', *New Literary History*, 33: 2 (Spring 2002), pp. 279–89.

[20] Harding, pp. 145–56.

granted as his gilded funeral carries on; however, both figures across the page are given the same battle accoutrements: 'Banner and shivered crest' lie beside the fallen woman, and Lord Murray too has 'Banner and dirge' at his grave (5, 8). These prominent elements in each poem initiate new lines and sentences and ultimately mix with the mortality of each figure, 'thy dust' (23, 60, 11). Hemans ensures mixing takes place through shared language and present-tense verbs, including 'Mingling' voices of sorrow and dust that 'blends' with that of another (21, 11). The manipulated text thus identifies and enacts a movement of war materials that resist their once-stable positions in elegiac or social conventions. These words—'banner', 'dust', and even 'stately'—that are shared between the dead figures attempt to merge the common materials and literature for male heroes with female participation in war, to momentarily overcome the notion of separate genders and genres (13, 1). This new materiality of war and gender constantly overlaps seemingly separate pages, words, items, and bodies that together provide new options for wartime participation, options beyond celebrating fame without the reality of dead bodies and beyond singling out women destroyed by war. Instead, both bodies are given access to the supposedly masculine space of the battlefield as equal actors to the point that gendered language and tropes overlap and undermine the importance of gender in determining distinct wartime roles. Because the woman has mixed with things like the 'crest' and 'spear' usually allotted to male soldiers, and because her text like her body shares space and language with Lord Murray's, Hemans momentarily creates more fluid, almost nonbinary modes of being and modes of writing during war (5, 4).

Hemans's material mixtures, of being and of writing, at once make and unmake distinct texts and specific notions of femininity and masculinity by virtue of repeated terms embedded in corresponding stanzas. Though the dead, unnamed 'form' is rescued and given agency by the surrounding bright 'Gleams', readers soon lose sight of the body in the battlefield cacophony of 'trumpets' and 'Trampling' horses' feet. The form dissolves first into light, blended with that of Lord Murray, then into sound until 'Woman on the Field of Battle' ends with the warrior's 'dust'. Initially reminiscent of Sir Harry Smith's dematerializing 'mould' and 'it', this final note of decay turns again towards movement and making as the end of each poem is again tied in a knot on the page. The woman warrior's 'dust' is compounded by her 'love', 'deep soul', and 'thought' (lines 53, 58, 59) in the closing quatrain, which mirror 'soul', 'thoughts', and 'Love' at the end of 'To the Memory of Lord Charles Murray' (22, 15). The second poem merges with and again sets in motion the body and matter of the first poem thanks to the map of shared language and corresponding structures. Further, the 'Love' at the end of the second poem corresponds not to the titular hero but to his mother, which unites and elevates the diverse, often overlooked roles for women during war. As three bodies are now mixed on the periodical page, the page itself undergoes unmaking, similar to that strange moment of textual instability in Sir Harry Smith's memoir. The 'thought' of 'love' in the first poem extends in the second to 'thoughts a record keep'. Here it is suggested that the 'record'—in the mind, in the 'thoughts' of Lord Murray's mother—is a rival to the seemingly traditional elegy on the page. The mental 'record', with its potential for other 'treasures', destabilizes the printed text by making room for other modes of representing or remembering war beyond the familiar war song that filled Romantic print culture (21).

Hemans's language continues to hint at the decay of print and of bodies before they ultimately mix and recreate one another with materials like 'soul', 'love', and 'thought'. Shared language constantly guides readers' gazes, especially the familiar 'dust' and 'Banner', but in the middle of these overlapping poems, the multifaceted phrase 'mould heroic' is added to the repeated term 'dust' (11). Not only does 'mould' resurface in Smith's *Autobiography,* which was not printed until 1901, but Hemans evokes a dual event of making and unmaking with this term, a term that Smith only uses to denote a pre-made, distinct form. While Lord Murray's 'dust blends with mould heroic here', Hemans primarily establishes a union of earth and decaying bodies; bodies disintegrate and moulder, but 'blend' into something new 'here' at both page and gravesite (11). Moreover, according to the *Oxford English Dictionary,* 'mould' is also 'something which gives shape, form, or character to something else; an established pattern'. The productive tension between 'decayed remains' and the giving of form embodies Hemans's moving text and the exchanges between bodies and diverse matter, recasting rigid conceptions of gender and writing during war. Indeed, like the frame or form used in papermaking, the 'mould' of paper or body has the potential to make, unmake, and mix.[21] For instance, before 'mould heroic', readers have thrice seen 'dust' repeated above on the page, primarily referring to the woman warrior and connecting her with Lord Murray. At the end of her text, the dust is activated as her 'love … *Pours* on the dust' (58–60, emphasis added). The agential dust now overtakes or pours into Lord Murray's poem, meeting and making other types of love, mould, and thought, as noted above. Out of the moldering bodies and separate texts come new combinations of being and writing, traced by readers as their eyes follow overlapping materials and language that challenge rigid, gendered conceptions about wartime participation.

Finally, Hemans's structural use of questions and implicit answers across both poems fully force the carefully chosen, shared terms and materials of each poem to perpetually move across the page, assembling a new war text with each series of questions. The question and answer structure, adapted from

[21] 'Mould', *Oxford English Dictionary* (2018), entries 11.a, 2.c, 9.d. These are contemporary definitions as well.

many other periodical war poems, further undermines the unequal, gendered expectations readers and writers have for wartime participation while proposing alternative avenues for voice. As I mention above, Hemans includes proof of wartime 'work' in 'Woman on the Field of Battle' not through an account of battle but through circulating items and sounds like 'Banner and shivered crest' and 'the trumpet's note' (5, 29). In fact, her narrator puts these telling materials into motion by beginning the poem with a question:

> Gentle and lovely form,
> What didst thou here,
> When the fierce battle-storm
> Bore down the spear? (1–4)

The alternating meter and punctuation here embody the tension in the rest of the poem between question and answer, boundary and transgression.[22] The shared language of 'Banner and shivered crest' is subsequently used to answer this question, which, because of its prominent repetition in both poems, asserts that these typically masculine materials are applicable to both genders and genres of ballad or elegy during war (5). Still, the speaker continues to acknowledge the difficulty present in breaking gender boundaries. 'Yet', despite her contributions to war, the woman is described as 'strangely, sadly fair', thus returning to a more expected, feminine description (9). Like Smith's account of the 'delicate' woman disguised in military regalia, this tension quickly leads the narrator to another question: so lovely yet valiant, 'How gave those haughty dead / A place to thee?' (15–6). The place on the battlefield, like the place on the same page as the male elegy, is crucial for Hemans to establish. In implicit responses, Hemans's quatrains circulate among 'farewell' songs, connections with 'brave men', and an unstoppable 'glow' (24, 38, 50). But the question of how gendered place was or can be given to the woman by men is never fully answered in this poem alone. In fact, 'charger[s]' enter, 'Trampling thy place of sleep' (33–5). This sudden intrusion does not lead to a memorial like Lord Murray's whose 'Banner and dirge met proudly o'er thy grave', lifted by helping hands across the page, or even to acceptance (8). After a long dash, the cavalrymen again ask, 'Why camest thou here?' (36). The narrator's question is answered, it seems, with another question, briefly undermining the stability of both narrator and text. Unlike many periodical elegies or ballads about fallen heroes, Hemans's descriptions increasingly fail to shed light on the questions posed and thus prompt readers to look for possible answers elsewhere on the surrounding pages, an important creation of materially moving the gaze.

[22] In her edition of Hemans's texts, Wolfson notes that 'The starkly alternating dimeter and trimeter lines of 'Woman' mime the drumbeat of a funeral dirge' (p. 457, n1).

Although Hemans's unnamed woman warrior does not answer any of the questions herself, as Jane Alice Sargant's characters do, Hemans does manipulate the structures of her paired poems in order to guide readers towards an answer about gendered place. Hemans's stanzaic form in 'To the Memory of Lord Charles Murray' stresses the status of this poem as a response or relief to the repeated questions and heroic materials in 'Woman on the Field of Battle'. Although the two poems—ballad quatrains and Venus and Adonis sestets—do not make a perfect fourteen-lined sonnet, I read the sestet stanzas of 'To the Memory of Lord Charles Murray' as sonnet-like responses to the questions put forth in 'Woman on the Field of Battle', which is placed prominently just above readers' eyes on the top of the periodical page. Helen Luu similarly finds that Hemans's repetitive 'contest of voices' throughout *Records of Woman*, published a year after these paired poems, 'formally contests the dominant ideology and its concomitant constructions of femininity'.[23] There are also four questions in the first poem and four sestets in the second that affirm Hemans's reciprocal structure. In response, the second poem details Lord Murray's memorial service filled with the repeated 'Banner and dirge' plus things like a 'noble rite' and 'trophies' that never appear in the above ballad (8, 7, 2). In one sestet's ending couplet, Lord Murray's 'dust' is linked to that 'mould heroic', a pronounced volta that exposes the unnecessary difference between male and female memorials (11). The woman too is 'dust' twice in her poem, but she is never named a hero. The answer to 'How gave those haughty dead / A place to thee?' is, it seems, that they did not (15–6). Indeed, the narrator realizes that the woman warrior 'Should have [been] crown'd' with flowers brought by 'Friends', a hypothetical, feminine version of the 'trophies' and funeral procession going on across the page (18). Yet the conditional tense, thrice repeated, suggests the loss or failure of separate, gendered events and texts. Instead of a distinct place on the battlefield or page, 'Woman on the Field of Battle' turns to a blend of trumpets, dust, and glowing light that is poised to generate other, varied forms of being and of writing during war. The woman's body fluidly moves between notions of femininity and masculinity just as her text and its connection to Lord Murray's suggests it is not a standalone battlefield ballad one typically finds in periodicals, making both texts look beyond restrictive gendered forms and expectations. The questions and unifying sestet answers constantly mix diverse materials while overlapping each page, prioritizing movement to best direct readers towards new conceptions of war, namely, the need to eschew gender as a prerequisite.

While Hemans uses the printed page to map movements between supposedly opposing bodies and texts to uncover half-hidden voices that

[23] Helen Luu, 'Fantasies of "Woman": Hemans's Deconstruction of "Femininity" in *Records of Woman*', *Women's Writing*, 21: 1 (2014), p. 51.

counter limited ideologies of wartime participation, Sargant's post-Waterloo page similarly challenges those ideologies by filling up with copious amounts of quoted speech from men and women. Sargant's simply titled 'Ballad' in her 1818 *Sonnets and Other Poems* relays the parting of two lovers before war through another series of questions and answers that ultimately give way to the rocks and waves of the seaside setting, materials that consume the destroyed bodies of both speakers.[24] The wartime relationship between the speakers and their nonhuman counterparts is first established in a series of questions like 'Will sorrow's tear-drops stay?' (line 28). Both speakers repeatedly compare one another to natural materials 'like the blue-bell, modest flow'r, / That only loves the shade' and rocks 'amid the billowy main' until both characters merge with 'insensible' nature or are 'Dash'd 'gainst the rocks' (53–4, 33, 67, 103). In its reliance on dialogue, nature, and the ballad's oral connections, 'Ballad' embodies one way 'print often found itself re-oralized ... and rewritten' in a continuous loop during the Romantic period.[25] As Celeste Langan has argued, texts not only slip in and out of printed and oral mediums, but print also 'transmits' oral content by presenting moments of speech, song, or storytelling. Although the sights and sounds of oral tradition risked destabilizing silent, 'normativizing' print, mixing print with oral influences and vice versa made possible other material transmissions among gendered bodies, voices, and nonhuman nature. Much like Langan's 'audiovisual hallucinations', the oral reappears in the printed 'Ballad' through Sargant's mnemonic use of parallel dialogue between war-torn lovers and a related transmission of nonhuman nature from symbols to active forces.[26] In brief moments when print and oral, human and nonhuman blend, Sargant offers an account of war that moves beyond gendered affect and generic expectations of war ballads. Indeed, the transformative role nonhuman materials play during war helps mix and even eliminate gender from the text's oral features.

Sargant forcibly unites oral and printed forms through quoted dialogue, repeated in a series of questions and answers, in order to make and mix human

[24] All quotations from 'Ballad' are taken from Sargant, *Sonnets and Other Poems* (London: George Smallfield, 1818), pp. 46–56.

[25] Celeste Langan and Maureen N. McLane, 'The Medium of Romantic Poetry', in *The Cambridge Introduction to British Romantic Poetry*, eds. James Chandler and Maureen N. McLane (Cambridge: Cambridge University Press, 2008), p. 243.

[26] Celeste Langan, 'Understanding Media in 1805: Audiovisual Hallucination in "The Lay of the Last Minstrel"', *Studies in Romanticism*, 40: 1 (Spring 2001), pp. 70, 50, 53, 69. Maureen N. McLane similarly points out that citing or evoking orality provided ballads with a 'bodily presence' that print denied. *Balladeering, Minstrelsy, and the Making of British Romantic Poetry* (Cambridge: Cambridge University Press, 2008), pp. 60, 76–8. See also Ruth Finnegan, *Oral Poetry: Its Nature, Significance, and Social Context*, reissued (Bloomington: Indiana University Press, 1992), pp. 160–1 and Langan and McLane, 'The Medium of Romantic Poetry', pp. 243–7.

and nonhuman affect. For sixty-two lines, 'Ballad' weaves between the voices of Anna and her beloved sailor, who repeat one another's words and syntax—almost verbatim—as they debate lovers' constancy during war. At one point the unnamed sailor establishes a relationship between human emotions and nonhuman rocks that Anna later repeats and revises so she might blend her wartime experiences with his.

> VIII.
> 'On yonder rock's cold flinty breast
> The cheering beams shall play;
> Awhile it then shall gaily glow,
> Warm in the genial ray;—
>
> IX.
> 'But when amid the billowy main,
> The god of day shall rest,
> Cold as before, it then shall be,
> Unblessing and unblest.
> ...
> Wilt thou forget to love?' (lines 29–44)

The sailor's wartime fears about the possibility of physical and emotional change are drawn out by repeating contrasting terms 'cold', 'glow', and 'warm', all features of the seaside rocks. Anna's answer to these particular concerns draws on the sailor's exact language, which at once establishes a mnemonic form and instigates human and nonhuman mixing.

> XVI.
> 'That rock, indeed, true emblem is
> Of what my heart would be,
> If thou, forgetful of thy vows,
> Shouldst cease to think on me.
>
> XVII.
> 'Soon would it lose all vital heat,
> And cold in death remain;
> Alike insensible to all,
> To pleasure, or to pain'. (61–8)

In linking the repeated rock to her heart, Anna revises her beloved's fears to reflect her own vulnerability and establishes a link between both gendered bodies and the seaside rocks.

At first seemingly symbolic of constancy, the rocks become connective tissue between gendered wartime expressions and hold the place of oral mnemonic structures through their pointed repetition. Like repeating the same or related language to assist memory in an oral story, the rocks—and elsewhere waves and blue-bells—suggest important turns in the narrative and its possible oral delivery. In one study of the ballad form, Alan Bold notes that 'ballads are schematic story-containers sturdy enough to retain their basic shape despite repeated usage by different people', an idea echoed by Langan and McLane.[27] It is the mixture of men's and women's voices during war—voices that reuse and revise the same materials and language—that Sargant finds significant enough to recirculate on the page and possibly long term in readers' memories. Such 'mnemonic repetition' is, however, unnecessary because of print's inherent reliability and 'repeatability' (Langan, p. 55). Yet Sargant relies heavily on repetition of voice—complete with quotations—and materials like rocks, water, and flowers in order to create affinities between gendered responses to and fears of war. For instance, there is a risk that both Anna and the sailor might turn 'cold', become 'Unblessing and unblest', or unresponsive like the rocks, the most repeated material that helps mark oral moments and amalgamations of affect.

To explore the relationship between human and nonhuman affect during war, Sargant shifts the role of nature from literary and mnemonic symbols to dynamic 'thing-power', in Jane Bennett's term (p. xvi). Rocks in particular merge with human bodies, an exchange that offers alternative embodiments of wartime participation that look beyond gender into the posthuman. Never fully out of sight, the seashore rocks are first invested with the power to represent warm and cold emotions. In the quatrains quoted above, the unnamed sailor maps warm and cold emotions onto the rocks, but he adds verbs like 'play', 'glow', and 'rest' that suggest agency (lines 30, 31, 34). Anna's response similarly allows for 'That rock' to control her emotions; without the sailor's love she will 'lose all vital heat' and become 'Alike insensible to all' as she assumes the rocks to be (61, 65–7). The coldness and roughness of the rocks are potentially transferred to Anna as she repeatedly brushes against rocks in the text. In the parallel dialogue, then, nature is already moving and potent, which complicates Anna's use of the rocks as an 'emblem' (61). They create and enact her 'insensible' state of sorrow

27 Alan Bold, *The Ballad* (London: Metheun & Co. Ltd, 1979), p. 15. Langan and McLane also note that, because of print, 'poetry no longer had to serve the needs of information storage, but could rather range more freely, untethered by age-old requirements of mnemonic repetition'. Still, poets' uses of exclamation, personification, and apostrophe are other devices related to orality aimed to 'abolish our consciousness of the print media' (pp. 247, 245).

while containing the possibility for 'play', for movement and change into other wartime emotions or states of being beyond gender. Indeed, the rocks do manifest their thing-power against human bodies and minds. On his return from battle the sailor, in excited impatience, jumps into the water to swim to Anna. Suddenly he is 'Dash'd 'gainst the rocks that lurk below, / He sinks — to rise no more!' The rocks, 'with a certain effectivity of their own' now 'lurk' instead of 'glow' (Bennett, p. xvi). Not only have the rocks changed again, but they have mixed with darker water instead of the earlier sun 'beams', which suggests yet another, potentially threatening, affect from the rocks (30). Whereas Hemans's bright gleam merges human and nonhuman material to combat rigid gender roles, Sargant's shifting mixtures of nonhuman nature propose what Favret describes as a global wartime affect with impact beyond the human. The long dash and other protruding punctuation in these two lines dramatize the physical breaking, the dashed body, that the rocks co-create. As the sailor's body is 'Dash'd' on the rocks, it breaks up and disappears into the waves and rocks, themselves pieces of something once much larger. In this interchange of human and nonhuman matter, Sargant avoids the common tropes of heroic battlefield deaths and wandering women that rarely bend the material realities of gender or genre or war. Unlike the broken body and man-made 'bark' that disappear from the page, the rocks remain and pose active possibilities for warmth or threats of harm before and after war. By inserting nonhuman nature into war narratives as active participants, 'Ballad' seems to widen concepts of war and war writing not only to mix men's and women's verbal debates on the subject but also to include and remind readers of the autonomy inherent in nonhuman things that can transform or outlast individuals as well as society.

The dashed body and rocks ultimately overtake the lovers' dialogue as the 'thing-power' of the rocks reverberates across Sargant's pages in active, even destructive, language. Anna—watching the sailor's breaking, his death, unfold—becomes 'crush'd' and her 'heart / One refuge hath— / To break at once' (120–1). Like the 'Dash'd' sailor, Anna's heart and seemingly her body are 'crush'd' and broken, descriptors that also pertain to the rocks and their potential to harm. Sargant's manipulation of the changing rocks with such repeated, destructive language helps orient readers in an understanding of war that makes space for and even prioritizes the role of nonhuman matter. The similar mnemonic language of 'crush'd' and 'Dash'd' grinds and mixes human and nonhuman affect so that distinct genders, voices, and oral or printed texts are blurred. Momentarily, human speech and bodies disappear, the break or pause dramatized by yet another long dash at the end of the line and stanza. At this moment Anna dissolves into the harsh, 'insensible' qualities of the rocks used in her earlier dialogue, which suggests their persistent force. The heart 'crush'd' by a rocky blow causes a permanent mental change: 'And reason knew no more' (126). As Kate Singer has pointed out, madness may be read as 'the dissolution of a sentimental ... subject' into matter, in this case into the similarly insensible rocks (p. 184). Thus, in her madness, Anna takes on the vibrant potentiality of the rocks that she has seen 'glow', 'warm', 'lurk', 'break', and turn 'cold', even 'insensible'. In this language that spreads across the lengthy ballad, the rocks are seen quickly to remake their affect or status, moving beyond the symbolism used by Anna and the sailor. Anna, too, re-enters and recasts the diffused materials of body, text, and language so that they reveal ongoing, post-war changes and exchanges between human and nonhuman.

Anna is in fact able to speak for a final time, but her language and the page are changed and unstable because of her continued exchanges with the rocks. Though mad, she 'sits and sings' about a 'burn' and 'fever' in place of her earlier 'drooping sad' insensibility (129, 151, 156, 21). An extreme revision of the warm and cold rocks that mapped earlier emotions, this burning bodily response to breaking causes Anna to launch into song rather than speech. Moreover, she 'plaits her long, dark hair, / With many a wreath of *simple flow'rs*' instead of blue-bells, a clear break from the earlier moments where mnemonic oral forms appeared in print (130–1, emphasis added). As she sings a new song with new language that better fits her situation, Anna enacts the potential of oral and printed ballads to loop perpetually in and out of different modes and variations of making, like oral performance, manuscript, and print. Rocks and waves and flowers not only hold the place of orality in print but also instigate material changes in bodies and texts that expand opportunities for war poetry and wartime participation. Indeed, the closing scene and clipped song is set on the edge of 'the lonely shore' where readers anxiously anticipate glowing or perhaps lurking rocks; this liminal space—like that overlap of print and orality—is fertile enough to encourage the continued mixing and recasting of seemingly distinct bodies, voices, and matter into a new mode of war writing that is structured to encourage readers to question contemporary ideologies of gender and nonhuman nature.

Sargant puzzles with her layers of voice—from mnemonic repetition to quotations to nature's shared affect—and, like Hemans, she leaves untidy, unnamed characters throughout her war verse. Yet, the new avenues for voice and the blended, sometimes nonbinary, options for wartime participation mapped onto these three poems' language and structures suggest that expected materialities needed revision post-war. Seemingly stable war songs or elegies were fissured and filled with gendered bodies, nonhuman natures, battlefield accoutrements, and silent responses that could repeatedly overlap and mix on the page by guiding readers' gazes. In the few post-Waterloo texts surveyed here, Hemans and Sargant share an attempt to materialize voices from overlooked corners of war poetry through manipulations of the printed page.

Shared language, juxtaposed genres, and quoted speech contribute to more dynamic war texts where typically distinct materials like women and spears, love and rocks, print and orality might play and interpenetrate. Resisting distinct bodies and texts like those found in Sir Harry Smith's memoirs or countless periodical songs allowed Hemans and Sargant to propose a more blended, sometimes posthuman, approach to war and war writing. Readers' gazes are guided in and out of mouldering, dematerializing bodies, texts, and things in order to create new, moving mixtures of wartime matter and affect. By moving seemingly separate bodies between and beyond gender, supported by shifting generic structures, Hemans and Sargant subtly critique expected materialities of war and war poetry that relied on gender distinctions to determine one's role and place during war.

Bibliography

Anonymous. 'Dirge on the Death of Lord Nelson'. *The Morning Chronicle* (8 November 1805). In *British War Poetry in the Age of Romanticism: 1793–1815*, ed. Betty Bennett. New York: Garland Publishing, 1976, p. 350.

Bainbridge, Simon. *British Poetry and the Revolutionary and Napoleonic Wars*. Oxford: Oxford University Press, 2003.

Behrendt, Stephen. *British Women Poets and the Romantic Writing Community*. Baltimore, MD: Johns Hopkins University Press, 2009.

Bennett, Betty, ed. *British War Poetry in the Age of Romanticism: 1793–1815*. New York: Garland Publishing, 1976.

Bennett, Jane. *Vibrant Matter: A Political Ecology of Things*. Durham, NC: Duke University Press, 2010.

Blackwood, William. Letter to Felicia Hemans, 27 September 1827. Blackwood Archives, National Library of Scotland. MS 30310, ff. 282–83. Excerpts reprinted in *Felicia Hemans: Selected Poems, Letters, Reception Materials*, ed. Susan J. Wolfson. Princeton, NJ: Princeton University Press, 2000, p. 457, n. 1.

Bold, Alan. *The Ballad*. London: Metheun & Co. Ltd., 1979.

British Review, 15 (January 1820), p. 299.

Chappell, Warren and Robert Bringhurst. *A Short History of the Printed Word*. 2nd ed. Vancouver: Hartley and Marks Publishers, Inc., 1999.

Craciun, Adriana. 'Romantic Poetry, Sexuality, Gender'. In *The Cambridge Companion to British Romantic Poetry*, eds. James Chandler and Maureen N. McLane. Cambridge: Cambridge University Press, 2008, pp. 155–77.

Dugaw, Dianne. *Women and Popular Balladry, 1650–1850*. Chicago, IL: University of Chicago Press, 1996.

Favret, Mary. 'Coming Home: The Public Spaces of Romantic War'. *Studies in Romanticism*, 33: 4 (Winter 1994), pp. 539–48.

——. *War at a Distance: Romanticism and the Making of Modern Wartime*. Princeton, NJ: Princeton University Press, 2010.

Feldman, Paula. 'Women Poets and Anonymity in the Romantic Era'. *New Literary History*, 33: 2 (Spring 2002), pp. 279–89.

Finnegan, Ruth. *Oral Poetry: Its Nature, Significance, and Social Context*, reissued. Bloomington: Indiana University Press, 1992.

Harding, Anthony John. 'Felicia Hemans and the Effacement of Woman'. In *Romantic Women Writers, Voices, and Countervoices*, eds. Paula L. Feldman and Theresa M. Kelley. Hanover, NH: University Press of New England, 1995, pp. 138–49.

Hemans, Felicia. *The Siege of Valencia*. 1823. MS Eng 1227. Houghton Library, Harvard University, Cambridge, MA.

——. 'Woman on the Field of Battle' and 'To the Memory of Lord Charles Murray'. In *Felicia Hemans: Selected Poems, Letters, and Reception Materials*, ed. Susan J. Wolfson. Princeton, NJ: Princeton University Press, 2000, pp. 455–7.

——. 'Woman on the Field of Battle'. *Blackwood's Edinburgh*, 22: 132 (November 1827), pp. 585–6. Images produced by ProQuest as part of *British Periodicals*, at www.proquest.com.

Langan, Celeste. 'Understanding Media in 1805: Audiovisual Hallucination in "The Lay of the Last Minstrel"'. *Studies in Romanticism*, 40: 1 (Spring 2001), pp. 49–70.

Langan, Celeste and Maureen N. McLane. 'The Medium of Romantic Poetry'. In *The Cambridge Introduction to British Romantic Poetry*, eds. James Chandler and Maureen N. McLane. Cambridge: Cambridge University Press, 2008, pp. 239–62.

Luu, Helen. 'Fantasies of "Woman": Hemans's Deconstruction of "Femininity" in *Records of Woman*'. *Women's Writing*, 21: 1 (2014), pp. 41–57.

Matho. 'An Elegy on War'. *The Protestant Dissenter's Magazine*, III (1796), pp. 32–3. Reprinted in Bennett, p. 183.

Mayne, John. 'Nelson—A Dirge'. *The Gentleman's Magazine*, LXXIV (September 1812). Reprinted in Bennett, p. 446.

McLane, Maureen N. *Balladeering, Minstrelsy, and the Making of British Romantic Poetry*. Cambridge: Cambridge University Press, 2008.

Peterson, Linda. 'Nineteenth-Century Women Poets and Periodical Spaces: Letitia Landon and Felicia Hemans'. *Victorian Periodicals Review*, 49: 3 (Fall 2016), pp. 396–414.

Quarterly Review, 16 (June 1812), pp. 309–10.

Robinson, Mary. 'Llwhen and Gwyneth, written in the year 1782'. In *The Poetical Works of the late Mrs. Mary Robinson*, vol. II. London: Richard Philips, 1806, pp. 22–9.

Ryan, Brandy. '"Echo and Reply": The Elegies of Felicia Hemans, Letitia Landon, and Elizabeth Barrett'. *Victorian Poetry*, 46: 3 (Fall 2008), pp. 249–77.

Sargant, Jane Alice. 'Ballad'. In *Sonnets and Other Poems*. London: George Smallfield, 1818, pp. 46–56.

Scoto-Britanus. 'Thomas and Kitty'. *The Courier* (22 January 1796). Reprinted in Bennett, p. 170.

Singer, Kate. 'Limpid Waves and Good Vibrations: Charlotte Smith's New Materialist Affect'. *Essays in Romanticism*, 23: 2 (2016), pp. 175–92.

Smith, Harry Sir. *The Autobiography of Lieutenant-General Sir Harry Smith, Baronet of Aliwal on the Sutlej G.C.B. Edited with the addition of some supplemental chapters by G.C. Moore Smith, M.A. In two volumes.* London: John Murray, 1901.

——. *Autobiography of Sir Harry Smith.* MS Add. 7036. Cambridge University Library, Cambridge.

Wolfson, Susan. *Borderlines: The Shiftings of Gender in British Romanticism.* Stanford, CA: Stanford University Press, 2006.

Zeiger, Melissa F. *Beyond Consolation: Death, Sexuality, and the Changing Shapes of Elegy.* Cornell, NY: Cornell University Press, 1997.

Chapter Four

Vibrant Art on the Grand Tour in Anna Jameson's *Diary of an Ennuyée*

Holly Gallagher

In Anna Jameson's *Diary of an Ennuyée*, first published in 1826, the unnamed narrator, a dispirited female traveler, moves through the locales of France and Italy, surveying the objects of the Grand Tour. Though she laments an unrequited love as she leaves England, her encounters with objects and spaces animate her. As Jameson's narrator journeys to Paris, she rather dramatically reveals that she suffers from sickness, but she hopes that traveling will revive her: 'Here begins, I hope, a new era. I have had a long and dangerous illness; the crisis perhaps of what I have been suffering for months. Contrary to my own wishes, and to the expectations of others, I *live*'.[1] Moments like this, beyond a histrionic display of sentiment, show a general movement towards reanimation; they often present the narrator coming to energetic life through a lively interest in the objects that she encounters—paintings, sculpture, ruins, the landscape, and people that she sees. The ennuyée experiences more than a distraction from heartbreak through objects, though; her encounters on the Grand Tour, and especially Italy, often situate her among things that mingle in unexpected ways and transform her own fragmented and disconsolate history. In the reflective space of her diary, the ennuyée begins to synthesize this material world she moves in, to understand herself as part of that world of objects, and to challenge the art viewers and artists who instead perceive materiality from a distance. She gradually appreciates the aesthetic dynamics of her unpredictable relationships with things rather than aiming to see objects with the trained eye of a connoisseur. Within such musings, her recognition of the liveliness of matter develops into an alternative aesthetic appreciation, a recognition of shared affect between vibrant human and nonhuman bodies.

[1] Anna Jameson, *Diary of an Ennuyée* (Boston, MA: Ticknor and Fields, 1857), p. 24.

Ultimately, the diarist experiences art objects not just as momentary pleasures, or as symbols of the past, or even as a way to affirm the authority of the seeing eye/I; rather, she shows how experiencing the aesthetic vibrancy of objects can alter one's sense of self in the world. As the diarist begins to 'see' by considering how her body interacts with other bodies, her subjectivity becomes a connectedness with the world around her.

While not overtly antagonistic, Jameson defies the idea of who can contribute to discussions of art and other objects on the Grand Tour. As an uneducated woman of the middle class, Jameson also transgresses publication conventions with her initially anonymous publication. Her diary asserts the authority of a woman to define the meaning of art and objects, an initiative that Laurie Kane Lew also reads as Jameson establishing a new feminized, middle-class perspective. She explains that though Jameson writes about 'high art', she focuses on well-known pieces and avoids the 'largely masculine (and self-assured) world of high culture that [Joshua] Reynolds … addressed'.[2] Likewise, Jennifer Krisuk asserts that Jameson offers a way for women to enter into a conversation about art by validating alternative ways of experiencing it from the art education monopolized by male viewers.[3] In this essay, I argue that Jameson's attention to the ways that Grand Tour objects take on unexpected roles and interact with unlikely bodies challenges prevailing modes of aesthetic perception as something that happens to a dominant viewer who determines the tastefulness of a static object. Instead, Jameson shows that the *experience* of art forms a dynamic existence within a conglomeration of vibrant things and subverts the male gaze and subjectivity that is allied to the Grand Tour.

The ennuyée's records of art are personal recollections scattered throughout her diary. For example, when looking at objects in Florence's Pitti Palace, she explains that had she visited Italy 'in the character of a ready-made connoisseur', she would not have had the same experience of wonder and attentiveness from the things she encountered because 'as the eye becomes more practiced, the taste becomes more discriminative and fastidious … [and a] thousand things which once had power to charm, can charm no longer' (p. 297). Her understanding that the eye that has not been trained to see objects in a particular way leads to greater 'pleasures' suggests that the process of discovering materiality produces a deeper sense of connectedness among human and nonhuman bodies and a different affective experience of the Grand Tour. Following Jane Bennett's proposition of the 'active, earthy, not-quite-human capaciousness' of matter, I understand the diarist as recognizing and

[2] Laurie Kane Lew, 'Cultural Anxiety in Anna Jameson's Art Criticism', *Studies in English Literature*, 36: 4 (1996), pp. 829–56, 834.

[3] Jennifer J. Krisuk, 'Reclaiming Spaces of Learning in Anna Jameson's *Diary of an Ennuyée*', *Women's Writing*, 22: 4 (October 2015), pp. 411–27.

contemplating the unexpected vibrancy of the materials that she encounters.[4] While many of the artifacts she confronts may be understood in terms of human creation from one perspective, Jameson's diarist observes the material world understanding the influence that objects have beyond their intended human purpose, exemplifying Bennett's argument about how *objects* become *things*, or 'vivid entities not entirely reducible to the contexts in which (human) subjects set them, never entirely exhausted by their semiotics' (p. 5). The narrator demonstrates that art writing should be more than an absolute formal assessment of quality; instead, she shows how artifacts reveal their capacity to unsettle human viewers in unexpected ways and to shape networks composed of things from diverse spaces and times. As such, she reflects how objects that are often neglected can also be things of aesthetic vibrancy: '[a]fter all, what place is like Rome, where it is impossible to move a step without meeting with some incident or object to excite reflection, to enchant the eye, or interest the imagination?' (p. 259).

While discussions of artifacts often center on the object's intended meaning or how it affects viewers, the diarist understands how things, such as artworks, can initiate a more pervasive web of experience comprised through a variety of human and nonhuman bodies. Examining the lives of things in this way is not an antiquarian's re-creation of past spaces or an objectification of materials from other cultures; instead, it reveals a sense of how discrete things interact to form conglomerations. Such an interest in the interactivity of things can be understood through Bennett's description of assemblages, which she uses to consider networks of blackouts or hurricanes as 'ad hoc groupings of diverse elements ... that are able to function despite the persistent presence of energies that confound them from within' (pp. 23–4).

Furthermore, while art is usually said to affect its viewers, Jameson shows how the experience of art is not and should not be limited by the connoisseur's classification of objects; instead, she reflects on how art and material things emit a thingly power that is in excess of human aesthetics. Her attention to an object's vibrancy allows her to see the affective flows among humans and nonhumans. Thus, the ennuyée thinks about her 'morocco-bound diary, regularly ruled and paged, with its patent Bramah lock and key' not as a guidebook, but as a material object that has the potential to disrupt traditional modes of travel and viewing. In playful mockery of the trend of keeping a diary 'to record and preserve all the striking, profound, and original observations—the classical reminiscences—threadbare raptures—the poetical effusions—in short, all the never-sufficiently-to-be-exhausted topics of sentiment and enthusiasm', she instead invites her readers to engage in more intimate reflections with such material things, which diminishes the privilege

[4] Jane Bennett, *Vibrant Matter* (Durham, NC: Duke University Press, 2010), p. 3.

of the cultured viewer (p. 17). As if anticipating Bennett's call for a 'cultivated, patient, sensory attentiveness to nonhuman forces operating outside and inside the human body', the diarist 'learn[s] how to induce an attentiveness to things and their affects' (p. xiv).

Jameson wrote her *Diary* at a time when interest in the art of Old Masters, and especially Italian art, was common in the growing middle classes, who were increasingly able to embark on the Grand Tour. Consequently, a variety of guidebooks by writers such as John Chetwode Eustace and Joseph Forsyth were published to instruct travellers, especially the untrained art viewer, on how to perceive artworks and nature.[5] By the time Jameson was writing her travel diary, the art objects, landscapes, and city spaces of the Grand Tour had been described and, at times, reproduced for armchair travellers as well as continental tourists. However, the ennuyée proposes that her diary communicates something different about objects than other travel records: 'I have no intention of turning my little Diary into a mere catalogue of names which I can find in every guide-book' (p. 67). Instead, the ennuyée describes the experience of going on the Grand Tour and coming into contact with the objects that one might have already read about or seen reproduced and thus have certain expectations of; rather than focusing directly on hierarchical subject–object interactions, though, she frequently considers herself among the groupings of artworks, people, nature, and artifacts that she encounters. By reading the gallery space as a new materialist assemblage of human and nonhuman bodies, Jameson's narrator suggests a vibrant aesthetics that depends on the evolving relationships between human and nonhuman in space, and, as her gallery experiences are expressed in her 'little Diary', her circulation of this object proposes consideration of new aesthetic assemblages of reader, book, and the human and nonhuman bodies they encounter.[6]

Though the narrator often considers whether her taste in artworks is acceptable, she is also critical of guidebooks that advocate conventional, formal assessments, showing the connoisseur of art as mechanically trained. By this point in the century, such connoisseurs were sometimes satirized in writing and cartoons, yet the implications of their prominent vision still held weight in British culture.[7] Similarly, as the diarist observes a connoisseur of art looking

[5] John Chetwode Eustace's *A Classical Tour through Italy* was first published in 1813 and in its seventh edition in 1841. Jameson refers to Eustace's *Classical Tour* in her *Diary*. Joseph Forsyth's *Remarks on Antiquities, Arts, and Letters: During an Excursion in Italy, in the Years 1802 and 1803* was first published in 1813.

[6] See also scholarship on the human and nonhuman bodies in gallery spaces: Thora Brylowe, *Romantic Art in Practice: Cultural Work and the Sister Arts, 1760–1820* (Cambridge: Cambridge University Press, 2018), p. 25; Janine Barchas, *What Jane Saw*. University of Texas at Austin, 2013, 2016, at www.whatjanesaw.org.

[7] For example, in the Thomas Rowlandson cartoon 'Connoisseurs' (1799), a group of

intently at an artwork in the Tribune, she rejects his viewpoint as a perfunctory viewing habit. In her amusing representation of such expert men, she describes how this unnamed English connoisseur perceives a sculpture of Venus in the learned manner of the educated viewer:

> Here comes a connoisseur, who has found his way, good man! from Somerset House to the Tribune at Florence: see him with one hand passed across his brow, to shade the light, while the other extended forwards, describes certain indescribable circumvolutions in the air, and now he retires, now advances, now recedes again, till he has hit the exact distance from which every point of beauty is displayed to the best possible advantage, and there he stands—gazing, as never gazed the moon upon the waters, or love-sick maiden upon the moon! (p. 298)

Here, the diarist mocks the connoisseur's performance as an art-viewing specialist in the premiere museum space of Somerset House in London. Beyond her intentions to parody, though, the way she caricatures this connoisseur suggests that such viewing practices actually separate subjects from objects rather than demonstrate an experience of being affected by material things. Her critique addresses the limitations of approaching materiality and its affective potential from a predetermined perspective. Though the connoisseur seems to perceive the painting with his whole body, his movement is clichéd and seems more of a theatrical display than reactive, embodied engagement. In her portrayal, however, the ennuyée's attention to the body of the critic as if *he* was the work of art places him as merely one within a group of aesthetic bodies in the museum space. She questions the authority and the authenticity of this trained viewer of the art object, which throws into relief the vital presence of the gallery itself and her own more attuned discernment of the human and nonhuman bodies assembled in the art museum space. The diarist's sense of the interactions of bodies in the museum promotes an aesthetic experience of art objects that adapts Bennett's 'impersonal affect', as not 'a spiritual supplement of "life force" added to matter', but 'a vitality intrinsic to materiality' of both human and nonhuman bodies (p. xiii). In comparison with the connoisseur's deficiency, her own affective response to his body in relation to the artworks he moves among shows a Romantic absorption and empathetic response to vibrant matter.

Here, and in similar moments in the museum space, the narrator's reinterpretation of the objects she sees follows Valerie Hartouni's ideas about the

elderly art critics eagerly examine a painting of a voluptuous Venus and Cupid, and their fervent expressions mock the clichéd disposition of an engrossed critic, suggesting that their deep analysis here is actually a licentious mindset.

inversion of sense perception: 'Seeing is a set of learned practices, a set of densely structured and structuring interpretive practices, that engages us in (re)producing the world we seem only to passively apprehend and, through such engagement, facilitates the automatic, if incomplete, operation of power'.[8] Hartouni's description of seeing as a passive 'operation of power' helps explain the diarist's resistance to the museum experience that she ridicules and her investment in an alternative interpretation of the gallery space as feminist assemblage. As a substitute for the hierarchical mode of viewing she mocks, her *Diary* suggests the possibilities for feminist assemblages, where any human or nonhuman object has potential agency and aesthetic value. While the narrator's inclusion of things not considered in other Grand Tour guidebooks is in part a way to carve out a space for original observations, it is also a reconsideration of the dominant perspective of the British male spectator who surveys the continent, affirming his subjectivity and thus control over the interpretation of the object. Feigning that her records will remain confidential—'Now if my poor little Diary should ever be seen! I tremble but to think of it!' (p. 164)—the diarist records her encounters with things as personal moments of discovery and reflection rather than a more formal guide to appropriate responses of good taste. Her approach anticipates a particular response to her 'poor little Diary' as an object disregarded for its female authorship, and, in the early editions of *Diary* before Jameson's authorship was discovered, her feigned male editor's preface authenticates the book as a notable record of a deceased woman's travels, describing how it was 'published exactly as it was found' to show 'a real picture of natural and feminine feeling'.[9] Such references to her physical book as a collection of a woman's private feelings that could circulate in the world indicates that Jameson considered *Diary* an uncommon thing that might unsettle readers' expectations and, thus, enact feminist assemblages that draw attention to the liveliness of unexpected things.

In rejecting the regulation of guidebooks and the high knowledge of the connoisseur, the ennuyée frees herself from some of the lessons of perception that hinder her from engaging with art and spaces on a bodily level. In

[8] Valerie Hartouni, *Cultural Conceptions: On Reproductive Technologies and the Remaking of Life* (Minneapolis: University of Minnesota Press, 1997), p. 3.

[9] From 1821 to 1825, Jameson did travel to Europe, mostly Italy, as governess for the children of Edward Littleton, and she describes her journey through the eyes of a fictional narrator. While the fictional diarist leaves an unnamed love, Anna Brownell Murphy left behind a broken engagement to lawyer and jurist Robert Jameson, whom she then married in 1825. *Diary* is a fictionalized version of her travels, and the intertwining of life and fiction also comes through in the diarist's narrative arc in her writing art history. Jameson published the early editions of *Diary* anonymously and uses a fictional unnamed editor to frame the book as an authentic collection of private records. Anna Jameson, *Diary of an Ennuyée* (London: Henry Colburn, 1826), p. 12.

her writing, she often appreciates the estimation of educated eyes and the refinement of exquisite taste, but her experiences of objects are not narrated by these standards. In her reconsideration of artworks as a result of her personal engagement with them, the ennuyée experiences something akin to Walter Benjamin's idea about an artwork's aura as an aesthetic presence, reminiscent of religious experience and threatened by the modern development of the technologies of reproduction.[10] For her, though, the aura results from a shared affect that happens between the physical art object and her body, emanating not from a 'spiritual supplement', but the 'material vibrancy' of both bodies involved (Bennett, p. xiii). Though sometimes the narrator is familiar with an artwork, having seen an engraving in a published reproduction, when she encounters the physical art object, or '*originalissimo*', she responds to the affective quality of the work, such as the first time she sees Titian's *Venus of Urbino* in the Tribune at the Uffizi Gallery: 'In the multiplied copies and engravings of this picture I see everywhere, the bashful sweetness of the countenance, and the tender languid repose of the figure are made coarse, or something worse: degraded, in short, into a character altogether unlike the original' (p. 103). The 'coarseness' that the diarist observes suggests the lack of vibrancy, which is lost even in copies. Here, the aura of the *originalissimo* strikes the diarist and calls on her own affective body to resonate with the object: 'I felt while I gazed a sense of unalloyed and unmingled pleasure, and forgot the cant of criticism' (p. 86). Similar to Benjamin's description of aura, a kind of intersubjective experience, a thing gazing back at the viewer, and Bennett's explanation of 'thing-power' as the 'vitality intrinsic to materiality … *not* the raw material for the creative activity of humans or God', the diarist comes into contact with these things as aesthetic experiences that emerge from the art object's agency (p. xiii).

Alternatively, a number of the celebrated works of art disrupt the diarist's expectations in absence of their material affect. At such moments, the diarist does not limit her judgment of art to an assessment of form: her ideas about the artwork respond to the art object as a potentially vibrant thing in an assemblage. For example, when she sees Rudolph Schadow's *Filatrice* (*The Spinner*), she acknowledges that the sculpture is 'exquisitely natural and graceful', yet she expresses disappointment because she is unmoved by the work: 'This beautiful figure has repose, simplicity, nature, and grace, but I felt a *want*—the want of some internal sentiment' (p. 190).[11] The narrator praises the formal elements,

[10] Walter Benjamin, 'The Work of Art in the Age of Mechanical Reproduction', in *Illuminations: Essays and Reflections*, trans. Harry Zohn, ed. Hannah Arendt (New York: Schocken, 1968).

[11] Goethe's poem describes the passion and melancholy that Margaret experiences as she waits for Faust.

'simplicity' and 'grace', of the sculpture, but the 'want of internal sentiment' comes from the work's self-absorption and detachment. This desire for the spinner to have a different disposition is not just the narrator's impression that the artist misunderstands the subject, as it also shows her desire for the art object to have a provocative access point for viewers to engage in an experiential way. This interest in the affective poignancy of objects is a desire to think about objects as doing something beyond representing objective visions of the world; her response considers the possibility for an object's affect to move the art experience beyond the hegemony of the viewer.

While the ennuyée often approaches objects as things that may surprise her with their independence, she does sometimes assume the position of a subject appraising the object. Such a moment occurs at the Florentine church of the Santo Spirito when she approaches a painting as an expert observer; nonetheless, her authority as a viewer is challenged. At first, she sees a painting of the Virgin 'said to be possessed of miraculous powers' and ridicules this idea as superstition. In an attempt to belittle the object's significance, the narrator deems it just average—'not destitute of merit as a painting'—yet she views with disdain 'her grateful devotees, having decorated her with a real blue silk gown, spangled with tinsel stars, and two or three crowns, one above another, of gilt foil' calling the effect 'the oddest imaginable'. While the diarist, from the point of view of a distanced observer, sees this act of adornment as 'senseless bad taste, such pitiable and ridiculous superstition', the painting's devotees interact with the art object in an unexpected way, suggesting that potential of the art object's vitality. Jameson shows how, after scorning the devotee's extravagant and unwarranted reverence for this artwork, the narrator's experience changes in relation to the artwork when she observes a particularly moving response to it. She observes a poor woman who walks 'a pale and delicate boy' to the painting, then 'prostrated herself before the picture, while the child knelt beside her, and prayed for some time with fervour'. By the time that the woman teaches the child an Ave Maria—'repeating it word for word, slowly and distinctly, so that [the diarist] got it by heart too'—the diarist's reserve has diminished, and she describes being 'strongly affected' by their presence. Her involvement in this intimate encounter shifts her criteria for appraising objects and transforms her relationship with the things involved. Though she still maintains, from a Protestant standpoint, that the woman's religious devotion is 'mistaken in its object', she begins to see the vibrancy in the artwork that makes it 'no longer an object to ridicule'. In moments such as this, Jameson observes art as neither object nor subject, but it intervenes as an actant, a term Bennett shares with Bruno Latour, that identifies a human or nonhuman source for action.[12] Though the diarist initially identifies this painting in formal

[12] Bennett adopts Bruno Latour's concept of 'actants' as that which is 'neither an object

terms as one of the churches' two 'fine pictures' in a 'Guido-like style', she comes to appreciate the artwork not in terms of accepted aesthetic qualities but because it is an actant that influences bodies in unexpected ways, and she 'returned home rejoicing in kinder, gentler, happier thoughts' (pp. 105–6). The diarist then rejects a conventional art interpretation and quotes Wordsworth to promote such an individualized, affective experience: 'To the traditionary sympathies / Of a most rustic ignorance,— / This rather would I do, than see and hear / The repetitions wearisome of sense, / Where soul is dead, and feeling hath no place'.[13] Such reconsideration of material objects as potentially transgressive challenges the ideal of the cultivated observer of traditional art criticism and cultural guides who remain prominent through the century from John Ruskin to Walter Pater. While Jameson does appreciate and encourage such aesthetic education, she also confronts the *exclusive* privilege of the trained eye that controls cultural authority through judgments of good taste. Her diary entries disrupt the acceptance of this subject-centered aesthetics and present art spaces as assemblages in which art objects function as actants, often affecting other bodies in unexpected ways.

Writers of the Grand Tour, such as Eustace and Forsyth, often notice the aesthetic qualities of nature in addition to artworks, and the diarist, likewise, appreciates natural objects, though her nonhierarchical approach leads to a more bodily experience of things. When she arrives in Geneva, she approaches the space around her by 'drinking in the soul of things' like others who have 'viewed nature less with their eyes than their hearts'.[14] Here, the ennuyée, like Bennett's vital materialist, looks closely 'to linger in those moments ... fascinated by objects, taking them as clues to the material vitality that they share with them' (Bennett, p. 17). At the same time, in again referencing Wordsworth's speaker in the *Excursion*, who also describes 'deeply drinking-in the soul of things', the diarist places herself in company with Romantic poets as her experiences 'elevate [her] mind to a level with the sublime objects round [her], and excite [her]'. She has no qualms about declaring her own ability to fathom the sublimity of natural things, which she describes in terms of their overwhelming vitality, as she suggests her responsiveness to that vibrancy, her 'enthusiasm', allows her to realize their agentic powers. The natural things affect the diarist not simply in an emotional way of feeling joy or sadness, but rather,

nor a subject' but an 'intervener' (Latour, qtd. in Bennett, p. 9). *Politics of Nature: How to Bring the Sciences into Democracy*, trans. Catherine Porter (Cambridge, MA: Harvard University Press, 2004).

[13] Wordsworth, 'Book Fourth: Despondency Corrected', *The Excursion* (London: Longman, Hurst, Rees, Orme, and Brown, 1814), lines 613–15, 19–20.

[14] Wordsworth's speaker discusses his relationship with natural objects as one in which he absorbs creative insight: 'Thus deeply drinking-in the soul of things / We shall be wise perforce' ('Book Fourth: Despondency Corrected', *The Excursion*, lines 1265–6).

as Bennett describes impersonal affect, as becoming imbricated into a dynamic flux of vital materiality. Even as the diarist exclaims 'how deeply they have penetrated into [her] imagination!', she also emphasizes that it is the 'value of [her] own enthusiasm' that allows her to form an interconnection with natural things rather than the superiority of her mind (p. 31). As a young, unnamed woman reflecting on such intimate relationships with natural objects, the diarist diminishes the exclusive authority of the Romantic eye/I and demonstrates the capacity for other travellers to experience natural objects vibrantly.

Furthermore, as the diarist envisions a vital materialism, in which 'the status of the shared materiality of all things is elevated', she promotes an equality between her body and the natural things she encounters: 'If I could but infuse into you a portion of my own existence, as you have become a part of mine—if I could but bid you reflect back my soul, as it reflects back all your magnificence, I would make you my only friend, and wish no other; content "to love earth only for its earthly sake"' (Bennett, p. 13; Jameson, p. 31).[15] Here the diarist imagines a shared affect with materiality in which she will 'infuse' into the natural objects 'a portion of [her] own existence': notably, she conceives of the dynamic fluidity between these bodies—'you reflect back my soul, as it reflects back all your magnificence'—as collective rather than hierarchical. The diarist's Romantic communion with nature positions her as a vital materialist whose shared affect with natural things inspires her to reflect on their interdependence: as Bennett writes, '[t]his sense of a strange and incomplete commonality with the out-side may induce vital materialists to treat nonhumans—animals, plants, earth, even artifacts and commodities—more carefully, more strategically, more ecologically' (p. 17). Jameson shows the narrator as less of an intentional agent who has decisive power to control outcomes of the assemblages of which she becomes a part and imagines herself as something like an actant, or just one of many 'infuse[d]' bodies with potential agency within the assemblage. Through the kind of affective exchange with nature that she imagines, the narrator sees herself as entangled, and, at the same time that human and nonhuman bodies remain separate, she also suggests a blurring of their individual purposes, much like a 'knotted world of vibrant matter' (Bennett, p. 13). The diarist thus rejects the idea that she is purely a discrete individual in control of her own experiences and considers the way her existence melds with the world around her.

[15] The narrator quotes Byron's speaker in *Childe Harold's Pilgrimage*, Canto III, when he asks: 'Is it not better, then, to be alone, / And love Earth only for its earthly sake?' (stanza 71, lines 671–2). However, Jameson revises Byron's sense of isolation. In the diarist's musing about her interactions with the world that she moves in, she resembles Byron's speaker's broader reflective relationship with his surroundings: 'I live not in myself, but I become / Portion of that around me; and to me / High mountains are a feeling, but the hum / Of human cities torture' (stanza 72, lines 680–3).

The narrator's search for the 'least vaunted' things prompts her to consider as well her interactions with those forgotten remnants, isolated fragments, or objects often overlooked as mundane (p. 27). As the celebrated Italian ruins were extensive, they often reached beyond the knowledge of travelers or their guidebooks, and so part of the Romantic appeal of ruins was 'discrimination rather than comprehensiveness' in determining what was 'illegible or unrecognizable'.[16] For the ennuyée, these enigmatic objects often entice her with their unknown histories, and, in attempting to decipher them, she becomes an actant in the assemblages of which they are a part. When she passes the Pontine Marshes on her way to Naples, the narrator considers such an assemblage of nonliving fragments and the living things around them as an intermingling of past and present:

> At every hundred yards, fragments of masonry are seen by the road side; portions of brick work, sometimes traced at the bottom of a dry ditch, or incorporated into a fence; sometimes peeping above the myrtle bushes on the wild hills, where the green lizards lie basking and glittering on them in thousands, and the stupid ferocious buffalo, with his fierce red eyes, rubs his hide and glares upon us as we pass. No—not the grandest monuments of Rome—not the Coliseum itself, in all its decaying magnificence, ever inspired me with such profound emotions as did those nameless, shapeless vestiges of the dwellings of man, starting up like memorial tombs in the midst of this savage but luxuriant wilderness. (p. 199)

Though the ennuyée describes the things she encounters as timeworn, like the 'decaying magnificence' of the Coliseum, she still responds with fresh 'profound emotions' as becomes part of new assemblages with these actants. She describes how the world grew around these material remnants of the past, although this assemblage 'not governed by any central head: no one materiality or type of material has sufficient competence to determine consistently the trajectory or impact of the group' (Bennett, p. 24). During this excursion in Gaëta, she considers antiquarians' attention to the vitality of things in time: 'Antiquarians, who, like politicians "seem to see the things

[16] Rosemary Sweet, *Cities and the Grand Tour: The British in Italy, c.1690–1820* (New York: Cambridge University Press, 2012), p. 101. Other scholars who have examined the interest in ruins during the Romantic period include: Jonathan Sachs, who discusses how Byron uses the ruins of Rome to conceptualize subjectivity in *Romantic Antiquity: Rome in the British Imagination, 1789–1832* (New York: Oxford University Press, 2010) and Sophie Thomas, who discusses the complex relationship between ruins and Romantic historicity in 'Assembling History: Fragments and Ruins', *European Romantic Review*, 14 (2003), pp. 177–86.

that are not", have placed all along this road, the sites of many a celebrated town and fane—"making hue and cry after many a city which has run away, and by certain marks and tokens pursuing to find it;" as some old author says so quaintly' (Jameson, pp. 198–9).[17] Here, the narrator recalls that the antiquarian envisions the past lives of things and the way they interact with other bodies. Jameson, likewise, thinks beyond the isolated object and resists idealizing perception of the object as eternal and unchanging. In such environments, the narrator moves within assemblages of fragments with the understanding that they have 'a distinctive history of formation but a finite life span' (Bennett, p. 24). By noticing 'certain marks and tokens' of 'a city which has run away', the narrator imagines how those assemblages evolve through time and space.[18] However, unlike the antiquarian who privileges an organizing human power that has departed, the diarist calls attention to the ongoing dynamic *shi* of the assemblage, 'the mood or style of an open whole in which both the membership changes over time and the members themselves undergo internal alteration', and considers how the *distributed* power of assemblages causes the composition to change (Bennett, p. 35). Even after years of decay, the diarist sees the fragments as evolving vital matter interacting with new things, 'peeping above' the living vegetation and accommodating green lizards that 'lie ... on them in thousands'. She considers how objects and people grow around fragments of the past, which might at one moment consist in a 'mild and ephemeral effluence of good vibes, and at another in a more dramatic force capable of engendering a philosophical or political movement' (Bennett, p. 35).

Additionally, although the ruins she sees in Gaëta are understated compared with 'the grandest monuments of Rome', the fragments affect the diarist more than impressive and intact structures with an available, specific history. Grander 'monuments' that indicate a kind of materiality with a known story are similar to the kind of matter that Bennett calls 'human social structures' with 'human meanings "embodied" in them' (p. xvi). The forgotten ruins that the diarist observes, 'like memorial tombs', call to mind a human narrative that is no longer available. In her descriptions of the landscape as 'savage' and a 'wilderness', the absence of a given narrative allows for her own integration

[17] 'Seem to see the things that are not' is probably a loose translation of Plato's *Phaedrus*: 'Things are not always what they seem; the first appearance deceives many; the intelligence of a few perceives what has been carefully hidden'. Jameson likely read this quote from seventeenth-century English historian Thomas Fuller (1608–61) in the 'Antiquarian'. Fuller appealed to writers of the Romantic period, as his work considered ruins and imaginations of the past.

[18] Here the diarist, again, references Fuller and quotes from the 'Antiquarian diligence' entry of 'Specimens from the Writings of Fuller', a collection of quotations from various published works edited by Charles Lamb, which first appeared in *The Reflector* in 1811.

into the assemblage. In quoting Alexander Pope's *Imitations of Horace*—'In vain they toil'd, in vain they bled, / They had no poet—and are dead'—she suggests that only a poetic account can communicate the historic vibrancy of things encountered, which endorses the expressive language and excerpted and original poetry of her diary (p. 199). As the diverse constituents of an assemblage, these less celebrated and unfamiliar fragments, the 'nameless, shapeless vestiges of the dwellings of man' fascinate the ennuyée, and she engages with them in a material connection and with her creation of narrative space.[19] As an actant among a collection of actants rather than an object or subject, the narrator shifts through these different assemblages, in which agency is distributed rather than governed by a human. As she later describes in an original poem in her journal entry, her integration with things around her leads her to discover their vibrancy: 'We wandered through bright climes, and drank the beams / Of southern suns: Elysian scenes we view'd, / Such as we picture oft in those day dreams / That haunt the fancy in her wildest mood' (p. 201). In drinking in the sunbeams of affective and aesthetic scenes, the narrator intervenes in the construction of art canonicity by reconvening groups of things as art experiences, instead of reinforcing distanced museum experiences or only established pieces of art. While the museum connoisseur assumes a position of 'central head' in determining a long-term aesthetic quality of art objects, the narrator suggests the changeability of vibrant things as an alternative to more static notions of aesthetics.

Thus, though the narrator appreciates the antiquarians who attempt to reimagine the past, she also emphasizes that historical spaces and things can only be perceived through their interactions with the present. In this way, the things of the past cannot be discrete, stagnant objects, but they are malleable and change in relation to the assemblages of which they become a part. Writing specifically about art objects, Erin Manning explains that the 'manner of experience' is an object's quality rather than a particular form, arguing that 'quality is how the world comes to expression, how it is felt, how it is lived, and how it does its living'. Manning's premise, that 'everything changes in

[19] See also the following scholarship on the significance of ruins and fragments in Romantic literature: Sophie Thomas discusses fragments and ruins as materials on the unstable boundary between the visible and the invisible in *Romanticism and Visuality: Fragments, History, Spectacle* (New York: Routledge, 2007); Tim Fulford reconsiders Romantic poetry not through dematerialization but through rematerialization by looking at reinscription on the landscape ('The Materialization of the Lyric and the Romantic Construction of Place: Bards and Beasts on Dartmoor', *Romanticism*, 22: 1 [April 2016], pp. 15–32); and Bradley Depew argues for a reconsideration of Wordsworth's *Essays upon Epitaphs* as an overlooked text that makes a case for the significance of the epitaph as poetic genre ('Wordsworth on Epitaph: Language, Genre, Mortality', *ELH*, 79: 4 (Winter 2012), pp. 963–88).

kind', complicates the attempt to conceptualize an object outside of time, removed from experience.[20] For a similar reason, in *Diary*, Jameson's narrator frequently laments the limitations of reproduced engravings and written records to describe encounters with artworks and ruins; her personal understanding in the form of her diary offers an alternative assemblage, paying attention to the medium of her book, to express the experiences of things in museums or churches. Her project of reimagining assemblages of art on the Grand Tour proposes the personal and transient experience of shifting formations of art agglomerates of human and nonhuman actants. In also envisioning the *shi* as the 'dynamic force emanating from a spatia-temporal configuration rather than from any particular element within it', the diarist observes how the fragments of human and nonhuman bodies develop into a 'dynamic force' as an alternative, all-encompassing aesthetic experience of the interactions of bodies (Bennett, p. 35). Following this, she considers how the imbrication of viewer and artwork collapses the formal distinction of the museum world, which often appears detached from the life that goes on around it, and considers the 'art of time', or 'the proposition art can make to a world in continual composition' (Manning, p. 51).

The ennuyée often describes such objects, bodies, and spaces as working together in an aesthetically symbiotic way as 'picturesque', clearly suggesting an affinity with the cultural standard of vision promoted by writers and artists such as William Gilpin; however, Jameson subtly modifies the concept of the picturesque into a kind of aesthetics of vibrant matter. Although the aesthetic ideal of the picturesque evolved over the late eighteenth through the early nineteenth century, it was generally used as 'a term expressive of that peculiar kind of beauty, which is agreeable in a picture'.[21] In seeing the world through the ideals of the picturesque, the diarist's active perception would be somewhat limited, so she reworks the picturesque with special attention to the vibratory resonance of things within an assemblage in order to render them equally lively and changing rather than replicable and static.[22] The ennuyée's reaction of surprise when experiencing the Vesuvian eruption at night because she 'never beheld any thing so wildly picturesque' shows how her particular

[20] Erin Manning, 'Artfulness', in *The Nonhuman Turn*, ed. Richard Grusin (Minneapolis: University of Minnesota Press, 2015), pp. 46–7.

[21] William Gilpin, *An Essay Upon Prints: Containing Remarks Upon the Principles of Picturesque Beauty* (London, 1768), p. 2.

[22] While Gilpin's discussion of picturesque beauty promotes the idea of vibrant materiality in that 'objects *in themselves* produce infinite variety' because '[t]hey are varied ... by *combination*', he also develops a hierarchy, as he singles out certain things as particularly vibrant: 'among all the objects of art, the picturesque eye is perhaps most inquisitive after the elegant relics of ancient architecture'. William Gilpin, *Three Essays: On Picturesque Beauty: On Picturesque Travel: And on Sketching Landscape*, (London, R. Blamire, 1794), pp. 42–6.

approach to the picturesque as an affective engagement with bodies leads her to a vital materialist's understanding of the ways that human and nonhuman things act together:

> My ears were by this time wearied and stunned by the unceasing roaring and hissing of the flames, while my eyes were dazzled by the glare of the red, fierce light: now and then I turned them for relief to other features of the picture, to the black shadowy masses of the landscape stretched beneath us, and speckled with shining lights, which shewed how many were up and watching that night; and often to the calm vaulted sky above our heads, where thousands of stars, (not twinkling as through our hazy or frosty atmosphere, but shining out of 'heaven's profoundest azure', with that soft steady brilliance peculiar to a highly rarified medium,) looked down upon this frightful turmoil in all their bright and placid loveliness. (p. 218)

The diarist moves through the landscape as if moving through an aesthetic assemblage, reacting to the vibrant visual details and, at the same time, imparting the perspective of other bodies, such as the stars that look down on her. In addition, her interest in minimizing human centrality and highlighting the vibrancy of nonhuman bodies aligns with Bennett's emphasis on the material agency of assemblages, which counters 'the human tendency to understate the degree to which people, animals, artifacts, technologies, and elemental forces share powers and operate in dissonant conjunction with each other' (p. 34).[23] Though she experiences the scene with a 'painter's eye', her interest in this 'wildly picturesque' scene does not assume Gilpin's sense of the picturesque with a 'fixed' position that is the 'best' point of view.[24] Instead, she moves through different assemblages of humans and nonhumans, such as the 'great numbers of the Austrian forces … on the mountain, assembled in groups, some standing, some sitting, some stretched on the ground and wrapped in their cloaks, in various attitudes of amazement and admiration' (p. 219). This new picturesque complicates the artist's detached perspective and suggests a kind of materialism in which the diarist herself is in movement like

[23] Tim Fulford discusses how travelers' momentary experiences of the picturesque were 'socially dangerous' because tourists could quickly pass through the scene and then move on to another, which provides an interesting perspective on the potential detachment from things. See *Landscape, Liberty, and Authority: Poetry, Criticism, and Politics from Thomson to Wordsworth* (New York: Cambridge University Press, 1996), p. 141. See also John Whale, 'Romantics, Explorers, Picturesque Travellers', in *The Politics of the Picturesque*, eds. Stephen Copley and Peter Garside (Cambridge: Cambridge University Press, 1994), pp. 175–95.

[24] Gilpin, *Three Essays*.

the vibrancy of matter.[25] Additionally, the periodicity of the narrator's diary entries indicates her ever-changing engagement with things and the continual transformation that her travels entail.

In the midst of this Vesuvian excursion, and arguably the climax of her diary, the narrator reveals her intention 'to approach near enough to a stream of lava to have some idea of its consistency, and the manner in which it flowed, or trickled down' (p. 219). Like other things she has encountered on her tour, she sees the lava as tantalizing and, although she later remarks on the hazard that this particular thing presented to her body, she explains that she was 'infinitely too much interested to have been alive to danger' (p. 220). While the lava threatens to consume her physical body, the attraction she has to this thing also has the capability of consuming her mind and suggests the potential of assemblages to override the self. Even when her guide persuades her to turn back when a 'shower of red-hot fragments' just misses her, she regrets having 'come thus far, and to be so near the object [she] had in view, and then to run away at the first alarm!' (p. 222). In moments such as this, rather than having a fear of losing her self in the material world, the diarist animates by developing 'a more refined sensitivity to the outside-that-is-inside-too' (Bennett, p. 120).

Not long after her Vesuvian adventure, the ennuyée leaves Italy heading home to Britain where her former lover resides. Her dread of returning to the indifference of her unrequited love parallels the sense of leaving vibrant things she encountered in Italy. As she travels north, quickly moving through the cities of the Grand Tour, her response for the things around her greatly diminishes, as she declares 'my mind is dull, and my eyes are dim, and I am scarce conscious of any thing around me' (p. 339). Correspondingly, she predicts falling back into the conventional practice of privileging her position as a viewing subject: 'London or Paris we may prefer, as comprehending in themselves all the intellectual pleasures and luxuries of life' (p. 340). In anticipating 'intellectual pleasure' and 'luxuries of life', she envisages returning to an environment where human bodies and good taste dictate interactions with objects. While the ennuyée laments leaving the vibrant things she encountered in Italy, which she remembers affectively as one would 'love a friend' and 'not as in general we are attached to places and things', her death at the end of

[25] Ron Broglio's argument that the picturesque 'overturns a prevailing notion of the Romantic subject' and that the technologies of representation were used to 'undermine a Romantic sense of self' presents a mode of viewing the kind of painterly and poetic picturesque that Jameson envisions. He looks at the Simplon Pass section of *The Prelude* to argue that at times Wordsworth's relationship with landscape is not always read through human terms, sometimes representing a human–nonhuman assemblage following Deleuze and Guattari. See *Technologies of the Picturesque: British Art, Poetry, and Instruments, 1750–1830* (Lewisburg, PA: Bucknell University Press, 2008), p. 86.

her diary represents the fatality of resuming her former languid life where she was less attuned to the vibrancy of things.

Bibliography

Barchas, Jane. *What Jane Saw*. University of Texas at Austin, 2013, 2016, at www.whatjanesaw.org.

Bennett, Jane. *Vibrant Matter*. Durham, NC: Duke University Press, 2010.

Benjamin, Walter. 'The Work of Art in the Age of Mechanical Reproduction'. In *Illuminations: Essays and Reflections*, trans. Harry Zohn, ed. Hannah Arendt. New York: Schocken, 1968.

Broglio, Ron. *Technologies of the Picturesque: British Art, Poetry, and Instruments, 1750–1830*. Lewisburg, PA: Bucknell University Press, 2008.

Brylowe, Thora. *Romantic Art in Practice: Cultural Work and the Sister Arts, 1760–1820*. Cambridge: Cambridge University Press, 2018.

Byron, George Gordon, Lord. *Childe Harold's Pilgrimage, Canto the Third*. London: John Murray, 1815.

Depew, Bradley. 'Wordsworth on Epitaph: Language, Genre, Mortality'. *ELH*, 79: 4 (Winter 2012), pp. 963–88.

Eustace, John Chetwode. *A Classical Tour through Italy*. London: J. Mawman, 1813.

Forsyth, Joseph. *Remarks on Antiquities, Arts, and Letters: During an Excursion in Italy, in the Years 1802 and 1803*. London: Cadell and Davies, 1813.

Fulford, Tim. *Landscape, Liberty, and Authority: Poetry, Criticism, and Politics from Thomson to Wordsworth*. New York: Cambridge University Press, 1996.

——. 'The Materialization of the Lyric and the Romantic Construction of Place: Bards and Beasts on Dartmoor'. *Romanticism*, 22: 1 (April 2016), pp. 15–32.

Gilpin, William. *An Essay Upon Prints: Containing Remarks Upon the Principles of Picturesque Beauty*. London: J. Robson, 1768.

——. *Three Essays: On Picturesque Beauty: On Picturesque Travel: And on Sketching Landscape*. London: R. Blamire, 1794.

Hartouni, Valerie. *Cultural Conceptions: On Reproductive Technologies and the Remaking of Life*. Minneapolis: University of Minnesota Press, 1997.

Jameson, Anna. *Diary of an Ennuyée*. London: Henry Colburn, 1826.

——. *Diary of an Ennuyée*. Boston: Ticknor and Fields, 1857.

Krisuk, Jennifer J. 'Reclaiming Spaces of Learning in Anna Jameson's *Diary of an Ennuyée*'. *Women's Writing*, 22: 4 (October 2015), pp. 411–27.

Latour, Bruno. *Politics of Nature: How to Bring the Sciences into Democracy*, trans. Catherine Porter. Cambridge, MA: Harvard University Press, 2004.

Lew, Laurie Kane. 'Cultural Anxiety in Anna Jameson's Art Criticism'. *Studies in English Literature*, 36: 4 (1996), pp. 829–56.

Manning, Erin. 'Artfulness'. In *The Nonhuman Turn*, ed. Richard Grusin. Minneapolis: University of Minnesota Press, 2015, pp. 45–80.

Sachs, Jonathan. *Romantic Antiquity: Rome in the British Imagination, 1789–1832*. New York: Oxford University Press, 2010.

Sweet, Rosemary. *Cities and the Grand Tour: The British in Italy, c.1690–1820.* Cambridge: Cambridge University Press, 2012.

Thomas, Sophie. 'Assembling History: Fragments and Ruins'. *European Romantic Review,* 14 (2003), pp. 177–86.

——. *Romanticism and Visuality: Fragments, History, Spectacle.* New York: Routledge, 2007.

Whale, John. 'Romantics, Explorers, Picturesque Travellers'. In *The Politics of the Picturesque,* eds. Stephen Copley and Peter Garside. Cambridge: Cambridge University Press, 1994, pp. 175–95.

Wordsworth, William. 'Book Fourth: Despondency Corrected'. *The Excursion.* London: Longman, Hurst, Rees, Orme, and Brown, 1814.

Part Two

Transgressive Things

Chapter Five

Hester Stanhope, '*Un être à part*'

Material Transgression and Belonging in the East

Jillian Heydt-Stevenson

'All the gates were shut, but all opened for me, and not a word said'.

—Catherine Lucy Wilhelmina Powlett,
The Duchess of Cleveland, *The Life and Letters of Lady Hester Stanhope*[1]

Perhaps then we can understand Object-Oriented Feminism as a perturbation of human and world, as a freedom to move through that door between inside and outside at will, noting the differences but not being limited by them.

—Ian Bogost, 'Object-Oriented Feminism: At the 2010 Society for Literature Science and the Arts Conference'[2]

[1] Catherine Lucy Wilhelmina Powlett, Duchess of Cleveland, *The Life and Letters of Lady Hester Stanhope* (London: John Murray, 1914), p. 138. Hereafter cited in the text as 'Cleveland'. Many of Stanhope's letters, but not all, and not all uncensored, can be found in this edition, published in 1897 by her niece. Additional correspondence is unpublished. There is no standard edition available. I have also consulted the Bruce Family Letters, which are in manuscript at the Bodleian Library, Oxford (*Papers of the Bruce Family, 18th–20th Century*).

[2] Ian Bogost, 'Object-Oriented Feminism: At the 2010 Society for Literature Science and the Arts Conference'. The quotation, part of Bogost's response to Katherine Behar's panels on object-oriented feminism at the 2010 conference on Society for Literature Science and the Arts, can be found at http://bogost.com/writing/blog/object-oriented_feminism_1/. Part of this quotation can also be found in Behar's 'An Introduction to OOF', in Katherine Behar, ed., *Object-Oriented Feminism* (Minneapolis: University of Minnesota Press, 2016), p. 8.

> A gate opens or closes a threshold that's taken for such because in this place a law is reversed: on this side a given rule rules, on the other a different law begins.
>
> —Michel Serres, *Statues: The Second Book of Foundations*[3]

When gates closed in England to Hester Lucy Stanhope (1776–1839), Eastern portals opened. Born into aristocratic power and wealth, she lived as an adult with and served as political advisor to her uncle, Prime Minister William Pitt.[4] After his death in 1806, estranged from her immediate family and refusing to marry for money and status, she left Britain in 1810 and traveled through Greece, Turkey, and Syria with her doctor and biographer, Charles Meryon, and her lover, the wealthy Michael Bruce, ultimately making Syria her home until her death in 1839.[5] There she established an independent life, earned the admiration and fear of the Ottomans, the Druze, and the Bedouins, and, outside of any official British diplomatic status or even permission, became a political power in the East: entitled 'Queen Hester', she was even thought by some to be the reincarnation of the third-century queen of Palmyra, Zenobia. Alexander Kinglake, visiting her in Syria in 1834, asserted that 'You may suppose how deeply the quiet women in Somersetshire must have been interested, when they slowly learned … that the intrepid girl who had been used to break their vicious horses for them was reigning in sovereignty over the wandering tribes of Western Asia!'[6] Kinglake did not exaggerate: before Ibrahim Pasha invaded Syria (1832), he sought Stanhope's neutrality, for she wielded enough power in the south to make him fearful. Thus, her travels in the East and her residence there offered scope for her to actualize her dynamic potential in the specifically material world of Eastern politics and war.

[3] Michel Serres, *Statues: The Second Book of Foundations*, trans. Randolph Burks (London: Bloomsbury, 2015), p. 47.

[4] For biographical details, see Kirstin Ellis, *Star of the Morning: The Extraordinary Life of Lady Hester Stanhope* (London: HarperCollins, 2008); she describes the Stanhope family's penchant for 'imperiousness, extravagant behaviour, and quixotic ambition' (p. 14); hereafter cited by author's name. Other biographies include Lorna Gibb's *Lady Hester: Queen of the East* (London: Faber and Faber, 2005); John Watney's *Travels in Araby* (London: Gordon Cremonesi, 1975); and Frank Hamel's *Lady Hester Lucy Stanhope: A New Light on her Life and Love Affairs* (London: Cassell & Company, 1913).

[5] Some parts of Syria that Stanhope lived in are now Lebanon. I will throughout refer to the country as it was constituted during her lifetime: under Ottoman rule, Syria included what is now modern Syria, Lebanon, Jordan, parts of Turkey and Iraq, Palestinian Authority, the Gaza Strip, and Israel.

[6] Alexander William Kinglake, *Eothen: Traces of Travel Brought Home from the East* (Cologne: Könemann Verlagsgesellschaft mbH, 1997), pp. 77–8.

Though now unfamiliar to most, Stanhope's intellectual and physical heterodoxy made her well known during the nineteenth century when periodicals printed some of her letters and then when Charles Meryon published three volumes each of the *Memoirs of the Lady Hester Stanhope, as Related by Herself in Conversations with her Physician* (1845) and the *Travels of Lady Hester Stanhope* (1846): these accounts relate how the material conditions of the East—the desert, the warring tribes, the volatility of Ottoman rule, and the Bedouin and Turkish acceptance of Stanhope as a cross-dressing military power—emancipated her to exist outside the limits of what Enlightenment thinking or the Romantic era would have defined as acceptable female thought and corporeality.[7] In 1810, Stanhope, having refused to marry her lover Michael Bruce, was reminded by her friend General Oakes of the 'customs of the World, and of our Country in particular'.[8] That 'Country', however, was not her concern. To Stratford Canning in 1813, she claimed that the British 'imagination' is 'as miserable as their humanity is bounded ... . Let the great learn from [the Arabs'] hospitality and liberality. ... I cannot regret past hardship, as it has given me the opportunity of seeing what is so curious and interesting, the manners and customs of the most free and independent

[7] Charles Lewis Meryon, *Travels of Lady Hester Stanhope, forming the Completion of her Memoirs narrated by her Physician*, 3 vols., unabridged facsimile (Chestnut Hill, MA: Elibron Classics, Adamant Media Corporation, 2005), II: pp. 181–2. Also see his other series, which I do not refer to in this essay: *Memoirs of the Lady Hester Stanhope, as related by herself in Conversations with her Physician*, 3 vols. (Cambridge: Cambridge University Press, 2012, Digital Reproduction). Hereafter, I refer to Meryon's *Travels* in the body of the text as '*T*', and include both volume and page number.

Feminist scholars on travel have not focused on Stanhope's experiences as often as one might expect. Further, when they do, they seem preoccupied by the inconsistencies in her identity and by her 'eccentricities'. For example, Vassiliki Markidou argues that Stanhope's travels in Greece 'failed to achieve a unified self' (p. 53), in 'Travels Off-centre: Lady Hester Stanhope in Greece', in *Women Writing Greece: Essays on Hellenism, Orientalism, and Travel*, eds. Vassiliki Kolocotroni and Efterpi Mitsi (Amsterdam and New York: Rodopi, 2008), pp. 39–54. Even Billie Melman, whose excellent *Women's Orients, English Women, and the Middle East, 1718–1918: Sexuality, Religion, and Work* (Ann Arbor: University of Michigan Press, 1992, 1995) covers dates from 1718 to 1918, relegates Stanhope to a metaphor: women travelers, like 'the remains of Lady Stanhope ... had to be exhumed, sorted and brought to light' (p. 7). Melman's logic for excluding Stanhope is that her scholarly interest lies in less well-known travelers. Yet, when she mentions Lady Hester, she twice describes her as 'eccentric' (Melman, pp. 1, 333). Several publications on Stanhope are primarily short biographies; for example, see Bettina L. Knapp, 'Lady Hester Stanhope (1776–1839)', in *Great Women Travel Writers from 1750 to the Present*, eds. Alba Amoia and Bettina L. Knapp (New York: Continuum, 2005), pp. 38–54. There is a film about Stanhope, *Queen of the East*, from 1995 and another in pre-production, currently titled *The Lady Who Went Too Far*, a title inexplicably implying criticism of Stanhope.

[8] General Oakes to Lady Hester Stanhope, 26 July 1810. MS. ENG. d.2835, fol ?. *Papers of the Bruce Family, 18th–20th Century*. Bodleian Library, University of Oxford.

people in the world' (Cleveland, p. 168).[9] Thresholds that in England barred the material incarnation of her desires opened in Syria, offering her the opportunity for an embodied movement that changed both her own body and the spaces she traversed.

This essay discusses the volatile, interwoven ways Stanhope experienced transgressive materiality: physically she interacts with her environment in ways thought 'scandalous' (through exercise, travel, sex, and battle); she unexpectedly intermingles with materials (clothing, antiquities) and, in doing so, transgresses expectations of the inherently stable body; and she functions materially in a way that is itself heterodox in so far as she seeks an experience that radically imbricates her with the material world rather than via representations of herself (through autobiography or portraits of her).[10] To demonstrate these ideas, I draw on two of Jane Bennett's notions of material 'vitality': 'the capacity of things—edibles, commodities, storms, metals—not only to impede or block the will and designs of humans but also to act as quasi agents or forces with trajectories, propensities, or tendencies of their own', and, second, her work on assemblages—those 'living, throbbing confederations that are able to function despite the persistent presence of energies that confound them from within'.[11] Further, Diana Coole and Samantha Frost envision a new materialist ontology as 'creating new concepts and images of nature that affirm matter's immanent vitality'; as one that 'avoids dualism'; and as a way of acting and thinking that 'espous[es] a monological account of emergent, generative material being'.[12] As

[9] Stanhope's contrast here between the emancipation she finds among the Arabs and the freedom England offers recalls Castel-Forte's observation in *Corinne, or Italy* of 'how much the English in general are slaves to the customs and habits of their country' (Raphael, Book 4, Chap. i, p. 50) ['et vous savez d'ailleurs combien les Anglais en général sont asservis aux mœurs et aux habitudes de leur pays.—' (Balayé, p. 90)], as well as evoking Corinne's repeated statements throughout the novel that in order for creativity and valor to flourish, a nation must be free, as when she says, that 'in an age more proud and free than Tasso's, Petrarch, like Dante was the courageous poet of Italian independence' (Raphael, Book 2, Chap. iii, p. 30) ['Dans un siècle plus fier et plus lire que celui du Tasse, Pétrarque fut aussi comme Le Dante, le poëte valeureux de l'indépendance italienne' (Balayé, p. 62)]. Germaine de Staël, *Corinne, or Italy*, trans. Sylvia Raphael (Oxford: Oxford University Press, 1998); Madame de Staël, *Corinne ou l'Italie*, Édition de Simone Balayé (Paris: Gallimard, 1985).

[10] Granted, there are portraits of her, most from after her death; yet, when Meryon uses charcoal to extol her in a poem he writes on the walls of one of Ba'albek's inner temples, Stanhope insists he 'efface the whole; and she declared she never had consented, when living with her uncle, to be praised in verse, or portrayed in painting' (*T*, III: p. 25).

[11] Jane Bennett, *Vibrant Matter: A Political Ecology of Things* (Durham, NC: Duke University Press, 2010), pp. viii, 23–4.

[12] Diana Coole and Samantha Frost, 'Introducing the New Materialism', in *New Materialisms: Ontology, Agency, and Politics*, eds. Coole and Frost (Durham, NC: Duke University Press, 2010), pp. 1–43, 8.

I focus on gender transgressions in this essay, I also draw on object-oriented feminism (OOF), which Katherine Behar explains

> originated as a feminist intervention into philosophical discourses—like speculative realism, particularly its subset OOO, and new materialism—that take objects, things, stuff, and matter as primary. ... Where an ontologist might speculate, describing the world, 'This is the way things are', object-oriented feminists and feminist new materialists engage in the world using experimental praxis, 'This is a way of being with things'. Or more simply, 'This is a way of being things'.[13]

I hope also to demonstrate that Stanhope herself becomes a kind of object-oriented feminist, enacting transgressive materiality when she creates what I will call 'gender contact zones'.[14] These, reassembling assemblages, occur when she enters into religious and political places prohibited to women; in the interactions between her and the people she meets dynamic metamorphoses arise allowing objects to breathe more vitality into these spaces and rendering her more object-like in this destabilized environment. Her own material energy and force, occupying male and female zones simultaneously, stimulate nonbinary states of being that precipitate a number of gender contact zones: her entry into battle and politics, her cross-dressing, her tour of a Christian monastery, her journey to Ba'albek, and her leadership of an archaeological expedition in which she orders her men to smash an ancient statue dating from the time of Herod.[15] As these zones spark with renewed vitality, assemblages

[13] Katherine Behar, 'Introduction', in *Object-Oriented Feminism*, ed. Katherine Behar (Minneapolis: University of Minnesota Press, 2016), pp. 1–36, pp. 3, 13.

[14] Mary Louise Pratt coined the term 'contact zone' to 'foreground the interactive, improvisational dimensions of colonial encounters' in which 'subjects are constituted in and by their relations to each other'; and though there are overlaps between my term and hers, by appending 'gender' to the term, my examination becomes more specific (*Imperial Eyes: Travel Writing and Transculturation* [London and New York: Routledge, 1992], p. 7). Further, my gender contact zones are to be differentiated from Susan Wolfson's 'hot' and 'temperate zones' in *Borderlines: The Shiftings of Gender in British Romanticism* (Palo Alto, CA: Stanford University Press, 2006), which, she argues, any woman author occupied, the former constituting women's writing that 'advanced the new philosophies of rights and liberty' and the latter 'host[ing] the home genres, conduct, sentiment, children, cookery' (p. 15). If categorized according to Wolfson's schema, Stanhope would occupy the 'hot zone'. However, I would emphasize that although Stanhope 'advanced' her own 'rights and liberty' she did not always do that for others, as say, Mary Wollstonecraft did. I am arguing for a zone in which binaries collapse.

[15] Perhaps the most famous example of a gender contact zone occurs when Stanhope is the first Western woman to cross the desert to visit Palmyra, a geographical passage I have discussed elsewhere. See my essay, 'The Last Ruins of Palmyra', *ELN*, 54: 1 (2016), pp. 93–112.

emerge among what Bennett would call 'ad hoc groupings of diverse elements, of vibrant materials of all sorts' (p. 23). Stanhope's heterodox materiality further galvanized what I call a 'slippery' textual presentation of her, one that emerges from the interactions among and the perspectives within texts that describe her. These male-authored letters and accounts of her life belittle the ways she empowers herself materially; ironically, however, the inconsistencies in these accounts (even though they all abuse her) and the discrepancies in how her major biographer, Meryon, presents her undermine each other, reminding readers that she is a 'non-totalizable sum' (Bennett, p. 24) of both matter and text, human and nonhuman. Such textual accounts, rendering her more than one thing, ironically fortify our sense of her deviating material power.[16] In trying to know her, we become entangled in a material flow that suspends reification. That is, she remains not impenetrable or withdrawn in the sense that Timothy Morton would argue—'incapable of being (fully) accessed'—but a dynamic materiality that is difficult to access, all the more vibrant for the challenge offered.[17]

I. Gender Contact Zones: An Assemblage in Eden of Hens, Monks, Cocks, and a She-Ass

Stanhope's capacity to transgress materially a predetermined female sexual identity enables her to enter religious and political terrains consecrated only to men and then to interact with others, instigating transformation in these gender contact zones.[18] One of these, the monastery of Mar Antaniûs (St. Anthony),

[16] While I argue that Stanhope and textual representations of her stand outside of binary constructions and that what is most positive about her is her undefinability, for Markidou Stanhope occupied liminal spaces between 'masculinity and femininity, tradition and cosmopolitanism (racial, national, and class) centrality, and (gender and textual) eccentricity' (p. 53).

[17] Timothy Morton, 'All Objects Are Deviant: Feminism and Ecological Intimacy', in *Object-Oriented Feminism*, ed. Katherine Behar (Minneapolis: University of Minnesota Press, 2016), p. 65.

[18] It may be important to note that while Stanhope transgresses gender boundaries, she does not transgress those of class. John Brenkman argues that in adopting as a critical paradigm the '"holy trinity of literary criticism"'—race, class, and gender—critics often strive, as Anthony Appiah and Henry Louis Gates Jr. so long ago advised, to find the '"multiple intersections"' among these three (p. 121). However, in reading Stanhope, one has generally to abandon any typical cause and effect relation that would join these three. Instead, this nexus of gender contravention and class [un]consciousness speaks to her desires for the materialization of a particular identity formation. In Syria, she is entitled 'Queen Hester', and she fully embraces such patriarchal attention—the status and homage offered—with enormous pleasure. We cannot forget, however, that she does end her life in poverty, choosing to do so rather than give up her independence and return to England. John Brenkman, 'Extreme Criticism', in *What's Left of Theory: New Work on the Politics*

which she visits while journeying from Ehden to Tripoli, was most legendary for the founder's 'manifestation of his anger towards anything of the female sex that presumes to cross the threshold of this holy place'. So severe was this misogyny that the monastery kept even the 'hen-fowls ... cooped up, lest they should stray into the sacred precincts, whilst the cocks run at large' (*T*, III: pp. 36, 37). The doctor wryly concludes that this discrimination was 'the chief reason that induced Lady Hester to turn out of her road to visit it' (*T*, III: p. 36). While he disparages the idea that Ehden—or as he transcribes it, 'Eden'—is the 'ancient paradise ... some travelers [have] fancifully supposed', the name place becomes significant in so far as Stanhope's presence inverts that first 'fall';[19] her interaction with the monks transmutes this place into a gender contact zone, wherein upon her arrival and impact, absolute patriarchal authority is recharged with zoetic vitality. At St. Anthony's, Lady Hester's male entourage is invited to reside in the monastery while she is boarded fifty yards distant from the action; however, as if in testimony to her desire to recover Eve's power, Stanhope sends a letter to the superior 'announcing her intention of trying the Saint's gallantry, ... saying that she would, on the following day, give a dinner to him and to the shaykhs, who had escorted her from Eden, in a room of the monastery itself' (*T*, III: p. 37). Here she draws on material powers (the shaykhs) to assert her own material presence inside this male sanctum.

Materially fortifying her point and unequivocally connecting herself to the female animal world St. Anthony has renounced, she arrives for dinner riding a '*she-ass* into the very hall of the building' (*T*, III: p. 38, emphasis original); she and the animal, conjoined here as transgressive interlopers, penetrate masculine territory, touring every room 'where she could put her head' (presumably the ass also swerves her head into these forbidden spaces); and, in doing so, she triggers a momentary altercation between the two parties of monks, those 'who were for and against her entering' (*T*, III: p. 39). That the friars were not united suggests that, for a few moments, the visitor and inhabitants enter into a surprisingly extemporaneous and collaborative gender contact zone. In his response to OOF, Ian Bogost has suggested that 'one of the goals and victories of feminism involves making insides and outsides accessible and welcoming, whether they involve rights, ideals, identities, or everyday practices' (qtd. in Behar, p. 8).[20] As a kind of OOF practitioner,

of Literary Theory, eds. Judith Butler, John Guillory, and Kendall Thomas (New York and London: Routledge, 2000), pp. 114–36.

[19] Throughout Stanhope's letters and Charles Meryon's memoirs of her, Turkish and Arabic names and places are both misspelled and spelled in various configurations. I will reproduce the ones they use and then, if necessary, add a note with the proper spelling for clarification.

[20] The quotation can also be found at http://bogost.com/writing/blog/object-oriented_feminism_1/.

Stanhope makes the inside of this monastery accessible. And that the floor did not open beneath her feet and 'swallow her up', as the monks anticipated, demonstrates how her very materiality must have vitally affected in some measure the community's superstitious 'woman-hating' (*T*, III: p. 38). That is, this gender contact zone rouses the monks to see that their material foundations remain structurally firm—their floors do not literally collapse and the earth does not literally 'swallow' them or her, propelling them down into hell—even though female 'animals' have clomped across them; nevertheless, a woman has dynamically reconfigured their space, allowing for a spectrum of subject–object possibilities, ones that do shake those foundations. Her visit, partially cracking the patriarchal edifice, helps repair that original fall in so far as it redistributes energies that in readings of the biblical story find Eve a perpetrator of harm rather than, as in Stanhope's case, a jubilant transformer. Predictably, some called her courageous and others sacrilegious but, either way, her behavior increased knowledge of her existence and substance in Syria, since her visit 'soon spread through the mountain, and was long the topic of general conversation' (*T*, III: p. 39). When they leave there and arrive in Tripoli, Meryon explains that 'The report of Lady Hester's approach had spread through the city, and the streets through which she had to pass were lined with spectators' (*T*, III: p. 40). Stanhope's material presence thus introduces fluidity into a stagnant space, altering its—and her—ontology. Who knows but that afterwards they let the hens roam with the cocks?

Desert Assemblages: Dress and Weaponry, Camels and Air

Dress itself becomes a gender contact zone for Stanhope, one which liberates her to express her transgressive materiality. Stanhope, trying to identify why, in the East, she could contravene custom and fully incarnate her being, claimed in 1838 that '[t]he Arabs have never looked upon me in the light either of a man or of a woman, but as un être à part' (Cleveland, p. 378).[21] She reveals in 1812 to General Oakes that she is 'A woman in man's clothes, a woman on horseback—everything directly in opposition to the Arabs' strongest prejudices, and yet never even a smile of impertinence—[they] let me go where I will. If it was as it is in England, it would be quite impossible to get through with it all'; to her friend, Sarah Fernandes, she writes in 1813, 'You have heard, I suppose, that I am dressed as a man; sometimes as Chief of Albanians, sometimes as a Syrian soldier, sometimes as a Bedouin Arab … and at other times like the son of a Pacha' (Cleveland, pp. 138, 144).[22] The cultural distance

[21] She said this to the German Prince, Hermann von Pückler-Muskau.

[22] Sarah Fernandes, courageous herself, 'was mulling over a speculative venture to manage a farm on … Lampedusa'; to explore this possibility she traveled there alone with her son while her husband, the Deputy Commissariat General of Malta, stayed behind (Ellis, p. 102).

between this Englishwoman and her Arab friends offers her an autonomy she would not have had in England or as a Syrian woman, but it also bequeaths a sense of belonging with others in this country. That latitude empowers her coherently to 'out' her transgressive desires in external, material form. Stanhope wants to breathe, move, shoot, and, above all, to ride: her clothes materially free her to ride astride her horse (shocking Europeans), rather than sidesaddle. As Kaja Silverman writes, 'Clothing exercises [a] profoundly determining ... influence upon living, breathing bodies ..., affecting contour, weight, muscle development, posture, movement, and libidinal circulation'.[23] In Eastern conditions, rigid bodily and material lines become fluid, liberating her to live fully in her body, kinesthetically.

Dressed like a chief's son, Stanhope's transgressive materiality frees her to move fluidly between and among binaries of gender and culture and human and nonhuman things (see Fig. 8a).[24] In the following letter to Sarah Fernandes, she capitalizes on her outfit's strange and powerful aspects, which transform a woman's supposedly delicate frame into a vigorous body capable of donning materials that are 'coarse', 'thick', 'immense', 'large', and heavy—a cloak made of 'carpeting'—and adept at going to war with a twelve-foot long spear (see Fig. 8b, that offers a sense of the length and heft of such a weapon). In the following description, we first see the headdress emerge, fashioned from

> A square handkerchief made of coarse cotton and silk, folded from corner to corner, this put over a red nightcap, or skull crown, as if to protect it from a shower of rain, with one corner behind, and one on each side, like an old-fashioned wig; round the head to bind it on, are several rows of thick cord, as big as two fingers, made of horse or camel's hair, put round three or four times. A shirt, a pair of large drawers, and a thing of the coarsest materials, sometimes cotton (white), or sometimes silk (red), not unlike a bedgown, fastened with a leather belt, over that a pelisse of curly white sheepskin, the leather dressed white, or orange colour, or copper colour, and over that a sort of immense cloak with armholds

[23] Kaja Silverman, 'Fragments of a Fashionable Discourse', in *On Fashion*, eds. Shari Benstock and Suzanne Ferriss (New Brunswick, NJ: Rutgers University Press, 1994), p. 190.

[24] CAJS Image Collection LBO BON 5060 LBO302CAJS. University of Pennsylvania Libraries. *Fils de Cheik*, http://hdl.library.upenn.edu/1017/d/holyland/lenkin_5060; *Cheik Bédouin*, http://hdl.library.upenn.edu/1017/d/holyland/lenkin_5060. Economic and social concerns enter into this decision to cross-dress since not only would military action be difficult to realize in nineteenth-century women's apparel, but, as she says, she cannot even afford it. As she reports in 1812, 'to dress as an Englishwoman ... would cost me two years' income'; and 'to dress as a Turkish woman would not do, because I must not be seen to speak to a man' in public (Cleveland, p. 117).

Figure 8a: *Fils de Cheik*. Maison Bonfils. Photograph. University of Pennsylvania.

> (called abba), made of a sort of carpeting, of two different sorts, one with stripes of black and white, six inches wide, or a white sort, with gold on the right shoulder … then a large pair of yellow boots, and a lance twelve feet long decorated with black feathers. (Cleveland, p. 145)

Here, in this gender and cultural contact zone, various fabrics, metals, feathers, and other substances overlap and flow into one another, forming a dynamic materiality where objects give way to others. Stanhope's garb's material interactions mirror her own gender and cultural fluidity as we encounter, Merleau-Ponty-like, folds within folds: a folded handkerchief, itself folded over a red nightcap, drapes its corners behind in a mode likened to an old-fashioned British wig, an analogy intertwining Eastern and Western fashions.[25] The thick coils which 'bind' her headdress will yield to an uncoiling when she

[25] See Coole, who argues that Merleau-Ponty 'entertained a rather richer sense of the

Figure 8b: *Cheik Bédouin*. Maison Bonfils. Photograph. University of Pennsylvania.

disrobes; this material undoing echoes how the clothing itself unravels rigid definitions of the known and foreign and bespeaks the endemic potentiality of matter to flow and move, wrapping itself around other materials. In coiling the foreign Bedouin (cords of camel hair), the English domestic (a night-cap, a pair of large drawers, a bedgown), the female (a pelisse), the male (a wig and skull crown), the animal (sheep, feather, and hair), and her own body (her fingers form the measure), she creates a materiality that emerges energetically as a multiply charged being, moving amid East and West, male and female, and 'temperate' and 'hot zones'.[26] Her sketch of this attire makes its otherness touch 'normality', makes the former more familiar and the latter productively stranger. Her clothes and her body within them join, in Merleau-Ponty's

fold, which is indicated by the references to coiling, labyrinths, hollows, watermarks, soft flesh, and vortices, and for which his inspiration may have been Leibniz' (Coole, p. 109).

[26] Again, Wolfson's phrases (p. 15).

words, 'in a circuit with the world', wherein humans, animals, fibers, colors, and textures flow together.[27]

As 'an embodied humanity enveloped in nature' (Coole, p. 113), Stanhope describes her clothing and correlatively herself as '*the true thing*' (Cleveland, p. 151, emphasis original): these emphatic words, more than just a reference to the ensemble's authenticity, remind readers of how things have agency. As these clothes are the true thing, giving her the dynamic power to remake her life and to move through portals inaccessible to almost every Westerner and every woman, so is she the *true thing*—that is, not only does she constitute a being apart, uncontained by gender binaries, whether cultural or biological, she is also a 'thing' apart, given that she shares materiality with the things she wears. In *Vibrant Matter*, Bennett asserts that a '[v]ital materialism'—one that empowers matter, rendering it 'lively' and one that 'minimizes' the subject–object split—could 'set up a kind of safety net for those humans who are now … routinely made to suffer because they do not conform to a particular (Euro-American, bourgeois, theocentric, or other) model of personhood' (p. 13). The unconventional, nonconforming materialism that Stanhope enacts not only minimizes the split between her own materiality and that of the Eastern 'social skin' she wears and the desert she rides through, but it also minimizes the gap between East and West as it affirms a bond with the people who make and wear these articles.[28] Stanhope shows us a way 'of being with things' and a way of 'being things' (Behar, p. 13).

Enveloped in her clothing and in the desert, at one with her horse and her lance 'twelve feet long [and] decorated with black feathers' (Cleveland, p. 145), she transgresses both Eastern and Western gender roles in action and in thought, which in turn strengthens the 'heterogeneous assemblage' she participates in with the Arabs and Turks; as Bennett explains, 'bodies enhance their power' when 'the concept of agency' gets 'distributed across an ontologically heterogeneous field, rather than being a capacity localized in a human body or in a collective produced (only) by human efforts' (p. 23). Such a phenomenon creates another gender contact zone when she makes 'an experiment upon the good faith of the Arabs' by visiting Mahanna El Fadel, who commanded 40,000 men: 'I sent for him, and spent a week with my people in their tents, and marched three days with them'; having 'disarmed' her servants, she claims she 'put [herself] into the hands of God and the great Emir, which succeeded admirably' (Cleveland, p. 148). Her statement, that the Bedouins are her

[27] Maurice Merleau-Ponty, *Nature: Course Notes from the Collège de France* (Evanston, IL: Northwestern University Press, 2003), p. 209.

[28] For use of the term 'social skin', see Terence Turner, 'The Social Skin', in *Reading the Social Body*, eds. C.B. Burroughs and J. Ehrenreich (Iowa City: University of Iowa Press, 1993), pp. 15–39.

people, does not constitute an act of colonial appropriation because she also belongs to them; in this assemblage, geography, travel, weapons, Ottomans, Bedouins, and Stanhope enter into a 'throbbing confederation', one that is 'able to function despite the persistent presence of energies that confound [it] from within' (Bennett, pp. 23–4).

While Stanhope glories in her power, she simultaneously takes and concedes authority as she prepares to journey to Palmyra, another gender contact zone. She writes that 'I have great confidence in the Arab chief; the Pasha sent an express for him almost at the same moment as mine arrived, and his answer was, "The Queen [Hester] must be served first". Mahanna waits my orders, just as Lord Paget with his cavalry would do yours were you to command a great army'; Palmyra, she says, will be the 'the seat of my empire' (*T*, II: pp. 181–2). As Lord Paget with his cavalry, she will exert power, but in this gender contact zone, made vibrantly tense via differences in material culture, Stanhope will also concede by 'disarm[ing] her servants' and abdicating power, forming, in Bennett's words, 'an open-ended collective' (Bennett, p. 24). In contrast, in a comment typical of much commentary on Stanhope, Lesley Blanch interprets Lady Hester as seeking dominance and incapable of 'collective' exchange: he says she 'was not so much seeking fulfilment as a woman, as seeking escape from her own nature: she craved power rather than love'.[29] Blanch defines 'nature' here in essentialist gender terms, rendering Stanhope's materiality not only deviant but solidified into one 'craving'. By contrast, I argue that the gender contact zones of cross-dressing and warfare, by virtue of offering multiple material options she can embody, help her incarnate her 'nature' in an assemblage.[30]

The desert stimulates a dynamic human–object alliance. Writing to Henry Williams Wynn in 1813, Stanhope claims that if 'your uncle ... Lord G., and the dear General, could breathe the air of the desert, they would then have no pains in their stomachs'; she goes on to make humans coextensive with the animals—'even the horses sniff as if taking snuff, it is so pure they quite live upon it' (Cleveland, p. 150). Coole contends that 'Existence ... is

[29] Lesley Blanch, *The Wilder Shores of Love* (London: Panther, 1954), p. xiv.

[30] See Sara Mills's *Discourses of Difference: An Analysis of Women's Travel Writing and Colonialism*, which theorizes women's travel writing from a feminist perspective, noting that all too often earlier critics have labeled women travels as 'feminine' or as merely escaping from 'boredom and depression' (London and New York: Routledge, 1991), pp. 34, 35. Ulrike Brisson explores how Mary Kingsley 'broke traditional gender rules and adhered to ideals of femininity at the same time' in 'Fish and Fetish: Mary Kingsley's Studies of Fetish in West Africa', *Journal of Narrative Theory*, 35: 3 (2005), p. 326. Hester Stanhope, in contrast, cannot be categorized as 'feminine' or as balancing femininity with rule-breaking. This is why I discuss her as someone who herself materially constitutes a gender contact zone.

an internally productive, *form*ative process wherein meaning and matter are irreducibly interwoven' (Coole, p. 101, emphasis original), a conception that describes specifically how 'the air of the desert' and its war-vitality engenders Stanhope's life-force: she rides with the Bedouins, 'drinking' into her body the living land and its vital population as she is 'surrounded with one hundred lances. What a sight it is at night to see horses, men, and camels repair to the tents, no one can have an idea of it but those who have seen it. One morning twelve thousand camels belonging to one tribe were carried to drink at once' (Cleveland, p. 149).[31] Arguing for 'the active, self-transformative, practical aspects of corporeality as it participates in relationships of power', Coole and Frost find that 'bodies exhibi[t] agentic capacities in the way they structure or stylize their perceptual milieu, where they discover, organize, and respond to patterns that are corporeally significant' (pp. 19, 20). Stanhope's transformative ability to 'structure' and 'stylize' her physicality and in turn to be shaped by it empowers her to respond materially to her new world, intertwining herself with it and participating in it; her very corporeality renders her a willing and accepted contributor to Eastern life, partially because she is able to join those other things—Turks, Bedouins, desert landscapes, horses—in a pulsing cultural and geographic assemblage.

An Assemblage in Ascalon:[32] Gold, Camping Equipment, and Statues

I have argued that once through the Syrian gate, Stanhope enters a zone where a different 'rule rules' and where a 'different law begins' (Serres, p. 47): a new materialist zone. Crossing that threshold into a zone where human and nonhuman objects interact and interfuse with each other allows her to contravene gender rubrics and participate in an assemblage made of the people and things of the East. In these gender contact zones, the dynamic process of folding, unfolding, metamorphosis, and coiling characterizes Stanhope's material life in Syria. In addition to her male attire and her experience at St. Anthony's, another gender contact zone emerges in her voyage to an archaeological dig at Ascalon. This assemblage tracks the folding and unfolding of political maneuverings that unsettle distinctions between Eastern and Western engagements with materiality—in this case, ancient artifacts. She initiates such a zone when, after being bequeathed a secret manuscript revealing that hoards of gold were buried in Ascalon, she discloses the document to the Sublime Porte, promising that if the Turkish government supports her expedition, she will give

[31] Stanhope to Mr. Henry Williams Wynne, 15 January 1813. She visits the Sheikh Muhannâ al-Fâdil. Dick Douwes explains that Muhannâ, the leader of the Hasana, 'the most powerful tribal group in the area to the east of Hama and Homs … acquired a nearly legendary status for his bravery' (Douwes, p. 32).

[32] The contemporary spelling for Ascalon is Ashkelon or Ashqelon. At one time the Arab village of al-Majdal or al-Majdal Asqalan, it was conquered by Israeli forces in 1948.

them the gold.[33] The Porte agrees, opening another 'portal' into a gender contact zone by sending from their 'secret court' a 'Capugi Bashi' to invest Stanhope 'with greater authority over the Turks than was, probably, ever granted even to any European ambassador'; he delivers 'imperial orders, empowering her to demand what she might want' from the Pashas of Acre and of Damascus and from 'all governors in Syria' (p. 94).[34] While this might seem like the antithesis of assembly, I argue that it is not, given that Stanhope uses this power in unpredictable, surprising ways, ways that allow the assemblage of Syrians, Turks, Christians, and this British woman to remain plastic in their interactions.[35] As they journey, for example, Eastern royalty folds into Western as Queen Hester stays in a tent of 'vast magnitude' that once housed the Princess of Wales (*T*, III: p. 126), yet royal materials give way to plebian as Stanhope abdicates traveling in a palanquin 'covered with crimson cloth, and having in front six large gilded balls, glittering in the sun', in favor of riding an ass (*T*, III: pp. 128–9). Then, in another turn, once at Ascalon, she chooses not to camp with the men but withdraws with her women attendants to a nearby cottage, veiling herself in traditional Turkish female garb and visiting the site only once a day to give orders. In contrast, in the camp, objects are emancipated from categories, as over two hundred participants, a 'host of cooks, and loads of shovels, pickaxes, baskets, and whatever was necessary for excavat[ion]' are gathered (*T*, III: pp. 145, 149). Such a rich assemblage—a miscellany of pulsating individual energies and collaborative dynamics—transforms the archaeological site into a 'scene of showy gaiety almost as lively as a race-course' with 'couriers … coming and going every day from and to Jaffa' (*T*, III: p. 158).

Out of the chaotic abundance of nonhuman and human components they dig up—foundation walls of a temple, human bones, 'marble shafts of pillars', a 'Corinthian capital', 'earthen phials', vases, and 'a bottle of lapis specularis'[36]—they unearth 'a mutilated statue' buried under 'six or eight feet' of 'mould and rubbish' (*T*, III: pp. 160, 161), an exhumation that generates material destruction and transformation:[37] this marble artifact,

[33] 'Sublime Porte' is the name for the Ottoman Empire's seat of central government.

[34] When the pasha orders the 'astute, false, and insinuating' (*T*, III: p. 147) Mohammed Aga, the governor of Jaffa, to escort her, she in turn invites her trusted allies, Mâlem Musa Koblan, the Austrian consul, Signor Catafago, and her dragoman Giorgio to accompany her (Ellis, pp. 244–5).

[35] For a discussion of this word 'plastic' in relation to OOF, see Behar's 'Facing Necrophilia, or "Botox Ethics"', in *Object-Oriented Feminism*, pp. 128–30.

[36] *Lapis specularis* is presumably a type of blue glass.

[37] Robyn Le Blanc points out that they had made an important find in discovering 'our only architectural evidence of a temple in Ascalon in the early nineteenth century' (*The Public Sacred Identity of Roman Ascalon*, Ph.D. Dissertation, University of North Carolina, Chapel Hill, 2016, ProQuest 10119897). Neil Asher Silberman notes that Stanhope's and Meryon's archaeological dig and their 'historical analysis' of these excavations proved

> of colossal dimensions and of good execution …, was headless, and had lost an arm and a leg; but was not otherwise disfigured. It seemed to have represented a deified king: for the shoulders were ornamented with the insignia of the thunderbolt, and the breast with the Medusa's head. There was every reason to believe that, in the changes of masters which Ascalon had undergone, the place in which we were now digging had originally been a heathen temple, afterwards a church, and then a mosque. The statue [almost seven feet tall] probably belonged to the age of the successors of Alexander, or it might be that of Herod himself. (*T*, III: pp. 161–2)[38]

The religious multiplicity of the site and the statue's dismembered state and uncertain provenance create a space wherein materials intertwine in dynamic momentum. Its colossal size renders it tangibly and visually impressive—an object that makes us feel its presence like a flash of lightning does—hence the thunderbolt insignia on its chest. Into this vibration enters Stanhope, who orders Meryon to 'go this instant: take with you half a dozen stout fellows, and break it in a thousand pieces!' (*T*, III: p. 166). When she orders him to throw the wreckage into the sea, the statue, already in fragments, is emancipated from inert stillness and dark burial under 'mould and rubbish' to experience a fluid materiality as it floats with the Mediterranean's waves.[39]

Although Stanhope's decision to shatter the statue seems rigid and unequivocal, her further order—to have the statue 'thrown into the sea'—renders her relationship with matter more flexible and dynamic if we consider

'uncannily accurate' when 'the British School of Archaeology at Jerusalem' began digging at the same site in 1921. In other words, Stanhope and Meryon, had, in 1815, 'correctly analyzed the structure at a time when pure archaeological analyses were unknown', and their dig at Ascalon could 'be rightfully called the first modern excavation in the history of archaeological exploration of the Holy Land' (Neil Asher Silberman, 'Restoring the Reputation of Lady Hester Lucy Stanhope', *Biblical Archaeological Review*, 10: 04 [July–August 1984], pp. 68–75, at http://cojs.org/restoring_the_reputation_of_lady_hester_lucy_stanhope-_neil_asher_silberman-_bar_10-04-_jul-aug_1984/).

38 Cornelius Vermeule and Kristin Anderson explain that 'The cuirassed statue … discovered by Lady Hester Stanhope and destroyed on her orders in April 1815 was of a standard type used along the coast of Asia Minor, especially in Pamphylia, to represent Septimius Severus', 'Greek and Roman sculpture in the Holy Land' (*The Burlington Magazine*, 123: 934 [1981], pp. 7–19, 12).

39 These lines resemble those of Felicia Hemans's in 'The Widow of Crescentius' (1823), where she describes how Hadrian's tomb, its 'fair forms by sculpture wrought' now 'Have found, like glory's self, a grave / In Time's abyss, or Tiber's wave' (*Selected Poems, Prose and Letters*, ed. Gary Kelly [Peterborough, Ont.: Broadview Press, 2002], lines 47, 51–2). Hemans's lines, as she indicates in her notes to 'The Widow', allude to a passage from *Corinne, or Italy*, which she quotes. I discuss Stanhope's reference to de Staël's passage in the body of this essay.

that in this line she alludes to *Corinne, or Italy*, where the narrator says that 'The most beautiful artistic monuments, the most wonderful statues, have been thrown into the Tiber and are hidden beneath its waters ... [and] when you think that ... a keener eye would see them through the waters, you experience an indescribable emotion' (Raphael, pp. 81–2).[40] Such a reference acknowledges Stanhope's cognizance of this monument's exceptionality—as she says, this find 'wd. have made some noise, & many travelers come to have visited it' (Ian Bruce, p. 338)—and reveals that although she destroys and inundates 'Herod', she holds open the possibility, like Corinne's narrator, that one could be more than human—unhuman—in being able to see through aqueous materiality and contact submerged matter. In *Corinne*, such a thrilling connection (that 'indescribable emotion') includes allowing one's 'thoughts to find companionship in physical objects' (Raphael, p. 82).[41] Stanhope's transgression is thus three-fold. First, she destroys what the West considers valuable. Second, she potentially alludes to a female writer who herself intimates that humans can find an *esprit de corps* with the nonhuman. Third, when Stanhope breaks 'Herod' into a thousand pieces in order to maintain 'with the Porte all the merit of my disinterestedness' (*T*, III: p. 165), she makes this choice so she can preserve her material place in the assemblage of Eastern society. In other words, while she acknowledges her own problematically transgressive materiality by referring to her decision as a 'crime',[42] she does not want 'Malicious people' to 'say I came to search for antiquities for my country, [instead of] ... for treasures for the Porte' (*T*, III: pp. 166, 165), a response that would endanger the material interfusions in which she participates in the East. Meryon explains that inhabitants of the East 'look with indifference ... on the works of the ancients as specimens of architecture, and do not understand how others can be so eager in researches after what they despise'; they also 'are strongly possessed with the idea that the Franks who come among them have no other object than to seek treasures concealed in ancient ruins' (*T*, III: 1, pp. 90–1). Though understanding this logic, he is appalled, reasoning with her that 'lovers of the fine arts' would appreciate

[40] 'Les plus beaux monuments des arts, les plus admirables statues ont été jetées dans le Tibre, et sont caches sous les flots. Qui sait si, pour les chercher, on ne le détournera pas un jour de son lit? Main quand on songe que les chefs-d'œuvres du génie humain son peut-être là devant nous et qu'un œil plus perçant les verrait à travers les ondes, l'on éprouve je ne sais quelle émotion qui renaît à Rome sans cesse sous diverses formes, et fait trouver une société pour la pensée dans les objets physiques, muets par-tout ailleurs' (Balayé, pp. 135–6).

[41] The context in *Corinne* for this statement is that such experiences of the transcendent nonhuman (seeing through the water deep into the Tiber) occur especially in Rome.

[42] This can be found in Ian Bruce, *The Nun of Lebanon: The Love Affair of Lady Hester Stanhope and Michael Bruce. Their Newly Discovered Letters* (London: Collins, 1951), p. 338.

it and that 'future travelers would come to visit the ruins of Ascalon', which would become a memorial to her own 'enterprise' (*T*, III: 3, p. 165). She, however, eschews a memorial—a static commemoration—to herself. Instead, Stanhope chooses a living, experiential materiality, for in maintaining her loyalty to Eastern sensibility, her so-called crime allows her to retain the physical freedom she shares with the people and the desert. Further, her capacity to 'shatter' Western values recalls her dynamic capacity to shatter gender expectations and reconfigure and regenerate a new materiality wherein she can fluidly perform roles such as warrior, politician, prophet, and hermit.[43]

When she chooses to fracture the statue, her transgressive materialism further unsettles cultural and gender ideologies of matter's organization since once her enemy—Mohammed Aga—sees the wrecked statue, he cannot 'conceal his vexation'; Meryon speculates that 'it is probable that Lady Hester had read what was passing in his mind, and had thus prevented many an insinuation against her' (*T*, III: p. 166). And although the actual expedition comes up empty of gold, destroying the statue 'establish[es] Lady Hester's popularity throughout Syria' (*T*, III: pp. 167–8). It does so in a way that reinforces matter's vitality: the report circulates that when Stanhope broke open its chest, it 'was found full of gold—half of which was given to the pasha, and the other half kept by Lady Hester' (*T*, III: p. 166). Thus, its demolition precipitates metamorphosis when it is said to be the vessel of treasure. In this way, Herod evolves into a new materiality—one with gold in his belly—while the 'real' one, empty and hungry, slips through historical fingers. In contrast, the British, wanting that materiality as possession, were infuriated that this prize slipped through their fingers. When word reached England, they did not know or understand her 'motives' and thus 'naturally … decried her conduct' (*T*, III: p. 166). Her rethinking of materiality in Eastern political terms functions like a Bacchanalian ceremony, which seems only to annihilate, but, in fact, doubles for her, as it does in Greek mythology, as a 'fertility' ritual to engender her continuing re-creation in Syria, replenishing her dynamic materiality, her celebrity, and her political *éclat*.

[43] Of course, her 'crime' against these ancient materials also invites questions of a historical and political nature, which I do not have the space here to address: for example, has she abjured what Eric Gidal has called, in regard to the Elgin Marbles, the 'subjective aesthetic experience homologous with the historical fate of the objects it comprises' (p. 114)? Should her actions be differentiated from Lord Elgin's 'vandalism' (Thomas, p. 23)? And how does her deed stand in relation to recent destructive acts, for example, ISIL's demolition of sights sacred to the Syrians, such as Palmyra? I discuss these issues in the current book I am completing, *Palmyra and London: Romantic-Era Engagements between the East and West*. See also Eric Gidal, *Poetic Exhibitions: Romantic Aesthetics and the Pleasures of the British Museum* (Lewisburg, PA: Bucknell University Press, 2001) and Sophie Thomas, *Romanticism and Visuality: Fragments, History, Spectacle* (New York and London: Routledge, 2008).

II. Slippery Textuality in the Gender Contact Zone: An Assemblage of Women: The Old, the Pythoness, the Prophet, and the She-Thing

As I have shown, Stanhope's transgressive materiality is one that snakes through cracks in Eastern and Western notions of the female gender and of British national identity: she is '*un être à part*'—a difference that simultaneously ensures her belonging in Syria. In this section I discuss how attempts to represent Stanhope textually ultimately fail, and for intertwining reasons. In ways similar to how humans strain to dominate objects, many Western men who write about Stanhope struggle to subjugate her when they attack her material force. Nonetheless, these attempts to undermine her dynamic materialism backfire; their failure arises from the fact that, although her doctor, lover, visitors, and ultimately the Victorian public are almost all united in their scorn, their derisive judgments vary widely.[44] These contradictory accounts thus work against each other, and in aggregation they create what I am calling here a slippery textual materiality.

The effect of such inconsistency is, I suggest, ironically positive, since the contradictions work to challenge any one view a reader might adopt: thus, even as her critics attempt to affix her force and motion into inert and known forms, and even as they try homeopathically to prevent British women from admiring her physical and intellectual power, the sheer miscellany of their interpretations pull the ground, as it were, out from under each other's feet, rendering them and our grasp of her unstable.[45] Tangling with dynamic materiality in print also entangles readers within it, even if the purported claim is to stabilize or reject such fluidity. For example, in reviewing Meryon's *Memoirs* of Stanhope's life, *Tait's Magazine* reassures 'respectable village matron[s]' in 1845 that they need not 'have envied' her, since this 'Queen of the Desert ... was, in fact, a pitiable old woman, playing, or trying to play, an absurd, incongruous, and therefore a paltry part'.[46] Hermann Pückler-

[44] In contrast, see Vassiliki Markidou, who argues in 'Travels Off-centre: Lady Hester Stanhope in Greece' more bilaterally than I do, when she claims that Meryon's travel narrative 'forces the reader to oscillate between [Meryon's] authoritative masculine voice controlling the public document ... and [Stanhope's] feminine voice registered in private documents' (p. 41). *Women Writing Greece: Essays on Hellenism, Orientalism and Travel*, eds. Vassiliki Kolocotroni and Efterpi Mitsi (Amsterdam and New York: Rodopi, 2008), pp. 39–54.

[45] There are of course exceptions. For one example, see Alphonse de Lamartine, who respects her 'elevated, mystic, and obscure, though sustained, connected and powerful conversation', in *Travels in the East, Including a Journey in the Holy Land* (Edinburgh, 1850), p. 123.

[46] William Tait, ed., Review of *The Memoirs of the Lady Hester Stanhope*, *Tait's Edinburgh*

Muskau brands her by contrast as a 'Pythoness', and Alexander Kinglake's derision mocks her as a 'Lady Prophetess' with a 'wilful nature'.[47] Byron said of Stanhope that he did 'not admire "that dangerous thing a female wit"', and that she was no 'different ... from other she-things'.[48] Enfolding her among the 'she-things', it seems, reduces her from a dynamic to a debased materiality, where a thing, which is multifaceted, gets reduced merely to a gender category; taken on its own, the phrase can be seen as only objectifying both a 'she' and a 'thing'. However, when we see this moniker contextually, in his description of his lover Margarita Cogni, she-thing refers to a throng of traits: 'a very fine animal, of considerable beauty and energy, with many good and several amusing qualities but wild as a witch and fierce as a demon' (XI: p. 336). Byron's descriptors suggest that a 'she-thing' is actually more complex because more varied—especially ontologically—and more contradictory. The other textual judgments (pythoness, prophet, pathetic, admirable), when considered individually, each 'fix' her in one way and thereby stand in contrast to a rich and liberating point of view such as OOF or feminist materialism offer. Taken together, however, these responses offer a lively spectrum of possibilities as to who Stanhope might or might not be, and this is why their 'slipperiness' gives us some insight into the mystery of Hester Stanhope. This cross-contamination—altogether positive—of materiality leaks into and through nonhuman serpentine textuality and interpretation.

While the slippery materialism in these texts emerges from the inconsistencies among them, in Meryon's *Travels* and *Memoirs* such oleaginous shifts develop from discrepancies within his text, those arising from the multiple points of view he engages: first, as he adds his own opinions toward her and the Arabs, both filtered through his gender and class prejudices; second, as he censors and then records in his volumes Stanhope's observations in letters; third, as he supplements his perspective with those of others' via transcriptions of her conversations with them; and fourth, as his version of events almost always conflicts tonally with her epistolary record. These four add to the narration's metafictional complexities and the frictional competition between Stanhope's story and Meryon's. Further, he dematerializes her by redirecting attention to his own exploits. Additionally, Lady Hester herself generates a slippery materiality given the unreliability of her own correspondence,

Magazine, XII: pp. 433–96, 434, at https://books.google.com/books?id=9eERAAAAYAAJ&vq=Stanhope&source=gbs_navlinks_s.

[47] See Cleveland for quotations from Hermann Pückler-Muskau (p. 374) and from Kinglake (p. 294); Kinglake's tone is sometimes difficult to pin down, though he seems to want to typecast Stanhope.

[48] George Gordon, Lord Byron, *The Works of Lord Byron: Letters and Journal* (London: John Murray, 1922), I: p. 302. This letter of 1810 was written to John Cam Hobhouse.

which presents a varying self, by turns or sometimes simultaneously virtuous, arrogant, heroic, vengeful, and humble.[49]

In Meryon's works, textual and material fluidity come together—as if in trying to describe a materially sinuous person, his texts themselves become a kind of materiality also in motion. Meryon's text-in-motion occurs most often when, in gender contact zones, Stanhope manifests differing facets of her material being, dissimilarities that also affect the energies in these assemblages. The zones she creates, however, with their varying gendered and cultural dynamisms, are effective as transformative spaces precisely because they are not stable. In other words, when he describes her (in varying ways) in each instance, it is as if she is that one description and nothing more. He can neither accept the multiplicity of her being nor gather those pieces together to try to form them into a unified whole. As a result of his resistance, when Stanhope's energies fly in different directions, his representations of her and of himself become more hackneyed. Yet the end result is that her transgressive materiality becomes more dynamic simply because (like the critics' judgments I discussed above) he offers so many versions of her. For example, on their journey to Ba'albek, they are forced to travel through plague-ridden areas, which necessitates taking their own supplies and sleeping in tents. He reports that at the last minute he had to find an extra mule to carry cheese, tea and sugar, syrups for sherbet, and fuel for Lady Hester, whose 'sex and delicate health necessarily prevented her from submitting to the privations to which men could willingly subject themselves' (*T*, III: p. 2). His fulsome and hackneyed language reduces her to one thing: the fragile flower. In fixing her, he becomes his own cliché: the heroic masculine traveler and man of feeling who is elevated by his 'humane tears' for the pitiable woman, such that he rejects any plasticity possible among potential and varying configurations of gender and of East and West: as Deborah Weiss has argued, 'The female suffering at the foundation of sentimental culture was, then, essential to the British understanding of what made a nation and its people civilized'.[50] And yet, in assuming this identity as an English man, probably because it is an identity he believes is fixed and therefore stable, he cannot envelop himself in his environment; as a result, unlike Stanhope, Meryon experiences an

[49] Her love letters to Michael Bruce form an exception to this. For example, on 9 October 1813, she writes, 'Were I to tell you all I feel dearest, I realize it would only make you low, so I will only say I am tolerably well & will do all I can to be better. Take care of yourself for my sake. I shall never cease to pray for you … . God never will be deaf to my prayers. … Adieu dearest, dearest love, HLS'. 'Letters from Lady Hester Stanhope to Michael Bruce, 1813–17', MS ENG. C 5758. *Papers of the Bruce Family, 18th–20th Century*. Bodleian Library, University of Oxford.

[50] Deborah Weiss, 'Suffering, Sentiment, and Civilization: Pain and Politics in Mary Wollstonecraft's *Short Residence*', *Studies in Romanticism*, 45: 2 (2006), pp. 199–221, 201.

agonistic relation to objects which he sees as pitting themselves against him: in trying to secure the mule, his 'riding dress' makes it 'scarcely possible' for him 'to walk', and the heavy 'brace of pistols in [his] girdle' tire him; the path foils him and he loses his way; robbers, leopards, and screaming jackals threaten him; a deep ravine sucks him down as he wanders in the night's 'abyss'; plague-infected food terrifies him; and then germs attack, infecting his feet with 'an intolerable erysipelatous heat and itching' (*T,* III: pp. 4, 5, 6, 8).[51] Objects, disregarded and excluded from the environmental assemblage he travels through, become threatening and thus entities to dominate, just as Stanhope becomes a being whose diversity must be reduced only to the part that he can comfort and thus overshadow.

Nevertheless, Stanhope and the text slip out of his hands, so to speak, since once he returns to camp he finds he is no longer the hero, for his failures in 'masculine' leadership and protection have seriously compromised the company's domestic vulnerability: before leaving to get the mule, he had neglected to entrust the food hamper keys to someone at the camp, causing, in his absence, the servants to break into the provisions, leading (in his opinion) to 'unnecessary waste'—that is, a loss of food. To solve the problem, Stanhope, apparently no longer a delicate flower, orders the company to eat hard and dry meat dumplings, refusing to 'abate one tittle of her resolution'. He takes on another role now: she is the general (no more and no less) and he is the lackey, for he has to 'enforce the order for their consumption by eating them [the dumplings] myself' and to control the grumbling, crying, and rebelling camp: there is more dissension among 'Christians, Drûzes, and Mahometans', he says, than he 'had hitherto experienced' (*T,* III: pp. 9, 12–3). In another slip, he concedes that she made the right decision, for no one starved and 'no one fell ill' (*T,* III: pp. 9, 12–3). Whoever Stanhope is now glides again through his fingers. As their travels become even 'more dangerous', she is neither a frail blossom nor an unreasonable tyrant, but is—like an 'easternized' Anne Elliot—'a woman whose composure of mind was never ruffled by real danger, and whose sleep was never broken by the apprehension of false' (*T,* III: pp. 13, 13–4).[52]

The very textual materiality of the *Memoirs*, *Travels*, and letters that gives us access to Stanhope's thoughts and actions challenges and controverts itself; such slipperiness encourages us to see her prismatically, to see the dynamic materiality in these gender contact zones. In doing so, they spark us to see

[51] Caused by streptococci, erysipelatous is a serious bacterial infection accompanied by inflammation.

[52] After Louisa falls and is concussed, Captain Wentworth wants Anne to care for her: 'if Anne will stay, no one so proper, so capable as Anne!' (Jane Austen, *Persuasion* [New York: Norton, 1995], p. 77).

how writers' representations, in trying to limit her materiality, free it from their grip. In this sense Stanhope's evasions from fixity reflect the contingency and movement of her decisions, actions, and embodiments, a kinesthesia which makes her appear as though she withdraws—as though she is unknowable—because they cannot see and thus cannot represent her dynamic materiality. The unpredictable folding and unfolding of identities I am exploring contrasts to the logic of OOO: Tim Morton argues that all objects withdraw, rendering them deviant, 'in so far as they exist in difference from themselves. This is because they are riven from within between what they are and how they appear' (p. 73). Morton brings a feminist slant to OOO when he links this thought to Luce Irigaray's ideas; for her, 'at least one entity, known as woman, falls outside the logical Law of Noncontradiction, insofar as female physicality cannot be thought either as one or as two but as a weird touching between one and two, a loop-like self-touching denigrated as narcissism' (p. 73). Thus, self-difference resembles Irigaray's notion of woman's deviation from male logic. My point, however, is that Stanhope's dynamic materiality—in part thanks to its slipperiness—materializes here even against the work of these authors. Narrators strain to represent her as deviant, but only in the most conventional sense of endeavoring to make her a failed example of her gender; in their attempts, they reveal how what makes her transgressive is what also allows her to slide through their representational grasp.

Multiple materialities collide and metamorphose during Stanhope's life in the East. As she modifies the objects she interacts with, so do they transform her. Whether it is the snap of a spear or the roughness of a camel or the invigorating desert air, these nonhuman materialities help create a vibrant interweaving of energetic encounters and, in these gender contact zones, Stanhope joins assemblages that are sometimes troubled, but always buoyant.

Bibliography

Appiah, Anthony and Henry Louis Gates Jr. 'Editors' Introduction: Multiplying Identities'. *Critical Inquiry*, 18 (1992), pp. 625–9.

Austen, Jane. *Persuasion*. New York: Norton, 1995.

Bennett, Jane. *Vibrant Matter: A Political Ecology of Things*. Durham, NC: Duke University Press, 2010.

Blanch, Leslie. *The Wilder Shores of Love*. London: Panther, 1954.

Bogost, Ian. Comments published 5 November 2010 in response to panels organized by Katherine Behar on Object-Oriented Feminism. Society for Literature Science and the Arts Conference (28–31 October 2010), at http://bogost.com/writing/blog/object-oriented_feminism_1/.

Booth, Marilyn, ed. *Harem Histories: Envisioning Places and Living Spaces*. Durham, NC: Duke University Press, 2010.

Brenkman, John. 'Extreme Criticism'. In *What's Left of Theory: New Work on the Politics of Literary Theory*, Essays from the English Institute, eds. Judith Butler, John Guillory, and Kendall Thomas. New York and London: Routledge, 2000, pp. 114–36.

Brisson, Ulrike. 'Fish and Fetish: Mary Kingsley's Studies of Fetish in West Africa'. *Journal of Narrative Theory*, 35: 3 (2005), pp. 326–40.

Bruce, Ian, ed. *The Nun of Lebanon: The Love Affair of Lady Hester Stanhope and Michael Bruce. Their Newly Discovered Letters*. London: Collins, 1951.

Byron, George Gordon, Lord. *The Works of Lord Byron: Letters and Journals*. London: John Murray, 1922.

Cleveland, Catherine Lucy Wilhelmina Powlett, Duchess of Cleveland. *The Life and Letters of Lady Hester Stanhope*. London: John Murray, 1914.

Cleveland, William L. and Martin Bunton. *A History of the Modern Middle East*, 6th ed. Boulder, CO: Westview Press, 2017.

Coole, Diana, 'The Inertia of Matter'. In *New Materialisms: Ontology, Agency, and Politics*, eds. Diana Coole and Samantha Frost. Durham, NC: Duke University Press, 2010, pp. 92–115.

Coole, Diana and Samantha Frost. 'Introducing the New Materialism'. In *New Materialisms: Ontology, Agency, and Politics*, eds. Coole and Frost. Durham, NC: Duke University Press, 2010, pp. 1–43.

Douwes, Dick. *The Ottomans in Syria: A History of Justice and Oppression*. London and New York: I.B. Tauris, 2000.

Ellis, Kirsten. *Star of the Morning: The Extraordinary Life of Lady Hester Stanhope*. London: HarperCollins, 2008.

Gibb, Lorna. Lady Hester: *Queen of the East*. London: Faber and Faber, 2005.

Gidal, Eric. *Poetic Exhibitions: Romantic Aesthetics and the Pleasures of the British Museum*. Lewisburg, PA: Bucknell University Press, 2001.

Hamel, Frank. *Lady Hester Lucy Stanhope: A New Light on her Life and Love Affairs*. London: Cassell and Company, 1913.

Hemans, Felicia. 'The Widow of Crescentius'. In *Felicia Hemans: Selected Poems, Prose and Letters*, ed. Gary Kelly. Peterborough: Broadview, 2002.

Heydt-Stevenson, Jillian. 'The Last Ruins of Palmyra'. *ELN*, 54: 1 (2016), pp. 93–112.

Kinglake, Alexander William. *Eothen: Traces of Travel Brought Home from the East*. Cologne: Könemann Verlagsgesellschaft mbH, 1997.

Knapp, Bettina L. 'Lady Hester Stanhope (1776–1839)'. In *Great Women Travel Writers from 1750 to the Present*, eds. Alba Amoia and Bettina L. Knapp. New York: Continuum, 2005, pp. 38–54.

Lamartine, Alphonse de. *Travels in the East, Including a Journey in the Holy Land*. Edinburgh: Chambers, 1850.

Le Blanc, Robyn. *The Public Sacred Identity of Roman Ascalon*. Ph.D. Dissertation. University of North Carolina, Chapel Hill, 2016. ProQuest 10119897.

Markidou, Vassiliki. 'Travels Off-centre: Lady Hester Stanhope in Greece'. In *Women Writing Greece: Essays on Hellenism, Orientalism and Travel*, eds. Vassiliki Kolocotroni and Efterpi Mitsi. Amsterdam and New York: Rodopi, 2008, pp. 39–54.

Merleau-Ponty, Maurice. *Nature: Course Notes from the Collège de France*. Evanston, IL: Northwestern University Press, 2003.

Melman, Billie. *Women's Orients, English Women and the Middle East, 1718–1918: Sexuality, Religion and Work*. Ann Arbor: University of Michigan Press, 1992, 1995.

Meryon, Charles Lewis. *Memoirs of the Lady Hester Stanhope: As Related by Herself in Conversations with her Physician*. 3 vols. Cambridge Library Collection. Cambridge: Cambridge University Press, 2012, doi:10.1017/CBO9781139344494.

——. *Papers of Charles Meryon*. 3 files. MS 5687. File 1: 19. The Wellcome Library.

——. *Travels of Lady Hester Stanhope, forming the Completion of her Memoirs narrated by her Physician*. 3 vols., unabridged facsimile. Elibron Classics: Adamant Media Corporation, 2005.

Mills, Sara. *Discourses of Difference: An Analysis of Women's Travel Writing and Colonialism*. London and New York: Routledge, 1991.

Morton, Timothy. 'All Objects Are Deviant: Feminism and Ecological Intimacy'. In *Object-Oriented Feminism*, ed. Katherine Behar. Minneapolis: University of Minnesota Press, 2016, pp. 65–81.

Papers of the Bruce Family, 18th–20th Century. MSS. Eng. b. 2067, c. 5740–72, d. 2834–48, e. 2994–3004; Facs. d. 302; Photogr. c. 71, d. 13, e. 9. Bodleian Library, University of Oxford.

Philipp, Thomas, ed. *The Syrian Land in the 18th and 19th Century: The Common and the Specific in the Historical Experience. Berliner Islamstudien*. Stuttgart: F. Steiner, 1992.

Pratt, Mary Louise. *Imperial Eyes: Travel Writing and Transculturation*. London and New York: Routledge, 1992.

Serres, Michel. *Statues: The Second Book of Foundations*, trans. Randolph Burks. London: Bloomsbury 2015.

Silberman, Neil Asher. 'Restoring the Reputation of Lady Hester Lucy Stanhope'. *Biblical Archaeological Review*, 10: 04 (July–August 1984), pp. 68–75.

Silverman, Kaja. 'Fragments of a Fashionable Discourse'. In *On Fashion*, eds. Shari Benstock and Suzanne Ferriss. New Brunswick, NJ: Rutgers University Press, 1994, pp. 183–96.

Staël, Madame de. *Corinne ou l'Italie*, trans. Sylvia Raphael. Oxford: Oxford University Press, 1998.

——. *Corinne ou l'Italie*, Édition de Simone Balayé. Paris: Gallimard, 1985.

Tait, William, ed. Review of *The Memoirs of the Lady Hester Stanhope. Tait's Edinburgh Magazine*, 12: August, 1845, pp. 483–96, at https://books.google.com/books?id=9eERAAAAYAAJ&vq=Stanhope&source=gbs_navlinks_s.

Thomas, Sophie. *Romanticism and Visuality: Fragments, History, Spectacle*. New York and London: Routledge, 2008.

Turner, Terrence. 'The Social Skin'. In *Reading the Social Body*, eds. C.B. Burroughs and J. Ehrenreich. Iowa City: University of Iowa Press, 1993, pp. 15–39.

Vermeule, Cornelius and Kristin Anderson. 'Greek and Roman Sculpture in the Holy Land'. *The Burlington Magazine*, 123: 934 (1981), pp. 7–19.

Watney, John. *Travels in Araby of Lady Hester Stanhope*. London: Gordon Cremonesi, 1975.

Weiss, Deborah. 'Suffering, Sentiment, and Civilization: Pain and Politics in Mary Wollstonecraft's *Short Residence*'. *Studies in Romanticism*, 45: 2 (2006), pp. 199–221.

Wolfson, Susan. *Borderlines: The Shiftings of Gender in British Romanticism*. Stanford, CA: Stanford University Press, 2006.

Chapter Six

'The Redundancy of Copious Nothings'

Fictional Offspring, Or, the Reproductions of Female Vanity

Mary Beth Tegan

In a fraught little fable originally intended to preface the novel *Cecilia* (1782), Frances Burney takes pains to distinguish her '2^{d} offspring' from the 'redundancy of copious nothings' produced at the Temple of Vanity.[1] Gendered as a feminine space, the Temple of Vanity arises in 'the early ages of Authorship' when 'Genius instituted the school of Letters, & inspired its Disciples' but soon 'suffered' Vanity 'to become the self-nominated Patroness of his thence polluted seminary' (Burney, pp. 943–4). Vanity's influence grows, the two engage in a 'vigorous contest', and Genius retreats from 'the promiscuous herd' with a few elect favorites, 'whose intellectual faculties he had rarified by sparks of his own immortal fire'. The 'youthful Author' of Burney's tale eyes the Temples of Genius and Vanity at a 'humble distance': the first radiant but distant, the second promising easy access and an extravagant welcome. Where Genius inspires, Vanity spreads miasmically, supporting the reproductions and the metamorphoses of her many acolytes. '[T]oo inebriated' by Vanity to perceive his 'Glory' or 'to consider *her* inferiority', the aspirant soon loses sight of the Temple of Genius (emphasis added). The cautionary strain in Burney's allegory is clear and the preface's omission at the novel's release telling, for it makes boldly manifest the affective traces of writerly ambition and critical reception.

Burney's projection of authorial anxiety is dense with metaphors of pollution, animation, and reproduction—images that recur among the literary reviewers who labored to characterize the 3,378 new novels published between 1780 and

[1] From a letter to her sister, Susan Burney, after the publication of *Evelina*. Qtd. in Justine Crump, *A Known Scribbler: Frances Burney on Literary Life* (Toronto: Broadview Press, 2002), p. 143; Frances Burney, *Cecilia*, ed. Peter Sabor (New York: Oxford University Press, 1988), pp. 943–6.

1829.[2] The proliferation of women's fiction gave rise to accounts both fanciful and flip. Clara Reeve imagines 'the press groan[ing] under the weight of Novels', while in Edward Cave's grotesque vision of 'worthless books', objects become the 'offspring ... of circulating libraries or their venal authors'.[3] Widely viewed to be a corrupting 'feminized space', the circulating library becomes strangely fertile—a site, argues Jacqueline Pearson, where the 'book, the library and the female body become disturbingly identified'.[4] Hannah More envisions the library as a 'breeding ground' for 'seducing books'; the scene she paints is one of reproductive mayhem, the effects of which are heightened by ambiguous pronouns and a confusion between subject and object:

> Who are those ever-multiplying authors, that with unparalleled fecundity, are overstocking the world with their quick-succeeding progeny? They are NOVEL-WRITERS—the easiness of whose productions is at once the cause of their own fruitfulness, and of the almost infinitely numerous race of imitators to whom they give birth. (p. 92)[5]

Pronominal uncertainty in this passage raises questions about the agents of novel reproduction, a conflation of authors with things that echoes Cave's topsy-turvy formula above. Libraries, books, and NOVEL-WRITERS are all imbued with generative powers but, as at the Temple of Vanity, their quick-succeeding progeny is 'redundant'—a race of imitators destined to reproduce the same.

The satirical use of 'birth topoi' to characterize uninspired literary production was predominant for most of the eighteenth century, a function, according to Terry Castle, of the neoclassical will to 'preserve a distinction between functions of the body and functions of the mind'.[6] Procreative metaphors were never positive, applying only to 'bad' writers; the 'one who conceives and brings forth', argues Castle, 'is nowhere in control, but rather is subject to a purely spontaneous animal function' (p. 202). John Dryden mocks the

[2] Anthony Mandal, 'Fiction', in *The Cambridge Companion to Women's Writing in the Romantic Period*, ed. Devoney Looser (Cambridge: Cambridge University Press, 2015), pp. 16–31. On the proliferation of women's novels and their reception, see also Jacqueline Pearson and William St Clair.

[3] Edward Cave, in *Novel and Romance 1700–1800*, ed. Ioan Williams (London: Routledge, 2010), p. 272.

[4] Jacqueline Pearson, *Women's Reading in Britain, 1750–1835: A Dangerous Recreation* (Cambridge: Cambridge University Press, 1999), p. 165.

[5] Hannah More, *Strictures on the Modern System of Female Education*, ed. Gina Luria, 2 vols. (Shrewsbury: Garland Press, 1974), I: p. 164.

[6] Terry Castle, 'Lab'ring Bards: Birth *Topoi* and English Poetics, 1660–1820', *Journal of English and Germanic Philology*, 78 (1979), p. 202.

poet who is '"swell'd" with pride or "big with hymn"', and Samuel Johnson dismisses even Shakespeare's '"strain[ed] faculties"' as he '"laboured"' in the production of tragedy (p. 200). 'The poetic birth, for Johnson as for Pope and the others, draws attention to itself in a context of failure, grotesquerie, vacuity, futility', concludes Castle (p. 200). This view is consistent with that of later reviewers who deplore the 'unparalleled fecundity' of women novelists, and it would seem that Burney adopts their assumptions wholesale in her gendered allegory about Vanity and the perils of literary ambition.

And yet in a letter to her sister Susan, written when *Cecilia* was a mere twinkle in her eye, the novelist's musings about her offspring are mostly positive, illuminating the dynamic between literary labor, vanity, and the sympathy of others. Burney begins gaily, with allusions to the '*flummery*' that '*turn[s] the Head of an Authoress*' and her triumphant sense of '*Consequence*' from the admiration of Dr. Johnson, the prominent Bluestocking Mrs. Cholmondeley, and Mrs. Thrale. The last becomes the 'Goddess of [her] Idolatry' due to praise that 'not only delights at *first,* but proves more & more flattering every Time it is considered!' (Crump, p. 143). Burney returns to Thrale's '*eloge*' often as she weighs the risks and rewards of continuing to write, and Thrale's sympathetic appraisal is the source of 'temptations' both potentially 'destruct[ive]' and '*almost* irresistible' to the young author (p. 143).[7] Conscious that the introduction of a second novel 'would no longer be a *Young Lady's first appearance* in public', Burney resolves that the 'wisest Course' is 'to bid an eternal adieu to Writing' (p. 143). Not only is the concern with 'redundancy' apparent in her reflections, but she worries that 'between either the Friends or the Foes of the *Eldest,* the 2^{d} would stand an equally bad chance, & a million of *flaws* which were overlooked in the former, would be ridiculed as villainous & intolerable *Blunders* in the latter' (p. 143). Burney's hyperbole here anticipates the fear of judgment encoded in her later allegory but, despite the tangle of negative and positive affect, the letter's dominant note is buoyant. Susan Stanford Friedman argues that in the hands of a woman writer, the childbirth metaphor 'expresses a fundamental rebellion' against 'historical realities' and the 'division of creativity and procreativity' with the 'male text'.[8] In this light, Burney's references to her progeny appear 'genuinely subversive', her vacillations indicative of the dangers *and* pleasures of literary labor (Friedman, p. 59). Exposing her '2^{d} offspring' to the public gaze is both tempting and terrifying, her shifting feelings a mirror of others' responses to the things she holds dear.

[7] Burney owns to being 'urged on by an impulse irresistible' in the allegory, but this she associates with the 'Quakers of Literature' who are 'neither blinded by self Love nor allured by Ambition' (p. 945). It is my contention that this thinly conceived third sect is also 'polluted' by Vanity, though its negative characterizations are evaded.

[8] Susan Stanford Friedman, 'Creativity and the Childbirth Metaphor: Gender Difference in Literary Discourse', *Feminist Studies,* 13: 1 (Spring 1987), p. 58.

Vanity's influence is only tacitly acknowledged in Burney's letter, but her Temple looms large in the allegorical preface. A fickle and fluid passion, vanity is dependent on the communication between bodies and things and imbued with the affective judgments of others. In *The Transmission of Affect,* Teresa Brennan defines affect as the 'physiological shift accompanying a judgment', observing that affects are ambiguous, resisting the 'meanings' identified with feelings because 'any evaluative (positive or negative) orientation toward an object' may be felt by the bodies involved.[9] Burney's aspiring author is 'inebriated' by positive affect at the Temple of Vanity—pleasurable but nebulous feelings generated by her own 'copious nothings' and the proximity of the corrupting 'promiscuous herd'. The approbation of others causes the 'heart to swell and dilate itself', observes Adam Smith, enhancing one's self-complacency, while ridicule or censure diminishes the self (and its offspring) with even greater force because pain is 'a more pungent sensation' than pleasure.[10] At stake in the attachment of affects to things is nothing less than the substance of selfhood, which is 'altogether insufficient to support [it]self', according to David Hume.[11] Personal identity depends upon vanity or pride—terms Hume uses interchangeably—which binds the self amid the swarm of shifting affects and agential objects.

Consider the matter of Burney's imaginative landscape—the Temples' visual grandeur, the personified passions, and vanity's physiological effects. All highlight the tendency of 'things' to 'take on a new life in the romantic period'—a state, as Bill Brown suggests, of 'indeterminate ontology where things seem slightly human and humans seem slightly thing-like'.[12] Books are children and authors are animals, and one (or an other) is reproducing 'vain things' in abundance: nothings 'as full of [them]selves as [they] are empty of every thing else'.[13] Such 'modern metamorphoses' enact contemporary theories of sympathy, Jonathan Lamb argues, occurring 'between the human and the non-human'

[9] Teresa Brennan, *The Transmission of Affect* (Ithaca, NY: Cornell University Press, 2004), p. 5.

[10] Adam Smith, *The Theory of Moral Sentiments*, ed. Knud Haakonssen (Cambridge: Cambridge University Press, 2009), pp. 61–62, 141.

[11] David Hume, *A Treatise on Human Nature*, eds. David Fate Norton and Mary J. Norton (Oxford: Oxford University Press, 2005), p. 228. It is worth noting here that the moral philosophers of the eighteenth century are not united in their deployment of the term 'vanity': where Smith and the Edgeworths distinguish it from 'pride', Hume and Hutcheson often use the terms interchangeably.

[12] W.J.T. Mitchell, 'Romanticism and the Life of Things: Fossils, Totems, and Images', in *Things*, ed. Bill Brown (Chicago, IL: University of Chicago Press, 2004), p. 240; Bill Brown, *A Sense of Things: The Object Matter of American Literature* (Chicago, IL: University of Chicago Press, 2003), p. 13.

[13] Jonathan Lamb, *The Things Things Say* (Princeton, NJ: Princeton University Press, 2011), p. xii.

when 'confusion amidst the world of objects destabilizes personal identity'.[14] But sympathy is too passive for the affective charge of assembled things in this strangely fertile, feminized space.[15] *Vanity* is the mother of ontological confusion, the begetter and disrupter of identity, the end and the beginning of 'promiscuous', novel ambitions. Affirming the latent 'gaiety' of Burney's writerly fable, this essay reframes the creative, destabilizing powers of vanity in order to consider how the passion lends substance to Humean 'no-things' or selves (p. 169). For the undeniably material nature of Humean subjectivity is striking and suggestive: if objects and affects are constitutive of character, then the ontological disruptions of vanity allow for a reassessment of women's 'labour'd Nothings' (Castle, p. 199) and the small but sustaining vanities that people their lives.

The Man in the Mirror: Vanity and Material Subjectivity

From the Latin *vanus,* for 'empty', vanity is an 'indirect passion', according to Hume, dependent upon the pleasure associated with external objects and the feelings of others that generate a positive self-image. The absence of an independent, internal source for the passion's creation and maintenance is suggestive, and this lack is implicit in its very nomenclature. But the flimsy foundations of vanity render it no less 'requisite in a character' (p. 381). For Hume, the self is an entity that has no real substance, a 'no-thing' like vanity that depends upon things for its tenuous existence (p. 169). A fiction that arises through our reflections on the perceptions and associations that pass through our minds, the self is a mere habit of mind causing us to mistake 'identity' for a string of related objects or impressions. 'Myself am the proper object of pride or humility' (p. 216), he writes, indicating that the self is the end-product of vanity or humility, both of which are generated in turn through the pleasure or pain occasioned by one's reflection on proximate things. These self-constituting objects may be one's own possessions or the palpable impressions absorbed from the 'minds of men [which] are mirrors to one another' (p. 236). Hume's grammatical construction is striking since

[14] Jonathan Lamb, 'Modern Metamorphoses and Disgraceful Tales', *Critical Inquiry*, 28: 1, *Things* (Autumn 2001), p. 133.

[15] Eighteenth-century moral philosophers and pedagogues present a surprisingly nuanced picture of the workings of vanity, examining its imbrication with sympathy, its link to social virtues and transgressions, and, in the case of Hume, its role in the constitution of personal identity. It is worth noting that Humean sympathy is considerably more embodied than than that conceived by Smith, who is 'suspicious of sympathy' (Mullen, p. 26); so too are the Edgeworths, who draw upon his work. To counter its uncertain, erratic influence, Smith 'constructs a subjectivity whose behaviour and judgements are inherently socialized, and yet one which is raised above the passions'—the impartial spectator (Mullen, p. 51).

'myself' serves generally as the object, not the subject, of a sentence. A case of form enacting content, the sentence underscores the argument's importance while also instigating the confusion that arises whenever affective transmission disrupts the Cartesian relationship between subject and object. The Humean self, then, becomes a subjective entity only through objects and the feelings they generate, a copious 'no-thing' in need of endless external mirroring.

The mirror's uses as a self-constituting object have long been recognized, and Hume enumerates additional 'mirroring things' that contribute to the making of pride or vanity, as well as that of the person:

> 'tis certain, that pride requires the assistance of some foreign object, and that the organs, which produce it, exert not themselves like the heart and arteries, by an original internal movement. ... [I]t languishes when unsupported by some excellency in the character, in bodily accomplishments, in cloaths, equipage, or fortune. (p. 188)

Arguing that pride depends upon external sources, Hume again inverts the subject–object construction in the ensuing discussion, identifying what is usually an 'object' of pride as its 'subject'—a telling reversal in that the object is agent of the affect produced. The 'subject' of vanity can either be a personal quality of mind (like wit or courage), a quality of the body (like strength or beauty), or any thing closely related to us. Thus, one's family, country, riches, and houses may all be subjects of vanity, though the more remote from the self they are, the less they reflect well upon it. This is why property, the most substantial relation that binds a man to inanimate objects, is first in the hierarchy of non-personal causes identified (p. 202). If we consider a family's country residence, for instance, the degree of pride a gentleman may take in it would depend upon whether he himself or a sibling owns the property, the rarity of the estate's beauty or size, and the frequency with which others might admire it (p. 192). And certainly one's progeny, born of the body but free to act independently, is a potent if unpredictable mirror.

Vanity ebbs and flows based on conditions that lend agential *force* to its extrinsic or material causes, as Hume suggests by his use of the term 'languish'. Indeed, vanity's power is determined by certain socio-relational conditions, including the extent to which the 'subject' (i.e., object or cause) is singular or peculiar to us, the degree to which it is obvious to others, and the role that 'custom and practice' play in settling the 'just value of every thing' and guiding our preferences (Hume, p. 192). In addition to the social forces determining vanity's strength is the 'subject's' durability (pp. 191–2). Because many causes are temporary and conditions determining their impact are liable to change, the satisfactions of vanity are fleeting and therefore in need of continual reinforcement. So, while *any* object possessed by a man is potentially capable of enhancing his vanity, its generative and replenishing powers are limited by the conditions outlined above. This interplay between the subjective social valuation of objects and the subjectivities they sustain is indicative of the inescapable materiality of self-constitution.

The Man in the Mirror: Mimetic Communication, or, the Force of Fellow-Feeling

Vanity's most significant cause, arguably, is the positive 'fellow-feeling' that circulates between bodies and things. On the accumulation of affective judgments inspired by property and persons, Hume writes: 'Our reputation, our character, our name are considerations of vast weight and importance; and even the other causes of pride; virtue, beauty, and riches; have little influence when not seconded by the opinions and sentiments of others' (p. 206). Because social 'sentiments' carry real 'weight', the things we strive to amass become effectually 'nothings' if not 'seconded' through the approbation of others. Smith highlights man's physical yearning for favorable notice also, observing the universal desire of men 'to stand in that situation which sets them most in the view of general sympathy and attention' (p. 70). When positive feelings come one's way, self-satisfaction is enhanced, while the negative feelings of others diminish one's sense of well-being. Vanity is the deeply felt disposition toward these transient feelings, originating with one's idea of oneself as 'the object of the observation and fellow-feeling of every body about him' (p. 62). Swelling or shrinking under the eye of 'every body', vanity vibrates to the regard—real or imagined—others give to its person and possessions.

This 'fellow-feeling', known by the moral philosophers as 'sympathy', is both social and material, feeding the vanity that awaits attention.[16] Smith observes that the 'stranger to society' would think nothing of his 'own character' nor the 'beauty or deformity of his own mind and face', but this changes in the company of men (p. 129). He writes,

> Bring him into society and he is immediately provided with the mirror which he wanted before. It is placed in the countenance and behavior of those he lives with, which always mark when they enter into, and when they disapprove of his sentiments; and it is here that he first views the propriety and impropriety of his own passions, the beauty and deformity of his own mind. (p. 129)

[16] Unlike Hume, Smith generally insists upon man's imaginative agency in his judgment of others and self, and yet he nevertheless emphasizes the physical sensation occasioned by moral judgment in a manner that anticipates Brennan's definition of affect.

Where the attention of Smith's 'natural man' is wholly occupied with the 'external bodies which either pleased or hurt him', social man attends to the 'mirrors' conveying other men's sympathy, the carrier of positive and negative affects that beget new objects. For the man in society experiences his passions as the objects of his thoughts—'things' that 'interest him deeply, and often call upon his most attentive consideration' (pp. 129–30). Man's moments of self-reflection are affected and effected by social responses to his person and behavior, and he thereby confronts impassioned objects that 'will now often become the causes of new desires and new aversions, new joys and new sorrows' (p. 129). These ever-changing objects—reflections of others' affects—are in fluid relation to one another: 'The object may evoke the affect, or the affect find the object', Silvan Tomkins argues.[17] In this field of ever-shifting feeling, the product of myriad mirroring objects, we find an explanation for identity's fundamental instability, its vain subjection to copious affect.

The precariousness of selfhood in the face of 'mimetic communication' is implicit in the abundance of metaphors suggesting bodily corruption. Referring to voluntary and involuntary corporeally-based forms of mirroring, Anna Gibbs writes: 'At the heart of mimesis is affect contagion … the bioneurological means by which particular affects are transmitted from body to body' (p. 191).[18] Affects are communicated rapidly and automatically through the 'synchrony of facial expressions, vocalizations, postures and movements' between two persons because when close by they tend 'to converge emotionally' (p. 186). Echoing Smith's emphasis on the mirror-like 'countenance', Gibbs, Brennan, and Tomkins highlight the ease with which we 'read' faces, tones, and gestures for affective information. Our most 'remarkable' human quality, according to Hume, is this 'propensity … to receive by communication [others'] inclinations and sentiments, however different from, *or even contrary to,* our own' (p. 206, emphasis added). But the involuntary nature of Humean sympathy, our susceptibility to 'emotional contagion' from without (p. 236) and the negative as well as positive affects, leaves us painfully pliant. We are buoyed energetically by the interest, excitement, or 'living attention' of others, writes Brennan (p. 24); we are depleted by the introjection of others' bad affect, a more likely event if we are socially subordinate and prone to the 'dumping' of others. Because personal vanity and identity are bound up with these circulating affects, most persons strive for a sense of affirmation, seeking unconsciously to minimize the residue of affects that diminish them. Megan Watkins observes that 'affects

[17] Silvan Tomkins, *Shame and Its Sisters*, eds. Eve Kosofsky Sedgwick and Adam Frank (Durham, NC: Duke University Press, 1995), p. 55.

[18] Anna Gibbs, 'After Affect: Sympathy, Synchrony, and Mimetic Communication', in *The Affect Theory Reader*, eds. Melissa Gregg and Gregory J. Seigworth (Durham, NC: Duke University Press, 2010), pp. 186–205.

are the corporeal instantiation of recognition' (p. 273), with the capacity 'to be retained, to accumulate, to form dispositions and thus shape subjectivities' (p. 269).[19] One's sense of self-worth reflects the pattern of accumulated affect, although the relational structure of affect transmission leaves one highly attuned to mirroring others. This 'constellation of affects' skews negative for women, whose limited self-'enhancement' opportunities and social function as mirrors leave them putative empty vessels for the projections of powerful men.[20]

The Woman in the Mirror: 'One Gay Assemblage'

The characters of women—'matter too soft a lasting mark to bear'—were considered to be more prone to the power of circulating affects and agential things.[21] Philosophers may speak of vain or proud men in their treatises, but poets and pedagogues worry more about women. In *Strictures on the Education of Young Women* (1799), Hannah More argues that vanity 'is uniformly to be controlled, as an active, a restless, a growing principle ... which not only mixes itself with all our faults, but insinuates itself into all our virtues too; and will, if not checked effectually, rob our best actions of their reward'.[22] Vanity's transmission is subtle and insidious, its power addictive; dependent on the support of external objects and others, its strength grows in a way that intensifies its need. This belief underscores the metaphor of intoxication employed by Richard Lovell and Maria Edgeworth, which evokes the pleasure of our vain reflections, as well as their apparently toxic consequences.[23] Writing of the 'patient' (p. 301) who has received quantities of praise 'too large and lavish' when young, the Edgeworths observe she 'languishes for want of the excitation which custom has rendered almost essential' to character, a 'disease' that 'succeeds to the intoxication of vanity' (p. 307). Like More's text, *Practical Education* (1800) reflects highly gendered assumptions about

[19] Megan Watkins, 'Desiring Recognition, Accumulating Affect', in *The Affect Theory Reader*, eds. Melissa Gregg and Gregory J. Seigworth (Durham, NC: Duke University Press, 2010), pp. 269–85.

[20] Similar to Watkins's account of the subject-in-process, Brennan defines the ego as a 'constellation of affects, grouped in clusters of associations (verbal and visual) around certain subjective fantasmatic positions' (p. 118). This unstable constellation is protected through the projection or dumping of one's negative affect upon others, the resistance of bad affect through discernment, and the 'enhancement' of its 'literal well being' through the addition of attention's 'actual living force' (p. 37).

[21] Alexander Pope, 'Epistle II. To a Lady. Of the Characters of Women', 1743, line 3, at https://www.ling.upenn.edu/courses/hum100/lady.html.

[22] Hannah More, *Strictures on the Modern System of Female Education*, ed. Gina Luria, 2 vols. (Shrewsbury: Garland Press, 1974), I: p. 38.

[23] Maria and Richard Lovell Edgeworth, *Practical Education*, ed. Gina Lurie, 2 vols. (New York: Garland Press, 1974), II: p. 307.

the mechanics of vanity, distinguishing it from pride through telling *prosopopoeia*: 'vanity cannot support herself without the concurring flattery of others', they write, but 'pride is satisfied with his own approbation' (p. 308). Emblematic of mainstream thought, the Edgeworths' construction associates self-complacency and substantive objects (i.e., real property) with masculine pride, while 'feminine' vanity and the self's constitution depend on superficial objects and empty praise.

And yet the necessity of pleasing is paramount for the eighteenth-century woman, who must catch the eye of 'the man without' as well as his sentiments.[24] Smith characterizes vanity as 'sprightly', 'gay', and often 'good-natured', observing that it drives a 'desire to oblige in all little matters' (p. 303). And most middle-class women were educated to 'oblige', for while the proud man might 'disdain to court your esteem', a woman had no such luxury (Smith, p. 301). The pedagogues seem to miss the inherently social and material nature of female vanity: its 'restless' 'insinuation' or 'intoxication', the reflections of others' affective judgments, the displacement of objectionable affect, and its active cultivation through cultural norms and expectations. *His* dependence upon *her,* an ostensible object, as the mirror that exaggerates his self-importance is doubly ironic, as her vanity becomes the concentrated force behind his pride of self. For male pride swells on the pleasure occasioned by his possession of the woman, a 'sight' for other, answering eyes as well. 'The vanity of power' Hume observes in many men is 'much augmented by the consideration of the persons, over whom [they] exercise [their] authority' (p. 205), and boosted again, presumably, by those who witness that asymmetrical relation. Male power may be 'enhanced' through the 'living attention' of his subordinates (Brennan, p. 37), but this requires a deflection of her attention to self, while her subordinate status leaves her vulnerable to the depletions of affective 'dumping' (Brennan, p. 37).

Smith claims 'the great secret of education is to direct vanity to proper objects' (p. 305), and most women were taught that a 'desire to oblige in all little matters' begins and ends with the home. Denied university educations, profitable occupations, and any obvious means of rising in the world but through marriage, women were forced to support vanity, and themselves, through things dismissed as trivial (Wollstonecraft, *Vindication,* p. 375). Late eighteenth-century women lacked land, houses, and wealth—durable objects that would enhance their value most in others' eyes—so they assembled comparably superficial objects for self-support. 'Pin money' in place of a proper

[24] Smith distinguishes between the morally sound character inspired by the 'impartial spectator' and that which only reflects the capricious 'man without', whose 'jurisdiction ... is founded altogether in the desire of actual praise and in the aversion to actual blame' (p. 150).

inheritance, jewelry, clothing, and bibelots: however sumptuous the personalty showered upon women of the upper and striving middle classes, its very mobility and transience rendered it a less effective 'prop' than real property. Women might be vain of their beauty or fashionable attire or manners, but the impermanence of all—the inevitability of aging or becoming outdated—limits their force as agential things. The *feme covert* had it little better than the *feme sole* and was dispossessed of her fortune or wages, her very identity under law. She could take limited pride in her family or home because her proprietary claims were negligible according to law and custom. Hume writes, 'the imagination naturally turns to whatever is important and considerable', and because 'the male sex has the advantage above the female, the husband first engages' and holds others' attention, even when it reaches him 'by passing thro' related objects' (p. 201). Whatever objects reflect well or poorly upon the pair, onlookers regard 'him with greater satisfaction' and 'with greater facility than his consort' (p. 201). Even in the case of children, whose maternal tie only is verifiable, the imagination's associative tendencies 'must strengthen the child's relation to the father, and weaken that to the mother' (p. 201). The very things a woman is *supposed* to want are insufficient supports to their vanity, including her offspring, her most obvious and intimate possession. Given the transience, the mediated nature, and the alleged triviality of things available to women, how are *they* to 'swell and dilate' (Smith, pp. 61–2) what Jonathan Lamb might call their 'thin subjectivity'?[25]

One means of proclaiming their presence in the face of diminishing affects and trivial nothings is for women to project or externalize 'conceit' and effect what I term a 'gay assemblage'. Writing on Deleuzian assemblage and the political import of 'affective fashion', Stephen Seeley demonstrates how human subjects might 'confront the nonhuman forces that compose them and through which they locate and seize the "lines of becoming" that traverse them'.[26] In other words, women can subvert the social norms prescribing what 'becomes' them by 'deforming' the things through which they are constructed and 'rearticulat[ing] the very ideals and norms of the feminine body itself' (p. 252). One such assemblage is suggested in the raptures of a fashionable Londoner in *The Twin Sisters; or, the Effects of Education* (1788), a three-volume-bound bit of miscellany that personifies 'copious nothingness'. Lady Priscilla Blomer, confidante and corrupter of the 'bad' twin Amelia, writes a letter lamenting her husband's interruption of her feminine conceits:

[25] Lamb defines 'thin subjectivity' as reflective of a state 'where nothing is owned, and nothing can simply be told from a secure position by a subject' (p. 28).

[26] Stephen D. Seeley, 'How Do You Dress a Body Without Organs?: Affective Fashion and Nonhuman Becoming', *WSQ: Women's Studies Quarterly*, 41: 1–2 (Spring/Summer 2013), p. 251.

> I shall never forgive him the loss of one this morning—I had been three hours planning the sweetest dress—The train was to be Circassian and azure—the body French and vermillion—the sleeves Italian and violet—and the trimmings—Oh! the trimmings! they were *one gay assemblage* of all sorts of things, and of all manner of colours! foils, French beads—and feathers: fringe, foliage, wreaths, and peacocks tails mingled and strayed in beautiful confusion, while dangling tassels elegantly swam on every side in light relief, as they sustain'd the gay festoons: and lo! this unlucky man demolish'd the whole idea ere 'twas well form'd in fancy's floating loom![27]

Lady Priscilla is extravagant in her description, and readers are clearly meant to see her husband's 'demolition' as justified, her excess distasteful, and her 'brilliance' superficial. And yet the superabundance of things described animates her character, lending energy to her vision of 'beautiful confusion' and highlighting 'one gay assemblage' in the chain of bodies that compose a woman's life. Captured in its unfinished state, before "twas well form'd', Lady Priscilla's dress mirrors the 'becoming-woman' who envisions it. Seeley emphasizes that Deleuze and Guattari's 'becoming-woman' is 'not a progression toward the dominant constructions of womanhood but is, instead, the process of deterritorializing one's body, mind, and desire from its capture and organization by a phallocentric economy that dictates the terms of femininity in advance' (p. 252). Her 'deterritorialization'—a blurring not only of subject–object but also human–nonhuman boundaries—is effected through her resistance to sartorial national integrity, the confusion of colors and countries, and the incorporation of animal parts.

Lady Priscilla's insistence on 'gaiety' is quite telling too: recall that Smith associates it with vanity, but it also connotes a commitment to social pleasure, promiscuity, and dissolution—euphemistically, even prostitution. Most striking, however, is her implicit assertion of affective need *and* resistance. Lady Priscilla chooses gaiety over filial tenderness, a sign of her desire for 'light relief': 'He will have it, that when I am a mother, all my present gay pursuits will yield to those of love and tenderness: for that my child will make an interest for him in my heart, and will not only plead in its own, but in its father's favour' (p. 138). Refusing the heart's occupation by father and son, Lady Priscilla occupies herself instead with 'a thousand brilliant thoughts and designs' (p. 137). Set side by side with a fashionable woman's 'conceits', Burney's investment in her literary offspring seems 'subversive' indeed (Friedman, p. 59). 'Like the 'gay assemblage' of 'fancy's floating loom' communicated by letter, the copious

[27] Anon., *The Twin Sisters; or, the Effects of Education. A Novel; in a series of letters.* (Dublin: Printed for H. Colbert, [1788] 1792), p. 138, emphasis added.

'nothings' of women are 'impossible to domesticate'; such romances were seen as inherently 'bad fictions', Lamb argues, 'from which *nothing* useful or benevolent can emerge' (p. 170, emphasis added). But the utility of bad fiction is in fact quite clear: 'nothings' divert readers and writers' affective attention from domestic cares, disrupting the projections of masculine prerogative.

The Power of Copious Nothings

The circulation of 'copious nothings' is therefore widely lamented by late eighteenth-century professional reviewers who fear the transmission of affect between women through novels (or between novels through women). Consider Wollstonecraft's 'demolition' of one lady's 'gay assemblage' in her 1788 review of *Edward and Harriet, or the Happy Recovery: A Sentimental Novel.* Dismissing the novel as a fictional farrago from line one, she declares it to be a 'heterogeneous mass of folly, affectation, and improbability', replete with 'metaphors and vulgarisms' (Wollstonecraft, 7: p. 19). Attacks on 'bad form' and excess abound in such reviews, a disembodied echo of the affective judgments assailing women's bodies and characters daily. Bad affect—harsh judgment, envy, shame—attaches more easily to women and their things, as Brennan argues and as Wollstonecraft implies in another review, on Charlotte Smith's *Emmeline* (1788): 'This story is much superior to the generality of mis-shapen monsters, daily brought forth to poison the minds of our young females, by fostering vanity, and teaching affectation'.[28] Here, as in Burney's imagery, one is struck by the aggressive physicality of the things assailing women—novels of monstrous proportions, unmanageable progeny, 'poisonous' passions. Fears about the corruption of mind and body are given palpable form, as the vanity associated with reading and writing novels makes (and unmakes) the characters of young women. The complex bond between women's bodies and their books is evident in Burney's attachment to her 'offspring', an interest that is proprietary, maternal, and material. But *Cecelia*'s proximity to the 'copious nothings' of the 'promiscuous herd' breeds anxiety over identifications that threaten the integrity of mother and 'daughter' alike.[29]

Corrupting 'feminized spaces' (Pearson, p. 165) like the circulating library are therefore regarded with keen distaste by novelists and reviewers dedicated to 'organizing a phallocentric economy' (Seeley, p. 252). Henry Mackenzie blames

[28] Brennan, p. 15; Mary Wollstonecraft, *The Works of Mary Wollstonecraft*, eds. Janet Todd and Marilyn Butler, 7 vols. (New York: New York University Press, 1989), VII: p. 26.

[29] Burney speaks figuratively here, but John Mullen cites an entry in Robert James's *Medicinal Dictionary* (1743–5) under 'Imaginatio' that concerns a pregnant woman's affective transference to her child: 'The improper and volatile "Desire" raised in the woman by reading the wrong books or thinking the wrong thoughts intervenes in the process of the reproduction of the social order' (p. 223).

'the wretched offspring of circulating libraries' for the 'debasement of the Novel', offering a brief history of the form's decline in his magazine *The Lounger*:

> All whose necessities or vanity prompted them to write, betook themselves to a field, which, as they imagined, it required no extent of information or depth of learning to cultivate, but in which a heated imagination, or an excursive fancy, were alone sufficient to succeed; and men of genius and knowledge, despising a province in which such competitors were to be met, retired from it in disgust, and left it in the hands of the unworthy. (p. 329)[30]

Here, as at the Temple of Vanity, the body reigns supreme; Mackenzie's field is abandoned by disgusted 'conscious craftsmen' (Castle, p. 201) and left to the uncontrolled fancies of women. Elsewhere, library users are threatened by 'filthy streams of spiritual and moral pollution' (Pearson, p. 164). The books in circulation are 'deformed' in a Deleuzian sense either by '"powder and pomatum between the leaves" or returned "soil'd and dog-ear'd" by a sluttish female borrower' (qtd. in Pearson, p. 165). Carriers of bodily residue and affective traces, women's novels have a sensual force born of women writers and readers' accumulated affect. Pleasure, anger, resistance, gaiety, vanity, venality: all and more are transmitted through the bodies involved. Elspeth Probyn argues writing is a 'corporeal activity' that 'takes its toll on the body that writes and the bodies that read', and the 'panting reader' in Wollstonecraft's review of *The Castle of Mowbray: an English Romance* (1789) is a prime example (7: p. 350).[31] Readers are meant to '"catch" the writer's interest' (Probyn, p. 76)—perhaps the one form of affect 'dumping' and introjection that is pleasurable for women.

Lamb argues that 'thin subjectivities' (p. 28) are easily overwhelmed by the things they encounter, but women's flimsy novels actually *support* the vanity selfhood requires. Indeed, one obvious attraction of sentimental novels was the 'infusion of vanity' from 'ninety-nine novels out of a hundred' (Wollstonecraft, 7: p. 82). Endless hyperbole, overwrought diction, a superfluity of improbable incident, powerful 'nobodies' who fascinate everybody: the very grandiosity of this fictional matter would appeal to readers 'deformed' (Seeley, p. 252) through identification with larger-than-life characters.[32] Lamenting the peculiar susceptibility of the female 'mirror', the Edgeworths observe that

[30] Henry Mackenzie, *The Lounger*, Saturday, 18 June 1785, qtd. in Williams, p. 331.

[31] Elspeth Probyn, 'Writing Shame', in *The Affect Theory Reader*, eds. Melissa Gregg and Gregory J. Seigworth (Durham, NC: Duke University Press, 2010), p. 76.

[32] Cf. Catherine Gallagher, *Nobody's Story: The Vanishing Acts of Women Writers in the Marketplace, 1670–1820* (Berkeley: University of California Press, 1994).

'[w]omen, who have been much addicted to novel reading, are always acting in imitation of some Jemima, or Almeria, who never existed, and they perpetually mistake plain William and Thomas for "*My Beverly!*"' (p. 297). The attraction of exalted or grandiose things is explained by Brown, who speaks to 'their force as a sensuous presence': 'thingness amounts to a latency (the not yet formed or the not yet formable) and to an excess (what remains … irreducible to objects)' ('Thing', p. 5). The extravagant excess of sentimental novels must attract the not yet formed, not yet formable 'becoming-woman' reader who eyes her future with dismay (Seeley, p. 252); feeling her own limitations, she might 'seize the lines of becoming' (Seeley, p. 251) and temporarily transform through the force of a sensuous presence.

Readers' emulation of fictional characters is a testament to the powerful 'latency' of things and the 'libidinal investments' made in 'empty, beautiful forms' or fantasy selves.[33] Consider the heroine of the 1791 translation of Françoise-Albine Benoist's novel *Aspasia; or, the Dangers of Vanity*. Her own identity is never disclosed; unnamed for the entirety of the novel, she agrees to take on the eponymous pseudonym at the urging of the man who seduces her:

> Of the 'goddesses of pleasure' the Baron says, 'Their manner of living is delicious, their society charming—There is not one of them so accomplished as yourself. You might eclipse them all, if you would follow my advice. … What are you?—What are the means of your existence, but precarious? I can see no way of your escaping from obscurity. If you had a name, a fortune, one might lament your error; and still leave you shackled by vulgar prejudices; but in your situation, favoured in the highest degree with all the gifts of nature, a decided character, a tender heart, a charming person, formed for love, and better than all that, a strong understanding'—I made a movement of surprise mingled with satisfaction. 'Yes, you are made for elevated sentiments; you shall be the modern Aspasia'.[34]

Because the unknown heroine lacks the objects—a name, a fortune—that would make her a 'somebody', 'Aspasia' functions as a fiction of selfhood that proclaims its own fictionality. 'What are you?', the Baron asks, crassly exposing the Humean 'custom and practice' that determines a 'subject' of vanity's value. But her desire to be known and singular is palpable, the fame

[33] Barbara Johnson, *Persons and Things* (Cambridge, MA: Harvard University Press, 2008), p. 59.

[34] Françoise-Albine Benoist, *Aspasia; or, the Dangers of Vanity. A French Story, Taken from Real Life*, trans. Anon. (London: Printed for J. Bew, No. 28 Paternoster Row, 1791), pp. 24–5.

she seeks assured. To escape from obscurity, she must both emulate *and* surpass the 'goddesses of pleasure'—become a 'gay assemblage' of the 'gifts of nature', the only property of which she is possessed. The fantasy of selfhood presented here is encouragingly empty, Aspasia's 'decided character', generic, illusory, and easily mirrored. Among the 'elevated sentiments' and adulation for which this cipher is 'made', a reader might 'swell and dilate' in vicarious 'satisfaction', pleasured by the positive feeling aimed at her 'like object', yet transmitted to her as well.

The 'wretched offspring of circulating libraries' not only possess the power to 'deform' the becoming-woman's character but, in the hands of the sufficiently vain, to reproduce themselves. Aspasia's account of the 'dangers' of vanity actually concludes quite happily: in retirement with her beloved, she writes when 'alone, and these memoirs ... are the fruit of [her] reflections and [her] amusements' (2: p. 319). Aspasia's 'fruitfulness' supports her vanity as nothing else could. Describing vanity's causes, Hume argues, 'All objects, in a word, that are useful, beautiful, or surprising ... may, by means of property, give rise to this passion' (p. 202), and one particularly suggestive example is that of the 'surprizing adventures' (p. 196) one might recount to her friends. The predictable amusements reproduced in Aspasia's composition are 'nothings' arrayed in abundance, supporting vanity with common intellectual property that nonetheless bears her name. The transmission of narrative desire between writer and reader is imagined by More, who illuminates a 'gay assemblage' in the making:

> A thorough-paced novel-reading miss, at the close of every tissue of hackneyed adventures, feels within herself the stirring impulse of corresponding genius, and triumphantly exclaims, 'And I, too, am an author!' The glutted imagination soon overflows with the redundance of cheap sentiment and plentiful incident; and by a sort of arithmetical proportion, is enabled, by the perusal of any three novels, to produce a fourth; till every fresh production, like the progeny of Banquo, is followed by
>
> Another, and another, and another! (p. 93)

More's sarcasm clearly undercuts the corresponding 'genius' of writer and reader, but her account is nonetheless provocative. Note the 'redundance' of sentiment and 'plentiful' incidents, the 'tissue' of hackneyed adventures: the 'glutted imagination' is overwhelmed by affect and the 'copious nothings' that pleasure its reader. 'Swelling and dilating' the reader's ambition, this particular confluence of things has material consequences. Wollstonecraft's review of the 1788 novel *Agitation* is also emblematic: 'From reading to writing novels the transition is very easy. ... A frivolous imagination diffuses itself on paper, and *gives life to* the scenes it has delighted to revel in' (7: pp. 19–20, emphasis added). Note the almost automatic animation of the page; the imagination is employed without will or intention, diffusing itself and reflexively recreating the scenes of other women's fantasies. The animated texts produce 'another, and another, and another!' automatically, effortlessly, even gaily.

Because of the 'period's constant elision of textuality and sexuality' (Pearson, p. 87), it is perhaps inevitable that 'birth topoi' in the review of women's novels take on a tenor both insulting and lewd. Critics complain often about the 'easy' imitation of novelists, and even Wollstonecraft conflates women writers' 'production' with questionable character: 'It has been sarcastically said, by a snarling poet, that most women have no character at all: we shall apply it to their production—Novels. The one before us, evidently written by a lady, is so like many other flimsy novels we have reviewed that we scarcely know how to characterize it' (7: p. 191). Echoing Pope's 'Epistle II. To a Lady' (1743), Wollstonecraft suggests that 'bad fiction' (Lamb, p. 170) is inseparable from its maker, and she shames literary mother and child alike. But lack of character in this instance also implies an absence of originality or creativity, the equation of which is testament to the Romantic turn in the birth metaphor's usage.[35] Wollstonecraft's irritation with the formulaic, mechanical nature of women's fiction is unmistakable in repeated allusions to 'flimsy' (7: p. 82). Among the many reviewers who employed this term, George Canning's description of the 'flimsy' novel is typical—a 'silly story, without weight, or art'.[36] But 'flimsy' has connotations beyond light and trivial. It referred also to a thin kind of paper used to multiply copies, a definition that subtly reinforces the mimetic communicability and self-propagating power of 'seducing books'.[37] In this sense novels have the power to corrupt character *and* to reproduce themselves through an apparently automatic reassemblage of other women's words. Writing of the copious popular fiction published by William Lane's Minerva Press from the 1790 to 1820, Elizabeth A. Neiman argues that 'when Minerva novelists "borrow" popular literary conventions they … forge connections among each other, creating a collective (or "generic") model of authorship'.[38] Given these material connections and the transmission of affect they occasion, I would argue in conclusion that women's literary offspring have greater force than their neoclassical counterparts. The birth metaphor resonates more strongly, means differently for women, not

[35] Castle demonstrates that the childbirth metaphor carries a positive valence again only with the rise of Romantic theories of spontaneous, organic creativity (pp. 203–5).

[36] George Canning, in *Novel and Romance 1700–1800*, ed. Ioan Williams (London: Routledge, 2010), p. 342.

[37] *OED*, 'Flimsy', B.2.

[38] Elizabeth A. Neiman, 'A New Perspective on the Minerva Press's "Derivative" Novels: Authorizing Borrowed Material', *European Romantic Review*, 26: 5 (2015), p. 634.

only, as Friedman suggests, because their procreative capacities honor the integration of body and mind but also because only *literary* offspring can be wholly claimed by women. Reflecting on their 'mothers' as no other form of property might, these 'productions of vanity' are durable, if not immortal, and peculiar to *them*, if not quite singular.

Burney's 'copious nothings', an image born of her fears for *Cecilia,* signal her sense that 'reading appears a solitary, transgressive, even masturbatory act whose impulses need to be redirected into a male-dominated, outward looking sociality (and, by implication, sexuality)' (Pearson, pp. 107–8). The widespread conflation of author and offspring, of novel and genital 'no-thing', is evidenced by the intercourse of literary reviewers who participate in the 'capture and organization' of women's bodies, minds, and desires (Seeley, p. 252). But 'nothings' matter immensely to the women who possess them, despite the cheapening disregard of socially-dominant others. Lamb accounts for the seeming disjunction of empty things and their powers of attraction:

> An unmediated meeting between a thing and a human will result therefore in these alternatives: either its emptiness will be derided as unmeaning matter, or its fullness (its faculty of being exactly what it is) will be worshipped. ... In the latter case the passions of the spectator ... are invested in the thing and instantly it is transformed ... absorb[ing] the impressions it has made on the human imagination, and there it stands the visible cause of its fantastic effects. (p. xii)

The critics of women's fiction dismiss copious nothings as 'unmeaning matter', in part to regulate female desire, in part because they fail to see meaning in their 'fantastic effects'. But the lovers of 'bad fiction' *depend* upon things pregnant with vanity; they are 'requisite in a character'. Possessed by a 'redundance of cheap sentiment', copious nothings transmit the powerful, accumulated affects of women, reproducing them with ever greater material force. The vanity 'fostered'—another form of the textual 'offspring' Burney envisions—has the power to swell and dilate thin subjectivities. More materially, vanity fosters the 'deforming' powers of authorial assemblage, demolishing the forms so 'becoming' to women, rearticulating relations between their bodies and things. Gaily upending gendered ontologies and objectifications, vain nothings are vital indeed.

Bibliography

Benoist, Françoise-Albine. *Aspasia; or, the Dangers of Vanity. A French Story, Taken from Real Life,* trans. Anon. London: Printed for J. Bew, No. 28 Paternoster Row, 1791.

Brennan, Teresa. *The Transmission of Affect.* Ithaca, NY: Cornell University Press, 2004.

Brown, Bill. *A Sense of Things: The Object Matter of American Literature.* Chicago, IL: University of Chicago Press, 2003.

——. 'Thing Theory'. In *Things.* Chicago, IL: University of Chicago Press, 2004, pp. 1–22.

Burney, Frances. *Cecilia,* ed. Peter Sabor. New York: Oxford University Press, 1988.

Castle, Terry. 'Lab'ring Bards: Birth *Topoi* and English Poetics 1660–1820'. *Journal of English and Germanic Philology,* 78 (1979), pp. 193–208.

Crump, Justine. *A Known Scribbler: Frances Burney on Literary Life.* Toronto, ON: Broadview, 2002.

Edgeworth, Maria and Richard Lovell. *Practical Education,* ed. Gina Lurie. 2 vols. New York: Garland Press, 1974.

Friedman, Susan Stanford. 'Creativity and the Childbirth Metaphor: Gender Difference in Literary Discourse'. *Feminist Studies,* 13: 1 (Spring 1987), pp. 49–82.

Gibbs, Anna. 'After Affect: Sympathy, Synchrony, and Mimetic Communication'. In *The Affect Theory Reader,* eds. Melissa Gregg and Gregory J. Seigworth. Durham, NC: Duke University Press, 2010, pp. 186–205.

Hume, David. *A Treatise on Human Nature,* eds. David Fate Norton and Mary J. Norton. Oxford: Oxford University Press, 2005.

Johnson, Barbara. *Persons and Things.* Cambridge, MA: Harvard University Press, 2008.

Lamb, Jonathan. 'Modern Metamorphoses and Disgraceful Tales'. *Critical Inquiry,* 28: 1, *Things* (Autumn 2001), pp. 133–66.

——. *The Things Things Say.* Princeton, NJ: Princeton University Press, 2011.

Mandal, Anthony. 'Fiction'. In *The Cambridge Companion to Women's Writing in the Romantic Period,* ed. Devoney Looser. Cambridge: Cambridge University Press, 2015, pp. 16–31.

Mitchell, W.J.T. 'Romanticism and the Life of Things: Fossils, Totems, and Images'. In *Things,* ed. Bill Brown. Chicago, IL: University of Chicago Press, 2004, pp. 227–44.

More, Hannah. *Strictures on the Modern System of Female Education,* ed. Gina Luria, 2 vols. Shrewsbury: Garland Press, 1974.

Mullen, John. *Sentiment and Sociability: The Language of Feeling in the Eighteenth Century.* Oxford: Clarendon Press, 2000.

Neiman, Elizabeth A. 'A New Perspective on the Minerva Press's "Derivative" Novels: Authorizing Borrowed Material'. *European Romantic Review*, 26: 5 (2015), pp. 633–58.

Pearson, Jacqueline. *Women's Reading in Britain, 1750–1835: A Dangerous Recreation.* Cambridge: Cambridge University Press, 1999.

Probyn, Elspeth. 'Writing Shame'. In *The Affect Theory Reader,* eds. Melissa Gregg and Gregory J. Seigworth. Durham, NC: Duke University Press, 2010, pp. 71–90.

St Clair, William. *The Reading Nation in the Romantic Period.* Cambridge: Cambridge University Press, 2004.

Sedgwick, Eve Kosofsky and Adam Frank, eds. *Shame and Its Sisters: A Silvan Tomkins Reader.* Durham, NC: Duke University Press, 1995.

Seeley, Stephen D. 'How Do You Dress a Body Without Organs?: Affective Fashion and Nonhuman Becoming'. *WSQ: Women's Studies Quarterly*, 41: 1–2 (Spring/Summer 2013), pp. 247–65.

Smith, Adam. *The Theory of Moral Sentiments*, ed. Knud Haakonssen. Cambridge: Cambridge University Press, 2009.

The Twin Sisters; or, the Effects of Education. A Novel; in a series of letters. By a Lady. Dublin: Printed for H. Colbert, No. 135 Capel-street, [1788] 1792.

Watkins, Megan. 'Desiring Recognition, Accumulating Affect'. In *The Affect Theory Reader,* eds. Melissa Gregg and Gregory J. Seigworth. Durham, NC: Duke University Press, 2010, pp. 269–85.

Williams, Ioan, ed. *Novel and Romance 1700–1800.* London: Routledge, 2010.

Wollstonecraft, Mary. *The Collected Letters of Mary Wollstonecraft*, ed. Ralph Wardle. Ithaca, NY: Cornell University Press, 1979

——. *A Vindication of the Rights of Woman.* In *The Norton Anthology of Literature by Women,* vol. 1. New York: Norton, 2007.

——. *The Works of Mary Wollstonecraft,* eds. Janet Todd and Marilyn Butler. 7 vols. New York: New York University Press, 1989.

Chapter Seven

Revolutionary Objects in Elizabeth Inchbald's *Nature and Art*

Mark Lounibos

Introduction: Objects/Chora/Chiasmus

At the beginning of Elizabeth Inchbald's 1796 English Jacobin novel *Nature and Art*, two young brothers, William and Henry, the 'sons of a country shopkeeper who had lately died insolvent', find themselves struggling in the competitive labor markets of late eighteenth-century London.[1] They subsist on odd jobs and errands but are frustrated in their search for more stable employment by a lack of resources and social connections. At wit's end, the younger brother, Henry, finally recalls a bit of training that might serve them in their desperation. Inchbald chooses to narrate this early turn of fortune by addressing the audience directly in the last sentence of Chapter II, emphasizing the moment's significance even as she freights it with irony. What was Henry's life-saving skill? 'Reader, Henry could play upon the fiddle' (p. 43).

This fortuitous recollection of musical ability is crucial, since Henry's subsequent success will not only raise their social position but also inaugurate a split between the brothers that will guide the novel's exploration of 'nature' and 'art'. The fiddle marks this tension because it is not only a specific material artifact of late eighteenth-century English culture but also an example of the conceptual drift that categorical distinctions like nature and art, object and subject, and rich and poor sought to police. Inchbald's engagement with materiality broadly construed emerges out of the novel's political commitment to observe and comment on the ways in which objects of all sorts, from the fiddle to, most importantly for this argument, women-as-objects, have served

[1] Elizabeth Inchbald, *Nature and Art*, ed. Shawn Lisa Maurer (Ontario: Broadview Press, [1796] 2005), p. 41.

the paradoxical function of exemplifying both the transgressive drift and the categories themselves. What has been described as the novel's unwieldy blend of didacticism, political radicalism, and conventional romance may be productively read as an acute sensitivity to the profound shifts in human and nonhuman relationships being driven by early industrial capitalism and the accompanying representational reassignments of material agents. Henry's 'fiddling' is only one example of how these border crossings unsettle conventional categories and metaphorically offer the possibility of a more productive relationship with materiality in which the vibrations set off by a bow and a string reverberate and ramify in ways that elude and perhaps even undo the binaries of objectification and exploitation. In this sense, Inchbald's engagement with materiality encompasses class, gender, and ecological exploitation in general.

The terms 'nature' and 'art' in this context refer to the nature/culture binary which still informs much of the contemporary debate regarding economic, social, and ecological justice. In the conventional reading of Inchbald's novel, 'nature' is Rousseauvian, innocent, and honest, while 'art' indicates human practices designed to identify and reinforce the divisions. Henry's untutored fiddling expresses his natural quality, even as the aesthetic pleasure it produces in listeners involves an art. The fiddle also exemplifies this distinction, being composed of natural materials, artfully synthesized into a musical object. Inchbald's explicit attention to material objects, along with her interest in the relations between these objects and human subjects, elides this conventional reading of the nature/art dichotomy and gestures towards a more revolutionary account of material agency.

Both nonhuman and human objects in the novel are notable not only for their productive power but also for the speed with which they are discarded, elided, or ignored by the human, primarily male, subjects profiting from their productivity. This disavowal occurs often at the very moment of exploitation itself and requires rapid shifts in categorization. Objects are afforded the richness and complexity of subjects only as long as such status is necessary for exploitation. Then, at the moment of plundering, they become bare, exhausted, objects again. Inchbald registers these shifts as a kind of conceptual chiasmus, where materiality crosses back and forth between the categories of object and subject. Rather than reifying these distinctions, Inchbald's attention, focused through the tension between nature and art, marks the two categories as reversible and fluid rather than fixed, in turn recognizing this fluidity as a function of materiality itself.

There is a distinction here between chiasmus in its classical rhetorical sense and the more revolutionary idea of a conceptual chiasmus. The classical chiasmus functions as a kind of illusion in which the reversal in syntax suggests a structural symmetry: ask not what your country can do for you, but what you can do for your country. By inverting the structure and fixing it, a new persuasive point is won. In contrast, a conceptual chiasmus works towards reciprocity by reversing and keeping open the passage.[2] As such, it instantiates a radical revolutionary perspective. Instead of a one-way trip, we have stochastic loops, returning, ramifying. They use language (irony, reversals, repetitions) to open the possibility of new perception and, in doing so, gesture towards the potential of revolutionary objects.

By narrating the ways that potentially vibrant human and nonhuman materiality is too often limited or impoverished, Inchbald's novel highlights the relationship between objectification and exploitation and suggests a more revolutionary attitude towards materiality itself, one where the agency of both isolated and aggregated things remains open to new forms and entanglements. To this end, the novel narrates a matrix of human/nonhuman agents, including, among other things, Henry and his brother William, their children, a fiddle, Rebecca Rymer, Hannah Primrose, a flock of sheep, counterfeit bills, prostitution, and a wig. Although my aggregation of humans, animals, social practices, and man-made items suggests yet another 'Latour litany', Inchbald's interest in materiality resists positing objects as either absolutely independent or purely networked and instead focuses on how such flattening often serves an exploitative agenda.[3] Similar, if slightly shorter and less varied, lists to the one above occur repeatedly in Inchbald's novel, and they serve to highlight the instability of such conceptual boundaries. They underline the transgressive fluidity of these nominally stable and discrete objects, for example the way plant, animal, and human material combine to activate the vibrations in a fiddle so that fiddle in turn becomes a violin when you play it a certain way, for certain people.

The very sequence in which these lists appear in the novel forms a chiasmus: beginning with natural objects, moving on to small consumer goods, then large-scale property, and finally returning to exhausted natural objects. This sequence reiterates the very process of exploitation itself: drawing from nature-as-object (raw material) to produce artful objects (consumer items) in order to acquire property (nature itself as consumer item) while the original materials are abandoned or destroyed. Objectification, exploitation, and disavowal of material conceive such agents as 'cheap nature', whose productivity comes at little or no cost.[4] It enacts a simultaneous production and erasure of difference,

[2] See for example, Leah Ceccarelli, *Shaping Science With Rhetoric* (Chicago, IL: University of Chicago Press, 2001).

[3] The term 'Latour Litany' was coined by the scholar Ian Bogost in homage to the philosopher of science Bruno Latour. Ian Bogost, *Alien Phenomenology, or What It's Like To Be a Thing* (Minneapolis: University of Minnesota Press, 2012). Latour's lists are deliberately nonhierarchical, or 'flat'.

[4] The concept of 'cheap nature' has been used by Jason Moore and others to refer to those resources and materials (including labor) whose costs are typically uncounted or

so that a sheep in the field, a woman nursing an infant, or a stream pushing a water wheel are first classified and defined individually before being redefined as a bundle of resources. In the logic of late eighteenth-century capital, accumulation, and industrial production, all are equally 'nature' and equally 'cheap'. Resisting and reversing this logic is the story of revolutionary objects in Inchbald's *Nature and Art*.

Inchbald's narrative depicts material agents both permeating and producing forms of human subjectivity, which in turn produce the very representational figures underpinning the subject/object divide. Although the novel is explicitly didactic, and the lists are in part a way for Inchbald to mark the failures of nascent consumer culture (one of the ways "art" is represented in the novel), her attentiveness to different forms of materiality also reveals an acute concern with the agency of these objects, in no small part because women would too often be counted among them. In this context, *Nature and Art* tells the story of revolutionary objects in order to show how the denial of women's agency is used to justify and facilitate their exploitation. The close attention Inchbald pays to logical absurdities inherent in such justifications confronts the reader with the difficulty of distinguishing between objects and subject. Inchbald's use of chiasmus suggests the revolutionary potential in allowing that binary to remain open to further reversals, to the possibility for emergent, recursive reciprocity. If this is the case with fiddles and wigs, it is even more so, in Inchbald's story, the case with women in the late eighteenth century.

As such, Inchbald's transgressive conceptual chiasmus invokes a third term, *chora*, as deployed by Rebekah Sheldon via Plato's *Timaeus*. Plato uses the term to identify the space where form is translated into matter and often refers to it as a kind of womb, assigning these potentially active agents the role of generative objects in the employ of human (white, male) subjects.[5] Sheldon, drawing on the work of feminist new materialism, identifies this locus with the emergent properties of both objects and relations themselves, creating an 'ontology of material-affective circulation' (p. 213). Inchbald's focus on precisely this circulation illuminates the arbitrary classifications instantiating early industrial exploitation by marking the moments of its representational incoherence. Inchbald's use of chiasmus is choratic in this sense because it challenges us to think of the reversal not as a singular event but an unending series of oscillations, irreducible to a finite temporal sequence.

undervalued in the logic of late capitalist economies. Jason Moore, *Capitalism in the Web of Life: Ecology and the Accumulation of Capital* (London: Verso, 2015).

[5] Sheldon argues for the term as a way forward between the often patrilineal assertions of object-oriented ontology (OOO) and the more nuanced but still ultimately formalist 'assemblage' theories of Jane Bennett and others, where qualities emerge primarily from objects rather than relations in themselves. Rebekah Sheldon, 'Form/Matter/Chora', in *The Nonhuman Turn*, ed. Richard Grusin (Minneapolis: University of Minnesota Press, 2015).

Reading *Nature and Art* with these terms in mind illuminates not only Inchbald's interest in the agency of objectified material but also how this material exists as contingent, circulating co-productions with revolutionary potential, along the lines of what Caroline Levine calls the 'loosely and unevenly collected arrangements' of objects and things ordering and disordering the political, the social, the literary, and the ecological elements of our existence.[6] It is precisely this messy, entangled, embodied, relational element that *Nature and Art* dramatizes. Inchbald's chiasmic lists focus on the links between human and nonhuman materiality, in particular their role in the exploitation of women, as a challenge to the taxonomies driving these violent practices. As laboring humans, women in early industrial England were continually conceptualized as objects or subjects, depending on their use value. In the characters of Hannah and Rebecca, Inchbald's novel offers a glimpse of laboring women that complicates and challenges this either/or categorization.

Inchbald's engagement with the era's debates on political and social justice also provides insight into contemporary discussions regarding new materialist criticism. For although many OOO readings coincide with justice on a human scale, such object-centered anti-anthropocentrism, however unintentionally, too often assumes an undifferentiated 'anthros' of whiteness, maleness, straightness, and so on, in much the same way that a focus on the Anthropocene casts the category of 'human' as a singular, agential force, rather than a historically situated set of species-level differentiations.[7] A chiasmic/choratic reading of *Nature and Art* suggests an alternative to the prioritizing urge in some current theoretical work even as it resembles Inchbald's own method for overflowing the representational boundaries defining and limiting human and nonhuman agents. Inchbald's focus on both the materiality of and the materiality among these human and nonhuman agents helps us read how politics has always been material or, as Jason Moore puts it, is 'already environmental history' (Moore, p. 11). Inchbald achieves such a focus via human protagonists who, because of their class and sex, are necessarily more intimate (and at times conscious of this intimacy) with their material surroundings. As Erin B. Taylor writes in *Materializing Poverty,* an ethnographic study of a barrio in Santo Domingo, 'we are socialized into a material world at birth'.[8]

[6] Caroline Levine, *Forms: Whole, Rhythm, Hierarchy, Network* (Princeton, NJ: Princeton University Press, 2015), p. 17.

[7] See, for example, Timothy Morton, 'They are Here', in *The Nonhuman Turn*, ed. Richard Grusin (Minneapolis: University of Minnesota Press, 2015).

[8] Erin B. Taylor, *Materializing Poverty: How the Poor Transform Their Lives* (Plymouth: Rowan and Littlefield, 2013), p. 20.

Raw Material/Artful Objects

Nature and Art engages with this socialized material intimacy and the rich, recursive fields of material affective circulation it generates by looking first at a fiddle. The fiddle is a vehicle for Henry's success, but it also contributes to the destruction of his relationship with his brother, William, who comes to see Henry's musical performances as beneath his station. Even though they are from modest origins, William always had a 'proud and disdainful mind' (Inchbald, p. 46). Perhaps even more galling, 'William could NOT play on the fiddle' (p. 43). Although Henry's talent helps his brother obtain a deanery, William's subsequent distancing from his brother becomes an inter-generational conflict across which Inchbald will draw her distinctions like a bow on a string. William exemplifies the rigid, classificatory practices of established English culture while Henry, enthusiastic and innocent, in turn suggests an experience in which humans and nonhumans form and reform representational boundaries in rich, vibratory arrangements. Inchbald's objects are often, if not always, already something more than what they seem to be.

For example, Henry's fiddle is also called a violin, both by the narrator and the character. In fact, it crosses back and forth between the two names on a regular basis throughout the early chapters of the novel. While today some distinguish a violin from a fiddle by reciting the joke that 'you don't spill beer on a violin', humorously marking the class distinctions and genres of music associated with each, the terms were often interchangeable in the eighteenth century. In Johnson's *Dictionary*, the fiddle is 'a stringed instrument of musick; a violin', while the entry for violin reads, 'fiddle; a stringed instrument of musick'.[9] This lexical reversal is less a sign of shifting social markers or the anxiety of class mobility than an emblem for the complex field of material relations informing the social sphere. By alternating between the two terms, Inchbald not only marks Henry's status shift, but she also addresses the fluidity inhering in the co-production of power, or 'capital', which the relationship between Henry and the fiddle exemplifies. The agile, nominal instability of the instrument (the words 'fiddle' and 'violin' are used interchangeably within a paragraph of each other in the novel), akin to the wild lexicological landscape that eighteenth-century English dictionaries sought to tame, immediately calls into question the very notion of coherent and compelling categories.

The violin/fiddle is, according to David Schoenbaum, an 'improbable object', one whose material composition includes not only 'trees and animal tissue' but also the labor and responsiveness of human agents. If 'spruce and maple are the instrument's primary materials, it also has vibrating strings that

[9] Samuel Johnson, *A Dictionary of the English Language*, 2 vols. (London: J.F. and C. Rivington, 1785).

are its motor, varnish that preserves the wood, glue that holds it together, and finally the neural processes that it activates in both the player and the listener'.[10] As an aesthetic object, assembled in turn from natural or raw material, the instrument is more than the sum of its parts, particularly when it interacts with specific human bodies. Otherwise limited by his class status and illiteracy, Henry is empowered by the fiddle, which, crucially, he retains even after it has served its apparent purpose.[11]

Henry leverages this technical skill through and with the violin in such a way that it becomes not merely a tool but an agent in his success. Nevertheless, as important as this co-producer of value is, it remains dispensable in the general milieu of capital accumulation in the novel. Henry's loyalty to the instrument contrasts with William's refusal to acknowledge Henry's role in his own success, which illuminates a more general cultural refusal to acknowledge the role of material labor, whether it is the labor of humans, animals, or nonhuman things, fields, or forces. This tension is in large part a crisis of representation. Inchbald's work is inarguably moral and didactic, but it is also an attempt to confront the contradictions inherent in the early industrial moment in England, where the labor of slaves abroad, women and children in the home (or, increasingly, the fields and urban spaces), animals, and environmental forces such as wind, water, and sun all remain relatively unaccounted for in the economic ledgers recording the production of wealth. These profoundly different forms of human and nonhuman material vitality and productivity become fungible in a classificatory calculus that distinguishes only in order to isolate, exhaust, exploit, and eliminate, as a vulnerable animal is separated from the herd by a predator.

By attending to the contradictions at the heart of these operations, Inchbald allows us to see Henry's facility with the violin as a kind of environment-making with revolutionary potential. His intimacy with his material surroundings (in other words, his capacity as a musician) is subversive to the ruling class precisely because it has the capacity to avoid classification. As such, it must be excluded from the category of acceptable behavior. The patron may enjoy the music, but the musician will not live in the same house. Henry's identity becomes bound up with the practices he employs and, through the material intimacy of his partnership with the fiddle, it presents an alternative to the

[10] David Schoenbaum, *The Violin: A Social History of the World's Most Versatile Instrument* (New York: W.W. Norton and Co., 2015), p. 2.

[11] Some of Henry's success may be chalked up to good timing. England in the late eighteenth century was a period when the opera flourished, and concerts were part of both public and private entertainment. Inchbald knew a great deal about this world; her stepson Robert had been listed as second violinist at a series of memorial concerts for Handel in 1784. Annabel Jenkins, *I'll Tell You What: The Life of Elizabeth Inchbald* (Lexington: University of Kentucky Press, 2003), p. 374.

rigidity of ruling class objectification. It illuminates instead the possibility of a form of life where use is freed from ownership, and there exists, perhaps, not only mutual acknowledgement, but even a measure of reciprocity.[12] Henry's violin/fiddle will literally save his life later in the novel, and this is because, as mentioned before, he does not discard the fiddle or leave it to gather dust on a shelf. Rather, it is imbricated with his subjectivity.

After Henry's wife dies, he takes his son (also named Henry) and his fiddle and sails with a party of Portuguese adventurers to an island off the coast of West Africa. When islanders attack, Henry saves his son's life and his own by pleasing the islanders with his music. Eventually, Henry's son escapes and finds his way to his uncle William, with a note from Henry begging that his estranged brother raise the boy alongside William's son (conveniently named William as well). Young Henry's natural upbringing is contrasted to that of the younger William, whose society upbringing, Inchbald notes, has had the curious effect of dehumanizing him, since 'when he imitated the manners of a man, he had something of [the brute] in his appearance—for he would grin and bow to a lady, catch her fan in haste when it fell, and hand her to her coach, as thoroughly void of all the sentiment, which gives grace to such tricks as a monkey' (Inchbald, p. 54). Sentiment, understood as self-conscious agency regarding one's intersubjective and affective experiences, was generally not extended to women and children precisely because they could not control it.

This distinction between the young Henry and William allows Inchbald to focus her exploration of revolutionary objects by examining the material culture of the upper class, and this section provides some of her sharpest satire on the contradictions implicit in ruling class categorizations. One of young Henry's first objects of wonder is the massive periwig worn by his uncle. Henry is first mystified by it, but when told it is an object used to distinguish the great from those inferior, he understands and tells his uncle that such a practice was common on the African island as well, where chiefs would ornament themselves with 'brass nails, wire, buttons and entrails of beasts … to give them importance' (p. 59). After learning to bow when addressing his uncle, Henry comes unannounced into his uncle's dressing-room and, seeing the wig on the table, is unsure which object to address. He finally chooses his uncle, but afterwards bows 'reverently to the wig' (p. 61).[13] From then on

[12] I gesture here towards the work of Giorgio Agamben, in particular *The Highest Poverty* (2013), his historical study of the concepts of use and property in early-modern monastic life, which offers a potential link between biopolitics and feminist new materialist thought. Giorgio Agamben, *The Highest Poverty: Monastic Rules and Forms-of-Life* (Palo Alto, CA: Stanford University Press, 2013).

[13] There is a conscious irony at work throughout Inchbald's delineation of the uncle's character, for he was earlier frustrated in employment in part because he 'could not dress

he also 'respected the ear-rings' of the Lady almost as much as he respected herself (p. 61), ironically identifying the inextricable commingling of human and nonhuman material inherent in class categorization.

Like the violin, wigs were assembled from an array of nonhuman material, including glue, wire, and animal hair and, like the partnership of violin and player, the concordance of wig and head produces a new kind of agent. Unlike the violin, however, the function of this material agent, via the human subject's ideological disavowal, is to police class distinctions while denying the labor power behind the very wealth it symbolically reinforces. For William, as a representative of the ruling class and gender, the assembled materials co-produce value, or positive outputs, for only one segment of the assembly: himself. This co-production of difference is a process where laboring material is awarded special status only for the time it takes to add value to the human subject and be returned to an abject, object state. Such a reversal seeks to profit from the fungibility of material categorization while eliding this slippage through an either/or frame, much the same way classical chiasmus seeks to make its point by simply reversing the syntax.

Henry's intimacy with materiality encourages him to afford the same status to the wig as he does his uncle, destabilizing the representational hierarchy into something reciprocal. As Inchbald frames it, the difference between an African island and a Dean's dressing room is the islander's acknowledgment of the material they incorporate. What the privileged (upper-class, white, male, English) subject does not recognize is the chiasmus itself. By highlighting it, Inchbald's novel perforates the apparent solidity of these relationships and reroutes them, choratically, through a field of material-affective intensities. The violin and wig both gesture towards the materiality of culture itself and, in particular, the degree to which we are figuratively socialized into our material relationships not only by human culture, but also by things themselves. Class, gender, and other sociohistorical identities involve both material and figurative environment-making, but they are then reinforced through a refusal to acknowledge that very collaboration.

This disavowal of mutual material reciprocity is of critical interest to *Nature and Art*'s Jacobinism. Inchbald suggests early in the novel that the vanity and blindness of manners are a result of individuals unreflectively taking their cues from 'surrounding objects …. [M]anners were not governed by (one's) mind, but were solely directed by external circumstances' (p. 74). This argument is indebted to the philosopher and novelist William Godwin, a frequent

hair' (Inchbald, p. 61). Furthermore, by the mid-1790s wigs had begun to fall out of fashion, in part because of Pitt's new tax on wig powder, but also due to shifting cultural mores. In the 1780s, Inchbald was, famously, the first woman to appear on stage with her natural hair, sans wig.

correspondent with Inchbald.[14] Godwin famously included a chapter in his highly influential work *An Enquiry Concerning Political Justice* (1793) entitled 'The Character of Man is Derived from External Circumstances', in which he argues for the contingent nature of personality. This Godwinian perspective illuminates the difference between the young William and Henry, but it also necessarily complicates that simple observation. Despite Godwin's insistence that all individuals ideally exert a sphere of discretion that filters and judges external phenomena, one's external circumstances are often part of the very basis for that individual judgment. Although Inchbald follows Godwin in valorizing the abstracted rational mind over the social and material conditions that, in their estimation, over-determine human character, it is nevertheless revolutionary even to acknowledge these material conditions as influential in the production of culture itself. Inchbald's satirical observations break open the conceptual boundaries separating objects from their own agency, and this is nowhere more apparent than in her use of lists.

Across the Chiasmus

The sequencing of the lists in Inchbald's novel may be thought of as a series of reversals and reiterations, suggesting how the process of objectification can become part of the emergent property of the object itself. As Brian Massumi puts it, 'the object as it happens, is not one. It is a recursively emergent, reiterative event'.[15] The lists exemplify a series of developmental stages, each one more dependent on objectification than the one before, until the last list reverses course to rest with an exhausted set of things, now the domain of both objects and subjects alike, as if to point towards the emptiness of consumption practices already developing in early industrial England.

The first list occurs in a pamphlet written by the older William in praise of God's providence. He names 'fields, wood, water, corn, grass, sheep, oxen, fish, fowl, fruit, and vegetables' (Inchbald, p. 69) as existing for man's use and contributing to a happy and free society. The younger Henry is pleased to hear this but is later puzzled to learn that there is also poverty and deprivation in England. He wonders why the Dean has omitted these from his list. This section is one of many satires on religious and upper-class hypocrisy, but it also functions as an entry point into how objectification enables exploitation. The objects here described operate as raw material 'providentially' suited for

[14] Godwin was also, for a time, a frustrated suitor for Inchbald's hand in marriage. The subtitle to his famous novel *Caleb Williams*, '*Things as They Are*' is a suggestive signpost for the study of materiality in the Jacobin novel.

[15] Brian Massumi, 'The Supernormal Animal', in *The Nonhuman Turn*, ed. Richard Grusin (Minneapolis: University of Minnesota Press, 2015), p. 12.

human exploitation, and Henry's innocent confusion at the arbitrary but powerful distinctions between wig and head, rich and poor, expresses this acutely.

A second list occurs soon after, during another discussion about the poor between the elder William and his peers. In that conversation, William explains that many of the problems confronting the lower class are caused by their attempts to emulate the wealthy, particularly when it comes to modes of dress. It is to their own detriment that they must always be clothed in 'stockings, a coat, and a waistcoat, a gown and a cap, and a petticoat and a handkerchief' (p. 76). Here the list of objects serves to mark the distinction between rich and poor. These consumer goods are the residue of wealth production due to the exploitation of the resources from the first list. The problem of the poor (as William argues) is that they mimic upper-class consumption without the necessary quality to sustain and embody it. The irony here is that while the poor are the producers of wealth, any attempt by them to express a connection to that wealth production through the mode of dress immediately requires the reinscription of an ideological barrier. They cannot afford such things; they should not buy such things; they themselves are things. For those who accept such a frame, the claims of the poor make as little sense as it would if a stream in a field requested a hat to shield itself from the rain.

The third list occurs later in the novel, after the introduction of the major female characters, Rebecca and Hannah, and is expressed directly by young Henry. It is recited when young Henry lectures his beloved Rebecca on the superficiality of English culture and expresses his priority for 'people' over 'things'. He writes that he pities those who seek happiness in 'fine houses, gardens, and parks … pictures, horses, money, and various things' (p. 122). He rejects precisely those objects which naturalize, through their apparent perdurability and force as status markers, the exploitation of cheap nature. These objects are not trifles, like jewelry or even a wig, but the very means of justifying the original exploitation by gesturing towards the idea of a stable, enduring class system. Fungible, exploited natures are given meaning through the transmission of culture in the form of horses, estates, gardens, and parks. By rejecting these markers, Henry aligns himself with a romantic nature, but, as we will see, this alignment is ironic, since Henry has his own still unrecognized debt to this vibrant, entangled materiality.

This irony becomes apparent with the final list, which occurs when the two Henrys, reunited after many tribulations, pass the stately manor where the younger William resides, now despised by his tenants and unhappy, and they view it no longer as a 'noble edifice' but as 'a heap of rubbish'. Rather than inhabit such a place, they instead would prefer the shelter of 'a bank, a hedge, a tree, a hill' (p. 149). This list of bare geographical features suggests a nonhuman environment. These are no longer raw materials available for human use but rather ecological features existing as objects for themselves first. It is as if the whole boom-and-bust cycle of resource exploitation were here narrated, bringing us back to the start, but with less than before, and it gestures toward the possibility of a paradigmatic shift where humans cede control over objects and simply exist among them.

Women and Revolutionary Objects

Inchbald's awareness of this ironic reduction accompanying exploitation becomes clear in the narrative's transition in its second half from the two sets of Henrys and Williams to the female characters Hannah and Rebecca. While Inchbald again uses these characters to critique the hypocrisy of the upper class, the narrative also deepens the exploration of nonhuman materiality and agency by exploring the liminal status of women in late eighteenth-century England. The stories of Rebecca and Hannah explore how women in the eighteenth century were subject to extraordinary representational mutations and reversals that classified and reclassified them as subject or object, nature or art, useful or useless, based on their productive potential and material relationships.

Rebecca's narrative arc will culminate in apparent success, but Hannah's is its dark mirror, revealing how the nominally settled divisions between objects and subject are, in fact, contingent; we see the women cross back and forth between these two categories, usually as a consequence of their use-value, where gender and class distinctions facilitate the exploitation of women as cheap nature. The second half of the novel presents the labor of women (not merely agricultural or menial labor but, especially, reproductive and sexual) as a crucial driver of both English industry (culture/art) and also of the very category of nature to which such labor is ultimately assigned. Women are subject to a representational strategy marking them as artful human subjects or natural objects depending on their specific location within the sequence of cultivation, exploitation, and dismissal, as seen most acutely in the seduction of Hannah by young William. By contrast, my choratic reading of Rebecca and Hannah attends to the transgressive elements implicit in Inchbald's account of these two characters.

The strong, ironic pivot from the more subtle consideration of nonhuman material agency and transgression is signaled by the narrator's plea to the liberal, unprejudiced reader that these two 'heroines may deserve your attention, just as the wild herb of the forest, equally with the cultivated plant in the garden, claims the attention of the botanist' (p. 81). As Theresa Kelley has shown, such flora-logical identifications are part of a long representational history that personifies women as flowering plants, with all of the resonances of beauty, cultivation, and delicacy. However, Inchbald explicitly associates the women with the 'wild herb' and not the 'cultivated plant'.[16] The wild herb is, crucially, not dependent on human cultivation and therefore identifies the women as artless and free. Yet the wild herb is not completely outside the realm of human activity, since these plants serve a significant role as food and health additives as well as a raw material for production, and although they were not cultivated, their use still required forage and gathering. This work was traditionally carried out by women, who would either use the material in the household or sell it at market. Here the women are both the natural objects and also laborers securing more natural objects. As such, the representation suggests that Rebecca and Hannah are not only gendered but also objectified.

The two women are individuated for the sake of Inchbald's didactic satire, but their differences also illuminate their relationships to material agency. Rebecca is the youngest and plainest daughter of a country curate. She is described as 'free of vanity' and a reader of the 'finest English books' (p. 79). Beloved by the virtuous Henry and guided by her own sense as it has developed in a relationship to texts, Rebecca enjoys a slow, modest courtship based on reciprocity and care. Hannah, the illiterate and beautiful daughter of a country cottager, has been conditioned to respond more instinctively to superficial and gendered attention, and young William cynically seduces her. She becomes pregnant, William ignores her pleas, and, in desperation, she abandons the infant in the woods, where it is found by Henry and given to Rebecca to nurture. Rebecca's nutritive labor, as with most good deeds performed by women in the novel, will go unrewarded but not unpunished, for when the child is finally discovered, Rebecca's culpability is assumed. This misunderstanding will briefly separate Henry and Rebecca, but Hannah's fate is more inexorable. Soon reunited with her child and determined to support them both, she finds work on a nearby farm, where her skin becomes so burnt and rough that her reflection is no longer recognizable. Despite her physical transformation, which mirrors her change from subject to object, she finds solace there with her son and works as a shepherd 'solely with the brute creation … a state she preferred to the society of human creatures' (p. 123). Significantly, though, this is represented as a contingent state rather than an expression of Hannah's determination to live in a harmonious relationship with her material environment.

As is well known, rural, agrarian labor in late eighteenth-century England waned as enclosures reduced common grazing area for the rural poor, who had for centuries depended on such shared spaces. Inchbald stresses Hannah's isolation and the degree to which this labor is ignored by those who profit from it. She also clarifies Hannah's objectification. Hannah is not merely

[16] Theresa Kelley, *Clandestine Marriage: Botany and Romantic Culture* (Baltimore, MD: Johns Hopkins University Press, 2012).

working 'with brute creation'; she is a part of brute creation, as witnessed by her wild appearance. She, along with the sheep and the fields in which they graze, form another field of material affordances with productive aspects, like Henry and the fiddle or William with his wig. However, in this case, because of the social and historical practices situating and constraining her position, Hannah's potentially vibrant and agentic field of material relationships is far more vulnerable to exploitation.

After the farmer dies, Hannah repeats the English industrial-age migration from country to city, as had the senior Henry and William at the beginning of the novel. The difference between the two cases concerns the way that gender and class categories deny Hannah the opportunity to form new material alliances that will help her prosper in the new setting. She has no fiddle; she will wear no wig. Instead she has a child and her body. She is refused work because she cannot make caps and gowns or preserve and pickle, because she is too pretty or too young. She finally obtains employment as a general servant until her employer learns of her child and fires her. As it was with Rebecca when she took in Hannah's abandoned child, to recognize the work of childcare is to wrestle with its cost. For women, too often that cost of their reproductive and nutritive labor is the fact that the very labor is itself hidden, or uncounted, in the first place precisely because these material relationships between mother and child are constructed as natural, involving no agency, no obligation for reciprocity, on the part of the actors who enjoy its fruits.

Desperate, Hannah finds work in a brothel. Soon after she is implicated in a forgery ring, captured by the police, and sentenced to death by the newly appointed magistrate, William, who fails to recognize Hannah. It is not until after her execution that he sees her name and town of birth in the paper and realizes what he has done. He sends for her child, his son, only to learn that he has killed himself after his mother's death. Finally moved by Hannah's plight, William wonders how his thoughts could have been absent from an 'object so pitiable' (p. 141). Only after the fact and absent the opportunity to reciprocate does the white, male subject express a sense of obligation and, even then, it is more distress at the loss of what the pitiable object's labor has produced, the son.

Although Inchbald encourages us to consider how much of Hannah's fate is tied to her sentimentalism, compared with Rebecca's more educated and rational judgments, she also offers Hannah as a stark illustration of female exploitation in the late eighteenth century. Reproductive, nutritive, caregiving, menial, and sexual labor, now typically recognized as crucial components of economic growth, has historically not been counted precisely because it has been lumped in with, or objectified alongside, nonhuman material. Hannah's value to William is only as a means to an end; her body is the vessel through which he achieves his sexual desire. Once he has his pleasure, he refuses to 'see' her, both literally and figuratively, and she bears his child and does the work of reproduction almost invisibly. In this sense she is an expression of Plato's conventional chora through which ideal form becomes matter, passing through the neutral body.

This sense of Hannah as a passive vessel is the representation that Inchbald resists. Her attention to Hannah's plight transgresses objectification by choratically intensifying our experience, arresting our interest. Hannah's status as a mother is only recognized in the moment she attempts to abandon the child, and her labor is only valued when she attempts to resist its coercive assumptions. Exploitation demands a non-reciprocal material transformation, a reversal where the dangerous border crossing is performed by agents with little power, in the service of the privileged. But there is the imagined alternative, an open, choratic chiasmus that Inchbald invites by highlighting the contradictions in Hannah's case and emphasizing the discordance of the novel's ending.

Hannah's story is a compilation of ironic reversals. She performs illegal sexual labor only after William has coerced her to perform it 'legally' for no compensation. Furthermore, the act that causes her trial and execution is precisely the attempt to circumvent the profoundly inequitable economic field of labor-value and financial reward. Counterfeit bills challenge the authority of a particular, arbitrary model of valuation and, to do so, in Hannah's case, was to condemn her. Crucially, again, in the very act of sentencing her to death, just as when he enjoyed her sexual labor, William does not see Hannah. She is undifferentiated and objectified. Women are represented through a conceptual chiasmus that temporarily assigns them as pseudo-subjects, extracts value, and then lumps them back in with the mass of undifferentiated objects collectively framed as nature. The brief glimpses of Hannah among 'brute creation' offer a messier model of material agency, and although it flirts with pastoral romanticism, its refusal to narrate the patterns of hierarchy suggest a way toward a more choratic understanding of how we conceptualize women's labor both in the Romantic period and today.

Soon after Hannah's execution, young Henry and his father are reunited and learn of the death of Lady Clementina, the younger William's mother, who had caught cold wearing a new-fangled dress and died the 'miserabilist object you ever heard of' (p. 146). This recurrence of the term 'object' to describe another dead woman is not accidental. While Inchbald certainly indicates that Lady Clementina, like Hannah, exhibits a lack of Austenian 'sense', there is also a chiasmic repetition at work. Inchbald's ironic engagement with the representative violence acting on Hannah produces a choratic reading by identifying the very forces producing this representation of woman as object and insisting we refuse to let the representation be settled or set. Inchbald invites us to cross the representational borders and recognize richer, more vital material effects in the partnership between and among humans, sheep, fiddles, and even bare hills. These are alternatives to the status quo suggested by Hannah's fate, and even to the apparent happy ending achieved by Rebecca, young Henry, and his father.

Conclusion

'Persons, not things' has been the younger Henry's mantra throughout the novel and, by the end, the three characters seem to have found happiness through a renunciation of the materialism of late eighteenth-century, upper-class culture, living by their own industry in a small hut on the seashore. The men fish, grow food, and sell the surplus at market; Rebecca tends the house, makes meals, and heightens the charm of conversation with taste and judgment; and all three agree that poverty is an enviable state if one is happy with simplicity. Yet a choratic reading complicates this conclusion, for the apparent moral of self-sufficiency and virtuous resistance to external circumstances sounds too much like Pangloss in *Candide*. While Henry suggests that 'It is the want of industry, or the want of reflection which makes the poor dissatisfied' (p. 153), their plan to support themselves 'independent of every person and thing but their own industry' only repeats the blindness of William and his peers. Compared to Hannah working alongside 'brute creation', Henry's pastoral vision obscures the degree to which poor, working women find their lives oriented by malnutrition, disease, and violence. The categories of object and subject, nature and art, male and female speak to the refusal by the dominant cultural and political narratives not only to value Hannah's labor and material agency equitably but even to think of measuring it in the first place.

The invocation of self-reliance by young Henry echoes the beginning of the novel, when the elder William and Henry mourn the loss of their father and console themselves with the thought that he had now, at least, avoided his creditors. The difference between the somber beginning and the 'happy' end is found in the way the characters acknowledge or refuse to acknowledge debt. Debt to one's creditors is unavoidable, but debt to objects and their material labor is unthinkable.

The Inchbaldian irony in the novel's 'happy' ending was not lost on her readers, however. Anna Barbauld wrote that she wished Inchbald had been kinder to young Henry, who 'in the end must be contented with poverty and his half-withered Rebecca'.[17] This deliberate acceptance of the 'half-withered' in all its forms recalls the bare, things-in-themselves list of 'bank, hedge, tree, hill' and also invokes Timothy Morton's rejection of romantic naturalism in

[17] Qtd. in Annabel Jenkins, *I'll Tell You What: The Life of Elizabeth Inchbald* (Lexington: University of Kentucky Press, 2003), p. 381.

favor of an embrace of the impoverished and ugly that urges us to come to terms with the uncanny otherness of materiality as an intrinsic element of our situation. Nevertheless, Inchbald's irony reminds us that the embrace of ugliness, even in all its creaturely difference, often repeats its own version of Romantic sublimity and elides the representational work, which is the task of the chora itself. To practice 'loving the thing *as* thing' must also mean recognizing not only the status, but the work of the 'thing' as well.[18]

Nature and Art invites us to attend the abject object in its rich, varied, existential plenitude. In this sense, the novel's choratic component becomes more apparent the less it refuses to work 'for us'. Like a stubborn mule, a broken hammer, or a reluctant mother, the novel gestures towards an undisclosed element within material itself: not only the relations among materials, but also the cascading, transgressive effects inaugurating and attending these phenomena. *Nature and Art* links together these moments of material transgression and challenges us to recognize that the object of revolution must be, in part, to recognize the revolutionary object.

Bibliography

Agamben, Giorgio. *The Highest Poverty: Monastic Rules and Forms-of-Life*. Palo Alto, CA: Stanford University Press, 2013.

Bennett, Jane. *Vibrant Matter: A Political Ecology of Things*. Durham, NC: Duke University Press, 2010.

Ceccarelli, Leah. *Shaping Science with Rhetoric: The Cases of Dobzhansky, Schrodinger, and Wilson*. Chicago, IL: University of Chicago Press, 2001.

Godwin, William. *An Enquiry Concerning Political Justice (1793)*, ed. Mark Philp. *Political and Philosophical Writings of William Godwin*, vol. 4. London: Routledge, 1993.

Inchbald, Elizabeth. *Nature and Art*, ed. Shawn Lisa Maurer. Ontario: Broadview Press, [1796] 2005.

Jenkins, Annabel. *I'll Tell You What: The Life of Elizabeth Inchbald*. Lexington: University of Kentucky Press, 2003.

Johnson, Samuel. *A Dictionary of the English Language*, 2 vols. London: J.F. and C. Rivington, 1785.

Kelley, Theresa. *Clandestine Marriage: Botany and Romantic Culture*. Baltimore, MD: Johns Hopkins University Press, 2012.

Kelly, Gary. *The English Jacobin Novel: 1780–1805*. Oxford: Oxford University Press, 1975.

Levine, Caroline. *Forms: Whole, Rhythm, Hierarchy, Network*. Princeton, NJ: Princeton University Press, 2015.

[18] Timothy Morton, *Ecology Without Nature* (Cambridge, MA: Harvard University Press, 2007).

Massumi, Brian. 'The Supernormal Animal'. In *The Nonhuman Turn*, ed. Richard Grusin. Minneapolis: University of Minnesota Press, 2015, pp. 1–18.

Moore, Jason. *Capitalism in the Web of Life: Ecology and the Accumulation of Capital.* London: Verso, 2015.

——. 'The Capitalocene Part I: On the Nature and Origins of our Ecological Crisis'. *The Journal of Peasant Studies*, 44: 3 (2017), pp. 594–630.

Morton, Timothy. *Ecology Without Nature: Rethinking Environmental Aesthetics.* Cambridge, MA: Harvard University Press, 2007.

——. 'They Are Here'. In *The Nonhuman Turn*, ed. Richard Grusin. Minneapolis: University of Minnesota Press, 2015, pp. 167–92.

Schoenbaum, David. *The Violin: A Social History of the World's Most Versatile Instrument.* New York: W.W. Norton and Co., 2015.

Sheldon, Rebekah. '"Form/Matter/Chora": Object-Oriented Ontology and Feminist Materialism'. In *The Nonhuman Turn*, ed. Richard Grusin. Minneapolis: University of Minnesota Press, 2015, pp. 193–222.

Taylor, Erin B. *Materializing Poverty: How the Poor Transform Their Lives.* Plymouth: Rowman and Littlefield, 2013.

Chapter Eight

Dancing with Ghosts in 'Isabella; or, The Pot of Basil'

Sonia Hofkosh

> Piteous she look'd on dead and senseless things,
> Asking for her lost Basil amorously …[1]

In his remediation of Boccaccio's tale about the passionate attachment of a young woman to the 'garden-pot' in which she has buried her lover's head, Keats dramatizes the intimacy between persons and things, or perhaps, more exactly, between personhood and thingness. By personhood I mean those features of subjectivity, such as consciousness and memory and desire, which have generally been considered integral to the experience of being human as well as to the cultural formation we call Romanticism. By thingness I mean neither the 'essential nature' of a thing that for Heidegger transcends its status as 'a represented object' nor an ontology oriented to objects as 'real' only in so far as they are immaterial, inaccessible, by definition 'deeper than our relation with [them]'.[2] Rather, I am interested here in how Keats understands

[1] 'Isabella; or, The Pot of Basil', in *The Poems of John Keats*, ed. Jack Stillinger (Cambridge, MA: Harvard University Press, 1978), pp. 245–63, lines 489–90. I am grateful to the editors of this volume and to Mary Favret for their helpful comments on drafts of this essay. The faults that remain are of course my own.

[2] Martin Heidegger, 'The Thing', in *Poetry, Language, Thought*, trans. Albert Hofstadter (New York: Harper & Row, 1971), pp. 165–86, 174, 167. Graham Harman, 'The Road to Objects', *continent*, 3: 1 (2011), pp. 171–9, 174. Also see Harman's concise account of OOO in *Immaterialism: Objects and Social Theory* (Cambridge: Polity Press, 2016) as 'a realist position that views objects of every sort as existing prior to their relations or effects' (pp. 42–3). I should note that I use the terms 'thing' and 'object' synonymously in this essay, though my thinking about the ghostly materiality of everyday life is informed by

the thingness of ordinary objects among which we practice our everyday lives, for example a poem in a book or a ceramic pot planted with a fragrant herb. Paper and clay are among the mundane materials with which we inevitably come into contact in our activities of daily living, those routines and rituals we perform, whether by habit, custom, or conviction, wherein the rhythms or patterns of our lives become recognizable to us as our own. As humans we exist in continual if also continually changing relation to mundane materiality, including, and not least of all, to the continually changing materiality of our own bodies. However unremarkable such encounters may be, however commonplace, when we turn the pages of a book to read a poem or we water the plant in a pot, we are touching the skin of things, and what we touch also touches us—touches us with both sensory and affective resonances.[3] Thus, though the lines I quote above from 'Isabella; or, The Pot of Basil' assume personhood and thingness as distinct categories of being with opposing qualities and capacities—the person is an active, speaking, feeling subject, while 'dead and senseless things' are by definition inert, unresponsive—I hope to show that Keats dramatizes a considerably more complex and less stable relation between human agency and 'the social life of objects' or, more broadly, 'the lively immanence of matter'.[4] I want to suggest that 'Isabella; or The Pot of Basil' stages this relation as a kind of ghost dance. At once what remains and what returns, both persistent and residual, the ghost takes many forms in Keats's poem, materializing at or as the shifting interface that subjectivity and the world of objects share. In addition I want to suggest that we dance with ghosts when we touch the skin of things and they thus also touch us in the recurring practices of everyday life; such a ghost dance conduces to what we might call the paranormativity (para: near to, beside, and yet also against or beyond) of everyday life, its very recursivity evoking the possibility of its own transformation.

My initial thinking about the relational drama Keats stages in 'Isabella; or, The Pot of Basil' draws on various new materialist figurations, for example

arguments that distinguish them along the lines that Heidegger sets out; see, for example, Bill Brown's influential discussion in 'Thing Theory', in *Things*, ed. Bill Brown (Chicago, IL & London: University of Chicago Press, 2004), pp. 1–16.

[3] I borrow this particular phrasing from Tom H. Fisher, 'What We Touch, Touches Us: Materials, Affects, and Affordances', *Design Issues*, 20: 4 (Autumn 2004), pp. 20–31. Also see Erin Manning, *Politics of Touch: Sense, Movement, Sovereignty* (Minneapolis: University of Minnesota Press, 2007); and Karen Barad, 'On Touching—the Inhuman That Therefore I Am', *differences*, 23: 3 (2012), pp. 206–23.

[4] Arjun Appadurai, *The Social Life of Objects: Commodities in Cultural Perspective* (Cambridge: Cambridge University Press, 1986); Diana Coole and Samantha Frost, 'Introducing the New Materialism', in *New Materialism: Ontology, Agency, and Politics* (Durham, NC & London: Duke University Press, 2010), pp. 1–43, 9.

Jane Bennett's in *Vibrant Matter*, which considers 'the extent to which human being and thinghood overlap, the extent to which the us and the it slip-slide into each other'. Bennett characterizes such relationality as a 'complicated web of dissonant connections between bodies', between human bodies, that is, and other corporeal forms, 'nonhuman or not-quite-human … circulating around and within human bodies'.[5] She elsewhere describes this 'web of dissonant connections' as an 'eccentric assemblage', and others who explore the relation of person and thing have posited similarly layered or looping models for this relation, such as Maurice Merleau-Ponty's 'intertwining' or Karen Barad's 'entanglement', constructions more likely to involve strands in tension or knots of resistance, than to resolve into harmony or synthesis.[6] Moreover, and what I want to highlight in reading Keats, these structures are dynamic, perhaps precisely in being transgressive, that is, in overlapping, twisting, or crossing lines, such as between person and thing or between human and nonhuman or not-quite-human bodies.[7] Phrases such as 'slip-slide into' and 'circulating around and within' in Bennett's formulation convey the mobility designed into these structure and figure relationality as an emergent pattern or process, unstable and yet ongoing, like the gestures of a dance or like the practices of everyday life.

It is through such repetitive, looping movement that Keats's poem performs the intimate transaction between the young woman and the 'garden-pot' that contains her lover's head and the plant she tends with such devotion: 'And so she ever fed it with thin tears, / Whence thick, and green, and beautiful it grew' (lines 425–6). The dissonance of this connection registers in the way the young woman 'withers like a palm' (447) while the plant in the pot grows so

[5] Jane Bennett, *Vibrant Matter: A Political Ecology of Things* (Durham, NC & London: Duke University Press, 2010), pp. 4, ix. Though it mines a more organic model than I want to engage here, see Jacques Rancière's discussion of the spider's web as a figure for Keats's poetry and by extension for the politics of the aesthetic more broadly in 'The Politics of the Spider', trans. Emily Rohrbach and Emily Sun, *SiR*, 50: 2 (Summer 2011), pp. 239–50.

[6] Jane Bennett, 'Systems and Things: A Response to Graham Harman and Timothy Morton', *New Literary History*, 43 (2012), pp. 225–33, 231; Maurice Merleau-Ponty, 'The Intertwining—The Chiasm', in *The Visible and the Invisible*, trans. Alphonso Lingis (Evanston, IL: Northwestern University Press, 1968), pp. 130–55; Karen Barad, *Meeting the Universe Halfway: Quantum Physics and the Entanglement of Matter and Meaning* (Durham, NC: Duke University Press, 2007). On the problematic of the 'subject–object synthesis' as a desideratum of Romanticism, see Paul De Man, 'The Rhetoric of Temporality', *Blindness and Insight: Essays in the Rhetoric of Contemporary Criticism* (Minneapolis: University of Minnesota Press, 1971), pp. 187–228, 199.

[7] See Barad, *Meeting the Universe*, on 'the lively dance of mattering' (p. 37) and Erin Manning, *Relationscapes: Movement, Art, Philosophy* (Cambridge, MA & London: MIT Press, 2009) on 'the dynamic cross-genesis of the body and its constructed environment' (p. 2).

abundantly, 'more balmy than its peers' (427). But it also registers as poesis, in the movement of the language itself across the lines of the poem.[8] 'And so she ever fed it with thin tears, / Whence thick, and green, and beautiful it grew': these lines strike a discordant note where the alliteration linking the contraries 'thin' and 'thick' puts the sound of the words in tension with their meaning, crossing likeness or identity with difference. Not unlike the 'or' in the title of the poem, which is suspended at or as the intersection of person ('Isabella') and thing ('The Pot of Basil'), the tendency of such conjuncture is provisional, unsettled. Does 'or' establish an affinity (it can be either one or the other, same difference) or mark an absolute divide (it can be only one or the other, mutually exclusive)? Or might it pivot, turning and returning to signify a mode of relation that could move beyond the binary of singular identities, such as person and thing or subject and object, towards an apprehension of other orders (or disorders) of being?[9]

'Isabella; or, The Pot of Basil' poses these questions not only as narrative, in retelling Boccaccio's 'old tale' (line 389) of the (in)tense relation between the young woman and the garden-pot, but also formally as craft, that is, in the particular arrangement of the words on the page. It is likewise in the particular arrangement of the words on the page that the poem enacts provisional answers to the questions about relationality that it poses. As a basic material of poetry, whether printed on paper or embossed as braille, digitized on a screen, or spoken aloud as invisible waves that vibrate in the ear, language is the medium through which we encounter the poem as a sensuous artifact; words, we could say, are themselves vibrant matter, and the operations of poetry, not unlike the axioms of philosophy, are necessarily proved upon our pulses. What we touch also touches us—with both sensory and affective resonances. For example, read (or read again) the word 'piteous', in the lines I quote as an epigraph from the poem's penultimate stanza:

> Piteous she look'd on dead and senseless things,
>   Asking for her lost Basil amorously;
> And with melodious chuckle in the strings
>   Of her lorn voice, she oftentimes would cry … . (489–92)

[8] For contrasting arguments about how and to what effect Keats's poetry registers the forces of materiality, see Forrest Pyle, 'Keats's Materialism', *SiR*, 33: 1 (Spring 1994), pp. 57–80; and Richard C. Sha, 'John Keats and Some Versions of Materiality', *Romanticism*, 20: 3 (2014), pp. 233–45.

[9] See Bruno Latour, *An Inquiry into Modes of Existence: An Anthropology of the Moderns*, trans. Catherine Porter (Cambridge, MA & London: Harvard University Press, 2013), on the effort to 'release' a plurality of ontologies from 'the crushing division between Object and Subject' (p. 182): he concludes that 'it always comes down to following ghosts' (p. 402).

As it is situated in the line, the word 'piteous' is grammatically uncertain or in flux; it can refer to how 'she look'd' as either a subject or an object or both, modifying how 'she look'd *on* dead and senseless things'—with feeling (pity, love) for what cannot itself feel—but also initially how '*she* look'd'—pitiable, arousing feeling in others, as indeed she does in the next and final stanza when she has died and 'No heart there was in Florence but did mourn / In pity of her love' (499). In the word 'piteous' the person who feels is entangled, perhaps inseparably, with the 'dead and senseless things' upon which she looks with such compassion and desire, her own emotion not so much projected onto as dispersed or distributed among them.[10] 'Piteous' stretches across the line as we read, crossing the line between person and thing, linking them, though with a somewhat disruptive or disorienting effect when the verb ('look'd') turns transitive (at 'on'), and we must shift our thinking, retrospectively rereading to adjust our understanding of how the word 'piteous' signifies in the line. Through its recursive sentence structures, the poem embeds such alienation effects into our experience of reading even at the level of the phoneme, the sound of its syllables.[11] When Isabella asks for her lost basil-pot 'with melodious chuckle in the strings / Of her lorn voice', it is not only the meaning but also the verbal texture of the language that articulates the tension or resistance thus embedded in the lines. Pronounced with its affricative 'ch' and plosive 'k', the word 'chuckle' contradicts its own descriptor ('melodious') by awkwardly straining against the otherwise flowing melody of the verse; we feel this strain in our own bodies in the act of reading—in our tongues, our throats, in our very breath. To read this poem (or even to hear it read) is to replicate within our own somatic experience the crisscrossing of the line between subject and object, between the active, speaking, feeling person and the 'dead and senseless things'—the world of objects, and also the words on the page—that speak to us in voices at once as familiar to us as our own and strangely dissonant.

The adjective 'piteous' is indeed strange and yet familiar too, for we are already rereading it by the time we come to the penultimate stanza, and the strain we surely feel in pronouncing these lines repeats the strain of another 'lorn voice' earlier in the poem, when the 'pale shadow' of Isabella's murdered lover appears in 'the drowsy gloom' (273) at the foot of her couch. When Lorenzo thus returns as a ghost, 'his lorn voice' (279) produces a 'strange sound' (281): 'For there was striving, in its piteous tongue, / To speak as when on earth it

[10] See Alfred Gell's formulation of 'distributed personhood', which postulates agency as enacted within or across a network of aesthetic contexts and social relations, in *Art and Agency: An Anthropological Theory* (Oxford: Oxford University Press, 1998).

[11] A term of art I borrow from Bertolt Brecht. See 'A Short Organum for the Theatre' (1949), in *Brecht on Theatre: The Development of an Aesthetic*, ed. and trans. John Willett (London: Methuen, 1964), pp. 179–205: 'A representation that alienates is one which allows us to recognize its subject, but at the same time makes it seem unfamiliar' (p. 186).

was awake' (282–3). In this earlier apparition, 'piteous' could mean pathetic in the sense of weak or inadequate, a different meaning of the same sound, which further—if in retrospect—bespeaks the dissonance elaborated in and across the lines of Keats's ottava rima stanzas. Like the looping reverberations of sounds and words and phrases that function as connective tissue throughout the poem—'O Music, Music ... O Echo, Echo' (435)—Lorenzo returns with a catch in his voice, perhaps a kind of stutter. As a ghost, Lorenzo appears as a body that is also not a body, or not a singular or stable one, but a body in motion, transformed or transformable, suspended (like the 'or' in the title of the poem) between person ('*his* lorn voice') and thing ('*its* piteous tongue'). Later I will look more closely at the appearances (and disappearances) of this body in motion and attend to the strain or 'striving' that echoes as a 'ghostly under-song' throughout (and beyond) Keats's romance. Through the unsettled, changing form of the ghost, the poem mobilizes the tension or resistance within structures of feeling (such as pity or love) that attach persons to things, personhood to thingness, human to nonhuman or not-quite-human bodies. These attachments at once enact and act against normative states of being or orders of experience, including those (such as consciousness, memory, or desire) usually attributed to individual human subjectivity as wholly distinct from mere objecthood. In the multiple incarnations of Lorenzo's ghost, including the haunting image of his severed head, 'Isabella; or, The Pot of Basil' conjures the paranormal within the intimate relation between persons and things; as a figure of that relation—that 'dissonant connection'—the ghost embodies the transgressive potential within the practices of everyday life, even, or even especially, within the practices of our own everyday lives as readers, which is to say as lovers of literary texts.[12] I suggest that it is in the routines and rituals that shape ordinary experience, 'the most banal and repetitive gestures of everyday life', such as turning the pages of a book to read a poem or watering a plant in a pot, that we may find ourselves, more like Isabella than we might like to think, dancing with ghosts.[13]

[12] On professional literary study as affective labor, see Deidre Shauna Lynch, *Loving Literature: A Cultural History* (Chicago, IL: University of Chicago Press, 2015). Also see Karen Swann, 'The Strange Time of Reading', *European Romantic Review*, 9: 2 (1998), pp. 275–82, where reading Keats (like gazing upon an image of his death mask) feels 'like hopeless love, or love, or mourning' (p. 275).

[13] Alice Kaplan and Kristen Ross, 'Introduction', to 'Everyday Life', *Yale French Studies*, 73 (1987), pp. 1–4, 3. See also Michel de Certeau, *The Practice of Everyday Life*, trans. Steven Rendell (Berkeley & Los Angeles: University of California Press, 1984), in which the practices of everyday life, including reading, can function subversively without being openly or directly challenging: what looks like assimilation can (or even necessarily will) transform the dominant order through strategies of adaptation, bricolage, or, more transgressively, poaching.

I

> The objects we have known in better days are the main props that sustain the weight of our affections, and give us strength to await our future lot. The future is like a dead wall or a thick mist hiding all objects from our view; the past is alive and stirring with objects, bright or solemn, and of unfading interest.[14]

> You crave to let history haunt you as a ghost or ghosts, with the ungraspable incorporation of a ghostly body, and the uncontrollable, sporadic, and unanticipatable periodicity of haunting, in the impossible frame of the absolute chance of the gift of time, if there is any.[15]

Let us begin our ghost dance with this pair of epigraphs. The first is from William Hazlitt's 'On the Past and Future', which was published in his *Table Talk* volume of 1821; the second is from 'Ghostwriting', Gayatri Chakravorty Spivak's 1995 critical response to Jacques Derrida's *Spectres of Marx* (1994). You would not be wrong to think that Hazlitt and Spivak make a rather odd couple, but such strange coupling is precisely what I want to explore in the intimate relation between the young woman and the garden-pot depicted in Keats's verse romance. Though obviously quite different as to time and place and other determinative circumstances of their writing, these passages from Hazlitt and Spivak overlap or intersect across their significant differences in calling up ghosts. Both essays are concerned with the potential of objects or bodies from the past—one personal and the other political—to 'produce effects, alter the course of events', to act, in Jane Bennett's phrase, as vibrant matter (p. viii). What Hazlitt and Spivak may contribute to a new materialist account of the vitality of matter is an old materialist attention to the legacies of history, whether personal or political or both. In thus feeling backwards, appealing to a looping temporality by which traces of the past might return laden with affective force and transformative potential, Hazlitt and Spivak together offer a new approach to Isabella's passionate attachment to the pot of basil.[16] If that approach takes some detours or makes some strange moves, it may have to do so in order to reread that intimate relation as an effort to disrupt from within its structure of repetition the ongoing trajectory of the everyday.

[14] William Hazlitt, 'On the Past and Future', in *Table Talk; or, Original Essays*, vol. 1 (London: John Warren, 1821), pp. 43–64.

[15] Gayatri Chakravorty Spivak, 'Ghostwriting', *Diacritics*, 25: 2 (Summer 1995), pp. 64–84, 70.

[16] I borrow this phrase from Heather Love, *Feeling Backward: Loss and the Politics of Queer History* (Cambridge, MA & London: Harvard University Press, 2007).

In 'On the Past and Future', the author of *The Spirit of the Age* (1825) asserts the enduring power of objects, even or even most forcefully those remnants of the past that provoke feelings of 'bitter disappointment' (p. 51); Hazlitt understands such remnants as a 'real and substantial ... part of our being' (p. 46). While the future, he declares, is uncertain, 'may never come to pass at all, that is, may never be embodied into actual existence in the whole course of events', the past is 'downright and sensible', materialized in or as objects that are 'alive and stirring' and thereby also stir us, potent enough still to sustain 'the weight of our affections' and elicit our 'unfading interest' (p. 47). For Hazlitt, the past is never quite or only past but persists into the ongoing present, including into the unfolding present as he writes and extending into our reading as we turn the pages he has written. The essay itself instantiates the efficacy of residual objects by means of which we maintain 'our hold upon the past' (p. 48) into the present. For example, Hazlitt describes Rousseau's tendency 'to gather up the past moments of his being like drops of honey-dew to distil a precious liquor from them; his alternate pleasures and pains are the bead-roll that he tells over and piously worships; he makes a rosary of the flowers of hope and fancy that strewed his earliest years' (p. 49). Thus defending Rousseau's devotion to the memory of Madame Warens, the lover of his youth, as a potent mode of repetition, a way 'to live the first and best part of [life] over again, and once more be all that he then was', the essayist recalls his own more recently lost beloved:

> that face pale as the primrose with hyacinthine locks, forever shunning and forever haunting me ... those eyes dark with their own lustre, still bent on mine ... that form gliding before me like Oread or Dryad in fabled groves. (p. 51)

With its pale face swelling into reality, summoned into the essay in the very midst of its composition, this phantom figure—indeterminately human or nonhuman or not-quite-human—produces a 'real and substantial' effect in the essay itself, prompting a dramatic shift in Hazlitt's familiar style from conversational prose to a genre of impassioned apostrophe that according to Charles Lamb 'approximates to the finest poetry'. As Hazlitt finds 'the great charm' of *Confessions* to be Rousseau's attachment to the past as tangible objects such as a bead-roll or rosary, Lamb appreciates 'On the Past and Future' as 'the most valuable' essay in the *Table Talk* volume precisely for the way it 'maintains the reality [of the past] as a possession in hand'.[17]

[17] Lamb's review of *Table Talk* remained unpublished until it appeared in *Lamb as Critic*, ed. Roy Park (Lincoln & London: University of Nebraska Press, 1980), pp. 299–307. It is worth mentioning that Lamb also admired 'the paraphrase of Boccaccio's story' (an 'affecting revivial') as 'the finest thing' in Keats's 1820 volume (pp. 243–5).

For Spivak, to the contrary, the past appears 'ungraspable', yet her invocation of 'a ghostly body' also mixes memory and desire—'you crave to let history haunt you as a ghost or ghosts'. In *Spectres of Marx*, the ghostly body is a 'familiar, too familiar' object, the wooden table in *Capital* that 'has been worn down, exploited, overexploited', but Derrida turns to it again to 'take the chance, then, after so many glosses, of an ingenious reading'.[18] Marx describes the 'obvious, trivial thing' turning into 'a very strange thing' as a commodity: that table 'stands on its head and evolves out of its wooden brain grotesque ideas'.[19] In Derrida's re-enactment of this transformation, the ordinary thing 'becomes someone ... its body comes alive ... it appears to put itself spontaneously into motion', thereby generating a host of contradictions—as a 'bodiless body' it is at once too familiar and very strange, creaturely and artifactual, 'dead and alive at the same time' (pp. 188–92).

Spivak responds to this burlesque performance in *Spectres of Marx* by making another move, spinning Derrida's 'whirling dance of ghosts' (p. 161) in a different direction. She brings James Mooney's late nineteenth-century ethnography in *The Ghost-Dance Religion and the Sioux Outbreak of 1890* into her account of the ghost dance as 'a prayer to be haunted' (p. 78). Invoking the history of settler colonialism and its ongoing legacies of violence and injustice, she approaches the ghost dance as a communal ritual, a collective act of protest or resistance in which the ghostly bodies of 'ancestors real or imagined' (p. 70) are summoned as an intervention, for the sake of or 'as a future' (p. 71). Like Hazlitt, Spivak acknowledges that the future is an 'absolute chance' or, as in Hazlitt, something that 'may never come to pass at all', and so the ghostly bodies thus ceremonially summoned could only return phantasmatically, as an 'uncertain subjunctive' (p. 79)—'uncontrollable, sporadic, and unanticipatable'. And yet it may be only within such a state of uncertainty and doubt that the ritual to recall the bodies of the dead could represent a 'condition of possibility', an opportunity to imagine some alternative to an oppressive social and political order, to tap into some latent but powerful capacity for creating change (p. 77). Though this alternative may never actually materialize, though it may be available only in the shadowy form of a desire or a hope, 'ungraspable' or 'impossible', 'yet', Spivak contends, the effort to call it into being 'is the only way to go at moments of crisis' (p. 71).

But time is passing, even now, as you turn the pages to read this essay; the present is becoming the past as I linger so long and with such unfading interest on my epigraphs, which can themselves be considered 'rather ghostly',

[18] Jacques Derrida, *Spectres of Marx: The State of the Debt, the Work of Mourning and the New International*, trans. Peggy Kamuf (New York & London: Routledge, 1994), pp. 186–7.

[19] Karl Marx, *Capital: A Critique of Political Economy*, vol. I, trans. Ben Fowkes (New York: Penguin, 1992), p. 163.

as Marjorie Garber has proposed.[20] Derrida notes in *Spectres of Marx* that 'everyone reads, acts, writes with *his* or *her* ghosts, even when one goes after the ghosts of the other' (p. 174). Spivak also (parenthetically) avows her own 'possession' by another's ghosts when she turns to Assia Djebar's *Far from Medina* in 'Ghostwriting': 'The chief occasion for my essay is *Spectres of Marx*. I am so taken by these ghostwomen of Islam that I cannot end the piece without giving an account of my possession. (In fact, this entire piece is obsessed with the stakes that academics develop after years of work, peculiar "identifications" that drive their "life" ...)' (p. 80). Hazlitt's essay is similarly obsessed and possessed, not only haunted by the pale face and dark eyes of his lost beloved but also by the writing of others, 'to judge not only by its subject but by the sheer density of quotations'.[21] As quotation, sentences marked as extracted and repeated, words cut from other pages and pasted onto this paper here, my epigraphs function as material remnants or relics—in Susan Stewart's apposite phrase, 'quotation appears as a severed head'.[22] And don't we all, doesn't 'everyone', look upon such fine phrases like a lover? Surely Keats does when he rewrites 'old prose in modern rhyme' (156), 'venturing syllables' (151) that 'echo' (160) the 'eloquent and famed Boccaccio' (145) in 'Isabella; or, The Pot of Basil', the romance about which many readers have said what Derrida says of the spectres of Marx: 'it is again a question of the head' (p. 172).

Linking Keats's poem to the transformations of the ordinary object that 'comes alive' through a logic of commodity fetishism is not my idea. George Bernard Shaw famously commented a century ago that if 'Karl Marx can be imagined as writing a poem instead of a treatise on Capital, he would have written *Isabella*',[23] and a number of excellent readings have drawn on Shaw's speculation to examine the social critique the poem offers, for example, in its depiction of Isabella's murderous merchant brothers.[24] The broader relevance for Romanticism of Derrida's apparitional reading of Marx ('after so many glosses')

[20] Marjorie Garber, '"" " " (QuotationMarks)', *Critical Inquiry*, 25: 4 (Summer 1999), pp. 653–79, 658. Also see Deidre Lynch on 'quotation compulsion' in *Loving Literature*: 'words can haunt as much as apparitions do' (p. 199).

[21] David Bromwich, *Hazlitt: The Mind of a Critic* (New York & Oxford: Oxford University Press, 1983), p. 188. In the case of this essay, as in Hazlitt's writing more broadly according to Bromwich, the 'identification' is with Wordsworth.

[22] Susan Stewart, *On Longing: Narratives of the Miniature, the Gigantic, the Souvenir, the Collection* (Durham, NC and London: Duke University Press, 1993), p. 19; also, on words as things, see William Keach, *Arbitrary Power: Romanticism, Language, Politics* (Princeton, NJ and Oxford: Princeton University Press, 2004), pp. 23–45.

[23] George Bernard Shaw, 'Keats' in *John Keats Memorial Volume*, ed. G.C. Williamson (London: John Lane, 1921), pp. 175–6.

[24] See, for example, Kurt Heinzelman, 'Self-Interest and the Politics of Composition in Keats's *Isabella*', *ELH*, 55: 1 (Spring 1988), pp. 159–93.

has also been compellingly examined.[25] It could be said that in Keats's poem the role of the ordinary object that turns into 'a strange creature' is played by the herb that grows so vigorously in the garden-pot that also contains the severed head of Lorenzo (Derrida, *Spectres*, p. 190). Drawing 'life, from human fears' and tears as well as 'the fast mouldering head' (lines 429–30), the flourishing plant in the pot becomes a very strange thing; spreading its leaves so abundantly, 'more balmy than its peers / Of Basil-tufts in Florence' (427–8), it inspires the curiosity and wonder of Isabella's kin by seeming to grow 'as by magic touch' (459).

But my real interest here is in what the ghostly objects and bodies animated in the essays by Hazlitt and Spivak bring to the story Keats tells about the intimate relation between persons and things in 'Isabella; or, The Pot of Basil'. I layer or loop these essays together in a 'web of dissonant connections' which may, like the objects from the past that are 'alive and stirring' for Hazlitt or the communal version of the ghost dance Spivak evokes as a 'prayer to be haunted', gesture towards an alternative reading of Keats's poem. While *Table-Talk* does not appear in print in time for Keats to have read 'On the Past and Future', Hazlitt's significant influence on Keats's thinking and writing has been amply demonstrated.[26] We do not need to establish a clear and direct link, however, or even recall that Keats may have gleaned the idea of composing this particular poem from Hazlitt, to see in the way the essayist values lost objects as phantom bodies only a slightly less fervent attachment to relics of the past than Isabella's to the pot of basil that holds the cherished remains of her lover. Nor is Spivak's conjuring of the desire and hope collectively expressed in the ghost dance ritual of the Plains Indians irrelevant to the situation of the young woman yearning for her absent lover and calling to '[h]is image in the dusk' in her own 'prayer to be haunted': 'Spreading her perfect arms upon the air, / And on her couch low murmuring "Where? O where?"' (237–40).[27] We should acknowledge the crucial differences between the actual violence (that continues to be) inflicted on indigenous peoples by the catastrophe of settler colonialism and the virtual suffering of a young woman whose lover has been murdered by her brothers in a verse romance.

[25] See especially Orrin N.C. Wang, 'Ghost Theory', *Studies in Romanticism*, 46: 2 (2007), pp. 203–25, 204. Also David Simpson, *Wordsworth and Social Concern: The Poetics of Modernity* (Cambridge: Cambridge University Press, 2009); and Susan Wolfson, *Romantic Shades and Shadows* (Baltimore, MD: Johns Hopkins University Press, 2018).

[26] In addition to David Bromwich, *Hazlitt: The Mind of a Critic*, see for example, Duncan Wu, 'Keats and Hazlitt', in *John Keats in Context*, ed. Michael O'Neill (Cambridge: Cambridge University Press, 2017), pp. 159–67.

[27] Boccaccio construes this gesture as a 'prayer to be haunted' even more clearly: 'In the silence of darke night, as she lay afflicted in her bed, oftentimes would she call for Lorenzo, entreating his speedy returning to her'.

And yet we might consider Avery Gordon's proposition that 'in haunting, organized forces and systemic structures that appear removed from us make their impact felt in everyday life in a way that confounds our analytic separations', to consider what looking at the intimacy between person and thing in 'Isabella; or, The Pot of Basil' as a ghost dance affords to our reading or rereading of Keats's poem, of Romanticism, and of everyday life.[28] It may be that it is only when 'our analytic separations' are confounded, when the lines we commonly draw to understand the world in which we live and our own position in it become intertwined or entangled, that we can begin to imagine, and to move, in some other direction.

II

> In my present state of Health I feel too much separated from you and could almost speak to you in the words of Lorenzo's Ghost to Isabella
>
> Your beauty grows upon me and I feel
> A greater love through all my essence steal.[29]

What is the essence of a ghost? When Keats repeats the words of Lorenzo's ghost in a letter to his own beloved, is he speaking as himself or as another (fictional) being? Is he living or dead? Is he a person or a thing? Or does the apophatic 'almost' with which he posits the repetition intimate what will eventually become his habitual feeling that he is leading a posthumous existence, 'dead and alive at the same time'? If in this letter to Fanny Brawne the poet feels ('too much separated') like the ghost of Lorenzo, in another he identifies more closely with the living lover, though she, too, 'is soon to be / Among the dead' (446–7) and so proleptically turned into a ghost as well. When Keats expresses his passion for his 'dearest Girl' by declaring, 'I can

[28] Avery F. Gordon, *Ghostly Matters: Haunting and the Sociological Imagination* (Minneapolis: University of Minnesota Press, 1997), p. 19. See also Cathy Caruth, *Unclaimed Experience: Trauma, Narrative, and History* (Baltimore, MD: Johns Hopkins University Press, 1996, 2016): 'personal trauma is never wholly extricable from larger social and political modes of denial … the "individual" and the "collective" cannot be extricated from each other, in the destruction of experience, which can never be grounded in the unity of a single position or voice' (p. 121). Also pertinent here is Alan Bewell's suggestive allusion to 'the song of the Plains Indian Ghost Dance' at the end of his reading of 'Lamia' in 'Place, Emotion, and the Colonial Translation of Natures' (Unpublished Keynote Lecture, Literary Environments Conference, Griffith University, Gold Coast, Australia, 17–19 July 2017).

[29] To Fanny Brawne, ? Feb 1820. Keats's letters are quoted from *The Letters of John Keats, 1814–1821*, ed. Hyder E. Rollins, 2 vols. (Cambridge, MA: Harvard University Press, 1958).

think of nothing else … I am forgetful of every thing but seeing you again— my Life seems to stop there—',[30] he almost echoes the amnesia attributed to the woman in love with the pot of basil in his poem:

> And she forgot the stars, the moon, and sun,
>   And she forgot the blue above the trees,
> And she forgot the dells where waters run,
>   And she forgot the chilly Autumn breeze … . (lines 417–20)

Here the insistent repetition of the phrase 'and she forgot' creates an effect similar to the one it describes, as if the poet were so attached to that evocative sentence fragment that he forgets to move on, his progress stopped there or possible only recursively, in the form of anaphora. But what I want particularly to notice in the letters to Fanny Brawne are the shifts and turns, the crossings and recrossings, within the patterns of repetition Keats's writing puts into play as it moves, looping between real life and fiction, linking the feelings of a living man to those of a dead one and also to the experience of a woman barely as alive as the object that sustains the weight of her affections even as she herself withers, grows spectre-thin, and dies. In such movement, such loops and linkages across specific embodiments and disparate domains, we might discern the choreography of a ghost dance. Calling up the ghost both within and beyond 'Isabella; or, The Pot of Basil' and repeatedly crossing the line that separates the inside from the outside of a particular body or a particular text, Keats's writing registers both the dissonance of the connections it establishes and their transgressive possibilities.

'Spectres', Marc Redfield proposes, 'render uncertain differences between self and other, here and there, present and past (or future): they are neither the one nor the other, and both'. Orrin Wang asserts 'the tangible intangibility of a ghost cuts across' at least one binary central to philosophy, politics, and the definition of Romanticism, that is, 'the material versus the ideal'.[31] Neither the one nor the other and both, cutting across categorical binaries, the ambiguous ontology of the ghost makes it a paradigmatic example of Bill Brown's 'other thing', which is the capacity of any object, any particular body, to turn into something (or 'someone') else.[32] In Keats's verse romance, Lorenzo appears at the foot of Isabella's couch as 'a thing more deadly dark than all' (line 266), and also as 'a vision' (272), a 'pale shadow' (281), a 'Spirit' (321); when Isabella

[30] To Fanny Brawne, 13 October 1819.

[31] Marc Redfield, 'Spectral Romanticisms', *European Romantic Review*, 9: 2 (1998), pp. 271–3, 271; Orrin N.C. Wang, 'Ghost Theory', *Studies in Romanticism*, 46: 2 (2007), pp. 203–25, 204.

[32] Bill Brown, *Other Things* (Chicago, IL & London: University of Chicago Press, 2015).

exhumes his body ('the clay, so dearly prized' [339]) and severs his head, he is transfigured once again, into a 'jewel, safely casketed' (431) in the pot; when Isabella's brothers steal the pot to 'sift / This hidden whim' (465–6), they find a 'thing … vile with green and livid spot' (475) that is nonetheless still recognizable as Lorenzo. As a 'ghostly body', 'a very strange thing', at once so many things and 'such / A very nothing' (461–2), Lorenzo resists or disrupts the normative logic of identity and difference, not least the difference between living, feeling persons and 'dead and senseless things'. So it is not just the chameleon poet who shifts his shape, continually filling some other body; Keats's romance operates on the principle that identity (being 'someone', a particular body) is necessarily an ongoing process, a mode of being enacted through the recurrences of the everyday, especially an everyday that emerges, to borrow William Galperin's recent formulation, as a 'history of missed opportunities', a present that only manifests *as such* in ghostly returns of the past.[33]

It is time, or past time, to return to the poem (after so many glosses) in which, as I have been suggesting, Keats choreographs the intimate relation between the young woman and the pot with the decomposing head inside as a ghost dance. Lorenzo's 'ghostly body' (at once human and nonhuman or not-quite-human) instantiates this relation, mobilizes it, acts as its mediating figure, a figure *of* mediation, though crucially not between two wholly distinct or stable ontologies (person and thing, living and dead) but as the occasion of their intersection. The ghost acts as an interface, a site of contact or conjuncture where one mode of being touches and might be transformed by or into another, the circumstance whereby they become entangled or intertwined, if only for a time, or over time, over again, continually. We could say that in Keats's poem the ghost functions as an instance of what Richard Grusin has called 'radical mediation': 'the process, action, or event that generates or provides the condition for the emergence of subjects and objects, for the individuation of entities in the world'.[34] For Grusin, it is worth noting, all mediation is *re*mediation and so necessarily entails repetition or return within its most formative (or deformative) potentials.

Reading Keats's poem in terms of ghost dancing is one way to recognize its (unfading) interest in objects that are alive and stirring or in matter that becomes all the more vital or vivid as pale shadows of the past. We have learned

[33] William H. Galperin, *The History of Missed Opportunities: British Romanticism and the Emergence of the Everyday* (Palo Alto, CA: Stanford University Press, 2017). Galperin argues that in emerging in or as retrospection, the everyday is a characteristically Romantic formulation.

[34] Richard Grusin, 'Radical Mediation', *Critical Inquiry*, 42 (Autumn 2015), pp. 124–48, 137–8. See also Karen Barad's claim that 'distinct entities, agencies, events do not precede, but rather emerge from/through their intra-action'. Karen Barad, 'Quantum Entanglements and Hauntological Relations of Inheritance: Dis/continuities, SpaceTime Enfoldings, and Justice-to-Come', *Derrida Today* 3: 2 (2010), p. 267.

from Marjorie Levinson to see in Keats's characteristic sensuousness an (over) investment in 'aesthetic things' as signs of a social code he can never quite crack, a form of fetishism, or a kind of kitsch.[35] The ghost dance in 'Isabella; or, The Pot of Basil' mobilizes the efficacy and force of such artifactual desire by valuing the most 'obvious, trivial thing' precisely for its reproducibility—its capacity to return; the ghost dance embraces kitsch, then, not as distinct from a more authentic work of art but as the very work of art, of the artifactual. 'In kitsch', writes Walter Benjamin, 'the world of things advances on the human being; it yields to his uncertain grasp and ultimately fashions its figures in his interior'—perhaps more like a tango than a waltz, with agency or desire suspended (like the 'or' in the title of Keats's poem) between the world of things (advancing, yielding) and the human being (grasping, but uncertainly).[36] Such moves or turns repeat the shifting distribution of affect across lines such as 'piteous she look'd on dead and senseless things', discussed at the beginning of this essay, or the way Keats unfolds the scene in which Isabella, digging for Lorenzo's body, 'turn'd up a soiled glove whereon / Her silk had play'd in purple phantasies' (lines 369–70). The phrase '[h]er silk had play'd in purple phantasies' shifts desire between person and thing. That 'her silk' rather than her*self* is the designated fantasist here hints at the loop the poem slips between human agency and the efficacy of the object; when she kisses the glove 'with a lip more chill than stone' and 'put it in her bosom, where it dries / And freezes utterly unto the bone / Those dainties made to still an infant's cries' (371–4), the figural closeness of person and thing is expressly though also uncomfortably material, skin touching skin, the living and the dead meeting in a body that becomes something or someone else at the point of contact.

The soiled glove that still bears the traces of Isabella's hand also recalls Lorenzo's body, and Lorenzo's body, like the glove, also appears more vivid and alive in being thus recovered in a residual form; when he appears as a 'pale shadow' at the foot of Isabella's couch, 'the reality of his body is now eerily inescapable' in a way it had not been earlier in the poem.[37] More than a few readers have noted Lorenzo's passivity in the poem's opening stanzas, where he more than once determines to declare his love but repeatedly postpones doing it.[38] Keats invents this extended hesitation, emphasizing 'the meekness' (47)

[35] Marjorie Levinson, *Keats's Life of Allegory: The Origins of a Style* (Oxford & Cambridge, MA: Basil Blackwell, 1988), pp. 9, 19.

[36] See the account of tango as 'a state of becoming though alterity' in Erin Manning, *The Politics of Touch*, pp. 1–18, 3.

[37] Kelvin Everest, 'Isabella in the Marketplace: Keats and Feminism', in *Keats and History*, ed. Nicholas Roe (Cambridge: Cambridge University Press, 1995), pp. 107–27, 121.

[38] Bernard Beatty notes the 'timidity and tepidity' of both lovers in 'Keats's Salutary Weakness: A Reading of *Isabella*', *The Aligarh Critical Miscellany*, 8: 1 (1995), pp. 44–61, 46.

that prevents Lorenzo from acting on his desire; even the close and continual watch Lorenzo keeps on Isabella in these early lines is passively constructed as 'her full shape would all his seeing fill' (12). The lovers discourse only to their pillows, and they both fall sick with longing, Lorenzo 'waxing very pale and dead' (53) until Isabella says his name and he is thereby moved to avow his passion. To such inaction and delay, compare the sudden impact of the phantom at the foot of Isabella's couch: 'It came like a fierce potion, drunk by chance … // like a lance, / Waking an Indian from his cloudy hall / With cruel pierce …' (266–71). Though but a 'pale shadow' (281), Lorenzo's physical body is represented more forcefully and in more vivid detail in its residual state than when he was a living person: we are told about his 'glossy hair which once could shoot / Lustre into the sun' (276–7) only after it is marred by 'the forest tomb' (275). He is but a 'shadow now' (305), yet 'his eyes, though wild, were still all dewy bright' (289), and, as he asserts, he knows what a body knows and feels what a body feels—including love and pain. We might say that the dead Lorenzo is more alive than Lorenzo living, that he dies into life. As a ghost, he exerts a compelling force, instructing Isabella where to find his body and requesting (or is he demanding) that she go to mourn him there. As a ghost, even his disappearance offers evidence of the real and not just the reality effects of his presence: 'The Spirit mourn'd "Adieu!"—dissolv'd, and left / The atom darkness in a slow turmoil' (321–2). The ghost agitates the particles of the atmosphere. Moreover, if as a man alive, Lorenzo has trouble declaring his passion, as a ghost the 'strange sound' of his voice is forceful and dynamic, 'invad[ing]' the poem in Keats's contorted syntax, as Andrew Bennett has observed, which is thus repeated in 'the reading mouth', and again, as we have seen, beyond the pages of the poem, in Keats's letter to Fanny Brawne.[39] In the context of his argument, Bennett sees the intrusion of a character's voice into the descriptive frame of the poem as a sign of the poet's anxieties about audience and reception; in my argument here, such metaleptic transgression performs the effects described *in* the poem (as narrative) as effects *of* the poem (as material artifact).

And then, of course, there is the question of the head, that 'bodiless body', another ghostly incarnation of the lost Lorenzo. The scene in which Isabella, an ardent mortician, cuts off Lorenzo's head and lovingly grooms it has been singled out as among the most visceral in Keats's writing, conveying a more insistently sensuous intimacy than the more conventional metaphors the poet devises to describe the lovers' attachment earlier in the poem, such as when Lorenzo's 'timid lips grew bold, / And poesied with hers in dewy rhyme' (69–70), or where 'they seem'd to tread upon the air, / Twin roses by the

[39] Andrew Bennett, *Keats, Narrative, and Audience: The Posthumous Life of Writing* (Cambridge: Cambridge University Press, 1994), p. 88.

zepher blown apart' (73–4). Focusing on Isabella's tender care close-up and in detail—'She calm'd its wild hair with a golden comb, / And all around each eye's sepulchral cell / Pointed each fringed lash …' (403–5)—Keats calls our attention to the head, as if 'he can't help but grimly celebrate its presence, making it more than ever the object of our fascinated look'. Thus Leo Bersani and Ulysse Dutoit, describing Caravaggio's 'David with the Head of Goliath', remark the 'dilemma of a head whose prominence and power may be only increased by its separation from the body'.[40] Our own fascination with the remnant of Lorenzo that Isabella so lovingly tends, wraps in a 'silken scarf', and buries in the garden-pot attests to its 'prominence and power' in Keats's poem.[41]

Critical discussion of the head in the pot has tended to acknowledge its emphatic, even grotesque materiality and then move rather quickly to adduce its figurative significance. Thus it becomes 'an emblem of the power of illusion to make beautiful what is ugly' or 'an emblem of totally privatized emotion' or 'an emblem of class' or 'the missing signifier' or it is seen as 'so full a symbol, associated with containers of different kinds: wombs, eggs, and the earth that nourishes seeds'.[42] The head appears to be so full a symbol, we might agree, that it represents the symbolic itself—what Tilottama Rajan would call 'the nature of representation' or what Levinson identifies as 'the supplement' ('absolutely apparitional').[43] I abbreviate these important and complex readings here to point to how the pot with the decomposing head inside repeatedly appears by disappearing into its symbolic function, as a trope or a trace, its ghostly transfiguration precisely what sustains our 'unfading interest', if not also our love. As professional readers, or lovers, of literature, perhaps we are not so unlike Isabella hanging so dotingly over her pot of basil; indeed, 'we dwell on the head',[44] practicing as we do for our living, as part of our everyday routines and rituals, what Emily Apter has called the 'fetishism of reading—"a common reading disposition—seizing and worrying literary details"'—or what Arjun

[40] Leo Bersani and Ulysse Dutoit, *Caravaggio's Secrets* (Cambridge, MA: MIT Press, 1998), p. 89.

[41] Also see Regina Janes, *Losing Our Heads: Beheading in Literature and Culture* (New York: New York University Press, 2005), which links severed heads to 'becoming human' (p. 9).

[42] Tilottama Rajan, *Dark Interpreter: The Discourse of Romanticism* (Ithaca, NY: Cornell University Press, 1980), p. 129; Jeffrey N. Cox, '*Lamia*, *Isabella*, and *The Eve of St. Agnes*', in *The Cambridge Companion to Keats*, ed. Susan J. Wolfson (Cambridge: Cambridge University Press, 2001), pp. 53–68, 62; Diane Long Hoeveler, 'Decapitating Romance: Class, Fetish, and Ideology in Keats's *Isabella*', *Nineteenth-Century Fiction*, 49: 3 (1994), pp. 321–38, 324; Michael Lagory, 'Wormy Circumstance', *Studies in Romanticism* (1995), pp. 321–42, 341.

[43] Rajan, *Dark Interpreter*, p. 111; Levinson, *Keats's Life of Allegory*, pp. 144, 157.

[44] Hoeveler, 'Decapitating Romance', p. 329.

Appadurai has characterized as 'methodological fetishism', which 'return[s] our attention to the things themselves'[45] and to our intimacy with those things that are at once as familiar to us as we are to ourselves and as strange.

Perhaps we are not so unlike Isabella in her fervent attachment to the garden-pot or so unlike her brothers, who 'wonder'd much' (457) 'what the thing might mean' (460). Such wondering about the meaning of the thing is also a question of the head or of the ideas that evolve in and out of it, and it takes us back to the ghost dance as 'a prayer to be haunted', an effort to grasp the 'ungraspable' by holding on to the bodies we have loved and love still, even or inevitably as ghosts. Readers have widely understood the 'dissonant connection' between the young woman and the 'dead and senseless things' upon which she looks with such love and longing within the framework of an aberrant psychology; her passionate attachment to the pot with the head inside is usually 'pathologized'—diagnosed as 'obsessive', 'neurotic', 'irrational', or 'perverse'.[46] To think of it instead as dancing with ghosts allows us to consider other valences of this 'dissonant connection', maybe seeing it as a response to a traumatic history, perhaps an act of protest or resistance to the prevailing order, even a call for disorder, for the disruption of normative modes of relation between human and nonhuman or not-quite-human bodies, or between individual and collective experience, or between the repetitions of everyday life and the aberrations that challenge even as they are conscripted to its rituals and routines. If there is a pathology operating in the attachment of the grieving young woman to the garden-pot in Keats's poem, it may indeed be the pathology of (para)normativity. When she spreads her arms and calls to 'his image in the dusk', Isabella craves to let history haunt her as the ghostly body of her lost beloved. What possible or impossible futures might begin to take shape if we were to see this 'prayer to be haunted' as an invitation to transgressive forms of relationality and an embrace of the as yet unrealized potential of such dissonant connections?

[45] Emily Apter, *Feminizing the Fetish: Psychoanalysis and Narrative Obsession in Turn-Of-the-Century France* (Ithaca, NY: Cornell University Press, 1991), p. x; Appadurai, *The Social Life of Things*, p. 5.

[46] Hoeveler, 'Decapitating Romance' p. 331; Kathleen Beres Rogers, 'Breeding Scorpions in the Brain: Obsession in Keats's *Isabella; or, The Pot of Basil*', *Essays in Romanticism*, 19 (2012), pp. 33–47, 43; Kelvin Everest, 'Isabella in the Marketplace', p. 121; Rajan, *Dark Interpreter*, p. 102; Michael Sider, 'Isabella and the Dialogism of Romance', *Nineteenth-Century Contexts*, 22: 3 (2000), pp. 329–51, 345; Wolfson, *Reading John Keats* (Cambridge: Cambridge University Press, 2015), p. 55.

Bibliography

Appadurai, Arjun. *The Social Life of Objects: Commodities in Cultural Perspective.* Cambridge: Cambridge University Press, 1986.

Apter, Emily. *Feminizing the Fetish: Psychoanalysis and Narrative Obsession in Turn-Of-the-Century France.* Ithaca, NY: Cornell University Press, 1991.

Barad, Karen. *Meeting the Universe Halfway: Quantum Physics and the Entanglement of Matter and Meaning.* Durham, NC & London: Duke University Press, 2007.

——. 'On Touching—the Inhuman That Therefore I Am'. *differences,* 23: 3 (2012), pp. 206–23.

——. 'Quantum Entanglements and Hauntological Relations of Inheritance: Dis/continuities, SpaceTime Enfoldings, and Justice-to-Come', *Derrida Today* 3: 2 (2010), pp. 240–68, doi:10.3366/E1754850010000813.

Beatty, Bernard. 'Keats's Salutary Weakness: A Reading of *Isabella*'. *The Aligarh Critical Miscellany,* 8: 1 (1995), pp. 44–61.

Bennett, Andrew. *Keats, Narrative, and Audience: The Posthumous Life of Writing.* Cambridge: Cambridge University Press, 1994.

Bennett, Jane. 'Systems and Things: A Response to Graham Harman and Timothy Morton'. *New Literary History,* 43 (2012), pp. 225–33.

——. *Vibrant Matter: A Political Ecology of Things.* Durham, NC & London: Duke University Press, 2010.

Bersani, Leo and Ulysse Dutoit. *Caravaggio's Secrets.* Cambridge, MA: MIT Press, 1998.

Bewell, Alan. 'Place, Emotion, and the Colonial Translation of Natures'. Unpublished Keynote Lecture, Literary Environments Conference, Griffith University, Gold Coast, Australia, 17–19 July 2017.

Brecht, Bertolt. 'A Short Organum for the Theatre'. In *Brecht on Theatre: The Development of an Aesthetic,* ed. and trans. by John Willett. London: Methuen, 1964, pp. 179–205.

Bromwich, David. *Hazlitt: The Mind of a Critic.* Oxford: Oxford University Press, 1983.

Brown, Bill. *Other Things.* Chicago, IL & London: University of Chicago Press, 2015.

——. 'Thing Theory'. In *Things,* ed. Bill Brown. Chicago, IL & London: University of Chicago Press, 2004, pp. 1–22.

Caruth, Cathy. *Unclaimed Experience: Trauma, Narrative, and History.* Baltimore, MD: Johns Hopkins University Press, 1996, 2016.

Coole, Diana and Samantha Frost. 'Introducing the New Materialism'. In *New Materialism: Ontology, Agency, and Politics,* eds. Diana Coole and Samantha Frost. Durham, NC & London: Duke University Press, 2010, pp. 1–43.

Cox, Jeffrey N. '*Lamia, Isabella,* and *The Eve of St. Agnes*'. In *The Cambridge Companion to Keats,* ed. Susan J. Wolfson. Cambridge: Cambridge University Press, 2001, pp. 53–68.

De Certeau, Michel. *The Practice of Everyday Life*, trans. Steven Rendell. Berkeley & Los Angeles: University of California Press, 1984.

De Man, Paul. 'The Rhetoric of Temporality.' In *Blindness and Insight: Essays in the Rhetoric of Contemporary Criticism*. Minneapolis: University of Minnesota Press, 1971, pp. 187–228.

Derrida, Jacques. *Spectres of Marx: The State of the Debt, the Work of Mourning and the New International*, trans. Peggy Kamuf. New York & London: Routledge, 1994.

Everest, Kelvin. 'Isabella in the Marketplace: Keats and Feminism'. In *Keats and History*, ed. Nicholas Roe. Cambridge: Cambridge University Press, 1995, pp. 107–27.

Fisher, Tom H. 'What We Touch, Touches Us: Materials, Affects, and Affordances'. *Design Issues*, 20: 4 (2004), pp. 20–31.

Galperin, William H. *The History of Missed Opportunities: British Romanticism and the Emergence of the Everyday*. Palo Alto, CA: Stanford University Press, 2017.

Garber, Marjorie. '" " " (QuotationMarks)'. *Critical Inquiry*, 25: 4 (1999), pp. 653–79.

Gell, Alfred. *Art and Agency: An Anthropological Theory*. Oxford: Oxford University Press, 1998.

Gordon, Avery F. *Ghostly Matters: Haunting and the Sociological Imagination*. Minneapolis: University of Minnesota Press, 1997.

Grusin, Richard. 'Radical Mediation'. *Critical Inquiry*, 42: 1 (2015), pp. 124–48.

Harman, Graham. *Immaterialism: Objects and Social Theory*. Cambridge: Polity Press, 2016.

——. 'The Road to Objects'. *continent*, 3: 1 (2011), pp. 171–9.

Hazlitt, William. 'On the Past and Future'. In *Table Talk; or, Original Essays*, vol. 1. London: John Warren, 1821, pp. 43–64.

Heidegger, Martin. 'The Thing'. In *Poetry, Language, Thought*, trans. Albert Hofstadter. New York: Harper & Row, 1971, pp. 165–86.

Heinzelman, Kurt. 'Self-Interest and the Politics of Composition in Keats's *Isabella*'. *ELH*, 55: 1 (1988), pp. 159–93.

Hoeveler, Diane Long. 'Decapitating Romance: Class, Fetish, and Ideology in Keats's *Isabella*'. *Nineteenth-Century Fiction*, 49: 3 (1994), pp. 321–38.

Janes, Regina. *Losing Our Heads: Beheading in Literature and Culture*. New York: New York University Press, 2005.

Kaplan, Alice and Kristen Ross. 'Introduction'. 'Everyday Life'. *Yale French Studies*, 73 (1987), pp. 1–4.

Keach, William. *Arbitrary Power: Romanticism, Language, Politics*. Princeton, NJ: Princeton University Press, 2004.

Keats, John. *The Letters of John Keats, 1814–1821*, ed. Hyder E. Rollins. 2 vols. Cambridge, MA: Harvard University Press, 1958.

——. *The Poems of John Keats*, ed. Jack Stillinger. Cambridge, MA: Harvard University Press, 1978.

Lagory, Michael. 'Wormy Circumstance: Symbolism in Keats's *Isabella*'. *SiR*, 34: 3 (1995), pp. 321–42.

Lamb, Charles. *Lamb as Critic*, ed. Roy Park. Lincoln & London: University of Nebraska Press, 1980, pp. 299–307.

Latour, Bruno. *An Inquiry into Modes of Existence: An Anthropology of the Moderns*, trans. Catherine Porter. Cambridge, MA: Harvard University Press, 2013.

Levinson, Marjorie. *Keats's Life of Allegory: The Origins of a Style*. Oxford & Cambridge, MA: Basil Blackwell, 1988.

Love, Heather. *Feeling Backward: Loss and the Politics of Queer History*. Cambridge, MA: Harvard University Press, 2007.

Lynch, Deidre Shauna. *Loving Literature: A Cultural History*. Chicago, IL & London: University of Chicago Press, 2015.

Manning, Erin. *Politics of Touch: Sense, Movement, Sovereignty*. Minneapolis: University of Minnesota Press, 2007.

——. *Relationscapes: Movement, Art, Philosophy*. Cambridge, MA & London: MIT Press, 2009.

Marx, Karl. *Capital: A Critique of Political Economy*, vol. I, trans. Ben Fowkes. New York: Penguin, 1992.

Merleau-Ponty, Maurice. 'The Intertwining—The Chiasm'. In *The Visible and the Invisible*, trans. Alphonso Lingis. Chicago, IL: Northwestern University Press, 1968, pp. 130–55.

Pyle, Forest. 'Keats's Materialism'. *Studies in Romanticism*, 33: 1 (1994), pp. 57–80.

Rajan, Tilottama. *Dark Interpreter: The Discourse of Romanticism*. Ithaca, NY & New York: Cornell University Press, 1980.

Rancière, Jacques. 'The Politics of the Spider', trans. Emily Rohrbach and Emily Sun. *Studies in Romanticism*, 50: 2 (2011), pp. 239–50.

Redfield, Marc. 'Spectral Romanticisms'. *European Romantic Review*, 9: 2 (1998), pp. 271–73.

Rogers, Kathleen Beres. 'Breeding Scorpions in the Brain: Obsession in Keats's *Isabella; or, The Pot of Basil*'. *Essays in Romanticism*, 19 (2012), pp. 33–47.

Sha, Richard C. 'John Keats and Some Versions of Materiality'. *Romanticism*, 20: 3 (2014), pp. 233–45.

Shaw, George Bernard. 'Keats'. In *John Keats Memorial Volume*, ed. G.C. Williamson. London: John Lane, 1921, pp. 175–6.

Sider, Michael. 'Isabella and the Dialogism of Romance'. *Nineteenth-Century Contexts*, 22: 3 (2000), pp. 329–51.

Simpson, David. *Wordsworth and Social Concern: The Poetics of Modernity*. Cambridge: Cambridge University Press, 2009.

Spivak, Gayatri Chakravorty. 'Ghostwriting'. *Diacritics*, 25: 2 (1995), pp. 64–84.

Swann, Karen. 'The Strange Time of Reading'. *European Romantic Review*, 9: 2 (1998), pp. 275–82.

Stewart, Susan. *On Longing: Narratives of the Miniature, the Gigantic, the Souvenir, the Collection*. Durham, NC: Duke University Press, 1993.

Wang, Orrin N.C. 'Ghost Theory'. *Studies in Romanticism*, 46: 2 (2007), pp. 203–25.

Wolfson, Susan. *Reading John Keats*. Cambridge: Cambridge University Press, 2015.

——. *Romantic Shades and Shadows*. Baltimore, MD: Johns Hopkins University Press, 2018.

Wu, Duncan. 'Keats and Hazlitt'. In *John Keats in Context*, ed. Michael O'Neill. Cambridge: Cambridge University Press, 2017, pp. 159–67.

CHAPTER NINE

It's the End of the World as We Know It and I Feel Queer

Mary Shelley, Queer Affect, and Shapeshifting Through *The Last Man*

Kate Singer

If we know one thing about affects and their wily, sly, shifty ways, it is that they are as contagious as a local plague, 'sticky', as Sara Ahmed and Silvan Tomkins write, moving from person to person, circulated through and by objects, endued within local atmospheres and national climates.[1] Our feelings change from interpersonal encounters of myriad kinds, within spaces and their alterations, through our consumption of, submission to, and intra-action with things of all natures. How does such sharing work? What is the substance, force, and form of such affective transfer? We could say, as Brian Massumi does, that affect is both physiological and something more than that, an incorporeal materiality that takes into account the body and all the potential moves the body, or bodies in concert, might make, in actuality or in the abstract. Such a materiality—incorporeal and bodily, actual and virtual—suggests that our connections with other humans and other things are something more than the shock of face-to-face sensation. Affect, understood as such a substance and force, crosses perforated embodied boundaries with or without our awareness or sometimes our control, whether by the transmission of pheromones, hormones, or rhythms, as Teresa Brennan has written, or by what Jane Bennett tries to conceptualize as a shared 'impersonal affect' (p. xiii). Whether enlightening or toxic, we never remain the same in the slipstream of affect's restless ken; trans-corporeal affects transform

[1] Sara Ahmed, 'Happy Objects', in *The Affect Theory Reader*, eds. Melissa Gregg and Gregory J. Seigworth (Durham, NC: Duke University Press, 2010), p. 36; Eve Kosofsky Sedgwick and Adam Frank, eds., *Shame and Its Sisters: A Silvan Tomkins Reader* (Durham, NC: Duke University Press, 1995), p. 79. See also Teresa Brennan, *The Transmission of Affect* (Ithaca, NY: Cornell University Press, 2004) and Mary Favret, *War at a Distance: Romanticism and the Making of Modern Wartime* (Princeton, NJ: Princeton University Press, 2009).

bodies, things, and themselves, provoking us to reform our very notions of materiality. How might we describe a change that multiplies the potentiality of the body's night moves and strange shapes, its most meaningful and haunting ontologies?[2] Such material affects, autonomous and not, make us each last men, last people, last things, losing our bodies and ontologies as they change, as they offer a theory of change that reshapes what we know about and how we might enact revolution. If we believe in the existence of such affects, we are provoked to ask what it means to be lost in mutual affect, to reform, to lose our selves and our bodies—in one another, in the world invested with 'thing-power' (Bennett, p. 22), in worlds yet to come—without disaster? Might Mary Shelley's *The Last Man* (1826), while seemingly so predicated on plague-driven disaster, provide a post-apocalyptic survival guide, a potent endurance kit of affective materiality in a post-revolutionary, post-Waterloo Europe, that offers a theory and a praxis for how to change materially after disaster?[3]

Shelley figures such an affective materiality through the plague that catastrophically decimates world populations in *The Last Man*. Both nebulous matter and partially unaccountable force, the plague manifests a trumped up, politicized inversion, perhaps, of Wordsworth's 'motion and a spirit' that rolls through all things and men. Dozens of scholars have commented on the plague's special allegory. After book one's roman à clef with its domestic tranquility, love triangles, and eventual domestic disaster (Raymond's adultery with Evadne, the dissolution of his marriage with Perdita, and Lionel's departure from Windsor's English sanctuary only to fail in reuniting his sister and the Byronic quester), the plague arrives as if a metonymy for that disaster, coming as it does just after Evadne curses Raymond on the killing fields of Constantinople. Steven Goldsmith has remarked on the plague as 'the return of the repressed … feminine, annihilating force' of the Sibyl whose heterogeneous polyvocality both accedes to and disrupts the Apollonian patriarchal voice (pp. 138, 139). Orianne Smith more recently has argued that the plague presents the 'illocutionary force of a woman's curse' where 'vatic authority replaces patriarchal authority' (pp. 213, 217). The materiality of this force, however, is not simply the linguistic or promissory expression of unrepressed psychological feminine rage or the contagious, deconstructive

[2] All my living attention and heartfelt gratitude to students of my Posthuman Affect Theory and Love, Sex, and Death in the Anthropocene courses, especially Sarah Loftstrom, Sara Rottger, and Baruch Levine, for helping me ask questions and be among the things in new ways. Thank you, too, to my brilliant, warmly cunty co-editors, for being incisive and loving at once.

[3] For explorations of Romantic living after disaster, see Jacques Khalip, *Last Things: Disastrous Form from Kant to Hujar* (New York: Fordham University Press, 2018); Khalip, 'The Last Animal at the End of the World', *European Romantic Review*, 29: 3 (June 2018), pp. 321–32; and Chris Washington, *Romantic Revelations: Visions of Post-Apocalyptic Life and Hope in the Anthropocene* (Toronto: University of Toronto Press, 2019).

language of revolt. Rather, I argue, Shelley simultaneously figures *and* materializes the plague as an affective force. It performs, voices, and materializes the ability to affect bodies and be affected by them. These material transformations enact some things akin to the movements and rests of Massumi's Spinozan affect, while they also resemble Jane Bennett's triangulation of Spinoza, nineteenth-century naturalism, and vitalist theory into 'impersonal affect', the matter and energy shared among things, people, and all sorts of beings. However oriented to extinction, the plague's disease brings humans to their knees through an affect that initiates ontological change—from the human to the posthuman. Not only does Evadne's breathy curse manifest death and destruction on hetero-patriarchs starting with Raymond, not only does Lionel arguably become the last man and first posthuman, as Chris Washington argues in *Romantic Revelations*, but the plague also alters and allegorizes a material affective force of bodily and ontological change that operates throughout the novel, and not only through negative affects with an appetite for destruction.

If such affective force appears feminine when tied to the plague's laceration of Raymond's masculine, imperial energies or Lionel's normcore efforts to get the band of families back intact to Windsor, the plague—and other instances of transmogrifying affect—is actually tied to a larger, queer or queering affect that manifests in other, more loving moments and figures throughout the novel.[4] Sara Rottger reads the plague as a figuration of queer lesbianism born through Evadne's cross-dressing as both an architect and a militant: 'the plague represents an infectious force that collaborates with nature to supersede traditional modes of language and binaries, which allows Shelley to develop a model of lesbianism that revises societal tenets of emotional exchange, desire, and reproduction'.[5] For Rottger, the plague functions, in part, to locate moments of heterosexual oppression and points to the more opaque moments of lesbian affect represented by Evadne's, Idris's, and Lucy's entanglement. It is of a piece with other, similar forms of affect within the novel, especially those homosocial, potentially queer affects that circulate through Adrian and

[4] I am indebted to Amy Rodgers and Marjorie Rubright for the term 'normcore', meaning an affective atmosphere occurring within families that together replicate and enforce a hetero-white culture that pretends to radical identities but enforces normativity through forms of consumption tied to a familial, visiting culture much like eighteenth-century country gentry.

[5] Sara Rottger, '"Life Had Married Death": Erotics of Difference and Lesbian Reimagination in *The Last Man*', *The Paper Shell Review*, 8 (May 2018), pp. 54–66, 55. Working from Fran Michel's seminal article on lesbian panic in *Frankenstein*, Rottger argues that 'the plague materializes as an erotic, vaporous embodiment of the pent-up entanglement of panic and attraction that characterizes lesbianism in the novel. *The Last Man* presents a complicated perspective on lesbianism that demonstrates how its existence depends simultaneously on panic resulting from both male homosocial and heterosexual domains, as well as sexual energy between women and relations of difference' (pp. 58–9).

Lionel, and later among Lionel and all sorts of beings, affects that queer the anthropocentric great chain of being to offer other sorts of ontological relations or modes of being altogether. Such queering acts accordingly when it routes the biopolitical charge of heteronormative, anthropocentric reproduction of species but also when it brings into intimacy (bodily and affective) unexpected, nonbinary assemblages of beings, things, and affects.

At crucial points during the novel's beginning and end, there are loving kinds of transmogrifying affect in *The Last Man*, particularly within the exchanges of affect between Adrian and Lionel, amid the plague's rearrangement of human relations into various queer familial configurations (including the aforementioned feminine friendships and Lionel's and Adrian's queer family), as well as within Lionel's communion with animals, books, vegetal life, and sundry beings once humans have passed away. In the first pages of this resolutely posthuman novel, Shelley's narrator happily sheds his savage state-of-nature and his wolfish skin for a more civilized subject position in the republic. We might assume that with this act he successfully becomes an Enlightenment man of reason and feeling, a man who can argue passionately with Raymond about public works projects and save Adrian from a sudden and furious lovesickness over Evadne. Yet, Lionel's ontological alteration is, in fact, the first in a series of human–animal–vegetal transformations that occur in the wake of posthuman passions. These changes crescendo when Lionel's initial manning up gets reversed at the novel's very end, after the plague and ostensible death of all other humans, when our Omega Man realizes his savage nature in a deserted Rome saloon, buddies up with a dog, and the two ride off into a sea-faring sunset. Shelley's science fiction does not disappoint in making the inanimate animate when she writes Lionel but also Adrian, variously described to be serpent and spirit, as shapeshifters fueled by the magic of positive and negative affects. Affect itself becomes a force able to instigate material change in bodies and in being.

These positive affects, as material and life-altering forces, suggest what Eve Sedgwick has called the 'reparative impulse … to assemble and confer plenitude on an object that will then have resources to offer an inchoate self' (*Touching*, p. 149). The energies that circulate between Adrian and Lionel and later between Lionel and various nonhuman things offer such a reparative force through the plenitude of ontological options for Lionel beyond the savage animal/civilized man binary. Unlike Sedgwick's psychoanalytic frame that reconstitutes the Enlightenment subject, Shelley does not merely deconstruct the Western, male subject, as Goldsmith attests in his reading of the plague, but her novel also convenes what it might be to live in a series of shifting human, animal, and vegetal forms, as we are made and remade down to our very beings. This shapeshifting not only scrambles the usual anthropocentric hierarchies of human/animal/vegetal/incorporeal, vestiges in the chain of being, but also gives us a model of transformation through a special form of queering: the posthuman affect that begins with Adrian and Lionel's queer relationship, continues with the lesbian friendships and no-futurism of the plague, and culminates after Adrian drowns Lionel's attempts (and failures) to find real love for various beings of the inanimate world.

Shelley offers us strategies for how we might alter ourselves to live and love in what Fuson Wang, Elizabeth Effinger, and Washington have described as Shelley's frighteningly familiar post-apocalyptic, posthuman world. She suggests that the mechanism of such queer, revolutionary change stems from a potent form of affective materiality when she understands it as a jointly human–nonhuman force, a nebulous form of materiality and an ur-form of post-posthumanity. Cary Wolfe proposes a definition of the posthuman that 'comes both before and after humanism': an embodied existence that has always been coeval with animality, technology, and nature as well as 'a historical moment in which the decentering of humanity by its imbrication in technical, medical, informatics, and economic networks is increasingly impossible to ignore' (p. xv). Shelley's posthumanity does not simply decenter the human as the object or even the method of critical inquiry; she envisions a human–nonhuman relation in which the two are, if not entangled, then placed in close relationship. The motor and mover of these relations is affect: both a vital materiality that circulates within and among diverse beings as well as the mechanism by which those ontologies shift and reveal their interrelation. Such a material affect unlocks the post-posthuman power to transmogrify ourselves into ontological shapeshifters, changing our embodied being in the world.

***

As if recapitulating a Rousseauvian history of modern Western civilization, Lionel narrates his becoming-human at the start of the novel by first comparing himself to Romulus: 'I wandered among the hills of civilized England as uncouth a savage as the wolf-bred founder of Rome'.[6] Lionel's further descriptions of his youth paint him in ways reminiscent of Wordsworth's 'glad animal movements' as an unthinking roe in 'Tintern Abbey': 'My life was like that of an animal, and my mind was in danger of degenerating into that which informs brute nature .... I stood on the brink of manhood; passions, strong as the trees of a forest, had already taken root within me, and were about to shadow with their noxious overgrowth, my path in life' (p. 18). Lionel enacts the Rousseauvian conversion of a Wordsworthian boyish savage civilized into responsible, virtuous manhood with a Protestant duty to republican citizenship. Yet, Shelley demonstrates such a civilizing narrative precisely to undo it with Lionel's ultimate recourse to a savage, multispecies salon at the end of the novel.

[6] Mary Shelley, *The Last Man* (New York: Oxford, 2008), p. 14.

Other characters, moreover, are repeatedly allied with nonhuman ontologies, suggesting that Lionel may be only delusionally writing himself into a civilizing narrative. These other ontological alliances belie the civilizing narrative and reveal a more physical and metaphysical materiality at work in the novel.

While Verney's wolf is social with 'a band' or pack of 'others friendless like myself' in his 'war with civilization', his sister Perdita is a solitary daydreaming wanderer of the forest whose 'active fancy wove a thousand combinations' (p. 14). She is likewise associated with the nonhuman, here the typically fecund vegetal world: 'A sensation with her became a sentiment, and she never spoke until she had mingled her perceptions of outward objects with others which were the native growth of her own mind' (p. 17). Shelley echoes this famous passage from her mother Mary Wollstonecraft's *Letters Written During a Short Residence in Sweden, Norway, and Denmark*:

> Nature is the nurse of sentiment,—the true source of taste;—yet what misery, as well as rapture, is produced by a quick perception of the beautiful and sublime, when it is exercised in observing animated nature ... and the harmonized soul sinks into melancholy, or rises to extasy, just as the chords are touched, like the Aeolian harp agitated by the changing wind. (p. 39)

Perdita's ability to weave with sentiment near-infinite combinations of relations among human subjects and nonhuman objects resembles Wollstonecraft's harmonized soul that is nursed by nature in sentiment and whose chords are touched, agitated, and altered by the changing wind. Both passages suggest the power of the emotionally conversant human, the empath, to 'mingle' perceptions with the nonhuman objects of nature in a material way, such that the soul itself becomes a nonhuman thing touched as strings on an Aeolian harp.

Shelley, in a typically dialectical, Wollstonecraftian rhetorical flourish, makes one more turn to the argument about the relation between the human and nonhuman when she continues the description of Perdita: 'She was like a fruitful soil that imbibed the airs and dews of heaven, and gave them forth again to light in loveliest forms of fruits and flowers; but then she was often dark and rugged as that soil, raked up, and new sown with unseen seed' (p. 17). This additional description accomplishes two things. First, it redraws Perdita as nonhuman like Lionel—not simply an observer who, when the mood suits her, chooses to mingle her perceptions with external objects, but as already a part of the nonhuman, the soil in material interchange with the airs and dews that both produces fruits and flowers (useful and beautiful things) and remains a site of fertile potentiality for 'unseen' seeds. Although the first part of both independent clauses begins with a simile ('like a soil', 'as that soil') that preserves the space between human and thing, the second half of those clauses each continue with a second piece that forgets or erases that distance with a more metaphor-esque figure ('gave them in loveliest forms of fruits and flowers', 'and new sown with unseen seed').

Such play with simile and metaphor through two independent clauses, each split in two, speaks purposefully to Wollstonecraft's own dialectical reasoning and sinuous (if often unnoticed) syntax. Rewriting a passage from the very start of the introduction of Wollstonecraft's *Vindication of the Rights of Woman*, Shelley reverses her mother's critique of 'the flowers which are planted in too rich a soil' only to end with 'barren blooming' (p. 7): Perdita figures not blown flowers whose value depends on beauty and short-lived reproductive capacity but rather the sheer potentiality of the vegetal. Although Perdita's verdant capacity might seem to relegate her to the realm of the unthinkingly fertile domestic woman of the nineteenth century, in fact, her ability to be conversant with the nonhuman—and to grow/enhance it—is parallel to Adrian's own transfiguring power when he, a few pages later, transforms Lionel by strumming his mind with affect that is described as an Aeolian force.

A similar metamorphosis, though one that takes up less space in the novel, occurs between Perdita and Raymond. She, as the 'unseen seed', shortly becomes noxiously fertilized by Raymond's colonial imagination. Raymond describes himself as a musical instrument similar to the way Lionel will describe himself at the (helpful) strumming hands of Adrian: 'a stringed instrument with chords and stops' but with 'no power to turn the pegs, or pitch my thoughts to a higher or lower key' (p. 66). This characterization of Raymond's own 'tide of passion' serves as a microcosmic allegory for the plague itself, a miasma that may figure many things, but it especially figures a mass of negative, chaotic affects, a nonhuman force that is the inverse of Adrian's spirit.

Lionel's ameliorative alteration begins during his encounters with Adrian, even though he assumes that the son of a king who had injured his own father must be out to do the same to him. Mixing epic modes, Shelley's Virgilian hero looks down on Adrian's Miltonic one when teen wolf Lionel imagines Adrian at a distance, as an antagonistic, Satanic animal: 'His praises were so many adder's stings infixed in my vulnerable breast' (p. 23). In Adrian's saurian aura, Lionel's heart burns, his blood boils, and the air seems 'poisoned by his presence' (p. 23). Adrian gets Lionel's blood pumping with affects that bespeak a reactive response that may be less a Sedgwickean repressed homosexual desire than Lionel experiencing a transfer of animal vibrations, smells, stings, and pheromones through the air, seemingly negative affects that he receives against his will. After their first face-to-face meeting Lionel declares, 'I am now began to be human' (p. 29). Before he takes up such a status, however, a syrupy moment remakes them both, if temporarily, into nonhuman things. Adrian, 'imbued with the spirit of high philosophy', becomes a 'spirit' that gives 'a tone of irresistible persuasion to his intercourse with others, so that he seemed like an inspired musician, who struck, with unerring skill, the "lyre of the mind", and produced thence a divine harmony' (p. 26). Adrian here is not, or not merely, the human poet, a.k.a. the Percy Shelley of Mary Shelley's roman à clef—he only 'seemed like' a musician. Instead, we need to read this passage more literally: the spirit imbued with high philosophy, a partially nonhuman force, strikes Lionel's mind, now a partial thing, a human 'lyre of the mind'. Rather than seeing Adrian as the genius poet whose aristocratic biopower changes Lionel with its civilizing attention, we can read this Shelleyan fierce and wild spirit as an 'impersonal affect' that moves materially and autonomously amid minds and bodies, human and nonhuman.

Shelley is surely working from Samuel Coleridge's Hartleyan trope of the Aeolian Harp—echoed by Wollstonecraft in the *Letters* and by Percy in 'Ode to the West Wind', among other poems—which, Shelley Trower reminds us, vibrates with material resonance.[7] Shelley's figuration of this trope proposes what we might call a new materialist model for the transmission of affect, arising, perhaps, from her understanding of Hartley's vibrations that move within the body and without it via the aether and from Joseph Priestley's or Humphry Davy's models of gaseous stimulation. Culled both from the discourse of sensibility and from William Godwin's and Mary Wollstonecraft's associationist philosophy, vibration theory posited moving matter that circulated both within the body and outside of it, often into and through other bodies. More chemical branches of empiricist science and philosophy likewise searched for spirit-matter, such as Priestley's phlogiston, a fire-like element that circulated through bodies. Davy's experiments with air and ether, Michele Speitz has recently shown, reveal an affect that is nonhuman, material, contingent, and pervasive.[8]

Adrian's spirit, part of the spirit of the world, allows for a porousness of embodied boundaries not simply receptive to but also interacting with and changed by the material affects they receive. In *The Transmission of Affect*, Brennan turns our attention to mutual psychological and physiological exchange, especially through the exchange of hormones and pheromones (known to

[7] See Shelley Trower, 'Nerves, Vibration, and the Aeolian Harp', *Romanticism and Victorianism on the Net*, 54 (May 2009), at https://www.erudit.org/en/journals/ravon/2009-n56-ravon3401/038761ar/.

[8] See Michele Speitz, 'Affect and Air: The Speculative Spirit of the Age', in *Romanticism and Speculative Realism*, eds. Chris Washington and Anne C. McCarthy (London: Bloomsbury, 2019), pp. 37–56; Steve Mentz, 'Phlogiston', in *Elemental Ecocriticism: Thinking with Earth, Air, Water, and Fire*, eds. Jeffrey Jerome Cohen and Lowell Duckert (Minneapolis: University of Minnesota Press, 2015), pp. 55–76; G.J. Barker-Benfield, *The Culture of Sensibility: Sex and Society in Eighteenth-Century Britain* (Chicago, IL: Chicago University Press, 1992); and Richard Sha, 'The Motion behind Romantic Emotion: Toward a Chemistry and Physics of Feeling', in *Romanticism and the Emotions* (Cambridge: Cambridge University Press, 2014), pp. 19–47.

scientists as chemical entrainment) or the vibrations of rhythm. Unlike negative affects such as rage and anxiety that disrupt cognition and evoke chaos that then must be sorted through (usually by a mom), Adrian's spirit is the reparative spirit of love, akin to what Brennan calls 'living attention'. 'If I receive another's love', she writes, 'I receive their living attention; and this attention, logically, is a biological force in itself, as palpable an energy as adenosine triphosphate (ATP), the bioenergetic basis of life and consciousness' (p. 34). This living attention deeds energy to its recipient, gives life itself, and, in doing so, 'directs positive feelings toward the other by attending to the specificity of the other (rather than seeing her or him through idealizing or demonizing projections)' (p. 32). Karen Barad, in her essay on touching, grazes this notion that haptic attention intervolves (as Percy would write) one another: 'Is touching not by its very nature always already an involution, invitation, invisitation, wanted or unwanted, of the stranger within. … All touching entails an infinite alterity, so that touching the Other is touching all Others, including the "self," and touching the "self" entails touching the strangers within' (pp. 207, 214). Thus, Adrian's civilizing spirit organizes Lionel's rage by altering his life-force into a 'divine harmony'. Lionel converts from a raging and aggressive alpha into a subdued human, clearly heard, vibrating as a new song with the tender energies of attention. Such a reception of energy, which invokes and evokes all sorts of beings and others Lionel might transform into, reorganizes, remolds human being with the material vehicles of 'plastic' lyre strings. This transformation moves and bends being without violence and, I would argue, through a much less binary and agonistic method than Barad's self-others model suggests. Rather than the language of Other or even all Others, Shelley offers harmonics that resonate and reverberate without collapsing into essentiality.

Affect, then, for Shelley, is a transmission of this transversal energy, a constantly awakening force on the make at each moment—transformative in loving ways, as with Lionel and Adrian, and more initially destructive ways, as with Evadne and the plague. When we consider the plague moving through human bodies or the spirit shifting its nonhuman force amid nonhuman thing (lyre), we can intimate a mechanism for affect that transgresses human and nonhuman at once. For Lionel, this unstill affect is autonomic and transformational: 'my plastic soul was remoulded by a master hand, which I neither desired nor was able to resist' (p. 29). Affect here works autonomously, without Lionel's willful encouragement or opposition, as a disembodied hand that reshapes his being, as a substance easily shaped but then able to retain, perhaps momentarily, its new form.[9] Adrian's other-wordly nature, his close relation to spirit, within the additive context of the other animal and nonhuman

[9] See the *OED*'s first use of this definition of 'plastic' in 1803 to reference plaster of Paris.

metaphors that shape the novel, deed an explanatory mechanism to *Prometheus Unbound*'s own troping of spirits as nonhuman forces both within the mind and the world: 'and like lutes / Touched by the skill of the enamoured wind, / Weave harmonies divine, yet ever new, / From difference sweet where dischord cannot be' (III.3.36–9).[10] Spirit is affect as a nonhuman force that travels and that morphs Lionel's mind into a thing that likewise exudes nonhuman force, the music of the spheres.

***

Not strictly ethereal, the 'plastic soul' can be reshaped, as clay, wax, or another soft and formless material might be. Through these events of shapeshifting, Lionel and Adrian—and others within their proximity—become irrevocably liable and labile to transformations of all sorts, with humanity only one of many ontologies. This ontological familiarity and flexibility may explain their immunity to the plague's own affective ontology. Their mutual animal natures signal an affective queerness, or animacy, what Mel Y. Chen defines as unorthodox affiliations or exceptions to conventional orderings of species intimacy, sentience, locomotion, and agency. Chen, taking the idea of animacy from cognitive linguists, shows how cross-cultural grammars repeatedly reveal animation and agency constructed in a hierarchy, beginning with humans, animals, inanimates (natural and manmade), then finally incorporeals, which include abstract concepts, natural forces, states of being, and emotions themselves. Thanks to this hierarchy, when people are represented as something other than human, they are usually dehumanized. In Chen's partially Foucauldian reading, affect either regiments or disrupts these categories: 'If affect includes affectivity—how one body affects another—then affect, in this book, becomes a study of governmentality of animate hierarchies, an examination of how acts seem to operate with, or against, the order of things' (p. 12). Such a top-down structure was endemic to the Romantic period in the legacies of the great chain of being but also disrupted by various less anthropocentric discourses: sympathy directed to animals as a model for human behavior, versions of feminist and transgender botany that privilege plants as a means to recategorize human gender or sex relations, and writings on climate that give credence to the agencies of inorganic matter such as Shelleyan, Schellengian personifications of the Earth.

When the plague disrupts national boundaries and common flows of sympathy, it likewise permanently undermines the anthropocentric biopolitics

[10] For a discussion of the pagan and nonhuman roots of Percy Shelley's orphic song in *Prometheus Unbound*, see Suzanne L. Barnett's *Romantic Paganism: The Politics of Ecstasy in the Shelley Circle* (New York: Palgrave Macmillan, 2018).

that dominate the first part of the novel with tales of human reproduction and political desire. While the plague works to disrupt man's place at the top of the ontological food chain and thus opposes the norming domesticity of volume one with the affective disruption of volume two, the affects that circulate between and proliferate beyond Lionel and Adrian offer yet another queer alternative to the heteronormative family. The vibrations that recompose Lionel's bodily harmonics at the start of the novel bring into relation unexpected intimacies. These liquid, material currents queer the reproductive, linear drive of the roman à clef from the very start, creating an alternate spacetimemattering reverberating all the while like a beloved soundtrack looping through the novel's head and heart. We might say, then, that Adrian and Lionel allegorize a traveling affective materiality always on the make, one that queers human relationships, but, even further, queers the relationality of materiality more globally.

This interpenetration of man and environment might posit a radically queer sexuality verging on objectophilia, yet because such desire alters the very nature of its beings, it seems to evoke not sexual penetration or touch but an even more material and dynamic level of ontological change. Colin Carman has recently given us a way to think about the interdependence of eros and environment in Shelley's works.[11] The kissing of earth entangled with Adrian and Lionel's relationship reveals, for Carman, how sexuality might be triangulated and displaced through the environment. The changes in environment that are the subject of the novel, then, unfold the 'full … spectrum of human sexuality' as 'an extension of rather than a deviation from, nature' (p. 171). The novel, however, offers a more complex form of queer entanglement, one that is not necessarily based on human sexuality. The editor's reassembling and translating of the leaves she finds in the Sibyl's cave resonates with Chen's notion of queer as putting into relation new forms of difference via 'questions of intimacy, sexuality, and connectivity' (p. 12). Coming to the leaves as fragments of material text that are assembled with the palpating potential for future and further rearrangement figures Shelley's textuality as itself a queer event. It puts into relation odd intimacies of moving materials—altered both by human hands, climate, and the leaves' own self-altering decomposition—that assemble intervolved ontologies. Texts become leaves whose partial erosion has already pervaded the Bay of Baiae's atmosphere as posthuman affective materiality that has, even before the narrator has translated the leaves, affected her. Leaves are powerful as material events as they are when they become texts through the narrator's hands, the Sibyl's voice, and Lionel's posthuman narration. Textual and material hierarchies are upended, reanimated, and intertwined. Shelley's novel, with its harmonic play

[11] Colin Carman, *The Radical Ecology of the Shelleys: Eros and Environment* (New York: Routledge, 2018).

of text, voice, leaves, air, and water, queers our expected affiliations to instigate ontological confusion as a means of finding new powers to survive the death of humanity. The immense positivity of affect as living attention resounds the possibilities of material and ontological change. Although Shelley's novel begins with the transformation of one body into another, it quickly redoubles its shapeshifting, as we shall see, to explore a range of bodies and materialities. Adrian, we might recall, is soon after described by Lionel as a series of three birds: an eagle, a dove, and a lark. If, as Chen writes, 'Recentering on animality (or the animals who face humans) tugs at the ontological cohesion of "the human", stretching it out and revealing the contingent striations in its springy taffy' (p. 98), then Shelley shows how affective spirit-play stretches and bends this springy taffy at the center of all life.

***

At the end of the world, Adrian and Lionel finally have some time together, traveling through the wrecks of civilization to Greece, the Western home of homosexual love, but even this love gives way to even more diverse bodies in assemblage. This alternative family traces a line of flight through Europe, with Lionel's children in tow. Just as earlier instances of shapeshifting mixed and matched different ontologies, so the queer family entails various forms of affect, relationality, and orientation. After Adrian and Clara drown, the queer family—the cathexis of feelings among a small band of humans—dies with them, as Lionel's regret, George Haggerty argues, becomes the expression of queer love put under erasure.[12] But perhaps the queer family goes the way of all humans because, in the wake of Adrian's disappearance, Lionel is forced to find other affiliations, affections for things other than the humans who recapitulate a family closed off from other people and other beings. Queer humanism of the family with a reproductive future becomes substituted for another form of queerness that includes the nonhuman in a non-familial assemblage, though one with as much affective energy. What Lionel ends up finding, however grievously, is another form of queer affect, a kind bound to nonhuman affect that might remake his own. He does, momentarily, attempt to sympathize with the animals: 'I will discipline my sorrowing heart to sympathy in your joys; I will be happy, because ye are so. ... I have something beyond this, but I will call it a defect, not an endowment' (p. 459). Lionel tries—and fails—to bond with a family of goats and, while much has been made about the shepherd dog that Lionel befriends in Rome, the two have no affective exchange that mends Lionel's grief.

[12] George Haggerty, '"The End of History": Identity and Dissolution in Apocalyptic Gothic', *The Eighteenth Century*, 41: 3 (Fall 2000), pp. 225–46. Please see also Haggerty, *Queer Gothic* (Urbana, IL: University of Illinois Press, 2006).

We might chalk up these failures at animal sympathy, tendered as they are through anthropocentric feeling, to Lionel's total grief at Adrian's and Clara's deaths. Still Lionel privileges his relation with humans, maintaining the animacy hierarchy that sees humans and their affective pull as more valuable and sustaining than animal or plant life—the very life that provides environments for humans to traverse. Only through grief does Lionel begin to bond more thoroughly with what he calls 'all of living nature'. In the throes of overwhelm, he laments, 'Oh! Grief is fantastic; it weaves a web on which to trace the history of its woe from every form and change around; it incorporates itself with all living nature; it finds sustenance in every object; as light, it fills all things' (p. 446). The web of Lionel's affect aggressively bonds with all living nature, to consume it for its own ends—to reproduce human grief and the grief for humans. Yet even while Lionel's melancholy threatens to devour the nonhuman world with its life-in-death shape all light, the extensible intensity of Lionel's pain takes the place of Adrian's spirit. Other nonhuman embodiments, the pervasive, ever-growing spiderweb and light, powerful and nonhuman, paradoxically enliven him, propelling him to live on. Insisting that 'restless despair and fierce desire of change lead me on' (p. 470), Lionel takes up the mantle of affect as movement, an appetite for change, and a Spinoza-esque perseverance in striving to be. In the process, he transforms once again, here into creeper ivy: 'I would have wound myself like ivy inextricably round them. … I would have entered and been part of them' (p. 452). If Lionel's own affect alters his animacy into that of vegetal ivy, he ends the novel a 'wild-looking, unkempt, half-naked savage' once again (p. 457). With ruthless irony, Shelley returns to the vegetal ontology of Perdita but now without her, as Lionel only tentatively and impermanently inhabits plant life.

This trending down the ontological ladder of animacy occurs in Shelley through shapeshifting into and out of various materialities powered by the force of affect. Such a model speaks to a dynamic, fluid way of conceptualizing change that refigures current new materialist accounts of change, which are vague at best and still carry traces of masculine aggression at worst. New materialists, perhaps more than any other theorists, have done much to bring into relation human and nonhuman, and yet Shelley transgresses those boundaries perhaps even more so. Rebekah Sheldon's redrawing of the Platonic chora as a space of potentiality where matter is decomposed and comes into being does much to reinvigorate a Kristevan fecundity that needs no human agency to set it in motion. Barad's notion of 'cutting' suggests, alternately, that subjects and objects only come into being when matter is sliced and diced into different discursive-material forms in a variety of relations.[13] Her

[13] See Karen Barad, *Meeting the Universe Halfway: Quantum Physics and the Entanglement of Matter and Meaning* (Durham: Duke University Press, 2007); Rebekah Sheldon,

ontology, like Sheldon's, allows for the imagination if not the realization of myriad potentialities of matter in a myriad of relations, and both theorists envision matter as already in a smoorged human–nonhuman relation that is often anthropocentrically cut (to its own detriment) by human technologies and ideologies.[14] Matter has the possibility of being cut differently by humans and, more radically, by matter's own different, autonomous agency. Such 'cutting' on Barad's part still seems to carry with it the legacies of violent subject–object splitting or suturing, while Sheldon's chora manifests change without detailing a more resolute or helpful model, particularly in the case of political or environmental distress.

Shelley's theorizing offers a mechanism for agential metamorphosis that envisions changes that occur fluidly through affective transfer or sharing and not via Barad's more aggressive notion of cutting. Lionel's multiple shapeshiftings occur through affect's vibrations that carry attention and energy from one being to another, as in Perdita's and Adrian's harmonics, or through figurative language's transfer of embodiments, like creeper ivy's winding motion that eventually entangles (entering and becoming part of) human and nonhuman. While Washington has argued that such cutting can be a 'cutting together' that splices and entangles the threads of matter together and differently, Shelley's shapeshifting suggests that post-Ovidian transformations of ontology occur through excesses of affect and language that collect matter already in the air or moving among us, already a part of and in relation to said bodies.[15] As such it should be seen neither as an addition of foreign matter (such as vitalist fluid) nor as a joining of previously separated bodies of matter but rather as a reassemblage, a regeneration based on affect's force, directionality, and concentration. Shelley's feminist theory of transmogrification precludes the violence of separation or, as a result, binding; it resists the notion of separate or distanced objects that bespeak a caged, individualized, self-sufficient Enlightenment subjectivity and its phantasmic return in object-oriented ontology's own notions of withdrawal, which, I have argued elsewhere, repeat the most isolationist aspects of the egotistical sublime.[16]

Lionel's changeling materiality becomes more apparent as the shapes he takes become more fluid, rough, or elemental—as web, ivy, and unkempt

'Form/Matter/Chora: Object-Oriented Ontology and Feminist New Materialism', in *The Nonhuman Turn*, ed. Richard Grusin (Minneapolis: University of Minnesota Press, 2015), pp. 193–222.

[14] I take this term from Walt Kelly's *Pogo*, vol. 1 (New York: Fantagraphics Books, 2011).

[15] Chris Washington, 'Non-Binary Frankenstein?', in *Frankenstein in Theory: A Critical Anatomy*, ed. Orrin N.C. Wang (New York: Bloomsbury, forthcoming 2020).

[16] Kate Singer, 'Surfing the Crimson Wave: Romantic New Materialisms and Speculative Feminisms', in *Romanticism and Speculative Realism*, eds. Chris Washington and Anne C. McCarthy (London: Bloomsbury, 2010), pp. 111–32.

savage. Perhaps he truly embraces nonhuman affect when he seeks the 'still ploughing seedless ocean', that vatic archive of fluidity and protean form so reminiscent of Perdita as she is described at the start of the novel and when, like Mary Robinson's Sappho, she merges into the sea. The restless sea that has killed Adrian also succeeds him in fomenting those infinite nonhuman movements of the world. In the novel's last line, Lionel gives all his attention to those inanimate and incorporeal animacies when he promises: 'I shall witness all the variety of appearance, that the elements can assume—I shall read fair augury in the rainbow—menace in the cloud—some lesson or record dear to my heart in everything' (p. 470). Lionel pledges himself to be taught all their shapes, all the beings they take on, all their movements. Not just recording life in posthuman times for other humans, he re-cords, his heart made new once again by everything beloved to it, in loving, in attending to, all the elements.

Shelley's final nonhumans, the rainbow and cloud, of course reference Percy's figure of Iris, or the shape all light, from his last, unfinished poem, 'The Triumph of Life' and perhaps his other rainbows in 'To a Skylark' and 'The Sunset'. The shape all light doses Rousseau (already transfigured into a tree trunk) with a beverage that intoxicates and produces Rousseau's gothic version of the triumph—which is not unlike the parade of allegorical monster personifications in 'The Mask of Anarchy'. Mary's much more realist rainbow diffracts her husband's vision with a more thingly object, a rainbow that bends the anthropocentrism in his personification into an animated shape that is not humanized or monstrous but rather speaks to the more eluctive energy of affect and the rainbow of orientations it potentializes. These rainbows might, too, remind us of Wordsworth's lines, 'My heart leaps up when I behold / A Rainbow in the sky: / So was it when my life began; / So is it now I am a Man' (lines 1–4). Whatever we take to be Wordsworth's notion of natural piety, the rainbow persists through childhood and manhood, preserved in literature as that which continues to exist despite aging—that other kind of human shapeshifting—and that which incites affective movement. Here the heart also re-cords, up and out to the skies, though it resolves back in the body and memory of man. John Keats's own infamous use of the rainbow describes the sinuous and serpentine Lamia whose ontology partakes of 'some penanced lady elf, / Some demon's mistress, or the demon's self' (I.55–6). Hetero-patriarchal cold philosophy, in Book II of the poem, 'Unweave[s] a rainbow' (II. 237) and destroys Lamia, herself a shapeshifter who bridges the human and nonhuman with her unconventional sexuality.

Shelley's rainbow collects these ontological differences through a philosophy that does not critique so much as creates assemblages and relations among things, including the transfer from one thing to the next inherent in metaphor. Her queer flag paints a virtuality of ontologies, a Massumian materiality that conjures all the bodies that might exist, or perhaps all the potential ontologies that bodies might be transformed into during different moments of realized embodiment. If the rainbow in contemporary LGBTQIA+ culture has become a symbol of gender and sexual diversity, Mary Shelley's queer novel implies that the '+' intimates queer affects, intimacies, and ontologies that are born through change that includes the human, animal, vegetal, and the dewy incorporeal. Those material changes that occur thanks to affective attention, positive and negative, might even serve to eradicate the Foucauldian but still binary notions of normativity and difference, materiality and discursivity, providing instead shapes and relations of all varieties, corporeal, linguistic, and incorporeal.

Shelley's rainbow finally teaches the heart to re-cord the bows and vapors of nature, their affective materials and movements so close to a heart that itself beats as a nonhuman part within a changeable whole. If Lionel's rainbow promises the return of the heavenly covenant after apocalypse, it heralds a pact to learn and to tend to the nonhuman forces and things within and without us—not as if they have a secret language of their own we must translate, not as if they demand us to open ourselves to their sounds and sights, but as they remind us of all the variety of our beings, our queer, animal, plant ontologies, our candy hearts and corny brains, that have already moved and changed us with animacies all their own.

Bibliography

Ahmed, Sara. 'Happy Objects'. In *The Affect Theory Reader*, eds. Melissa Gregg and Gregory J. Seigworth. Durham, NC: Duke University Press, 2009, pp. 29–51.

Barad, Karen. *Meeting the Universe Halfway: Quantum Physics and the Entanglement of Matter and Meaning*. Durham, NC: Duke University Press, 2007.

——. 'On Touching'. *differences*, 23: 3 (2012): pp. 206–23.

Barnett, Suzanne L. *Romantic Paganism: The Politics of Ecstasy in the Shelley Circle*. New York: Palgrave Macmillan, 2018.

Bennett, Jane. *Vibrant Matter: A Political Ecology of Things*. Durham, NC: Duke University Press, 2010.

Brennan, Teresa. *The Transmission of Affect*. Ithaca, NY: Cornell University Press, 2004.

Carman, Colin. *The Radical Ecology of the Shelleys: Eros and Environment*. New York: Routledge, 2018.

Chen, Mel Y. *Animacies: Biopolitics, Racial Mattering, and Queer Affect*. Durham, NC: Duke University Press, 2012.

Effinger, Elizabeth. 'A Clandestine Catastrophe: Disciplinary Dissolution in Mary Shelley's *Last Man*'. *European Romantic Review*, 25: 1 (February 2014), pp. 19–34.

Goldsmith, Steven. *Blake's Agitation: Criticism and the Emotions*. Baltimore, MD: Johns Hopkins University Press, 2013.

Haggerty, George. '"The End of History": Identity and Dissolution in Apocalyptic Gothic'. *Eighteenth Century: Theory and Interpretation*, 41: 3 (Fall 2001), pp. 225–46.

——. *Queer Gothic*. Urbana, IL: University of Illinois Press, 2006.

Kelly, Walt. *Pogo*. Vol. 1. New York: Fantagraphics Books, 2011.

Khalip, Jacques. 'The Last Animal at the End of the World'. *European Romantic Review*, 29: 3 (June 2018), pp. 321–32.

——. *Last Things: Disastrous Form from Kant to Hujar*. New York: Fordham University Press, 2018.

Massumi, Brian. *Parables for the Virtual*. Durham, NC: Duke University Press, 2002.

Mentz, Steve. 'Phlogiston'. In *Elemental Ecocriticism: Thinking with Earth, Air, Water, and Fire*, eds. Jeffrey Jerome Cohen and Lowell Duckert. Minneapolis: University of Minnesota Press, 2015, pp. 55–76.

Rottger, Sara. '"Life Had Married Death": Erotics of Difference and Lesbian Reimagination in *The Last Man*'. *The Paper Shell Review*, 9 (May 2018), pp. 54–66.

Sedgwick, Eve Kosofsky. *Touching Feeling*. Durham, NC: Duke University Press, 2002.

Sedgwick, Eve Kosofsky and Adam Frank, eds. *Shame and Its Sisters: A Silvan Tomkins Reader*. Durham, NC: Duke University Press, 1995.

Sha, Richard. 'The Motion behind Romantic Emotion'. In *Romanticism and the Emotions*, eds. Joel Faflak and Richard C. Sha. Cambridge: Cambridge University Press, 2014, pp. 19–47.

Sheldon, Rebekah. 'Form/Matter/Chora: Object-Oriented Ontology and Feminist New Materialism'. In *The Nonhuman Turn*, ed. Richard Grusin. Minneapolis: University of Minnesota Press, 2015, pp. 193–222.

Shelley, Mary. *The Last Man*. New York: Oxford, 2008.

Shelley, Percy Bysshe. *Shelley's Poetry and Prose*, eds. Neil Fraistat and Donald H. Reiman. 2nd ed. New York: W.W. Norton & Co., 2002.

Singer, Kate. *Romantic Vacancy: The Poetics of Gender, Affect, and Radical Speculation*. Albany, NY: SUNY Press, 2019.

——. 'Surfing the Crimson Wave: Romantic New Materialisms and Speculative Feminisms'. In *Romanticism and Speculative Realism*, eds. Chris Washington and Anne C. McCarthy. London: Bloomsbury, 2019, pp. 111–32.

Smith, Orianne. *Romantic Women Writers, Revolution, and Prophecy: Rebellious Daughters, 1786–1826*. Cambridge: Cambridge University Press, 2013.

Speitz, Michele. 'Affect and Air: The Speculative Spirit of the Age'. In *Romanticism and Speculative Realism*, eds. Chris Washington and Anne C. McCarthy. London: Bloomsbury, 2019, pp. 37–56.

Trower, Shelley. 'Nerves, Vibration, and the Aeolian Harp'. *Romanticism and Victorianism on the Net*, 54 (May 2009), at https://www.erudit.org/en/journals/ravon/2009-n56-ravon3401/038761ar/.

Wang, Fuson. 'The Historicist Turn of Romantic-Era Disability Studies, or *Frankenstein* in the Dark'. *Literature Compass*, 14: 7 (July 2017), at https://onlinelibrary.wiley.com/doi/abs/10.1111/lic3.12400.

——. 'We Must Live Elsewhere: The Social Construction of Natural Immunity in Mary Shelley's *The Last Man*'. *European Romantic Review*, 22: 2 (April 2011), pp. 235–55.

Washington, Chris. 'Non-Binary Frankenstein?'. In *Frankenstein in Theory: A Critical Anatomy*, ed. Orrin N.C. Wang. New York: Bloomsbury, forthcoming 2020.

——. *Romantic Revelations: Visions of Post-Apocalyptic Life and Hope in the Anthropocene*. Toronto: University of Toronto Press, 2019.

Washington, Chris and Anne C. McCarthy, eds. *Romanticism and Speculative Realism*. London: Bloomsbury Academic, 2019.

Wolfe, Cary. *What Is Posthumanism?* Minnesota: University of Minnesota Press, 2009.

Wollstonecraft, Mary. *Letters Written During a Short Residence in Sweden, Norway, and Denmark*, eds. Tone Brekke and Jon Mee. New York: Oxford University Press, 2009.

——. *A Vindication of the Rights of Woman*, ed. Deidre Shauna Lynch. New York: W.W. Norton & Co., 2009.

Part Three

Materialities Sexual and Animal

Chapter Ten

John Barnet and the Materiality of Desire in James Hogg's *Justified Sinner*

David Sigler

New materialists have been largely wary of psychoanalytic thought, and the suspicion has been mutual.[1] Yet the materiality of the signifier and the Thing-ness of sexual enjoyment together enable a proliferation of differences, including sexual difference, that could show the mutual relevance of each tradition to the other. Freud himself once asserted that 'analysts are at bottom incorrigible mechanists and materialists', even as he worried that an emphasis on the autonomy of things might hinder research into human desire.[2] But what if we could learn to see materiality, and the difference it produces, as functions of desire? Romantic-era writing had, at times, a tendency to make that connection. The quintessential example would be Gil-Martin, the diabolical figure in James Hogg's 1824 novel *The Private Memoirs and Confessions of a Justified Sinner*, who can morph his face to match that of the person he is thinking about, specifically as an expression of his desire. The novel treats this as an astonishing superpower; even so, desire finds a way to ramify materially everywhere we look in Hogg's text. The protagonist Robert Wringhim, for instance, admits that his murderous thoughts 'made some impression on my heart' because 'a constant thinking of an event changes every one of its features'.[3] In this way, Gil-Martin's metamorphoses simply literalize the process

[1] Rick Dolphijn and Iris van der Tuin, 'Pushing Dualism to an Extreme', in *New Materialism: Interviews & Cartographies* (Ann Arbor, MI: Open Humanities Press, 2012), pp. 115–37; Slavoj Žižek, *Absolute Recoil: Towards a New Foundation of Dialectical Materialism* (London: Verso, 2015), pp. 8–15.

[2] Sigmund Freud, 'Psycho-analysis and Telepathy', in *The Standard Edition of the Complete Psychological Works of Sigmund Freud*, trans. James Strachey, vol. 18 (London: Vintage, 2001), p. 179.

[3] James Hogg, *The Private Memoirs and Confessions of a Justified Sinner, with 'Marion's*

according to which desire, as it ricochets between subjects, becomes material throughout the novel and generates difference. Yet it is difference materialized as repetition, in so far as characters begin to resemble their interlocutors both physically and in the mutual entanglement of their desires, as if desire were etched into the body.

This essay will focus on a particular iteration of this situation in *Justified Sinner*: the scene, early in the novel's second half, in which Robert's stepfather, the town reverend, fires his 'serving-man' John Barnet (p. 84). John, a groundskeeper of thirty-three years' employ, has been spreading rumours about Robert's paternity, implying that Robert was (and is) the elder Wringhim's illegitimate child. Robert tattles to his stepfather, who confronts his employee. Barnet has a frankness of manner that frustrates Wringhim. Barnet does his job but refuses to claim to like it—an attitude, much as in Melville's later 'Bartleby, the Scrivener', that soon confounds the entire relationship. As Wringhim endeavors to explain how his supposedly adopted son so closely resembles him, meeting sardonic resistance from John at every turn, the discourses of the interlocutors detach from each other according to incommensurate logics of desire, leaving a parallax gap. By 'parallax', I invoke Slavoj Žižek's interest in 'the confrontation of two closely linked perspectives between which no neutral common ground is possible', an arrangement that lends itself, as Žižek counterintuitively shows, to dialectical outcomes.[4] The Barnet scene addresses its parallax by moving (really sublating) the disagreement between the characters up to the level of the signifier, where its processes of meaning-making (e.g., legal, generic, racial, sexual, narrative, and moral) can function. The controversy over Robert's paternity begins to engage what Jacques Lacan calls the names of the father. Paternity in *Justified Sinner* is indeed something that registers in the body, as Barnet and Wringhim separately grant, but its materiality emerges only through their disagreement, as it appears in Robert's narration. It is as if the signifying process itself begins to generate its own jouissance, tying materiality to language at a moment when language seemed to present a flight from the body and its unbearable jouissance. Materiality, in this novel, is about how a relation or false whole emerges through the gap in and between subjects, once the missing element in the attempted relation becomes supercharged with jouissance (through the force of its very repression) and begins to function as a positive presence in its own right.

Throughout the scene, the characters' discourses dovetail unexpectedly at the moments at which they seem most irreconcilable. This very irreconcilability

Jock' and 'John Gray o' Middleholm', ed. Karl Miller (London: Penguin, 2006), p. 121. Further citations given parenthetically.

[4] Slavoj Žižek, *The Parallax View* (Cambridge, MA: MIT Press, 2006), p. 4.

becomes, paradoxically, the basis of a shared discursive field, in so far as processes of signification (e.g., resemblance, narration, denomination, terms of employment) begin to take on a jouissance of their own. For instance, Robert's report to his father, which initiates the whole dispute, transcribes John Barnet's insinuation quite accurately, but with two changes: it gets converted into standard English from Scots, and it transposes the terms 'father' and 'dad'. Barnet had said that 'There needs nae aiths to be sworn afore the session wha is your father, young goodman. I ne'er, for my part, saw a son sac like a dad, sin' my een first opened', which Robert reports as: 'no oath before a kirk session was necessary to prove who was my dad, for that he had never seen a son so like a father as I was like mine' (pp. 85, 86). This minor difference—the terminological shifts occurring within playing out only through synonyms—illustrates a gap between the interlocutors, marking differences of class and kinship. Yet it forces a common ground between the disputants that would otherwise not be available and gives that gap body in language. Because that parallax gap finds its materiality in language, it gets indexed to the characters' desires, yet because the gap is indexed to the desire, it becomes material.

In a few short pages, the scene proceeds through five tightly embedded levels of narration. We have:

1., Robert Colwan Wringhim arguing with John Barnet regarding his paternity. This leads him to

2., tell the story of the argument to his father the reverend, which leads the reverend to

3., tell Barnet the story of Lady Dalcastle's desiring gaze and its material effects, and then an analogous story of a woman's desire for a 'blackamoor' 'servant', both of which then

4., Robert describes in his 'Memoir', during which he might

5., parenthetically resolve to the reader that he will denominate the reverend to be his father—giving flesh to the signifying function.

The content at each level doubles and reduplicates itself with minor changes, much as we saw with the example of 'father' and 'dad'. Thus, we need to re-evaluate the role that John Barnet plays in this novel: far from being a point of moral and epistemological stability for the reader, he occasions a proliferation of paternal metaphors that finds itself subject to overlapping signifying processes. Desire becomes material as it traverses the tiers of this structure.

In this deliberately 'enigmatic and controversial novel', known for 'its ability to suggest rather than decide', John Barnet has been seen as a stabilizing force, a proxy for the reader and the implied author.[5] He has been referenced, when at all, just in passing. In the 1970s and 1980s, scholarly discussions of the novel would sometimes momentarily pause to admire his integrity: Barbara Bloedé, for instance, calls the Barnet scene 'one of the most significant passages in *The Confessions*' because 'a typical, straigforward [*sic*] Scottish peasant expresses his disgust at the Wringhims' hypocrisy'.[6] In this tradition of scholarship, John, objecting to the Wringhims' lies and hypocrisies, provides the novel's moral compass—an especially important role in a novel otherwise eager to confound the reader with undecidable situations, disjointed perspectives, unreliable narrators, and metafictional indulgences. I want to focus more on the unfolding of the debate—its turns of argument—than its function for the reader. Embodied materiality and language become entangled, in the Barnet scene, not when language collapses into the real of copulation, and not by following pathways of desire back to some somatic origin, but rather once the cut of the signifier becomes material.[7] The younger Robert Wringhim, inscribed triply into the scene as party to the dispute, its subject matter, and its narrator, finds himself subjected to his own signifying practices, a situation that becomes material in the gap between and across those layers. The gap, that is, begins to embody repressed jouissance on its own, and thus incites the disputants' desire. The asymmetry of the disputants' respective positions, as employer and employee and across two generations, makes possible this effect—which is anything but 'straightforward'.

The scene begins as Reverend Wringhim, dreading the awkward confrontation ahead, attempts to make small talk with John. Barnet is not having it: 'Well, John, this is a fine day for your delving work', says the employer; 'Ay, it's a tolerable day, sir', replies the employee (p. 86). This is a magnificent response, paradoxically affirming Wringhim's suggestion by correcting it and

[5] David Groves, 'Parallel Narratives in Hogg's *Justified Sinner*', *Scottish Literary Journal*, 9: 2 (1982), p. 37; Warren Fox, 'Violence and the Victimization of Women: Engendering Sympathy for Hogg's *Justified Sinner*', *Studies in Scottish Literature*, 32: 1 (2001), p. 165.

[6] Barbara R. Bloedé, 'James Hogg's *Private Memoirs and Confessions of a Justified Sinner*: The Genesis of the Double', *Études Anglaises*, 26: 2 (1973), p. 182. See also David Oakleaf, '"Not the Truth": The Doubleness of Hogg's *Confessions* and the Eighteenth-Century Tradition', *Studies in Scottish Literature*, 18: 1 (1983), pp. 60, 70; Ian Campbell, 'James Hogg and the Bible', *Scottish Literary Journal*, 10: 1 (1983), p. 23; Philip Rogers, '"A Name Which May Serve Your Turn": James Hogg's Gil-Martin', *Studies in Scottish Literature*, 21: 1 (1986), p. 92.

[7] By 'cut' I refer to the process by which a subject is alienated from sexual enjoyment and instead becomes enmeshed in signifying processes. See Jacques Lacan, *Seminar XI: The Four Fundamental Concepts of Psychoanalysis*, trans. Alan Sheridan (New York: Norton, 1978), p. 43.

ignoring the 'delving work' part altogether. Barnet will work for Wringhim, but he will not discuss that work, express approval of its conditions, or pretend to enjoy it; he will not seek to bond with his employer by grousing about it. Desire will become material through this gap.

Melville's Bartleby, an inheritor of this literary tradition, is obstinate but quite direct, speaking matter-of-factly of his preferences. John Barnet is quite the opposite, passive-aggressively shielding his employer from his inner thoughts but working all the same: 'Are you thankful in heart, John...?', asks the reverend; 'It isna aye the maist thankfu' heart that maks the greatest fraze wi' the tongue', replies Barnet (p. 86). Such a response, which cites a lack of correlation between tongue and heart, opens a gap between spoken expression and inner feeling through which the scene will proceed. The response remains equivocal about the division it creates: on the one hand, John will neither admit that he is thankful nor deny it, and he is not claiming not to be thankful; on the other hand, or in another reading, he seems ready to attest to his thankfulness, provided that he be allowed to acknowledge that such assurances are meaningless. Either way, he stops well short of an earnest testimonial: as Jacques Derrida would say of Bartleby's catchphrase, 'it cannot not lead one to suppose that there is some irony in the situation'.[8] Here, as with his 'tolerable day' assertion, John (like Bartleby) will not say either yes or no; unlike Bartleby, John refuses to disclose his feelings.[9] The gap between feelings and speech tests the limits of the employer–employee relation; its ramifications there become the subject of Robert's narration. The jouissance implied in Robert's paternity, then, begins to function as a master signifier in the scene—meaningless in itself but the anchor of the signifying chains that follow. Signification gives body to the question of what employers buy when they hire someone: do they buy just the labor itself or, additionally, access to the thoughts and impressions of the person hired? Barnet holds the former view, Reverend Wringhim the latter.

Wringhim charitably assumes that John's impertinence is a function of his poor reasoning skills, but he is entirely wrong about that. Much as Bartleby's acts of refusal effectively warp Melville's narrator's discourse, changing the terms of their relationship, John Barnet's 'innuendoes' flummox Reverend Wringhim, who seems unable to stop spelling out for John the ways that his discourse is insulting. He begins to assume—still wrongly—that John's equivocations are intentional but underhanded: that they are supposed to pass in discourse undetected, as a way for the laborer to keep his dignity. This,

[8] Jacques Derrida, *The Gift of Death*, trans. David Wills (Chicago, IL: University of Chicago Press, 1995), p. 76.

[9] Jacques Derrida, *Resistances of Psychoanalysis*, trans. Peggy Kamuf, Pascale-Anne Brault, and Michael Naas (Palo Alto, CA: Stanford University Press, 1998), p. 24.

though, is a full-on rebellion staged discursively, as Barnet weaponizes the gap between telling and thinking—an extension of the speech versus feeling dichotomy highlighted previously:

> 'your dark hints are sure to have *one* very bad meaning'.
> 'Hout na, sir, it's only bad folks that think sae' ... .
> 'That saying is ten times worse than the other, John; it is a manifest insult: it is just telling me to my face that you think me a bad man'.
> 'A body canna help his thoughts, sir'. (p. 87)

Reverend Wringhim is not obtuse and flatly says: 'John, I do not approve of these innuendoes'. As the conversation continues, he chastises Barnet for 'an arch malicious manner of vending your aphorisms', for being 'extremely audacious and impertinent', and for being a 'profane old man': 'I desire that you will not presume to break your jests on me' (pp. 86–7). Barnet, though, is not one to seek approval for his innuendoes. Such a gesture, as Žižek has explained with reference to Melville, challenges the culture of 'aggressive passivity' that makes us complicit in capitalist oppression (*Parallax*, p. 342).

Immanuel Kant's slippery essay 'What is Enlightenment?' seems to inform Hogg's (or John's) thinking in this scene. Hogg, we know, valued Kant's work and even once criticized Percy Shelley for inadequately studying the philosopher.[10] If, for Kant, 'the public use of one's reason must always be free, and it alone can bring about enlightenment among mankind; the *private* use of reason may, however, often be narrowly restricted'.[11] Kant sees professional constraint as the key to liberation: '*Argue* as much as you want and about what you want, *but obey*!' (p. 55). Such is the constitutive paradox of Enlightenment: 'a lesser degree of civil freedom provides enough room for all fully to expand their abilities' (p. 59). Barnet epitomizes this vision of Enlightenment: even when disgusted with his employer, he remains his 'serving-man'; he will never, for instance, resign in protest; all the while, though, he refuses to accept any delimitation of his thoughts or speech. This vision of obedient agency, to borrow a term from Martin Wagner, requires its subject to assume control of their circumstances through relentless critique.[12] Yet Kant's vision of Enlightenment cannot comprehend the matter-of-fact announcement that 'a body canna help his thoughts'. Such a statement stresses the primacy and

[10] James Bieri, *Percy Bysshe Shelley: A Biography* (Baltimore, MD: Johns Hopkins University Press, 2008), p. 718, n13.

[11] Immanuel Kant, 'An Answer to the Question: "What Is Enlightenment?"', in *Kant's Political Writings*, ed. Hans Reiss, trans. H.B. Nisbet (Cambridge: Cambridge University Press, 1970), p. 55.

[12] Martin Wagner, 'Obedient Agency: Concept and Narrative' (Invited talk, Department of German, Princeton University, 9 December 2017).

autonomy of the unconscious: it challenges the notion that one's thoughts can ever be one's own, in any 'private' sense.

Barnet appears to be subject to an internal gap that cordons his thoughts from his speech. Yet he brings that gap into contact with another intersubjective parallax between the worker's right to those unknowable and unspoken thoughts and an employer's right to keep their sexual life separate from their professional life. Frustrated at the instability of these nested parallax structures, Wringhim cuts to the chase: 'Did you ever say to anyone that I was the boy Robert's natural father?', he asks. Barnet answers: 'I hae said mony a time that he resembled you, sir. Naebody can mistake that' (p. 88). The answer is, as might be expected, quite slippery: it nonchalantly over-confesses—'mony a time'—but attributes the thoughts to a generalized impression, moving quickly from 'I' to 'Naebody'. Barnet is exploiting the gap between saying and thinking that has structured the exchange to this point: he readily confesses to *saying* that there was a resemblance but takes no responsibility for *thinking* so. As the conversation continues, he continues to take refuge in the autonomy of his thoughts, saying: 'Ye canna hinder me to think whatever I like, sir, nor can I hinder myself'. Thus Barnet, flipping Kant's division of public and private on its head, asserts his right to think with impunity but accepts that he might refuse to speak them: 'Ay, it may be, sir. I coudna say' (p. 88). Claiming to be prohibited from 'saying' allows him to think anything he likes; claiming not to know his own thoughts allows him readily to cop to the saying without confirming or disconfirming the thoughts.

Yet even if we cannot control our thoughts, Barnet suggests, sounding suspiciously Freudian, those thoughts can still make us morally 'bad'. Such a claim finds its support, ironically, in the junior Robert Wringhim, the very object of John's unchecked speculation: later in the novel, as Robert fantasizes about killing his brother, he defends himself to the reader by saying: 'These thoughts, I say, come upon me unasked' (p. 133). He acknowledges that 'I was become a terror to myself', marking his alienation from his desires (p. 187). Barnet's self-defense ('a body canna help his thoughts!') thus compromises the groundskeeper's putative role as the novel's moral compass; Robert, in his hypocrisy, is simply appropriating Barnet's self-protective strategies. As the distinction between John and Robert Jr. collapses, the other important distinction, between John and Robert senior, folds with it: Barnet makes his case by toggling between his interlocutor's thoughts ('only bad folks') to his own ('his thoughts, sir'), a sleight of hand that makes it seem like he has been exculpated by the very accusation he has been leveling at his employer. The 'sir', quickly appended as if respectfully, implies a parallel between the supposedly involuntary nature of thoughts and the coercion created through employment. The employment relation materializes a structural asymmetry between the disputants—an aporia that has been discovered already within

John Barnet, between his thoughts and words, not only between employer and employee. Whether it was installed there as an effect of the employment relation, or whether the labor disruption is an effect of this lack-in-being, becomes impossible to determine, but the alienation of the subject from his thoughts is understood to be inseparable from the material conditions of his labor.

As the situation stands, Wringhim is still defending polite conversation as an end in itself, while Barnet is sticking up for the autonomy of the unconscious. The employer defends the dignity of the symbolic, ironically by demanding that repressed material remain unacknowledged; the employee is asserting the primacy of the real, ironically by attempting to show how repressed material is already circulating at the level of signification. The situation leaves Wringhim in a predicament. He seems at first to be primarily worried about the spreading of rumors: he is trying to ascertain if and when Barnet has expressed his suspicions of Robert Jr.'s paternity. He seems more concerned about John's utterances than his thoughts. But because John is operating by implication and innuendo, his words seem strangely innocuous when taken to the letter; they receive their scandalous aspect only when seen as an expression of unuttered thoughts. Thus, Wringhim is compelled to undermine his own discourse: it is *he* who must let the real function at the level of the symbolic, just as it is Barnet who maintains that repressed material cannot be expressed in language. They have switched positions. What is happening here? To build on Tom Eyers's work, we might say that the real is asserting itself as the 'stubborn opacity of the material itself' by its very dependence upon 'the weird materialism of the signifier'.[13] Even as desire divides the mark of the signifier from the raw materiality of the real, it becomes realized through the processes of signification. It is as if the friction occurring within rhetorical processes sparks its own independent jouissance. This is very disturbing to Reverend Wringhim, both for the indemnity it seems to grant a desirer and for the way it presents subjectivity as subjection to something radically autonomous. Everything depends on whether (or not) the real can be integrated into the symbolic—and without resolving that unresolvable question, no common ground may be found between these perspectives. Below, I will suggest that this parallax nevertheless begins to function as a 'false whole', which attains its own materiality.

Wringhim, clearly flummoxed by the separation of speech from thought in Barnet's address, ingeniously invites John to speak about his thoughts: 'So, then, John, you positively think, from a casual likeness, that this boy is my son?' But John merely says that he will not have his thoughts regulated—not

[13] Tom Eyers, 'Lacanian Materialism and the Question of the Real', *Cosmos and History*, 7: 1 (2011), pp. 156–7.

because they are his own private thoughts, but precisely because they are not! John claims to be entitled to his subversive thoughts because they come from the unconscious: 'Man's thoughts are vanity, sir; they come unasked, an' gang away without a dismissal, an' he canna' help them. I'm neither gaun to say that I think he's your son, nor that I think he's no your son: sae ye neednа pose me nae mair about it'. Barnet here again insists upon separating words from thoughts, and so controlling his words would be pointless (hence: 'needna'). Thoughts, he says, go away without being dismissed, which is a fascinating thing to assert on the verge of a forced resignation. He is, it seems, not at all like his thoughts: he will be staying here until he is dismissed.

John points out that he has sold his labor, not his thoughts, to the Reverend: 'Auld John may dee a beggar in a hay barn, or at the back of a dike, but he sall aye be master o' his ain thoughts an' gie them vent or no, as he likes' (p. 89). It is a strangely Kantian thing to say in a conversation in which he has so emphatically insisted that he is not, at all, 'master o' his ain thoughts'. Wringhim does not openly accept this line of argument, yet he seems to give up on the regulation of John's thoughts and attempts instead to regulate his *speech*: 'If you do not promise to me, in faith and honour, that you never will say, or insinuate such a thing again in your life, as that that boy is my natural son, I will take the keys of the church from you, and dismiss you from my service' (p. 89). By tying John's 'service' to his speech, Wringhim effectively deprives him of the possibility of 'Enlightenment' in Kant's sense. Hence Barnet throws down his keys to resign his post. In so doing, John seems to cling to the notion that desire is immaterial: that his body and thus his labor are totally separate from his desire; they operate independently via the parallax formed around the unconscious. Yet we will find that Robert's narration of the scene exploits this gap, forcing desire into contact with the body to apprehend John's desire as a material factor. This happens at the symbolic level, through narrative structures, through stories of Robert's immaculate conception, and through the function of proper names.

John is introduced to the reader as 'the minister's man', a genitive that immediately proves ironic when, straight away, he expresses concerns about our narrator's character: 'I'm feared he turn out to be a conceited gowk' (p. 82). Why, I wonder, does Reverend Wringhim say 'no', rather than 'I disagree', in response? Perhaps he is alarmed that an employee would make such a frank assessment of his son's character unsolicited. Yet he is also rejecting Barnet's right to be 'master o' his ain thoughts'. We can detect both ideas in the two 'no's of his reply (as narrated by Robert—*les nons du père*, as it were): '"No", said my pastor, and father (as I shall henceforth denominate him). "No, Barnet, he is a wonderful boy"' (p. 82). Robert's words, added after the fact through his narration, intervene between two 'no's, which were spoken consecutively, but which did not actually repeat each other: the second one seems to refute

Barnet's assessment of the son's prospects, but the first one sounds more like a warning. It does not merely dissent from Barnet's assessment of Robert Jr., but it also reprimands him for his presumptuousness. The flat tone of the response only underscores the gap in power that constrains the two men's relationship. The narrator's voice detaches the first 'no' from the second. We had a gap (i.e., the unconscious) separating John's public thoughts and private words, which became materialized as a second gap separating John's labor from his desire; that gap now finds material expression in a third one, separating moral judgment from economic domination.

It is strange yet understandable that Robert would present his seeming stepfather primarily as 'my pastor' and only secondarily as 'father' in this scene, given the controversy that has begun to surround the issue of his paternity; it is stranger yet that he should say, as a parenthetical aside, 'I shall henceforth denominate him'. The tone of 'I shall henceforth denominate him' is noticeably formal and legalistic and focused peculiarly on the signifier of paternity rather than the signified.[14] If *no, no* indicates the new parallax that has emerged—signaling, on the one hand, *there's another way to see it* and, on the other, *because I'm your boss*—this strange parenthetical intrusion by our narrator literally mediates between these perspectives, rescuing the conflict for the symbolic level as their relationship begins to break down in the imaginary. It does so by bringing the discussion about the materiality of bodies to the level of the signifier. The implication seems to be that one only becomes a 'father' by being 'denominated' as such by the succeeding generation—that one needs to be hailed as a father in order to serve as one. That development, interestingly, makes the entire conflict moot.

If John Barnet is a subversive quasi-Kantian, the junior Robert Wringhim may be a Hegelian: he proposes that a person needs to be formally and publicly recognized as one's father in order for him to have served as one, as if acts of care become acts of fatherhood only in being retroactively recognized as such by their beneficiaries. Robert's parentheses attempt—and fail—to open up a level of metanarration at which such an act might become possible: Robert, who is already functioning as an autodiegetic narrator, here avails himself of an additional parenthetical metalevel at which he might interrupt the main task of narration to address us again, separately. It indicates his wish to extricate himself from the conflict, when of course his body—and his stepfather's obscene enjoyment in begetting it—is the very matter at hand. Robert has thus materialized as the signifier of his father's desire; yet his narration of the scene interrupts and represses that primal scene of paternal jouissance.

[14] That in itself is quite ironic from a Lacanian standpoint, as the signified would be the proper (though inverted) 'denominator' of the pseudo-Saussurean formulation S/s. See Lacan, *Écrits*, pp. 414–15.

The signifier becomes laden with jouissance through the repression of that primal jouissance. The work being done within the parentheses (performatively affirming the denomination) is different from the work being done *by* the parentheses: formally, it prioritizes Wringhim's function as father over his function as reverend, but its content still refuses to give him a name: he is termed 'father' rather than 'pastor' but not, for instance, 'Robert' or even 'Dad'. Hailed by his social role rather than a name, he has not really been 'denominated' after all.

Lacan warns that fathers, like rainbows, exist only in being named: 'the function of *being a father* is absolutely unthinkable in human experience without the category of the signifier. What can it mean *to be a father*?' (*Seminar III*, pp. 318, 292). Lacan is not making the banal point that a father is a socially constructed role; he is saying that 'father' gains its materiality by being a word. The term 'father' needs to be denominated as such in order to function, but that it cannot emerge as such unilaterally: this process is, he explains, 'what happens when you are in a relationship with the discourse of another' (p. 285). That captures what has quietly transpired in *Justified Sinner*. Robert, as narrator, tends to focus on people's roles rather than their identities—recall his description of Barnet as 'the minister's man'. At times, Robert's emphasis on social role enmeshes those it describes in layers of social interconnectedness, each person finding a place in relation to the others: e.g., 'I liked John Barnet, my reverend father's serving-man' (p. 84). Robert, in his capacity as narrator, not as a diegetic character, tends to corral unwieldy elements of the story and situate them within a symbolic network. His implication that 'father' is a name may, at first, seem to suggest the immateriality of the debate at the level of the signifier: if fatherhood is accepted as a mere social function or 'denomination', it matters much less who has sired our narrator. Yet it is actually a dialectical movement: a dispute about material bodies as they relate to desire finds its materiality in being narrated. There is thus a horrifying materiality—the jouissance of the father, treated as scandalous by everyone involved—built in to the symbolic circuit.

Once established, a signifier like 'father' takes on its own conceptual force and becomes inseparable from the material circumstance of fatherhood. It does not simply function as an element in language. It resists attempts to replace it with other signifiers, and in that sense a proper name (or 'denomination') complicates, rather than secures, questions of paternity. Lacan, mocking Bertrand Russell's discussion of proper names, said:

> [W]hat is in question in 'my grandfather is my grandfather' means … this personage is exactly the same as the one who is posted on the civil register as being demonstrated by the bonds of marriage to be the father of my father, in as much as it is precisely the birth of the latter that is

> at stake in the act in question. You see therefore the degree to which 'my grandfather is my grandfather' is not at all a tautology.[15]

To say that 'Émile Lacan' is 'my grandfather' is not a tautology, says Lacan, offering his own family as an example, because it demarcates a gap between the symbolic (of the social function and the name) and the real (of procreation, material bodies, and thus of sexual enjoyment).[16] Hogg is going even further in the same direction: while, in the best of cases, to say 'my father is my father' is not a tautology, as it suggests an alignment between the biological progenitor and the social role, in *Justified Sinner* it is precisely in order for Hogg to disavow that convergence that John Barnet enters into the narrative. Robert Wringhim's 'denomination' of his pastor as 'my father' only replaces what might have (wrongly) seemed a tautology with another: it enables him to 'name' his father something other than 'Robert Wringhim' and thus introduce a nominal gap between the identically-named father–son duo. Yet, by functioning as a confession that 'my father is my [biological] father', it acknowledges, rhetorically, the very transgression that John Barnet has alleged. The jouissance has relocated, through repression, to the level of the signifier.

The elder Wringhim, being a reverend, is concerned by any appearance of impropriety: better to have welcomed a fatherless boy than to have raised one's own bastard. Fearing professional ramifications, he presses for a statement of Barnet's suspicions: 'Tell me, dare you say, or dare you think, that I am the natural father of that boy?' Here again, *saying* and *thinking* are presented as alternatives—but alternatives that can substitute for each other, as thinking is presented in the syntax as equivalent to saying. Clearly, Barnet will not be assuaging his employer's concerns or taking a vow of silence—indeed, he immediately points out the resemblance between father and son. And so Wringhim, panicking, asserts that there might be a perfectly chaste explanation for the family resemblance: 'But, John, there are many natural reasons for such likenesses, besides that of consanguinity. They depend much on the thoughts and affections of the mother; and it is probable that the mother of this boy, being deserted by her worthless husband, having turned her thoughts on me, as likely to be her protector, may have caused this striking resemblance' (p. 88). There is no doubt that denying the resemblance would have been easier: *I simply don't see it!* Instead, Wringhim acknowledges the 'striking resemblance' and offers this preposterous explanation, which, as Michelle Faubert notes,

[15] Jacques Lacan, 'The Seminar of Jacques Lacan, Book IX: Identification, 1961–1962', trans. Cormac Gallagher, n.d., sec. 6 December 1961.

[16] Jacques Lacan, 'The Seminar of Jacques Lacan, Book IX: Identification, 1961–1962', trans. Cormac Gallagher, n.d., sec. 6 December 1961.

employs the quasi-scientific discourse of maternal impressions.[17] Maternal impressions theory was mostly discredited sometime in the sixteenth century and was, thanks to researchers like Gervase Markham, widely considered ludicrous in the seventeenth century; it remained ludicrous in the early years of the eighteenth century, as Ian Stevenson explains with reference to the works of J.A. Blondel.[18] The scientific backlash against maternal impressions theory made its way into satirical Scottish literature by the mid-eighteenth century, most prominently in *The Adventures of Peregrine Pickle* by Tobias Smollett (1751). Therefore, readers of Hogg's novel, even those who take seriously its historical setting in the early eighteenth century, are expected to see the explanation as comically self-serving.

Why does Wringhim reach for this preposterous explanation, which, to be certain, John Barnet is not buying? Wringhim's response begins to feel perverse. He turns himself into a pure object of a mother's predatory sexual gaze, granting Robert's mother sexual agency. The syntax in which he does so—i.e., his reformulation of the sexual scene through the passive voice—plays out like a childhood beating fantasy from Freud: *a mother is being deserted, and I am being looked at*; *a woman had sex not with me—certainly not me—but with her husband, whom I have deemed 'worthless'*.[19] Fantasizing about his own passivity, Wringhim imagines himself a fetish for another's enjoyment. The perversion wishfully displaces his 'bad' deeds onto a double, who can enjoy on his behalf—thus anticipating the central crisis of the novel's murder mystery. The cost of this perverse jouissance, however, is that Wringhim must claim to exist in the world in a distinctly Barnet-like way: he is simply 'doing the job' of a father, while a totally independent other agency, which refuses to be regulated by norms of propriety or responsibility, gets to run amok at the level of the real. His claims about the materiality of desire actually cut across the parallax structure that has forced him to make these claims. The father's recourse to maternal impressions theory gets materialized in and through Robert at the level of the murder plot, retroactively giving a Gothic edge to the dispute. The child is thus 'father' of the man at the scene of his own conception.

[17] Michelle Faubert, 'John Ferriar's Psychology, James Hogg's *Justified Sinner*, and the Gay Science of Horror Writing', in *Romanticism and Pleasure*, eds. Thomas H. Schmid and Michelle Faubert (New York: Palgrave Macmillan, 2010), p. 97.

[18] Ian Stevenson, 'A New Look at Maternal Impressions: An Analysis of 50 Published Cases and Reports of Two Recent Examples', *Journal of Scientific Exploration*, 6: 4 (1992), pp. 353–4.

[19] Sigmund Freud, '"A Child Is Being Beaten": A Contribution to the Study of the Origin of Sexual Perversions', in *The Standard Edition of the Complete Psychological Works of Sigmund Freud*, trans. James Strachey, vol. 17 (London: Vintage, 2001), pp. 181–6, 198–200.

Maternal impressions theory ambivalently separates speech and thought, and then thought from deeds: *no, no, I didn't have sex with her; she was merely thinking of having sex with me.* To the extent that Wringhim thus accepts the warrants of Barnet's discourse, the claim, however preposterous, signals Wringhim's tacit capitulation to Barnet's way of thinking. The swapping of positions, seemingly impossible from within a parallax, can happen because the novel will not let any character claim their own thoughts: the impasse becomes held in common. Desire, in Wringhim's discourse, seems to be a blend of 'thoughts' and 'affections' and their material consequences: indeed 'thoughts and affections' become his euphemism for 'unacted desires', to employ William Blake's term.[20] Wringhim's self-defense literalizes Blake's Proverb of Hell (i.e., 'sooner murder an infant in its cradle than nurse unacted desires') only to dissent from it: a woman's desire was supposedly written onto the countenance of a fetus, so that, in time, she could actually nurse her unacted desires. Once Reverend Wringhim, as 'her protector', agreed to raise the child as an alternative to leaving that baby to die, he signaled that he would sooner nurse 'unacted desires' than murder, by neglect, an infant in its cradle. He even 'had him christened in his own name, and nursed in his own premises' (p. 16). The explanation, seemingly aspiring to chivalry, makes family resemblance something that happens intragenerationally: the likeness discloses a pregnant woman's desire for Wringhim, rather than his son's inheritance from his father. It establishes a kinship built on the materiality of desire, as it ascends to the level of the signifier. Lacan once proposed that we should learn to think about kinship horizontally, partner to partner, instead of vertically, across generations, as a way to initiate new logics of belonging and identity.[21] Wringhim, who has been wary of unconscious effects through much of the debate, relies on the material effects of desire to propose a horizontal kinship structure, rooted in desire not heredity.

Barnet remains incredulous, however, so Wringhim offers a parallel example to support his claim: 'I have known a lady, John, who was delivered of a blackamoor child, merely from the circumstance of having got a start by the sudden entrance of her negro servant, and not being able to forget him for several hours' (p. 88). Hogg's investment in the early nineteenth-century Gothic manifests here, as the example strongly recalls Charlotte Dacre's *Zofloya, or the Moor* (1806)—an important echo given the way that Gil-Martin, ever shape-shifting, is secretly a manifestation of Satan. The example is interesting, not only for its insistence on the materiality of desire, but because the origins of skin pigmentation were just becoming an 'intense debate' within European

[20] William Blake, 'The Marriage of Heaven and Hell', in *The Complete Poetry & Prose of William Blake*, ed. David V. Erdman, newly revised ed. (New York: Anchor Books, 1988), line 67.

[21] Lacan, 'Seminar IX', sec. 6 December 1961.

scientific research at the time of Hogg's writing, following the discovery of the pigment cell in 1819 by Giosué Sangiovanni.[22] Even taken on its own terms, it is hardly a neutral example: it asks us to believe that a mother's sexual desire—something here that is not deliberate, but wildly out of her control, and certainly illicit for the ways it crosses boundaries of monogamy, class, and race—pigments the child's skin. The body of the child thus confesses the sexual desire, even if supposedly unfulfilled, of the mother. Yet the mother's desire disappears into the parallax gap separating Barnet from Wringhim.

Implicitly, it compares the 'master', as Robert Jr. has termed his father, to a person (euphemistically called a 'servant') who has likely been enslaved, deepening the Hegelian echoes of the conversation and allowing it to invoke long-standing debates in Great Britain regarding slavery. It is an outrageous example, socially, scientifically, and literarily: as Anne Mellor explains, it was much more common in the Romantic period—that great era of abolitionist literature—to read expressions of white male desire for black female bodies than vice versa: 'the very possibility that a white female might sexually prefer the black male body to the white male body was one that British culture in the late eighteenth century either denied or abhorred'.[23] Hence one might again wonder how such a transgressive model of bodily materiality could possibly be exculpatory in a white supremacist Scottish culture, given how it likens Robert Wringhim, the town reverend, to 'a blackamoor'? Reverend Wringhim takes refuge in this myth of desire's materiality, however it may figuratively blacken him, as a way of realizing a deeper, even more taboo wish: that of harmonious relations between employers and their servants. The wish materializes, at the level of the sexual, the bourgeois fantasy of fellowship with a domestic servant: the 'servant''s mere presence in the room is treated as intimate to the fullest extent. The mother in the example does not have to be in control of her desire: she is surprised by 'the sudden entrance' of her servant and is simply 'not able to forget him'.

Hogg's joke is that this 'blackamoor' example offers no proof at all: the blackness of the child is certainly not proof that desire, rather than biology, determines one's physical appearance, and nor does it prove that racial difference is an effect of desire. Hogg is seemingly satirizing the myth of Immaculate Conception: Barnet says, subversively, 'an' I had been the laird, I wadna hae ta'en that story in' (p. 88). In practice it would invariably be taken as proof of the mother's sexual congress with a 'servant', speaking euphemistically, of color. Yet

[22] Wiete Westerhof, 'The Discovery of the Human Melanocyte', *Pigment Cell & Melanoma Research*, 19: 3 (2006), pp. 183–93. The novel is of course set in the early eighteenth century, a time in which, as Westerhof notes, the origins of skin color were already being studied and theorized.

[23] Anne K. Mellor, 'Interracial Sexual Desire in Charlotte Dacre's *Zofloya*', *European Romantic Review*, 13: 2 (2002), p. 169.

as a way of cutting across the parallax that separates employer from employee, Wringhim dares to suggest that people are physically, materially shaped according to the pathways of their mother's (even momentary) desire. In such a situation, one cannot but act in conformity with one's desire; there can be no 'unacted desires'. And Barnet, for all of his stated skepticism, embraces this logic, too: he was the first to posit that thoughts will necessarily follow desires and thus be irredeemably involuntary. There are two scandalous consequences to this confluence of parallax discourses: Wringhim has effectively invited John Barnet to place himself in the pathway of Lady Dalcastle's desire and has insinuated that Barnet may be effectively enslaved. His jouissance uncovered and exposed, the groundskeeper recoils and departs from the novel permanently, although he keeps coming back through echoes of the scene in Robert's narration.

The dispute between John Barnet and Reverend Wringhim, in its turns of argument and again in its very irreconcilability, gives body to the Lacanian lesson that: 'The subject may well know that copulating is *really* at the origin of procreation, but the function of procreation as signifier is something else' (*Seminar III*, p. 293). Robert's efforts to 'denominate' his father at the level of narration, and thus realize his (step)father's paternity at the level of the signifier, give desire its 'maternal impressions'. John has been trying to read the materiality of the body (i.e., Robert's features) as a signifier of paternity, and thus trying to integrate repressed material into the symbolic. The debate between Barnet and Wringhim, as it explores discredited models for grasping the materiality of desire (e.g., 'Enlightenment' and maternal impressions), forces their parallax positions to collapse into each other through their joint reference to the unconscious. As Robert narrates this effect and traces its ramifications on his own murderous psyche, he brings paternity to the level of the signifier. Materiality is a short circuit between Barnet and Wringhim, appearing as jouissance through the excesses of language as their impasse is described and narrated. Hence it is at the level of Robert's acts of 'denomination' that Reverend Wringhim *becomes, really,* Robert's father. As Lacan explains:

> The point is that the sum of these facts—of copulating with a woman, that she then carries something within her womb for a certain period, that this product is finally expelled—will never lead one to constitute the notion of what it is *to be a father*. I'm not even speaking of the entire cultural cluster implied in the term *being a father*, I'm simply speaking of what it is *to be a father* in the sense of procreation. (p. 293)

Although Robert clings to the naïve view that his father was not *really* his father, that is, biologically, we discover that it *is* at that next level that one becomes 'a father'—which means that Robert was right to 'denominate' him as such. As we have seen, women's enjoyment is brought into this circuit conceptually but assiduously avoided rhetorically and is thus subsumed under a symbolic matrix that cannot fully account for it.

The disagreement appears to concern, on the one hand, a worker's rights to his thoughts and, on the other hand, a person's right to keep their sexual history private. As the two tempt fate by playfully accepting parts of the other's position, the question emerges as to what, if anything, is providing the terms for their exchange. They are haggling over something that neither can control: namely, how the signifier might be brought into contact with repressed material. As they attempt to give a materiality to the unconscious via the signifier, the parallax that opens between them annuls the exchanges of labor, money, and information that have structured their non-relation for decades. Their respective discourses swerve to avoid each other, and this very avoidance becomes their bond. The gap between them, never traversable, becomes positivized in the narration as a material factor in its own right: it is a fragment of discarded sexual enjoyment that embodies the division between the characters, as they haggle over it indirectly.

The Barnet episode suggests that systems of exchange, including desire, have a material basis, which needs to be acknowledged if we are to grasp how and why the exchange breaks down. Two perspectives, which seem so incompatible and each so self-protective, begin to cross *through* their very lack of equivalence, and so can be repurposed at the level of Robert's narration. To note how this process is contradictory is to activate questions in Lacanian psychoanalysis that have been dormant for some forty years. In his seminar of 14 December 1976, Lacan offers that:

> we are advancing here very gently towards the contradiction of what I call the *une bévue*. The *une bévue* is what is exchanged despite the fact that it is not worth the unit in question. *Une bévue* is a false whole. Its type, as I might say, is the signifier[.] ... All that sustains the difference between the same and the other is that the same is the same materially. The notion of matter is fundamental.[24]

Lacan's term *une bévue* is somewhat tricky, being a portmanteau of the German *Unbewusst*, meaning 'unconscious', 'unconsciously', 'wittingly', and 'unwittingly', and the French *une bévue*, roughly meaning 'a blunder' or 'an error due to ignorance'. The translator Cormac Gallagher calls it untranslatable: it 'cannot be reproduced in English', he warns (n. 1). The Barnet episode is Robert's 'confession' of this 'false whole'. As the two sides to the debate discover 'a *bévue*' between them that 'will not be perpetuated', the 'other as

[24] Jacques Lacan, 'The Seminar of Jacques Lacan, Book XXIV: *L'insu Que Sait de l'une-Bévue s'aile à Mourre*, 1976–77', trans. Cormac Gallagher, n.d., sec. 14 December 1976.

such' comes into its 'materiality' through 'the sign mimicking the other'.[25] That is, the temporary, unintentional, and provisional alignment of Wringhim's and Barnet's perspectives, which arises out of the parallax between them but cannot be sustained, begins to function as a fantasy. Yet that imagined whole retains the parallax gap as its authorizing condition, ensuring that this structure is never whole (i.e., it is not-all). As the *bévue* that entangles them proliferates throughout the novel, it also must 'cease' to be a *bévue* at the level of narration.

Joel Faflak has observed how 'psychoanalysis in [Hogg's] novel is haunted by its own indeterminacy', in the sense that 'the novel invents psychoanalysis precisely by marking its impossibility'.[26] In the Barnet episode, that impossibility takes a parallax form, and its parallax structures beget several others. Although this scene had appeared to assert the moral dignity of the Scottish laboring class, that dignity proves to be far from coherent, epistemologically, given Hogg's tendencies to link desire to signification and to embrace the material consequences. The dispute between Barnet and the Wringhims enables signification to develop its own materiality. As Lacan would put it: 'the point of view I am trying to maintain before you involves a certain materialism of the elements in question, in the sense that the signifiers are well and truly embodied, materialized, they are words that wander about and as such they play their role of fastening together'.[27] This materialism, which Lacan would call llanguage, emerges in the excess to signifying structures as they collapse. The Barnet dispute is only resolved across and through the novel's narrative processes of making meaning, as the gap that opens between narrative levels, separating the disputants in a movement that takes on significations of its own. Thus, it responds (in advance) to several central problems in Lacanian psychoanalysis: how does the signifier tie the subject, through desire, to new forms of materiality? What gives the subject its materiality, once it is alienated into language? And might jouissance find a way of returning through the commodification of labor and the alienation so occasioned? The John Barnet scene suggests an affirmative answer to that last question, as Hogg creates a labor dispute around the materiality of the body, even as the dispute itself, and its subsequent narration, materializes desire. Jouissance returns through the break in the signifying structures that would seek to delimit it, sexualizing the entire scene. The aporias at work here challenge bourgeois ideas of the body, destabilize the meaning of sexual reproduction, and upend Enlightenment models of moral duty in a highly compressed way.

[25] Lacan, 'Seminar XXIV', sec. 14 December 1976.

[26] Joel Faflak, '"The Clearest Light of Reason": Making Sense of Hogg's Body of Evidence', *Gothic Studies*, 5: 1 (2003), p. 100.

[27] Jacques Lacan, *The Seminar of Jacques Lacan, Book III: The Psychoses*, ed. Jacques-Alain Miller, trans. Russell Grigg (New York: Norton, 1993), p. 289.

Bibliography

Bieri, James. *Percy Bysshe Shelley: A Biography.* Baltimore, MD: Johns Hopkins University Press, 2008.

Blake, William. 'The Marriage of Heaven and Hell'. In *The Complete Poetry & Prose of William Blake*, ed. David V. Erdman, Newly revised ed. New York: Anchor Books, 1988.

Bloedé, Barbara R. 'James Hogg's *Private Memoirs and Confessions of a Justified Sinner*: The Genesis of the Double'. *Études Anglaises*, 26: 2 (1973), pp. 174–86.

Campbell, Ian. 'James Hogg and the Bible'. *Scottish Literary Journal*, 10: 1 (1983), pp. 14–29.

Derrida, Jacques. *The Gift of Death*, trans. David Wills. Chicago, IL: University of Chicago Press, 1995.

——. *Resistances of Psychoanalysis*, trans. Peggy Kamuf, Pascale-Anne Brault, and Michael Naas. Stanford, CA: Stanford University Press, 1998.

Dolphijn, Rick and Iris van der Tuin. 'Pushing Dualism to an Extreme'. In *New Materialism: Interviews & Cartographies.* Ann Arbor, MI: Open Humanities Press, 2012, pp. 115–37.

Eyers, Tom. 'Lacanian Materialism and the Question of the Real'. *Cosmos and History*, 7: 1 (2011), pp. 155–66.

Faflak, Joel. '"The Clearest Light of Reason": Making Sense of Hogg's Body of Evidence'. *Gothic Studies*, 5: 1 (2003), pp. 94–110.

Faubert, Michelle. 'John Ferriar's Psychology, James Hogg's *Justified Sinner*, and the Gay Science of Horror Writing'. In *Romanticism and Pleasure*, eds. Thomas H. Schmid and Michelle Faubert. New York: Palgrave Macmillan, 2010, pp. 83–108.

Fox, Warren. 'Violence and the Victimization of Women: Engendering Sympathy for Hogg's *Justified Sinner*'. *Studies in Scottish Literature*, 32: 1 (2001), pp. 164–79.

Freud, Sigmund. '"A Child Is Being Beaten": A Contribution to the Study of the Origin of Sexual Perversions'. In *The Standard Edition of the Complete Psychological Works of Sigmund Freud*, trans. James Strachey. 24 vols. London: Vintage, 2001. 17: pp. 179–204.

——. 'Psycho-analysis and Telepathy'. In *The Standard Edition of the Complete Psychological Works of Sigmund Freud*, trans. James Strachey. 24 vols. London: Vintage, 2001. 18: pp. 173–220.

Groves, David. 'Parallel Narratives in Hogg's *Justified Sinner*'. *Scottish Literary Journal*, 9: 2 (1982), pp. 37–44.

Hogg, James. *The Private Memoirs and Confessions of a Justified Sinner, with 'Marion's Jock' and 'John Gray o' Middleholm'*, ed. Karl Miller. London: Penguin, 2006.

Kant, Immanuel. 'An Answer to the Question: "What Is Enlightenment?"'. In *Kant's Political Writings*, ed. Hans Reiss, trans. H.B. Nisbet. Cambridge: Cambridge University Press, 1970, pp. 54–60.

Lacan, Jacques. *Écrits: The First Complete Edition in English*, trans. Bruce Fink. New York: Norton, 2006.

——. *The Seminar of Jacques Lacan, Book III: The Psychoses*, ed. Jacques-Alain Miller, trans. Russell Grigg. New York: Norton, 1993.

——. 'The Seminar of Jacques Lacan, Book IX: Identification, 1961–1962', trans. Cormac Gallagher, n.d. Unpublished manuscript.

——. *The Seminar of Jacques Lacan, Book V: Formations of the Unconscious*, ed. Jacques-Alain Miller, trans. Russell Grigg. Cambridge: Polity, 2017.

——. *The Seminar of Jacques Lacan, Book XI: The Four Fundamental Concepts of Psychoanalysis*, ed. Jacques-Alain Miller, trans. Alan Sheridan. New York: Norton, 1978.

——. 'The Seminar of Jacques Lacan, Book XXIV: *L'insu Que Sait de l'une-Bévue s'aile à Mourre*, 1976–77', trans. Cormac Gallagher, n.d. Unpublished manuscript.

Mellor, Anne K. 'Interracial Sexual Desire in Charlotte Dacre's *Zofloya*'. *European Romantic Review*, 13: 2 (2002), pp. 169–73.

Oakleaf, David. '"Not the Truth": The Doubleness of Hogg's *Confessions* and the Eighteenth-Century Tradition'. *Studies in Scottish Literature*, 18: 1 (1983), pp. 59–74.

Rogers, Philip. '"A Name Which May Serve Your Turn": James Hogg's Gil-Martin'. *Studies in Scottish Literature*, 21: 1 (1986), pp. 89–98.

Stevenson, Ian. 'A New Look at Maternal Impressions: An Analysis of 50 Published Cases and Reports of Two Recent Examples'. *Journal of Scientific Exploration*, 6: 4 (1992), pp. 353–73.

Wagner, Martin. 'Obedient Agency: Concept and Narrative'. Invited talk, Department of German, Princeton University, 9 December 2017.

Westerhof, Wiete. 'The Discovery of the Human Melanocyte'. *Pigment Cell & Melanoma Research*, 19: 3 (2006), pp. 183–93.

Žižek, Slavoj. *Absolute Recoil: Towards a New Foundation of Dialectical Materialism*. London: Verso, 2015.

——. *The Parallax View*. Cambridge, MA: MIT Press, 2006.

Chapter Eleven

Werewolf Wollstonecraft

homo homini lupus, or, Romantic Beast Wars

Chris Washington

I. Werewolf Bibliophilia

Near the end of his *Confessions* (1770), Jean-Jacques Rousseau writes that, in response to the radicality of his controversial writing, he was 'chased in the country as if I were a were-wolf'.[1] Derrida, in his last lectures, *The Beast and the Sovereign* (2009), points out that Rousseau's bibliophilia similarly leads him to compare himself to a werewolf at the end of volume one of the *Confessions*, except in that passage the translator of that edition renders 'werewolf' as 'outlaw'.[2] For Derrida this eccentric translation is actually serendipitous since it recalls how the figure of the werewolf in Rousseau links to sovereigns and beasts that are both exempted in classical legal structures by virtue of the former's supererogation of law and the latter's nonhuman, non-subject status: 'so the werewolf, the "true" werewolf, is indeed the one who, like the beast and the sovereign, places himself or finds himself placed "outside the law", *outlaw*, above or at a distance from the normal regime of law and right'.[3] On Derrida's reading, then, both the sovereign and the beast are irreducible in terms of both their discursive and material status under the law; their linguistic and conceptual but also their physical exemption from the law structures the very law that excludes them. The sovereign is the law but cannot be touched by the law—by either sociocultural interdiction or by laying hands on his

[1] Jean-Jacques Rousseau, *The Confessions*, trans. J.M. Cohen (New York: Penguin, 1953), p. 579.

[2] The French for 'outlaw' is *hors-la-loi,* and the French for 'werewolf' is *loup-garou.*

[3] Jacques Derrida, *The Beast and the Sovereign*, vol. I, trans. Geoffrey Bennington (Chicago, IL: University of Chicago Press, 2009), p. 64.

person—he can be killed but not legally sentenced to death. The beast, in contrast, exists outside the law and as such can be conscripted neither within it by the discursive force of the law nor by the physical force of legal murder. To put it in biopolitical terms, the beast can be killed but not murdered under the law, according to Derrida, and so perforce the sovereign and the beast exist paradoxically inside of the law by virtue of existing beyond the law because it is that very law that dictates their lawlessness, their exclusion from the parameters of the law.

This judicial bestiary at the heart of eighteenth-century politics has long been evident in Enlightenment social contract debates. Michel Foucault's and Giorgio Agamben's biopolitics, for example, turn on government's ability to regulate life via the transition from monarchal states to social-contract states. But rather than the Rousseau who obsesses Derrida, it is Thomas Hobbes who provides the most famous example of the human and the nonhuman in regards to social contract theory. Hobbes writes, in *De cive* (1642), '*homo homini lupus*', 'man is a wolf to (for) man'.[4] He explains this sociopolitical reality with an example taken from the Roman Empire. It was, he tells us, said by the 'Roman people' that 'all kinds are to be reckoned amongst ravenous beasts' even as these same people are themselves 'a beast of prey' as their Empire 'despoiled nations' and placed them in 'a specious bondage' (p. 89). Following this logic, citizens of any country are nothing more than beasts, nonhumans who prey on not only each other but other nations as well. Hobbes's rhetoric—beyond whatever he may think he is doing—makes plain the gender stakes of humans' wolfish nature: 'good men must defend themselves by taking to them for a sanctuary the two daughters of war, deceit and violence: that is, in plain terms, a mere brutal rapacity' (p. 90). War, '*bellum omnium contra omnes*', in Hobbes's famous assertion, appears, here, as the personified father of daughters whom men must shelter and guard to prevent their spread across the land.[5] Good men, those wolves, must become mini-sovereigns and fulfill their hetero-patriarchal duties by adopting 'deceit and violence' and by this means forestall war's afterbirths; they must restrain their own innate wolfishness by controlling their female offspring, the very deceit and violence that they themselves birth. Within the metaphor, then, men *are* war, ontologically speaking, and are *at* war, until they take on the sovereign mantle and control the feminine passions, their daughters, that have been created by their own wolfish natures, which would paradoxically suggest, then, that before deceit and violence are born of war they are innate to 'man'.

[4] Thomas Hobbes, *De cive*, ed. Bernard Gert (New York: Hackett, 1991), p. 89. My translation. The genitive and dative cases are both offered in order to capture fully what Hobbes means.

[5] Thomas Hobbes, *Leviathan*, ed. Edwin Curley (New York: Hackett, 1994), p. 76.

Hobbes's explanation blurs gender lines entirely in the very act of delineating them by associating the negative, uncontrollable passions of warfare with women that men, presumably because of their stronger will, can and must protect themselves from by protecting these feminine innate productions of their own loins. In other words, if we follow Hobbes's logic, in order to prevent war, men must control the women inside of them, those women who are, perhaps we can provisionally say, again on this logic, the real wolves. Deceit and violence are a 'brutal rapacity', a term important below but let us here note that 'rapacity'—which which comes from the Latin '*rapaces*', 'birds of prey'—circles back around to the ravenous beasts, the citizens who devour the citizens of other—and even their own—nation in order to establish and build empire. To ultimately prevent such wars Hobbes, and Rousseau in response to him, constructs a social-contract hetero-patriarchal politics—for Hobbes it is explicitly a monarch who must reign—that can restrain these women wolves in male clothing and prevent the war of all against all. We can therefore see the wolf as the figure at the heart of these politics that destabilizes gender and expresses, in its simultaneously human and nonhuman body, the paradox of a nonhuman humanity whose natural protective urges are also vociferously carnivorous.

But Derrida's reading of this politics adds another twist—that the werewolf and not the wolf is a figure for the sovereign that exceeds any law at all, a true 'out-law', we might say, more out-law than the outlaw of the wolf, more out-law, then, than the men and women who are war's beasts of prey. Derrida initially delinks the wolf and the werewolf, writing early in the seminar that, 'we will return at length to the werewolf, which is something else'.[6] Nonetheless, as Kelly Oliver points out, his mention of the 'she-wolf', so important, he says, to hold in mind, receives no recursive analysis as promised.[7] Oliver suggests something similar to what I want to claim here, that Derrida elides the figure of the 'she-wolf' because this is how he reveals 'sovereign phallic power' as a 'fabulous fake … all along'.[8] When Derrida does return to the figure of the werewolf it turns out that the werewolf, as seen in the quotation above, shares all the same qualities with the wolf, based on the translation of werewolf as 'outlaw'. The werewolf, perhaps unwittingly in Derrida's reading, morphs into another wolf, another beast man. And yet, I want to suggest that if we were to follow Derrida's logic to its own logical endpoint, then the werewolf or she-wolf would stand outside the wolf, outside the law of the father that is to say, and instead represent something else entirely. So, who, in such a politics, would

[6] Derrida, *The Beast and the Sovereign*, I: p. 11.

[7] See Kelly Oliver, 'Between the She-Wolf and Little Red Riding Hood: The Figure of the Girl in Derrida's *The Beast and The Sovereign*', *Derrida Today*, 4: 2 (2011), p. 280.

[8] Oliver, 'Between the She-Wolf', p. 280.

be 'true' werewolves, 'true' out-laws? As my reading of Hobbes above might already hint at, I want to say, at least provisionally, that the true werewolf is the werewolf that blurs both crosshatched gender lines and human and nonhuman lines. But, the added twist, the one Derrida cannot think, is that it is not Hobbes who fully theorizes this werewolf but Mary Wollstonecraft, an outlaw herself in Enlightenment debates.[9] In this sense, the woman-as-werewolf—the woman inside the man who makes *both* neither woman nor man—destabilizes hetero-patriarchal socio- and bio-politics entirely.

While elided in Derrida's lectures and often dismissed or rejected in her first foray into these debates, *A Vindication of the Rights of Men* (1790), her response to Edmund Burke's *Reflections on the Revolution in France* (1790), Wollstonecraft is nonetheless the first thinker of 'true' werewolf out-lawry in her final novel, *Maria: or, The Wrongs of Woman* (1792). Following on Kate Singer's reading of *Maria* and Wollstonecraft's work in general as developing what we now call 'new materialism', I want to argue that in *Maria* Wollstonecraft leverages that new materialism as a feminist critique of hetero-patriarchal society.[10] As we will see, Wollstonecraft's new materialist thinking scrambles gender across even human and nonhuman distinctions. Judith Butler, most famously, has provided an idea of the performativity of gender that has structured social constructivist accounts of it for quite some time.[11] But new materialism of the sort Karen Barad offers critiques Butler's story as decidedly one-sided, as championing social discursivity over the material reality of bodily matter that matters. Barad writes, 'perhaps the most crucial limitation of Butler's theory of materiality is that it is limited to an account of the materialization of human bodies ... through the regulatory action of social forces'.[12] What Barad calls 'agential realism', 'in contrast to Butler's more singular focus on the human body and social forces ... does not limit its reassessment of the matter of bodies to the realm of the human ... or to the domain of the social' (p. 209). Instead, on Barad's account '*matter is a stabilizing and destabilizing process of iterative intra-activity.* Phenomena come to matter through this process of ongoing intra-activity. That is, *matter*

[9] It may perhaps appear curious then that Derrida, who wrote so passionately and insightfully against what he calls 'phallogocentrism', returns, again and again, from *Of Grammatology* (1976) onward, to the work of Rousseau rather than Wollstonecraft, whom he appears not even to have read.

[10] Kate Singer, '"I feel it coming in the air tonight": Mephitical Vapors, Pestiferous Plagues, and the Psychosis of Materiality in Wollstonecraft and Shelley', *Romantic Psychosis*, ed. Elizabeth Fay, *Romantic Circles Praxis Series, Romantic Circles* (forthcoming).

[11] Judith Butler, *Gender Trouble: Feminism and the Subversion of Identity* (New York: Routledge, 2006).

[12] Karen Barad, *Meeting the Universe Halfway: Quantum Physics and the Entanglement of Matter and Meaning* (Durham, NC: Duke University Press, 2007), p. 209.

refers to the materiality and materialization of phenomena, not to an assumed, inherent, fixed property of abstract, independently existing objects' (p. 210, emphasis added). She arrives at this conclusion through her interpretation of Niels Bohr's double-slit experiment wherein light unaccountably presents itself, impossibly, as both a particle (entirely normal and expected) and a wave (completely abnormal and unexpected). For her this occurs because of what she calls 'quantum entanglement', when the subject and object intra-act to create new realities. As she puts it, 'entanglements are highly specific configurations ... [that] change with each intra-action. In fact is it not so much that they change from one moment to the next or from one place to another, but that *space, time, and matter do not exist* prior to the intra-actions that reconstitute entanglements' (p. 74, emphasis added). Quantum entanglements between a human and nonhuman create new spacetimes, new realities, even, we might say, new ontologies and as such exemplify the werewolf(ing) ontology of gender Wollstonecraft develops.

In her trenchant critique of Rousseau, Wollstonecraft links sovereignty to what she calls 'man', which examples how heteronormative, hetero-patriarchal politics rely on Hobbesian standard accounts of wolfishness but that also supplies her beginning move in envisioning a different ontology of gender politics: 'few women have emancipated themselves from the galling yoke of sovereign man'.[13] The sovereign's 'galling yoke' enchains women's bodies as yoked beasts, and these bodies are put to use as sexual, reproductive, and domestic labor by men. Richard Sha describes this power dynamic well: 'heteronormativity has its price: the reduction of sex to reproduction and the consequent reduction of human beings to beasts'.[14] In promulgating the connection between sovereignty, man, and the father, Wollstonecraft thus diagnoses the problem of the social contract as a problem based on gender and sexual inequality and not exclusively 'social' equality, which for Rousseau, in any event, does not include women anyway. And so, while Eileen Hunt Botting, in her incisive study, argues that Wollstonecraft's main goal is to reimagine the family as 'egalitarian', what, we may well ask, is such a family to look like?[15]

To counter this microcosmic familial and macrocosmic state hetero-patriarchy, Wollstonecraft theorizes what I am calling, following the example of wolves and werewolves, not a family but a 'pack'. For Wollstonecraft this pack organizes various iterations of members of society not into a nuclear

[13] Mary Wollstonecraft, *A Vindication of the Rights of Woman*, 3rd ed., ed. Deidre Shauna Lynch (New York: Norton, 2009), p. 100.

[14] Richard C. Sha, *Perverse Romanticism: Aesthetics and Sexuality in Britain, 1750–1832* (Baltimore, MD: Johns Hopkins University Press, 2009), p. 7.

[15] Eileen Hunt Botting, *Family Feuds: Wollstonecraft, Burke, and Rousseau on the Transformation of the Family* (Albany, NY: SUNY Press, 2012), p. 1.

heteronormative, hetero-patriarchal family top-down sovereign state of affairs but into confederations bound by, radically enough, 'love'. The pack manifests as new spacetimes through quantum entanglements that produce this love between subjects and subjects, but it never strives to reproduce binaristic pairings that reproduce the sovereign family. A pack, as Wollstonecraft's texts demonstrate, emerges from processes of co-creation that iterate new subjects and objects without dynamic power structures structured around stable gender identities or human and nonhuman power relations. Wollstonecraft's Baradian pack is more than simply deconstructive in that for deconstruction the subject is always already not fully present; quantum entanglement merges the subject and object into something not always already there no matter how fully or not fully present. Quantum entanglement is always on the make; it iterates and finds; it laughs and hugs. The pack does not differ and defer in space and time—it is a co-created new space and time, what Barad calls a 'spacetimemattering'.[16]

The pack is a revolutionary response to the shortcomings of the revolutionary debates and events Wollstonecraft critiques, even those happenings that are seemingly progressive. In her now little-read *An Historical and Moral View of the Origin and Progress of the French Revolution and the Effect it Has Produced in Europe* (1794), she sketches a remarkable portrait of a pack iteration that depicts a negative exemplar of the pack concept that she here labels a 'concourse'. Recounting the march of women from Paris to Versailles to confront Louis XVI, she describes it with a plainspoken disgust that nonetheless marks the progressive destabilizing gender potentialities—and so egalitarian possibilities—of this assembly:

> The concourse, at first, consisted mostly of market women, and the lowest refuse of the streets, women who had thrown off the virtues of one sex without having power to assume more than the vice of the other. A number of men also followed them, armed with pikes, bludgeons, and hatchets; but they were strictly speaking a mob, affixing all the odium to the appellation it can possibly import; and not to be confounded with the honest multitude, who took the Bastille.—In fact, such a rabble has seldom been gathered together; and they quickly showed, that their movement was not the effect of public spirit. (pp. 196–7)[17]

[16] Karen Barad, 'Nature's Queer Performativity', *Qui Parle: Critical Humanities and Social Sciences*, 19: 2 (2011), pp. 121–58.

[17] Mary Wollstonecraft, *An Historical and Moral View of the Origin and Progress of the French Revolution and the Effect it Has Produced in Europe*, in *The Works of Mary Wollstonecraft*, eds. Janet Todd, Marilyn Butler, and Emma Rees-Mogg (New York: New York University Press, 1989), VI: pp. 1–236.

> At this juncture of the debate the tumultuous concourse of women arrived at Versailles: but it must not be unnoticed, that there was a number of men with them, disguised in women's clothes; which proves, that this was not, as has been asserted, a sudden impulse of necessity. There were besides men in their own garb armed like ruffians, / with countenances answerable, who, swearing vengeance against the queen and the body-guards, seemed to be preparing to put their threats in execution. (p. 201)

This concourse of ragtag ruffians seems an image of Hobbes's daughters of war come to life, with women playing out their deceit and violence by 'throwing off the' false 'virtues' of femininity they normally disguise themselves with and men adopting the guise of women as if signaling the deceitful and violent feminine nature inside of them. These cross-dressing transformations that make the innate, shall we say, material, indicate how biopolitical logic wolfs out in detriment to civil society all the while still adhering to the sovereign law of the father that designates women deceitful and violent and can only fault men for the same traits through gender contortions. Small wonder then that when this concourse arrives at Versailles, they fall under the charming sways of the king and wend their way back whence they come, violence averted because gender power roles have been—even if it might for a moment look the opposite—maintained.

While concourses like this Versailles one get derogatorily termed *'canaille'*, a pack of dogs, by society, Wollstonecraft figures her pack in *Maria* as potentially new communities of creatures that depend not on worn-out, war-ridden notions of sovereignty and social contract politics but on covenants of loving care for each member of the pack by each member.[18] For Wollstonecraft the pack surmounts the wolf's deeply gendered and anthropocentric politics. As *Maria*'s Jemima says, recounting her treatment by her masters, 'I was the filching cat, the ravenous dog, the dumb brute, who must bear all', as a result of which, she adds, 'I had not even the chance of being considered as a fellow-creature'.[19] Responding to and rejecting this biopolitics, Wollstonecraft writes that females may be construed as the 'brute creation'—a senseless, thoughtless, stupid animal as this term is used in eighteenth-century writing—but it is a brute creation that seeks to overthrow masculine sovereignty through a pack that outwits marriage, which is based on the model of state sovereignty defined

[18] For a deconstructionist reading of Wollstonecraft on Burke wherein Wollstonecraft charges Burke with figuring women as an infection in the body politic, see Tom Furniss, 'Nasty Tricks and Tropes: Sexuality and Language in Mary Wollstonecraft's *Rights of Woman*', *Studies in Romanticism*, 32: 2 (1993), pp. 177–209.

[19] Mary Wollstonecraft, *Maria: or, The Wrongs of Woman*, ed. Gary Kelly (Oxford: Oxford University Press, 2009), p. 95.

by the ideology that 'a man has been termed a microcosm; and every family might also be called a state' (*Rights of Woman*, p. 187). Replacing the binaristic logic of sex and gender, human and nonhuman, the social and the material, that founds and stabilizes the heteronormative, hetero-patriarchal privilege of the law of the father that orders the family, the pack thinks familial relations in terms of quantum entanglement.[20] Wollstonecraft theorizes marriage instead on the basis of friendship, 'the most holy band of society', and on a love that two people bring into being through discursive-material entanglement that, in turn, ontologically creates a new spacetime of being—and love (*Rights of Woman*, p. 33).[21] As Wollstonecraft writes of her prophecies contra those of Burke and Rousseau (and by implication Hobbes), 'a CROWD of authors [assert] that all is now right; and I, that all will be right' (*Rights of Woman*, p. 17). For Wollstonecraft whatever pack there will be is only in a future-to-come; the pack must trounce the social contract 'CROWD' whose big bad wolf laws desire to prevent the pack's formation. Wollstonecraft vindicates a pack that does not yet exist and this is why she foretells 'what will be', the to-come of the pack's futural spacetimematterings because any pack, any entanglement, can only be made in the future that is not the now of hetero-patriarchy.

Nor is a pack a prototype of those households she proposed to house and hold with Henry Fuseli and Gilbert Imlay and their lovers, nor even is it a constellation that necessarily requires a multiplicity—it can be many, or a two, or even a one because it defies the mathematical logic of Newtonian space and time. It is not necessarily based on sex either but rather from a love brought into being by two (or more) people through entanglement that defies two-ness to make more-ness of that two-ness because the love from that two-ness is incorporative. As she writes, when 'the rights of the most sacred friendship' are instituted in the family, 'a mutual care produces a mutual sympathy' (*Rights*, pp. 162, 161). We can hear a sympathetic reading of my idea of Wollstonecraft's pack in Julie Carlson's reading of the family in the Wollstonecraft circle because Carlson, also, sees in it a suggestive ontological possibility in that hers is 'a reading of a family of writers whose writings seek to defamiliarize what has counted as family in order to clear space for new species and manners of being'.[22] By refiguring a baggy, fluid family around friendship, mutual care, and love, rather than

[20] Perhaps it is no wonder then that, as Virginia Sapiro notes, Wollstonecraft often used metaphors from physics. Sapiro, *A Vindication of Political Virtue: The Political Theory of Mary Wollstonecraft* (Chicago, IL: University of Chicago Press, 1992), p. 162.

[21] Rousseau's notion of the complex relations of the state and the family is similar to Wollstonecraft's only, for him, they actually diverge because the state looks to foster citizens and the family as moral individuals.

[22] Julie Carlson, *England's First Family of Writers: Mary Wollstonecraft, William Godwin, and Mary Shelley* (Baltimore, MD: Johns Hopkins University Press, 2007), p. 13.

hetero-patriarchal sovereignty, Wollstonecraft radicalizes, differently than Hobbes's nihilistic thanatopolitics, the notion of the werewolf pack as a progressive figure for egalitarian political incorporation into an affiliated group. Or, at least, this is Wollstonecraft's vision of reconstructing a society wherein the 'law ... makes women property of their husbands' (*Maria*, p. 172).

II. Quantum Bibliophilia

Early in her meditations on her own imprisonment, Maria rewrites Rousseau's famous opening line from *The Social Contract* (1762) that 'man is born free, and everywhere he is in chains' as an interrogative about gender relations: 'was not the world a vast prison, and women born slaves?' (p. 73).[23] Wollstonecraft's response to this question, the scenes of Maria and Darnford in prison, I'll argue, indict and rewrite Rousseau's entire sociopolitical theory to think a pack—even if, in this novel, that notion ultimately fails to coalesce. Wollstonecraft distinguishes Maria's, and women's, very real prison contrary to the gothic fictions circulating in her time, which she characterizes as 'abodes of horror ... castles, filled with spectres and chimeras, conjured up by the magic spell of genius to harrow the soul, and absorb the wondering mind' (p. 69). This first paragraph, then, provides a key to understanding the new materialism at work throughout the whole novel. On one hand, Wollstonecraft offers us the real in the material form of the prison's iron bars and walls and, on the other, the discursive represented by the gothic fictions that encage women as mere objects of men's dark terror and lust. The word 'chimera' here echoes Wollstonecraft's put-down of Rousseau's thinking in the second *Vindication*—'women, considered not only as moral, but rational creatures, ought to endeavour to acquire human virtues (or perfections) by the same means as men, instead of being educated like a fanciful kind of half being—one of Rousseau's wild chimeras' (pp. 42–3)—and illustrates how these gothic fictions are also metaphors for Rousseau's own supposedly nonfictional political theories and their own sovereign assertions of male dominance that Rousseau lasciviously fantasizes about in the corner.

Maria and Darnford are both declared out-laws and self-declared bibliophiles, which is to say that they are werewolves, and from this lycanthropy they co-write a pack love through the quantum entanglement of the materiality and the discursivity of the very love they bring into being through a discursive-material process of writing.[24] Once Maria, like a bird of prey, had

[23] Jean-Jacques Rousseau, *Du contrat social ou Principes du droit politique* (Paris: Union Générale d'Éditions, 1963), p. 9, my translation.

[24] See Singer's different reading of this new material exchange that loops Jemima, the

'devoured' her own small supply of English books, her jailer, Jemima, delivers to her Darnford's French edition of Rousseau's *Julie, ou la nouvelle Héloïse* (1761), an epistolary novel the margins of which Maria and Darnford use to write their own love letters (p. 75). Maria relates, 'to write these letters was the business of the day, and to receive them the moment of sunshine' (p. 83). Whereas in *Tristram Shandy* (1759–67) digressions are the sunshine of life, for Maria and Darnford the entanglement of the rewritten discursive epistolary text that materially manifests the sentiment of their affection is the sunshine of life and of love in that this entanglement both produces and is that love. Rousseau—whose novel is about the hopeless love between Julie and St. Preux recorded in their own letters—is, Darnford declares, 'on the margin of an impassioned letter', 'the true Prometheus of sentiment', the only one who 'possessed the fire of genius necessary to pourtray the passion, the truth of which goes so directly to the heart' (p. 81). However, their literal rewriting of Rousseau's own novel on that novel suggests something different. On the margin of a letter Darnford writes his comments, a letter that is, as yet, not a letter and has no destination, but becomes, once Maria reads it, a letter that reaches its destination and thereby conveys what Rousseau could not, the true sentiment of love but only by bringing that inexistent sentiment into being between Darnford and Maria. After she reads this note, Maria's reading of it, that is, *her* reading of the letter itself, transforms the letter into a letter and, as the word 'delineates'—an act of inscription—indicates, 'every glance afforded colouring for the picture she was delineating on her heart' (p. 82). She writes on her own heart his words, the discursive of the letter burning into the materiality of the heart, entangling the materiality of the letter with her own discursive subjectivity. Words that colour the heart, the novel tells us, write on the heart and write the heart; these words bring the heart, as both the figurative and literal of love, into existence. The not-yet love that is the metaphorical heart writes on the material heart, but only as and at the same time that the material heart writes the words sent to the heart, is it itself brought into being in order to be written on.

The allusion to Prometheus also presages Wollstonecraft's daughter, Mary Shelley's, subtitle to *Frankenstein; or, The Modern Prometheus* (1818) and her future son-in-law's lyrical drama, *Prometheus Unbound* (1820), and in the process also adds more books-to-come to Maria's and Darnford's circulating prison house library and, in this sense, signals, via this quantum bibliophilia, the pack's temporal defiance of typical Newtonian timeframes. Wollstonecraft is writing, and writing of, a future-to-come. In this regard, she is not unlike what Anne McCarthy says of Godwin, who, in his *Memoirs* (1798), McCarthy

nonhuman asylum, and its inhabitants into an assemblage that both defies and replicates the law of the father.

writes, 'entertain[s] a more painful counterfactual possibility: the existence of another future where his wife does not die and thus the possibility of a present where he is not writing her epitaph' and, even, then, envisions a Wollstonecraft as a future author.[25] Darnford's identification of Rousseau with Prometheus hails him as the god who delivers an unheralded theory of passionate sentiments to his readers via his runaway alternate-universe *X-File*, *Julie*, which publishers could not print quickly enough to sate demand. But just as Prometheus, who delivers the fires of life to human beings and is in turn cursed, Rousseau, Julie, and St. Preux find themselves damned—dead in the latter two's cases and chased, in the former's, like a werewolf, a bibliophile. If Rousseau is the true Prometheus of such sentimental, doomed love in the eighteenth century, then Maria's and Darnford's quantum bibliophilia co-writes a different sentiment entirely. In this rewriting, the future remains open rather than closed by death's fully-stopped ending, which is why Wollstonecraft's novel's own materiality mimics the choose-your-own-adventure materiality of the novel's content by offering myriad paths of continuance—what Maria, indicating the future-to-come nature of it, calls the 'never-ending, still beginning' of her and Darnford's and Jemima's pack (p. 88).

By writing on, around, and over *Julie*'s text, they do more than convert the novel to a palimpsest or place it under erasure; they capture, in letters, what the fiction of *Julie*'s sentiment cannot, the materiality of what quantum entanglement pack love could be. If *Julie* represents the discursivity of the love letter, then Maria's and Darnford's marginal commentary in that novel evinces the discursive-material writing that *writes* how to unlock their chains, those chimerical demands of society that insist they perform their intended gender roles, the man enslaved by deceitful feminine seduction and the woman who must be encaged by the law of the father in order to bottle up this uncontrollable falsifying impulse. Instead of the terrors of Rousseau's fictionalized gendered society of false sentiment and real shackles, quantumly entangled love finds hope in this hopeless place: 'a magic lamp now seemed to be suspended in Maria's prison, and fairy landscapes flitted round the gloomy walls, late so blank. Rushing from the depth of despair, on the seraph wing of hope, she found herself happy.—She was beloved, and every emotion was rapturous' (p. 90). The chimera is described as a 'half-being' in the second *Vindication* because it is a twisted creature, part beast and part female and, therefore, being not fully beast and sovereign, not beast nor sovereign, nor anything at all, except unvindicated women who are not women and thus evade set gender roles entirely. Maria's and Darnford's sunshiny writing transforms the chimerical wings into the seraphic and recalls us, via this allusion to the

[25] Anne C. McCarthy, 'Falling in Love with the Author in Godwin's *Memoirs* of Wollstonecraft', *Essays in Romanticism*, 25: 2 (2018), pp. 123–39.

Book of Revelations and what it says of the seraphim—they interminably chant 'which was, and is, and is to come'—that this quantum entanglement through bibliophilia, through werewolvery, scrambles Newtonian space and time in its proleptic spacetimemattering.[26] Their love is always to-come because each inscription of the letter on the material letter of the discursive text presses their love into a book but also instantiates that love in the process, the feeling of love emerging from its own material-discursive production of writing 'I love'. To feel it is to write it; to write it is to feel it—but both *both* at the same time in and as a moment that co-creates this new spacetime of love between Maria and Darnford.

So, while we find Wollstonecraft herself writing to Imlay that 'I have always been half in love with Rousseau. And I can't quit coming back to him no matter how much he repels me', that half-love blossoms into a more-than-full love as it circulates beyond two to cure other members of the pack's *pharmakon* misanthropy.[27] Jemima, we are told, was an 'outcast of society', 'who had been hunted from hole to hole, as if she had been a beast of prey, or infected with a moral plague' (p. 73). She fell, as a result, into the 'misanthropy of despair' (p. 75). Small surprise then Jemima becomes a bird of prey herself who 'despised and preyed on the society by which she had been oppressed, and loved not her fellow-creatures, because she had never been beloved' (p. 75). Maria's and Darnford's love radiates with post-apocalyptic power, though:

> So much of heaven did they enjoy, that paradise bloomed around them; or they, by a powerful spell, had been transported into Armida's garden. Love, the grand enchanter, 'lapt them in Elysium', and every sense was harmonized to joy and social extacy. So animated, indeed, were their accents of tenderness, in discussing what, in other circumstances, would have been commonplace subjects, that Jemima felt, with surprise, a tear of pleasure trickling down her rugged cheeks. She wiped it away, half ashamed; and when Maria kindly enquired the cause, with all the eager solicitude of a happy being wishing to impart to all nature its overflowing felicity, Jemima owned that it was the first tear that social enjoyment had ever drawn from her. She seemed indeed to breathe more freely; the cloud of suspicion cleared away from her brow; she felt herself, for once in her life, treated like a fellow-creature. (p. 91)

Left to rot in the prison house of an un-entangled language and materiality, the end of the world for them, they instead find a return to paradise, with

26 *Book of Revelations* 4: 8, King James Translation.

27 Mary Wollstonecraft, 22 September 1794, *Collected Letters*, ed. Janet Todd (Columbia, SC: Columbia University Press, 2004), p. 263.

the wizard Love's alchemy incanting this spacetime, ensorcelling Maria and Darnford and countering the evil mage, Rousseau, and his 'magic spell of genius' that fakes a fake love to perpetuate social inequality in the name of equality. If for Barad quantum entanglement is 'meta/physics', then we can see that on display here, as the discursive-materiality of love enraptures and en-wraptures all as fellow creatures through a kind of alchemical process that recalls Newton's obsession with the end of the world and the philosopher's stone rather than his physics bible, the *Principia*.[28] Women, we remember Wollstonecraft wrote in the *Vindication*, were viewed as another species, a brute one. But the magical love potion brewed between Maria and Darnford between the covers of *Julie* circulates its ecstasy in an atmosphere that affects all members of the werewolf pack, as Jemima here becomes a member and, now, 'the world contained not three happier beings' (p. 91). An outlaw no more since she gives over her jailer duties, her maintenance of the law, she transforms into an out-law like Maria and Darnford. Maria, Darnford, Jemima—all are, as it says of Darnford, 'unjustly confined' and are therefore beyond the law, but also out-laws beyond the outlaw; they are the true werewolves Derrida seeks as none possess sovereignty over the other or the power to gain sovereignty over the other (p. 79).

But the novel also foretells a darker tale. The outlaw, the false out-law, the sovereign with the lupine smile and bloody teeth, the wolf with the regal air of command over the wolf pack—the women, the children, the family, the nation—lays traps and tracks, hunts in the heat of the noonday sun and the lover's quiet moonlit night, hunts those out-law outlaws beyond his law, those werewolves who threaten to change his hetero-patriarchal society. The gothic dread they associate with Rousseau's maligning gender fictions still haunts their lives despite their love's sorcery: 'horror still reigned in the darkened cells, suspicion lurked in the passages, and whispered along the walls' (p. 91). As ever, the hetero-patriarchal wolf appears in sheep's clothing, peering through the guileless rhymes of childlike nursery nonsense meant to lullaby. No matter the circumstances surrounding them, there is, between Maria and Darnford, 'an animated conversation, in which love, sly urchin, was ever at bo-peep' (p. 91). The allusion, of course, recalls this doggerel verse:

> Little Bo-Peep has lost her sheep,
> And doesn't know where to find them;
> Leave them alone, And they'll come home,
> Wagging their tails behind them.

Prodigal sheep will return, the rhyme tells us, even though they are lost and prey for the hungry wolf, and yet, they have nothing to fear, since waywardness

[28] Barad, *Quantum*, p. 253.

always wends back home, kind of like a letter that always reaches its destination but only by going astray. The world of Bo-Peep runs on a spatiotemporal letter logic that disallows contingency and thus guarantees safety, where what you see is *is* how things are, a make-sense world immune to disguised under-the-surface *Twin Peaks* terror. Of course, this safety proffers an illusion, an innocent lamb life that, in fact, in reality, therefore, only guarantees that the sheep will not be alert to the danger of the wolf, a paradise that never notices its own rhythmic sways are the devil's seductions it whispers in its own ear to comfort itself. 'To play bo-beep', after all, has an older meaning: to be stood in the pillory. The wolf always comes in sheep's clothing.

III. *Les Pactes des Loups*

Godwin writes in a note at the end of *Maria*, quoting Wollstonecraft, that she crafted the book with a moral purpose in mind, that 'of exhibiting the misery and oppression, peculiar to women, that arise out of the partial laws and customs of society' (p. 178). The novel certainly performs the critique Godwin asserts, unrelentingly detailing the legal customs and judicial punishments meted out to women. But, more stringently than Godwin's 'partial laws', the novel lays bare the larger political discourse of sovereigns and beasts that exclude women from legal redress for their wrongs because the law functions precisely through its extra-judicial illegality. Thinking through that deconstructive knot is, Wollstonecraft says, to form a pack that creates a new discursive-material entanglement since the ontological entanglement of packness is a coming-into-being outside the law, out-law.

Indeed, Jemima declares her legal status that equates her with beastly sovereigns later in the novel when she recounts her own harrowing tale of being cast out in terms of starvation and carnal consumption: 'consider, dear madam, I was famishing: wonder not that I became a wolf!' (p. 104). We can see what Anne Mellor means when she writes that the novel's subtitle 'registers an important ambiguity'—'the wrongs done *to* women and the wrongs done *by* women'.[29] Jemima becomes a man, a beast who possesses the sovereignty to harm others. Preying wolfishly on a 'poor wretch' who lives in her master's house, Jemima has the little girl expelled from the home. Jemima's language of lacking 'fellow creatures' is indicative of Wollstonecraft's pack logic: one must have a group of fellow creatures, of fellow beasts, to form a pack. The sovereign, although a beast, has no pack because sovereignty requires mastery and control in order to be sovereign. 'Fellow creatures' upends such a model by suggesting that fellowship and creatureliness—being the 'brute creation'—abrogates the

[29] Anne K. Mellor, 'Righting the Wrongs of Woman: Mary Wollstonecraft's *Maria*', *Nineteenth-Century Contexts*, 19: 4 (1996), pp. 413–24, 417.

law of the father. Once they establish a household, 'Jemima insist[ed] on being considered as her [Maria's] housekeeper, and to receive the customary stipend. On no other terms would she remain with her friend' (p. 167). The pack chimes with Mellor's assertion that 'Jemima will be an equal partner (paid for her work) and co-mother in the raising of Maria's daughter, the "new woman" of the future'.[30] But, more importantly, Jemima, although she insists on domestic capitalism, shifts from her earlier wolfishness to someone capable of giving love and being loved, taken in by Maria in a new sorority of creatures who, while on the run, nevertheless band together as out-laws who are not predators but a pack that does not rely on unequal affection any more than unfair labor practices. No more wolves; no more sovereign capitalism.

Conversely, what the novel calls male 'packs' are authorized by the law and engage in fraternal predation of the female out-laws who have no other legal status and are, therefore, like the beast and the sovereign, both inside and outside the law—out-laws that are in-laws. Jemima captures this paradoxical in-law/out-law effect in her description of her times living on the street: 'I had been hunted almost into a fever, by the watchmen … whom I had unwittingly offended, giving the word to the *whole pack*. … Not content with receiving from us, *outlaws* of society (let other women talk of favours) a brutal gratification gratuitously as a privilege of office, they extort a tithe of prostitution' (p. 137, emphasis added). The watchmen pack, which derives its authority from the law, illustrates the paradox of the law. They are 'instruments' of the law but also in violation of it when they force women into prostitution for the watchmen's pleasure. But only by virtue of the watchmen's legal authority can these men act illegally, sanctioned by the law itself that purports to safeguard against illegality. The law, then, for Wollstonecraft, is always double, turning its inside outside and its outside inside; the law is illegal and illegal because of the law itself. The watchmen exemplify this same logic as they, too, are 'outlaws', only, unlike the women, they are outlaws within the law. Yet, the women's own out-law outlawry also allows for the watchmen to take advantage of them because they have no legal remedy or recourse in the face of illegal activity condoned and justified by the law outside of which the women stand.

This is why throughout the novel Wollstonecraft links women to both beasts and outlaws in order to advance her reformist views of marriage. At the end of the fragmentary novel, Maria makes a plea to the court to grant her a divorce and dismiss the criminal complaint brought by Mr. Venables against her and Darnford. Railing against the 'rigid laws which enslave women' in marriage that make them, as she says earlier in the novel, 'as much a man's property as his horse, or his ass', Maria says that 'after leaving what the law considers as my home, I was hunted like a criminal from place to place' (pp. 171, 140, 172).

[30] Mellor, 'Righting the Wrongs of Woman', p. 420.

The hunting metaphor does double duty here, drawing together the beasts of the previous comparison with the criminal, the outlaw running loose in this one. Her husband, she tells us in the same speech to the court, had become consumed by a 'rapacious avarice' that drove him. 'Rapacious' reinforces the outlaw aspect of Wollstonecraft's critique and recalls Hobbes's phrase that opens this essay and grounds Enlightenment politics: 'man is a wolf to man', a creature of 'mere brutal rapacity'. Like Jemima before she found a pack with Maria, Mr. Venables is a wolf, that is to say a hetero-patriarchal man. Her sovereign in marriage, as the court reinforces when it rejects her divorce plea, her husband is also a beast, a beast and the sovereign, and a beast because he is a sovereign and a sovereign because he is a beast. When the court denies Maria's request, it does so along these lupine logics since Mr. Venables has legal standing in the court despite any evidence for his claims whereas Maria must, the judge decrees, 'love and obey the man chosen by her parents and relations, who were qualified by their experience to judge better for her, than she could for herself' (p. 174). The hetero-patriarchal family, in its kingly sovereignty, can 'judge' better than she. Mr. Venables, who is the law of the father, the wolf who must be obeyed because the law cannot touch him, can yet wield the powers of that law precisely because the law does not apply to him. He is, literally, above the law because he, as sovereign and beast, writes and is the law.

Writing this, her final novel, Wollstonecraft does not get to finish showcasing any triumphalism over that law, and the novel we have disintegrates, as does the pack, as Jemima disappears except as a Force ghost hallucination of Maria's (no one's ever really gone), and Maria's and Darnford's letters arrive at a destinational nowhere, as does the novel. So it turns out Maria's and Darnford's letters do reach a destination of sorts but it is also a destination that allows for the letters to never reach a destination, to keep writing on, which is the contingent factor of epistolarity that, as Derrida reminds us, allows for letter writing (and being and love) at all. While Maria and Darnford do not finally form a pack in the novel(s) we have, Wollstonecraft's sketched multiple endings indicate that they might, in these continuous fragments that write on, that write their future-to-come-ness that permits any future whatsoever.

Of course, the novel also ends in disintegrative fashion because of the abrupt death of Wollstonecraft herself in the very instance where she and Godwin try to form a real-life pack. From fictional letters to autobiographical letters, then, it makes sense, perhaps, to turn to Wollstonecraft's and Godwin's letters to see letters that never reach their destination because the people writing them, and the letters themselves, are not done writing, not done writing the future-to-come of the pack and so, because of that very a-destinationality, model a future-to-come, however much it may never be in the very spacetimemattering that it is.

IV. *Entre nous*

While *Maria* illustrates Wollstonecraft's vision of how inescapable hetero-patriarchal law is, her and Godwin's letters provide a to-come of love that the pack requires through the letters' literal discursive-material example of quantum entanglement in the materiality of the epistolary page that finds its discursive voice in the letters—their very material heart. Here, in these letters, we can find a Wollstonecraft rewriting the family as pack to halt the beast wars of human wolf-men and, in this rewriting, writing what she is not able to do in *Maria*: a spacetimemattering ontology. This spacetimemattering is the future-to-come of the pack. The letters affirm that *dasein*, 'to be in the world', should be *mitsein*, 'to be with in the world'.

In her letters to Godwin, written between them throughout the course of the day from their respective offices, like an early version of emails that sustain an every-minute, increasing affection, Wollstonecraft often attempts to bridge the gaps between her and Godwin, the differences that, she fears, threaten their relationship—her everyday anxieties and his inability to coherently articulate his feelings and be anything otherwise than a reclusive Trekkie nerd. When she writes to him 'I want to see you—and *soon*—I have a world to say to you' (30), she theorizes packness and *dasein* as *mitsein*.[31] This idea of 'saying the world', so to say, finalizes Wollstonecraft's pack logic since, for her, it should be possible to 'say the world', what Derrida calls the 'whole world' and by which he means the whole self, the best self, the whole self of your being, to your mate and to your pack.[32]

In their letters to each other, Wollstonecraft and Godwin co-write, which is to say bring into existence, a quantum entanglement spacetimemattering they call 'live fire' that exemplifies the pack's ability to be a two-ness or an any-ness because the love they share is *pack* love and not hetero-patriarchal marriage love.[33] Wollstonecraft writes to Godwin regarding their previous evening spent together, 'if the felicity of last night has had the same effect on your health as on my countenance, you have no cause to lament your failure of resolution: for I have seldom seen so much live fire running about my features as this morning'. This live fire, it seems, means freedom and not just sex. Godwin

[31] Mary Wollstonecraft, 'Letter to William Godwin, Sept. 8, 1796', in *Godwin & Mary: Letters of William Godwin and Mary Wollstonecraft*, ed. Ralph M. Wardle (Lincoln: University of Nebraska Press, 1977), p. 30.

[32] For Cynthia Richards, Godwin's stoicism makes him largely incapable of connecting with Wollstonecraft, except in her dying moments when his writing confounds the distinction between their bodies. Richards, 'The Body of Her Work, the Work of Her Body: Accounting for the Life and Work of Mary Wollstonecraft', *Eighteenth-Century Fiction*, 21: 4 (2009), pp. 566–92.

[33] *Godwin & Mary*, p. 46.

writes back, 'I wish I had been a spectator of the live fire you speak of: I *shall* rejoice in our freedom. Send me the next time anybody comes my bottle of ink: you can fill an inkstand. Fill it as high, as your image at this moment fills my mind' (pp. 47–8). The inkstand-filling metaphor bespeaks of intellectual memory, authoring the head not the heart, as if it is Godwin's head writing back to Wollstonecraft's heart of live fire, which fits perfectly well with the image we have of them. Yet, the live fire Wollstonecraft *feels* running through her countenance is the result of her and Godwin's love, not just the lovemaking but the aftereffect of it that both exceeds and fulfills the discursivity of the letter's materiality to capture it. Both of them, in fact, seem surprised by the fire's live-ness, its living through them, as they both write, again and again, in the letters, '*entre nous*' (p. 14).

The entanglement of this *entre-nous* live fire completes the rewriting—or, more accurately, the writing over, writing away from—Rousseau's social contract theory of hetero-patriarchal life that *Maria* can never fully achieve. Wollstonecraft writes to Godwin, 'I called on you yesterday, in my way to dinner, not for Mary—but to bring Mary—is it necessary to tell your sapient Philosophership that I mean MYSELF' (p. 13). By needing to state to Godwin—himself here cast very clearly in a Rousseau-philosopher role—that by 'Mary' Wollstonecraft means bringing herself and not her servant, Mary, it indicates both a playfulness on her part and a certain cheeky wariness about Godwin's own stuffiness from his position as armchair sapient. This leads, for a moment, to a certain recursive Rousseauvian self-love evoked by self-pity. Wollstonecraft writes 'I will become again a Solitary Walker' (p. 15). She references, of course, Rousseau's posthumously published final book, *Reveries of a Solitary Walker* (1782), in which he claims, among other things, that, as he is unlike anyone else in the world—a theme continuing from the first page of his *Confessions*—he remains alone in the world. Godwin's return missive arrives swiftly with a bluntness common to him but an imperative passion atypical—'do not cast me off. Do not become again a solitary walker' (p. 17). The 'again' signals a regression, of course, but also a doubling-down on the precarity they perceive in their relationship, as if the past is a nightmare not only from which they have not awakened but that they might be actively strolling back toward. Simultaneously, the 'again' floats the suggestion that, even in marriage, they have, some time before, already, become solitary walkers, felt solitary because not united, felt and known that togetherness needs solitariness to to-gether. To-getherness, for them, must needs the idea of solitariness in order to revenant from it the possibility of a pack, which indicates the revenantal possibility of loneliness in togetherness, of how the pack defies binaristic logic since a one can be two and a two one. As such, the '*entre nous*' is a phrase said but not yet materially manifesting that they are *nous*.

Godwin spirits out the solution, no doubt recalling that Wollstonecraft has already thought of and proposed it in the second *Vindication*, namely that *entre nous* is a condition possible only through friendship in marriage, through, finally, packnesss, a radical challenge to the hetero-patriarchy of social democracies. Godwin writes,

> it is best that we should be friends in every sense of the word; but in the mean time let us be friends. I will be your friend, the friend of your mind, the admirer of your excellencies. All else I commit to the disposition of futurity, glad, if completely happy; passive & silent in this respect, while I am not so. (p. 17)

Here Godwin returns to 'we', to '*nous*', but returns to that *nous*-ness in friendship—Wollstonecraft's sacred fundament of a new ontology of werewolf pack marriage—and in doing so instantiates friendship materially since he friends not only her, her self, her, as he says, 'mind', but her, her *self*. In other words, friending her mind means actually taking her ideas to head and heart and putting them to practice; to 'friend' her mind *co-makes* friendship. The act of friending enacts friendship. If he then references 'futurity', then it returns to the future-to-come of the very pack society they are envisioning in the act of enacting this entanglement that this future-to-come future-to-comes since it may never be and that may-never-never-be-ness allows for their to be a to be (a letter must never reach its destination in order to be able to reach its destination). In that wise, without over-pressuring the word, what if we read Godwin's 'am' in the 'am not so' as 'being' being ontological? A few pages later it seems he himself has this ontological point in mind for both of them: 'you are—but I cannot tell what you are. I cannot yet find the circumstance about you that allies you to the frailty of your nature. I will hunt it out' (p. 23). He cannot tell what she *is*, her very being, and he remains, surprisingly, still, in this, his own fearsome grip, his fear, his hetero-patriarchy, a wolf: 'I will hunt it out'. They have to find what is *is* to-gether within and with-out(law) hunting.

And they do. Godwin prints his feelings as words: 'Look at the first page and return it—I do not intend to let you extend your skepticism to me—or you will fright away a poor weary bird who, taking refuge in your bosom, hoped to nestle there—to the end of the chapter' (p. 27). The metaphor of the nestling bird taking amorous and sexual shelter within Wollstonecraft combines into something more than this somewhat tawdry and pedestrian comparison with the pages of the sent book and, perforce, the very letter Wollstonecraft is reading. Dashing off the metaphor places the book's first page metaphorically on the page of the letter and the last page, the last page of the chapter, after the bird metaphor, enclosing, in other words, the bird

Godwin inside the book Wollstonecraft will read that is itself enclosed in the material surface of this paper. The letter is the book that contains Godwin's feelings in their very selves since the letter *is* his body. Such sentiments recur in Wollstonecraft's letters as well. She writes,

> now by these presents [she means his letter] let me assure you that you are not only in my heart, but my veins, this morning. I turn from you half abashed—yet you haunt me, and some look, word or touch thrills through my whole frame—yes, at the very moment when I am laboring to think of something if not somebody, else. Get ye gone Intruder! though I am forced to add dear—which is a call back—. (p. 33)

The letter, itself, infuses her heart with Godwin, himself, his words and not mere words but his body, the 'word' both a 'look' and a 'touch', the hand that wrote the letter present in the 'presents' it's penned, its presence in presents, rounding back, as Wollstonecraft puts it, calling back, to ontological entanglement. Letters become, she writes, kisses: 'fancy, at this moment, has turned a conjunction into a kiss; and the sensation steals o'er my senses' (p. 35). The conjunction, seen here as the connection of the semicolon—literally con-juncts—crossroads things occurring in Baradian spacetimemattering. 'Con-junct' invokes the Latin sense of the word, '*conjuge*', which can mean both and or 'husband' and 'wife' but here signals what Wollstonecraft and Godwin have, beyond those simple sighs, the embrace in the crossroads that kisses, a gender scrambling of societal expectations, a potentiality, therefore, that makes a marriage beyond societal notions of marriage, that makes a pack.

Letters continue, they continue, they may always continue. When Wollstonecraft writes that 'if your heart was in your mouth, as I felt, just now, at the sight of your hand, you may kiss or shake hands with the letter and imagine with what affection it was written', Godwin feels his heart in his mouth in her body through his letter, which is written in his hand and contains his hand, and his heart, his, their affection. He may feel it in her mouth because she feels it feels but only because she feels it in her mouth because 'his hand' that he writes it in letters. In her mouth her heart she feels it in through the body of his hand, the hand of his letters, his ink on the page, and his hand she feels in reading, and the hand they feel in the shake, her hand touching his hand by touching his ink on the page, his hand, and the heart that is the hand, the hand that writes the heart. In her mouth that is his hand that is their heart.

Bibliography

Barad, Karen. *Meeting the Universe Halfway: Quantum Physics and the Entanglement of Matter and Meaning*. Durham, NC: Duke University Press, 2007.

——. 'Nature's Queer Performativity'. *Qui Parle: Critical Humanities and Social Sciences*, 19: 2 (2011), pp. 121–58.

Botting, Eileen. *Family Feuds: Wollstonecraft, Burke, and Rousseau on the Transformation of the Family*. Albany, NY: SUNY Press, 2006.

Burke, Edmund. *Reflections on the Revolution in France*, ed. L.G. Mitchell. Oxford: Oxford University Press, 2009.

Butler, Judith. *Gender Trouble: Feminism and the Subversion of Identity*. New York: Routledge, 2006.

Carlson, Julie. *England's First Family of Writers: Mary Wollstonecraft, William Godwin, and Mary Shelley*. Baltimore, MD: Johns Hopkins University Press, 2007.

Derrida, Jacques. *The Beast and the Sovereign*, vol. I, trans. Geoffrey Bennington. Chicago, IL: University of Chicago Press, 2009.

——. *Of Grammatology*, trans. Gayatri Chakravorty Spivak. Baltimore, MD: Johns Hopkins University Press, 1976.

——. *The Post Card: From Socrates to Freud and Beyond*, trans. Alan Bass. Chicago, IL: University of Chicago Press, 1987.

Furniss, Tom. 'Nasty Tricks and Tropes: Sexuality and Language in Mary Wollstonecraft's *Rights of Woman*'. *Studies in Romanticism*, 32: 2 (1993), pp. 177–209.

Hobbes, Thomas. *Leviathan*, ed. Edwin Curley. New York: Hackett, 1994.

——. *Man and Citizen (De homine* and *de cive)*, ed. Bernard Gert. New York: Hackett, 1991.

McCarthy, Anne C. 'Falling in Love with the Author in Godwin's *Memoirs* of Wollstonecraft'. *Essays in Romanticism*, 25: 2 (2018), pp. 123–39.

Mellor, Anne K. 'Righting the Wrongs of Woman: Mary Wollstonecraft's *Maria*'. *Nineteenth-Century Contexts*, 19: 4 (1996), pp. 413–24.

——. *Romanticism and Gender*. New York: Routledge, 1993.

Newton, Isaac. *The Principia: The Authoritative Translation and Guide: Mathematical Principles of Natural Philosophy*, trans. Bernard Cohen, Anne Whitman, and Julia Budenz. Berkeley: University of California Press, 2016.

Oliver, Kelly. 'Between the She-Wolf and Little Red Riding Hood: The Figure of the Girl in Derrida's *The Beast and The Sovereign*'. *Derrida Today*, 4: 2 (2011), pp. 257–80.

Richards, Cynthia. 'The Body of Her Work, the Work of Her Body: Accounting for the Life and Work of Mary Wollstonecraft'. *Eighteenth-Century Fiction*, 21: 4 (2009), pp. 566–92.

Rousseau, Jean-Jacques. *The Confessions*, trans. J.M. Cohen. New York: Penguin, 1953.

———. *Du contrat social ou Principes du droit politique.* Paris: Union Générale d'Éditions, 1963.
———. *Julie, or the New Heloise: Letters of Two Lovers Who Live in a Small Town at the Foot of the Alps*, eds. Philip Stewart and Jean Vaché. Hanover, NH: Dartmouth College Press, 1997.
———. *Reveries of a Solitary Walker*, trans. Russell Goulbourne. Oxford: Oxford University Press, 2011.
Sapiro, Virginia. *A Vindication of Political Virtue: The Political Theory of Mary Wollstonecraft.* Chicago, IL: University of Chicago Press, 1992.
Sha, Richard C. *Perverse Romanticism: Aesthetics and Sexuality in Britain, 1750–1832.* Baltimore, MD: Johns Hopkins University Press, 2009.
Shelley, Mary. *Frankenstein; or, The Modern Prometheus*, ed. J. Paul Hunter. New York: Norton, 2012.
Shelley, Percy Bysshe. *Prometheus Unbound.* In *Shelley's Poetry and Prose*, 2nd ed., eds. Donald H. Reiman and Neil Fraistat. New York: Norton, 2002, pp. 202–85.
Sterne, Laurence. *Tristram Shandy*, eds. Joan New and Melvyn New. New York: Penguin, 2003.
Wollstonecraft, Mary. *Collected Letters*, ed. Janet Todd. Columbia, SC: Columbia University Press, 2004.
———. *Godwin & Mary: Letters of William Godwin and Mary Wollstonecraft*, ed. Ralph M. Wardle. Lincoln: University of Nebraska Press, 1977.
———. *An Historical and Moral View of the Origin and Progress of the French Revolution and the Effect it has Produced in Europe.* In *The Works of Mary Wollstonecraft*, eds. Janet Todd, Marilyn Butler, and Emma Rees-Mogg. New York: New York University Press, 1989, VI: pp. 1–236.
———. *Mary and Maria: or, The Wrongs of Woman.* Oxford: Oxford University Press, 2009.
———. *Original Stories, from Real Life.* London: J. Johnson, 1788.
———. *A Vindication of the Rights of Men.* In *A Vindication of the Rights of Men and A Vindication of the Rights of Woman.* Oxford: Oxford University Press, 2008, pp. 1–62.
———. *A Vindication of the Rights of Woman*, 3rd ed., ed. Deidre Shauna Lynch. New York: Norton, 2009.

Chapter Twelve

Phantasmion, or the Confessions of a Female Opium Eater

Donelle Ruwe

Sara Coleridge's *Phantasmion* (1837) is the first fairy tale novel in English and is also a rare example of a female opium narrative.[1] Sara Coleridge, a mother of two as well as the daughter of Samuel Taylor Coleridge, is a second-generation opium addict, and her writing often explores the negative impact of opiate use within a familial context. For example, she was the primary editor of her father's works, and she implied that his opium use was a direct cause of the *Biographia Literaria*'s unevenness.[2] Only in her children's novel *Phantasmion* does Coleridge fully celebrate the material effects of opium. Her protagonist experiences multiple bodily transformations, and this fluid materiality leads to maturity and a greater understanding of the political, social, and emotional world.

Phantasmion recounts the adventures of young Prince Phantasmion after his melancholic mother and distant father have died. After Phantasmion

[1] The following list exemplifies studies that discuss only male-authored, Romantic-era opium narratives: Alethea Hayter's foundational discussions of Coleridge, Crabbe, De Quincey, Keats, and Poe in *Opium and the Romantic Imagination* (Berkeley: University of California Press, 1968); John Barrell, *The Infection of Thomas De Quincey: A Psychopathology of Imperialism* (New Haven, CT: Yale University Press, 1991); and Christopher Partridge, *High Culture: Drugs, Mysticism, and the Pursuit of Transcendence in the Modern World* (Oxford: Oxford University Press, 2018). Peter Melville Logan's *Nerves and Narratives: A Cultural History of Hysteria in 19th-Century British Prose* (Berkeley: University of California Press, 1997) discusses multiple novels by women, but these novels are used as examples of nervous narrators; when he discusses opium narratives, he looks only at texts by men.

[2] For discussion of Coleridge's editorial work, see Donelle Ruwe, 'Opium Addictions and Meta-Physicians: Sara Coleridge's *Biographia Literaria*', in *Nervous Reactions: Victorian Recollections of Romanticism*, eds. Julia Wright and Joel Faflak (Albany, NY: SUNY Press, 2004), pp. 229–51.

has suffered through many 'sleepless nights' and days of 'dejection', his fairy guardian Potentilla, the insect queen, materializes out of a pomegranate tree and grants Phantasmion the powers of insects—variously, a butterfly's wings, a spider's sucker-feet, grasshopper legs, and a warrior ant's strength—and he sets off on adventures.[3] *Phantasmion* is famously convoluted, containing intermarriages, feuds, land wars, political intrigues, multiple sets of star-crossed lovers, secrecy, sorcery, poisoning, metamorphoses, disguises, embedded verses, and detailed landscape descriptions. By the end of the novel, Phantasmion has saved his homeland from invasion, won his true love, and rescued his mother's disinterred corpse.

My discussion of this female opium narrative centers on how *Phantasmion* presents the material effects of opium on the body, mind, and emotions. Coleridge challenges aesthetic positions that present the mind as a force that can transcend the material world through the imagination. In *Phantasmion*, the body and mind are inextricably linked and mutually constitutive and, further, a basic source of empathy or, to use eighteenth-century terms, the sympathetic imagination. *Phantasmion* offers multiple scenes of metamorphosis—actual material transformations of the protagonist's body from human to insect and back—as well as dreamlike scenes of phantasmagoria in which the landscape (and characters) are transformed. The fluid materiality of Phantasmion's body, which I suggest is, at least in part, a screen for the physical effects of opium use, is associated here with insects and involutes. The opium 'involute' is a term created by De Quincey to identify a type of waking reverie in which the associative faculty works at full pressure, and memories, impressions, and symbols join together in a euphoric complex of feeling and mental activity.[4] Involutes are a textual performance of a defined cluster of images, and they are obsessively and compulsively replayed throughout a text: once any piece of the image cluster appears, all of the elements of the image cluster must be played out.

A *female* opium involute, as demonstrated through Coleridge's *Phantasmion*, involves an intense fluidity of the physical body. Her involutes are typically triggered by breathing in or ingestion—material incursions of the outside environment breaching the boundaries of the body—and lead inexorably to transformations of the hero's body, emotions, and abilities. Phantasmion's material body becomes, variously, odd, monstrous, angelic, incapacitated, extraordinarily capacitated, super-powerful, transcendent, damaged, overconfident, radiant, and/or paralyzed. In what follows I explore what is at stake in Coleridge's presentation of a fluid materiality in terms of her use of the

3 Sara Coleridge, *Phantasmion* (London: Pickering, 1837), p. 10.

4 See Alethea Hayter for a complete treatment of De Quincey's concept of the involute, especially pp. 101–31.

involute and her human-to-insect metamorphoses. *Phantasmion*'s involutes deploy the physical intake of vapors and liquids as a means of knowledge-making, personal discovery, societal peacemaking, and emotional entrainment. Entrainment, as defined by Teresa Brennan, is the neurological process by which one group's nervous and hormonal systems are brought into alignment with another's.[5] In *Phantasmion*, as I suggest, at the same time that ingestion and breathing create entrainment, actual bodily transformations (as when Phantasmion's body crosses species and takes on insectoid attributes) create radical forms of empathy, especially when Phantasmion begins to experience the physical world not just as a human body with super-added insect powers, but as a lowly, speechless insect itself.

The Maternal Body and Opium

Sara Coleridge, as a mother and as a daughter of an opium addict, was particularly sensitive to the fact that a predisposition toward nervousness and opiate use is both environmental and hereditary. The influential medical text Thomas Trotter's *A View of the Nervous Temperament* (1807) explains that such predispositions are transmitted from parent to child through the parent's behaviors as well as through the nerves themselves, for the nervous system 'inherit[s] all the bad impressions of its progenitor, hoarded as it were in the structures of its nerves'.[6] This predisposition, writes Trotter, is a 'permanent state of body' and is 'the basis and *prime director* of the evolution of the foetus' (pp. 197, 202).[7] Coleridge was intensely aware not only of her own body but also that her body could have material effects upon the bodies of others.

It is useful to mention, here, that the material body of Sara Coleridge was surprisingly *present* to others, who often commented on her physical frailties and beauty. For example, her brother Hartley wrote that 'I fear it is too painfully evident that she has a body; and a body that is a sad burden and torment to her sweet soul'.[8] Dorothy Wordsworth and Sara's own siblings called her a little sylph, a fairy, or a visible soul.[9] She was painted to great

[5] Teresa Brennan, *The Transmission of Affect* (Ithaca, NY: Cornell University Press, 2004), p. 9.

[6] Thomas Trotter, *A View of the Nervous Temperament* (New York: Arno, [1807] 1976), p. 210.

[7] Although I do not know if Coleridge was familiar with Trotter's text, the way she phrases her cautionary discussion of opium use suggests a familiarity with *A View*. Both Trotter and Coleridge contrast opium as a 'palliative' to opium as a pleasure.

[8] Qtd. in Peter Swaab, *The Region of Sara Coleridge's Thoughts: Selected Literary Criticism* (New York: Palgrave Macmillan, 2012), p. 51.

[9] Beatrice Turner interprets Sara's role within the Wordsworth/Southey/Coleridge circle. Sara became the 'embodiment or spirit of a Romantic aesthetic' in which she was a 'half

acclaim by William Collins as 'The Highland Girl' (1818), and this painting hung above her father's desk until he died. Her family opposed her marriage; they felt her physical constitution was too delicate for marital duties. Indeed, as a young wife and mother she suffered nervous disorders and was under the continual care of a nurse. She had seven pregnancies: three miscarriages, twins who died within days of birth, and two living children, Hartley (born 1830) and Edith (born 1832). In these traumatic years, Coleridge discusses opium use in numerous diaries, in letters to her private nurse Anne, in her published children's poetry, and in a private essay 'Nervousness', based on her interpretation of the brain-science writings of Franz Joseph Gall and his disciple Johann Gaspar Spurzheim, the founders of phrenology. For Coleridge, the stakes were high for understanding her body through medical, familial, philosophical, and aesthetic means.

Coleridge's first attempt to publish a work about opium was the poem 'Poppies' in *Pretty Lessons in Verse for Good Children* (1834). Here she presents opiates within a domestic context as a home medicine.[10] This first-person poem contrasts the beneficial medical effects that Coleridge receives from the 'liquor' brewed from poppies to the innocent pleasure that her young son Herbert (Herby) finds in brightly colored poppy flowers. Such a poem would seem innocuous, given that opium was an everyday sort of drug used to treat major and minor ailments and readily available in many forms (including poppy-head tea, laudanum, lineaments, pills, and powders).[11] However, Coleridge's brother Derwent feared that 'Poppies' would dredge up their father's reputation for opium intake, and, indeed, Sara apologized to numerous correspondents for having published the poem.[12] *Phantasmion* likewise reflects

Spirit' (according to Dorothy Wordsworth) or 'Fairy' or 'ethereal being' (according to Hartley Coleridge). See Beatrice Turner, *Romantic Childhood, Romantic Heirs: Reproduction and Retrospection, 1820–1850* (New York: Palgrave, 2017), pp. 99–109.

[10] For additional discussion of 'Poppies', see Hannah Cowles Freeman, 'Opium Use and Romantic Women's Poetry', *South Central Review*, 29: 1 (Spring/Summer 2012), pp. 1–20.

[11] For discussion of domestic opium use, see Virginia Berridge, *Opium and the People: Opiate Use and Drug Control Policy in Nineteenth and Early Twentieth-Century England* (London: Free Association Books, 1999), pp. 21–37.

[12] In letters to family and friends, Sara apologized for publishing 'Poppies' in *Pretty Lessons*, claiming that she had been too sickly to deal with the manuscript. See Heidi Thomson, 'Sara Coleridge's Annotation in *Pretty Lessons in Verse for Good Children*', *Notes and Queries*, 58: 4 (2011), pp. 548–9. Coleridge was also apologetic regarding *Phantasmion*: as she notes in a letter to a friend, to write a fairy tale is 'the very way to be not read': see Dennis Low, '"The Very Way to be Not Read": The Creative Significance of Literary Inconsequentiality in Sara Coleridge's *Phantasmion*', *The Coleridge Bulletin*, 12 (Winter 1998), pp. 27–56. Thomson suggests that Coleridge's disavowals reveal a need to diplomatically handle concerns about S.T.C.'s opium use. Derwent Coleridge tried to prevent Joseph Cottle from printing a memoir that referenced S.T.C.'s opium use, and even asked Southey to intervene. Derwent edited the works of Hartley, an alcoholic, attempting to

(and deflects) autobiographical elements, such as the complicated intermarriages, feuds, and family relationships that resemble the Coleridge, Southey, and Wordsworth families.[13] This poppy poem marks Coleridge's first exploration of the gendered dynamic of opium. For the boy Herby, opium is about the visual—an object that is apart from him, a thing to play with, touch, and explore that, nonetheless, never breaches the boundaries of his own body. Coleridge emphasizes the visual in her stanzas about Herby: 'The poppies blooming all around / My Herbert loves *to see*'; 'He loves their *colours*'; and 'He *views* their clust'ring petals' (emphasis added).[14] By contrast, when Coleridge describes herself in this poem, she describes herself as ingesting poppy juice: 'She drinks the poppy's juice; / That liquor soon can close her eyes' (p. 71). Coleridge allows the juice to breach physical boundaries and materially alter her own physical body. As if to emphasize that for her poppies are not a visual object, the poppy juice shuts her eyes. Herby objectifies poppies; his mother ingests poppy juice.

In *The Transmission of Affect* (2004), Teresa Brennan notes that sight offers distance and autonomy. We tend to think of sight—for example, the ability to pick up bodily cues visually—as the essential manner by which we physically learn about the world around us, for we resist the idea that a foreign body can enter our own bodies and breach bodily integrity. In a larger sense, to insist upon sight as the primary force of entrainment is an attempt to maintain the dichotomy of self versus environment. The transmission of affect, however, undermines the dichotomy between individual and environment. When we resist entrainment, as when we emphasize sight over other senses, we often also objectify and deny our own negative emotions, projecting them onto others. In this process of affect denial, as Brennan notes, the feminine (women, feminized 'others') tends to carry negative affects for the other, and the negative affect of aggression, when directed to the object/feminine being, registers as anxiety and depression (Brennan, p. 15). We fundamentally situate the mother as the passive repository of all of the child's unwanted raging affects,

make something of value out of the shambles of his life. To paraphrase Judith Plotz, Hartley was the designated child genius and child of nature for the Pantosocratic circle, and he ran wild with devastating consequences. When Coleridge describes Herby she does not celebrate his precocity but rather worries that his nervous temperament might reflect hers and her father's. See Sara Coleridge's *Memoir and Letters of Sara Coleridge*, ed. Edith Coleridge (New York: Harper, 1874), p. 107.

13 For discussion of the interpersonal relationships of *Phantasmion*'s characters, see Hilary Newman, 'The Structure of Sara Coleridge's *Phantasmion, A Fairy Tale*', *The Coleridge Bulletin*, 42 (Winter 2013), pp. 39–48. As Peter Melville Logan astutely states of opium narratives, these works contain multiple layers of memoir, deflection, self-reflection, and denial self-reflection, and denial (pp. 1–12).

14 Sara Coleridge, *Collected Poems*, ed. Peter Swaab (Manchester: Carcanet Press, 2007), pp. 70–1.

and this situating of the mother is, Brennan writes, 'the foundational fantasy' and primal act of 'othering' (pp. 13, 15). We see the mother as the origin of our negative affects. Coleridge, in 'Poppies', has instinctively understood this dynamic. She suffers depression and anxiety; she wishes her son to understand her physical needs. He, however, seems content to leave his mother stewing in her own emotional and physical anguish while he goes out to gaze at poppies (and thereby symbolically conquer) the environment that he refuses to allow entrance into his physical body.

Coleridge's fantasy novel takes 'Poppies' one step further. It, too, was written for her children but, instead of a brief poem, *Phantasmion* offers a phantasmagoria of material effects. Like the mother of 'Poppies' who tries to defend her bodily needs to her child, this novel is also a natural extension of maternal preoccupations and writings. Coleridge, like many young mothers, kept a baby-book of sorts—she records Herbert's date of birth, weight, and physical condition. She records how often he breast-feeds, how many bowel movements he has per day, what happens to Herby when she eats pea soup ('after the first fortnight he was rather tardy in his bowels').[15] But about the time she is pregnant with Edith, she writes less about Herby's body and more about her own. Soon, comments about her children are followed by comments about her own body: 'Edith sucks no more today, alas! Since the 12th I have been going on very sadly. Disordered bile accompanied with derangement of the nervous system is my complaint. Stomach & bowels out of order ... weakness-nervousness-shiverings and glowings, etc.' (20 September 1832). By October, she requires opiates to sleep and, by January, she is taking sixty to seventy drops of morphine each night and has stopped menstruating. Unlike in 'Poppies', where little Herby is allowed to remain apart from the ingestion of poppy-medicinals, in her baby-book and then in *Phantasmion*, bodies are penetrable and fluid, and affect and physical sensation move from one body to another. When Edith no longer drinks breastmilk, it is Coleridge's body that suffers 'shiverings and glowings'. To withhold physical comfort turns against the withholder. To return to Brennan's insights, the mother's body becomes the repository of the negative affects of her child. In *Phantasmion*, however, this fluid materiality is an essential plot element. Phantasmion's insect metamorphoses are transformative—literally and figuratively—and his involute scenes are intense moments of feeling and, at their most extreme, of animism in which the material world around Phantasmion seems to have its own life and spirit.

[15] All quotations from Sara Coleridge's manuscripts, unless otherwise indicated, are from the Harry Ransom Humanities Center at the University of Texas at Austin.

Phantasmion, Insect Poetics, and the Mother's Body

In *Phantasmion* the body itself is the nexus of knowledge. Indeed, the radical transformations of *Phantasmion*'s body offer opportunities for knowledge and growth, as when Phantasmion's body becomes a composite of insect and human features and when Phantasmion's whole body metamorphoses from one species to another. The oddity of Coleridge's exploration of materiality and methods of entrainment is in her use of insect/human metamorphoses.[16] To appreciate the corporeality of the insect requires extreme levels of empathy, or an ability to 'feel' as an insect feels, to experience and appreciate its material presence. As Eric Brown explains, insects are troubling to both readers and writers. Insects are marked by the irreducible otherness of their physical bodies:

> The insect has become a kind of Other not only for human beings but for animals and animal studies. ... Second is the attention to insect form and materiality—that it is categorically the shape, the workmanship, the 'artificio' of the insect that mark its singularity. Moreover, this artful world of the insect draws on our own imaginative faculties; we understand it first poetically, as a fantastic realm overlaying but not representing our own. The insect world must be mediated—by art, artifice, technology—as an (almost) impossibly *different* creation.[17]

The insect body is marked by singularity, segmentation, monstrousness, and artificiality. Insects elicit superlatives—the grossest, the smallest, the most innumerable species (p. x). They are sexually fecund; they lack feeling; they are mindless; they swarm; they appear everywhere, and nothing can stand against them. They feed on us. They live in and on us. They exist in a state of radical autonomy: they are too many to be counted, and they cannot be destroyed. The insect kingdom exemplifies Jane Bennett's argument regarding the vibrancy of matter and its resistance to a simple presentation of the human

[16] Entomological verse is linked to Romantic botanical verse, a genre associated with women. See Ann B. Shteir, *Cultivating Women, Cultivating Science: Flora's Daughters and Botany in England, 1760–1860* (Baltimore, MD: Johns Hopkins University Press, 1996), especially pp. 59–78. Charlotte Smith's epic 'Flora' offers a precedent for botanical fairy and insect writing: the fairy queen Flora wages war against insect invaders. For discussion of 'Flora' see Donelle Ruwe, *Children's Poetry in the Romantic Era: Verse, Riddle, and Rhyme* (Houndmills: Palgrave Macmillan, 2014), especially pp. 56–65; for discussion of the papillionade, see pp. 167–94. The papillionade craze of 1805–30 includes many insect works such as *The Butterfly's Ball and the Grasshopper's Feast* (William Roscoe, 1805) and *The Insects in Council* (Susanna Watts, 1828). Coleridge's manuscripts include an incomplete papillionade.

[17] Eric C. Brown, 'Introduction: Reading the Insect', in *Insect Poetics*, ed. Eric C. Brown (Minneapolis: University of Minnesota Press, 2006), p. ix.

as an actant and the material world as acted upon. The segmented insect is in itself a heterogeneous assemblage whose agency is distributed across a heterogeneous field.[18] If, as Pliny the Elder notes, observing insects positions us as detached spectators, then *Phantasmion*'s celebration of fluid metamorphoses of human to insect and back positions us as full participants in the radical otherness of the material world.[19]

Phantasmion's first and last insect metamorphoses are instigated by the loss of his mother, and these scenes of physical metamorphosis mark his growth from a self-centered child who sees only his own bodily needs and pleasures, to his mature self who acknowledges his responsibilities to others as others—not just as extensions of himself. The young child Phantasmion, when he is told that his mother has died, denies it, saying that death is no more than clouds passing away; they simply vanish. When he is taken to see his mother's corpse, she is in a shroud, and he cannot see her face. He has yet to accept the reality of death, and he often sees his mother in his dreams. When Phantasmion first calls upon Potentilla, his guardian fairy and the queen of the insect kingdom, he does so hoping to see his mother again: '"Give me wings!" he cried; for still he had a vague hope that he might once more behold that heavenly face if he could but soar aloft' (p. 11). Phantasmion believes that his mother can still exist as a spirit though her physical body is gone. Potentilla waves her wand, and the air fills with butterflies, 'those angel insects pouring from every region of the heavens' (p. 11). Phantasmion, given the power of flight, soars into the sky. He plays with sea eagles, attacks vultures, pretends to be a bird of prey, and frightens a heron. But when he flies too high into a thin, unbreathable atmosphere, he plummets without control and is attacked by an eagle that shatters one of his pinions. He falls to earth and must walk all the way home.

It is telling that it is a lack of air that causes Phantasmion's Icarus-like fall. The inability to breathe, to share pheromones and engage in entrainment, is Phantasmion's first downfall. His lack of empathy is signified by his violent attacks on the other birds, and his physical punishment—the broken pinion—teaches him his first lesson about the egocentric use of his body. Phantasmion, though taking on the actual physical attributes of an insect, has not yet accepted a fellowship of sense and seems incapable of empathy with the other creatures of the air. Phantasmion resists entrainment even though he has taken on an insect's abilities.

In his final transformation, Phantasmion becomes fully insectoid and no longer can separate his own body from that of the insects. This transformation is also triggered by his mother's death, but this time by her actual corpse. The

[18] Jane Bennett, *Vibrant Matter: A Political Ecology of Things* (Durham, NC: Duke University Press, 2010), p. 23.

[19] For discussion of Pliny, see Brown, p. ix.

Figure 9: Larva of ant-lion. A photo-micrograph created by Arthur E. Smith and featured in Richard Kerr, *Nature through Microscope & Camera* (1909).

young adult Phantasmion does not suppose that spirit and flesh are separate and that his mother's spirit is somehow still alive. Instead, he rescues her remains. Phantasmion discovers that his enemy has unearthed his mother's coffin and now plans to burn her remains in a public gesture of scorn. Potentilla, to help Phantasmion rescue his mother's relic, offers him an insect metamorphosis, but this time she offers (and he accepts) the powers of an 'unwieldy' insect, the larva of an ant-lion (see Fig. 9).[20]

[20] Richard Kerr describes the ant-larva in *Nature through Microscope & Camera* (London: Religious Tract Society, 1909), pp. 92–7. Kerr supplies two micro-photographs and an extensive excerpt from René Antoine Ferchault de Réaumur (1683–1757), the author of a six-volume entomological encyclopedia, *Mémoires pour servir à l'histoire des insectes* (Paris: Académie Royale des Sciences, 1734–42).

The ant-lion larva moves backwards and digs a pitfall (a funnel-shaped trap) by circling backwards in sandy soil. At the base of the pit just beneath the sand, the ant-lion awaits its prey, small insects that tumble to the bottom of the pit. Phantasmion, driven by rage, agrees to this transformation. His wings vanish, and 'every vestige of his human form disappear[s]' (p. 329). Most of Phantasmion's transformations have mixed human and insect features, but the human is dominant. For example, when he has insect wings, he can retract them so that they are hidden from others. At another point in the story, his body has a cicada's drum that is hidden by clothing. This time, however, his entire body is a giant ant-lion. It is fully insectoid, ruled by insect instincts, and no trace of the human remains. The 'metamorphosed prince' digs a pitfall and lies in the bottom of the snare, with only the 'points of his horrid fangs … like two reaping hooks' remaining visible (p. 329). The first ranks of the enemy army fall into the trap, bringing with them his mother's coffin. Phantasmion, with difficulty, backs out of the pit, dragging his mother's coffin. His 'monstrous form' terrifies the soldiers, who shoot him with javelins and arrows, and Phantasmion realizes that his death is imminent.

Usually, Phantasmion can find an object upon which to vent his rage. This climactic scene is the first time that Phantasmion places his rage and anger in the appropriate location: himself. In Teresa Brennan's discussion of materiality, the feminized others are the typical objects onto which negative emotions are channeled. As Brennan states, the child locates the primal source of rage in the mother. She is the passive repository of all of the child's unwanted raging affects, and this situating of the mother is, Brennan writes, our primal act of 'othering' (p. 15). In Coleridge's novel, Phantasmion as an insect cannot 'utter any articulate sound', and he is so exhausted, he cannot 'command the motions of his monstrous body' (pp. 332, 333). Alone, isolated with only the corpse of his mother for company, he laments, 'Miserable man that I am … or rather miserable spirit of a man, imprisoned in a frightful crust, to what dire extremity have I been driven by mad rage! I have cast away my human form and faculties only to perish unavenged by arrows from mine enemy's quiver!' (pp. 332–3). Phantasmion, in his moment of extremity, has stopped 'othering'. He at last accepts that he himself is the source of his 'mad rage', and he does not project it onto his mother, who now is but a corpse. He lacks language (another primary distancing tool between humans and the environment) to speak to Potentilla and ask to be physically returned to a human form, and so he must remain part of the animal world until a fairy takes pity on him.[21]

[21] Margaret Anne Doody suggests that whenever Romantic-era women write sensuously of an 'alien and homely' insect, they demonstrate a deep, interconnected 'fellowship of sense'. Further, fairies, like insects, allow for the exploration of sensation and reflection, in that fairies exist beyond man-made regulation and human mortality. See 'Sensuousness in

Phantasmion can no longer maintain a false dichotomy between individual and environment. He is finally able to experience the power of a truly fluid materiality: he has become an insect and, in doing so, he understands that he is not separate from his environment and that his body defines his presence in the world.

Autobiography, Entrainment, and the Female Opium Involute

Phantasmion's plot and protagonist offer constant examples of fluid materiality in which the actual physical body metamorphoses. This fluidity also appears in the physicality of emotion exchanges (entrainment) as demonstrated through the novel's unique use of the opium involute. Its opium involutes are particularly physical. They engage all of the senses—not just the visual—and are often triggered by the environment's incursions past the boundaries of the body through vapors and liquids.

Phantasmion is very far from a traditional fairy tale in that it constantly moves away from abstraction and into the material specificity of bodies, bodily affect, and landscape. Most fairy tales rely on a standard set of archetypal landscape features: castle, woods, hut, and tower. Each of these has its own symbolism (woods offer danger and opportunities for transformation; towers represent a slowing of time and agelessness).[22] By contrast, *Phantasmion*'s landscape is unusually fleshed out for a fairy tale. Coleridge refers to and names mountain ranges, lakes, rivers, streams, caves, beaches, mines, and natural terrain. She offers the political history of each country and identifies their natural resources, imports, and exports. For Coleridge, as for many contemporary fantasy writers, the details of place are the essential building blocks of a world.

Phantasmion's landscape exemplifies the fluidity of the material world. It is perhaps inspired by an epic fantasy world, 'Jugforcia', that Coleridge's eldest brother Hartley developed in childhood and acted out with his siblings.[23] As Derwent Coleridge recalls of this childhood fantasy world, there was a field nearby from which,

the Poetry of Eighteenth-Century Women Poets', in *Women's Poetry in the Enlightenment: The Making of a Canon, 1730–1820*, eds. Isobel Armstrong and Virginia Blain (New York: St. Martin's Press, 1999), p. 24.

[22] On fairy tale setting, see Joyce Thomas, 'Woods and Castles, Towers and Huts: Aspects of Setting in the Fairy Tale', *Children's Literature in Education*, 17: 2 (June 1986), pp. 126–34.

[23] During his school years, Hartley created a second childhood epic. This one featured a young intellectual anti-hero who betrays his father, a man of gigantic stature. See Judith Plotz, 'The Annus Mirabilis and the Lost Boy: Hartley's Case', *Studies in Romanticism*, 33: 2 (Summer 1994), pp. 181–200.

> a small cataract would burst forth, to which he gave the name of Jug-force. The banks of the stream thus created, soon became populous,—a region—a realm; and as the vision spread in ever-widening circles, it soon overflowed, as it were, the narrow spot in which it was originally generated, and Jugforcia ... became an island-continent, with its own attendant isles—a new Australia, or newest Sea-land.[24]

Jugforcia is a juvenile Xanadu in which a forceful cataract reconfigures the landscape, creates ever-widening vision, and generates an entire fantastical continent. A natural event, a small cataract, becomes a region, then a realm, and finally a whole world. In effect, even in this fragmentary recollection of Jugforcia, the material world is literally a fluid thing that morphs from one form to another. A handwritten map of *Phantasmion* sketched by Coleridge herself offers yet another example of fluid materiality: the landscape of her childhood is transformed into the mountains, rivers, lakes, and seas of her fantasy world. This map manuscript (when flipped as a mirror image) is a mirror image of the Lake District (see Fig. 10).[25]

Just as the landscape of the novel is intensely tangible and secretly autobiographical, the characters are written to be intensely physical (unlike the typical flat dramatis personae of the fairy tale) and, as with the Coleridge family, extremely susceptible to vision-enhancing opiates. Although *Phantasmion* never mentions opium by name, its traces are everywhere, for eating and drinking bring altered consciousness, paralysis, strange transmissions of affect, and sometimes death. Phantasmion's father dies from poisoned honey. Phantasmion's childhood friends die from ingestions, one from poisonous fruit and the other from an infusion of medicinal leaves. As a young adult Phantasmion drinks from an enchanted stream that produces 'unnatural sleep' and strange dreams (p. 124), he is overcome by flower smells. He drinks a potion brewed by a jealous lover, 'a precious liquor ... [that] takes away all sense of toil and pain', and it causes him to experience ecstatic visions, 'new sensations', dazzling changes of forms, and to transfer his emotions from his true love to her rival (p. 246). The novel's arabesque plot is characterized by a recurrent image of a magical pitcher that is often filled with mind-, body-, and emotion-altering liquids, and, as Phantasmion discovers, the pitcher had long ago set in motion a series of events that destroyed his mother's happiness.

[24] Derwent Coleridge, 'Memoir of Hartley Coleridge', in *Poems by Hartley Coleridge with a Memoir of his Life*, ed. Derwent Coleridge, 2 vols. (London: Moxon, 1851), I: pp. xli–xlii.

[25] For analysis of the map's relationship to the Lake District, see Joanna E. Taylor, '(Re-) Mapping the "Native Vale": Sara Coleridge's *Phantasmion*', *Romanticism*, 21: 3 (October 2015), pp. 265–79.

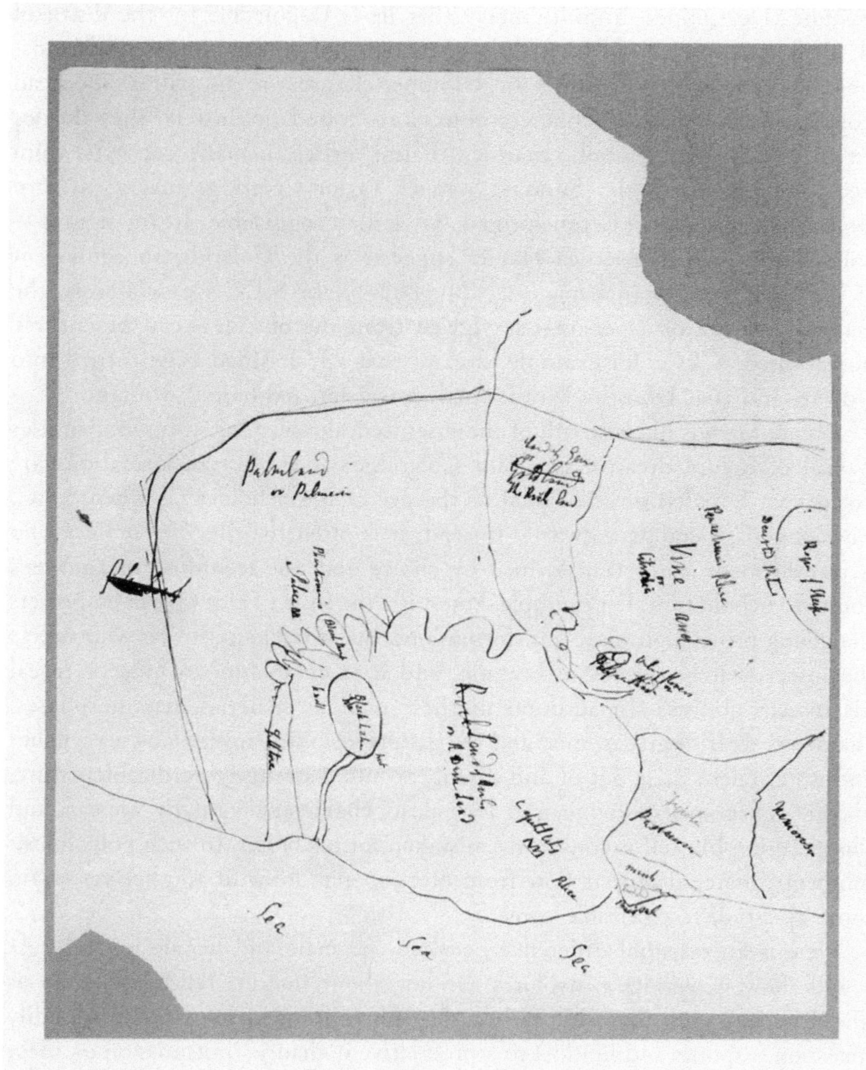

Figure 10: Map of *Phantasmion*.
Permission of the Harry Ransom Center, The University of Texas at Austin.

Perhaps the most consistent element of opium texts is the involute. Involutes, a knot of ideas that are obsessively replayed and rehearsed in texts such as *Confessions of An English Opium Eater*, are a type of image in which our deepest thoughts and feelings pass through us as 'perplexed combinations' of material objects. John Barrell suggests that De Quincey's texts return compulsively to the same places and images because he is attempting to hide a specific guilt that his imagination endlessly re-enacts. Barrell identifies an involute (De Quincey's guilt-fantasy that he is responsible for the death of his little sister Elizabeth) that links the bodies of young girls, sexual transgression, violence, sun/death, a locked upper-chamber room, palms, and head wounds. Although these concrete objects are found in clusters, they do not act in a consistent symbolic manner. 'Palms' arises in many contexts, from trees, to hands, to Palm Sunday. Samuel Taylor Coleridge invents a word for the phenomenon of transformed but still recognizable dream figures—polyolbiosis—which Alethea Hayter suggests is the Coleridgean equivalent of 'involute' and 'phantasmagoria' (pp. 203–5). In S.T.C.'s polyolbiosis, the material essence of a person—as viewed from the outside—can be entirely transformed. S.T.C., for example, dreamt that a friend had been turned into a dwarf and that Dorothy Wordsworth was a fat, red-haired woman.

Phantasmion is likewise full of the disguised, doubled, or suffused identities typical of opium dreams, but Sara Coleridge's identity transformations are not primarily based on the visual or the eye of the beholder (as when S.T.C. envisions his friend as a dwarf). Instead, it is often the dreamer *himself* who is transformed, *bodily* transformed by choice and not according to another's ability to behold him. For example, Potentilla the Insect Fairy Queen empowers the young prince's physical transformations, but it is Phantasmion who selects the insect that he wishes to become, and it is up to him to hide or reveal his insect's abilities. In addition to these obvious material metamorphoses, characters wear disguises, mist and fog distort visibility, mysterious sea witches and water fairies arise out of and disappear into a strangely permeable nature, ghostly reflections of living and long-dead characters regularly appear, and Phantasmion himself is constantly mistaken for his father. In such polyolbiosis moments, material objects flow from one concrete form to another yet retain some essential, recognizable core.

Here is an essential difference between the male and female involute. As I will show, Coleridge's involutes are not about interior reflections such as De Quincey's guilt fantasies; rather, they move from various forms of bodily ingestion (vapours and liquids) to a productive if chaotic transmission of affect and knowledge. *Phantasmion* insistently figures the material world as fluid and the mind as partaking of the body, which is particularly vivid in moments when the mind is influenced by opiates. Over time, Phantasmion learns to wield the transformations of his body as tools for understanding the treacherous political and emotional waters of his world. Phantasmion drinks or breathes or smells, has extraordinary visions, and reaches out to others, attempting to connect emotionally or physically with them.

Phantasmion's primary involute involves a silver pitcher. References to the pitcher are always accompanied by a standard set of objects and images that include the act of writing, liquids (as ice, frost, vapor, or water), intense colors, and flowers or plants. This involute pattern predates *Phantasmion* and seems to be drawn from Coleridge's first published work, her translation of Martin Dobrizhoffer's *An Account of the Abipones, An Equestrian People of Paraguay.* Dobrizhoffer (1717–91) was a Jesuit who in 1749 journeyed to South America and worked in Jesuit-sponsored settlements of the Guarany and Abipone peoples.[26] His book details the production of a native narcotic called the Herb of Paraguay. To quote Coleridge's translation of Dobrizhoffer: 'this nectar of Paraguay is ... what chocolate, coffee, Chinese tea, and spirits are to other nations' (1: p. 102).[27] Dobrizhoffer makes a direct comparison of *yerba de palos* or *caà-miri* to standard European intoxicants and argues that both European and American topers 'drink away their fortunes' through immoderate use (1: p. 104). He describes the herb's preparation as follows:

> The vessel in which it is taken is ... plated all round with silver. Into this vessel they put a common table spoonful of the herb, stir it up for some time with sugar and cold water, and then pour the hot water upon it. ... The herb thus prepared is strained through a silver pipe ... lest any particle of the herb, which is noxious to the stomach, should slip down the throat with the liquor ... green concrete balls of which are sometimes said to be found in the bowels of the deceased. ... [T]he warm water in which the herb has been steeped too long, cannot be drunk with safety to the health. Water of this kind grows black, and is only used by ink makers to deepen the blackness of their ink.
>
> The moderate use of this herb is wholesome and beneficial in many ways. For when taken with caution, it acts as a diuretic, provokes a gentle perspiration, improves the appetite, speedily counteracts the languor arising from the burning climate. ... On the other hand, it cannot be doubted, that by the immoderate and almost hourly use of this potation, the stomach is weakened, and continual flatulence with other diseases, brought on'. (1: pp. 103–4)

The physical effects of the Herb of Paraguay dovetail with many of the effects of opium: a weakened stomach, flatulence, perspiration, and vomiting. And, like

[26] See Ross Enochs, 'Catholic Missions to the Native Americans', in *American Indian Studies: An Interdisciplinary Approach to Contemporary Issues*, ed. Dane Morrison (New York: Peter Lang, 2000), pp. 195–216. The Jesuits opposed Spanish slave traders and founded havens for the Guarani in 1610. Unfortunately, as early as 1611, armed slavers traveled through the interior of Paraguay and captured Guarani who were concentrated in the missions. By 1628, only two of the eleven missions were intact. In 1767, King Charles III of Spain suppressed the order, the reductions collapsed, and the slave trade continued virtually unopposed (p. 199).

[27] In the Romantic era, coffee and tea were classed as anodynes. Trotter, for example, warns women against their overuse for fear of irrevocable damage to the female constitution.

opium, *caà-miri* has a creative aspect in addition to its effects on the body. Not only can its liquids be used in ink-making, it even creates green concrete balls inside the bodies of its imbibers. In effect, this brief description of the Herb of Paraguay offers a compelling example of how bodies and material objects can have a will of their own and be actants rather than objects acted upon.

This complex description by Dobrizhoffer gives Coleridge a pathway for understanding the fluid materiality of the body, the mind, and the writer who works with black ink. This passage as translated by Coleridge is the ur-text of *Phantasmion*'s involute: the silver vessel, the languor, the dangerous or medicinal liquor, writing (black ink), vivid colors (green concrete balls), and a text to be interpreted (or translated, in this case). Translation is the act of moving from text to text and, as a text moves from one author to another, it gains palimpsestic layers as traces of author and translator remain. In translation, as with involutes, the same sets of objects and images are recaptured in new shapes and forms, in this case through a new language.

The silver pitcher, the trigger for the *Phantasmion* involute, was made by the fairy Feydeleen, the spirit of all flowers. Her name alludes to the 'fey' power of having visions. Like the effects of laudanum on the Coleridge family circle, owning the pitcher becomes an obsession and causes feuds between the book's royal families.[28] The pitcher was made for Anthemmina, a young woman who loved Phantasmion's father. One day, Feydeleen appeared before Anthemmina and turned her earthen pitcher into a 'silver vessel engraved with curious characters' (p. 110). Whoever possesses the pitcher possesses Anthemmina and will become her husband. Phantasmion's father betrayed her, however, and so she married another king, and it is her daughter, Iarine, who is Phantasmion's love interest throughout the novel. In this origin story of the pitcher, the main elements of the involute are all in place. We see transmutations—earthenware to silver—and curious characters. We see flowers and liquids and portents and visions. We also understand that the pitcher offers real-world effects; royal families and individual bodies will be joined or destroyed.

The origin tale of the pitcher leads immediately to extended scenes of bizarre phantasmagoria. In the female opium narrative, these phantasmagoria lead to increasingly material effects. In the 1790s through the mid-nineteenth century, notes Terry Castle, the meaning of 'Phantasmagoria' gradually shifted from 'something external and public … to something internal or subjective: the phantasmic imagery of the mind'.[29] *Phantasmion*, by its very title, is linked to

[28] The connection of opium to a pitcher may be autobiographical. De Quincey had a crystal decanter of laudanum cut with water. At the height of S.T.C.'s opium use, he was drinking a quart of opium a week, or 20,000 drops a day. Such excessive amounts would be cut with water and poured into a pitcher.

[29] Terry Castle, *The Female Thermometer: Eighteenth-Century Culture and the Invention of the Uncanny* (Oxford: Oxford University Press, 1995), p. 29. In 1813 John Ferrier offered

growing speculation about the mind's capacity to create and embody ideas as external forms. *Phantasmion* offers both aspects of Castle's phantasmagoria—mental phenomena and external material phenomena—and, surprisingly, allows the protagonist to freely move between them or experience them both simultaneously. After he learns of the pitcher, Phantasmion's world fills with visual and visceral material transmutations. He sees a strange reflection in a stream, 'the graceful figure of a damsel, holding up a silver pitcher so that it concealed her face' (p. 119). As the picture fades, the sands form words: the names of Phantasmion, his father, his mother, and Iarine. Phantasmion attacks a birch tree, which screams like a human as 'blood-drops trickl[e] down its silver skin' (p. 122). At one point his foe suddenly metamorphoses into a woman writhing on the ground, twisting a silvery veil over her face (p. 123). Phantasmion wrestles his rival for the pitcher until 'an irresistible drowsiness came over him' (p. 121). The air is misty, time passes without his awareness, and the scenery alters each time he awakes. These phantasmagoria are classic involute moments in which, to repeat my earlier definition, the associative faculty works at full pressure to create a euphoric complex of image and feeling. In Coleridge's female narrative, the euphoric complex is particularly physical: writhing women, screaming trees, and blood drops. These scenes with the pitcher display unfettered desire, unfettered imagination, and unfettered metamorphosing of the material world. Time is subjective, place is permeable, and objects and feelings freely intermix.

The involute and its effects climax in a scene set in a mysterious cavern, home of an evil sorceress. This scene is a textbook example of the transmission of affect. According to Brennan, transmissions of affect arise most powerfully through smell; she discusses, for example, the way pheromones work in entrainment. In *Phantasmion* the sorceress brews a precious liquor in a cauldron, and Zelneth (a jealous lover of Phantasmion) successfully entices Phantasmion to try it. This gothic scene is set in a cavern with passages winding in every direction and lit only by the flickering red light of the cauldron's flames. The cavern's air is filled with disorienting 'steams of the liquor' and 'luscious vapour' (p. 245):

> [Zelneth] left the crystal basin on a table of rock just opposite to Phantasmion: he saw the liquor lie glowing and creaming in the bowl, like melted rubies frothed with pearl; he inhaled its sweet bewildering odour, and, scarce knowing what he did, the youth raised it to his lips and drank deeply. In a moment he was electrified with delight, a rapturous tranquility pervading his whole frame: he felt intoxicated with

a popular theory of phantasmagoria. He described phantasms as 'hallucinations' and attributed apparitions to poor digestion, diseased nerves, irregular circulation, or other 'peculiar' conditions of the sensorium (qtd. in Castle, p. 55).

> pleasure which sprang from no cause and tended to no object, yet was ever ready to be reflected and multiplied from all objects around: ... All thought of Zelneth, all thought of Iarine, all remembrance of the past, all anticipation of the future were completely suspended: he only knew that he was gazing on a sun of loveliness, in which a thousand beauties seemed to converge, while the feelings inspired by his own heavenly maid were mingled with his new sensations, though the object of them was veiled in his memory by a dazzling mist. ... [Phantasmion] beheld fantastic petrifactions, which hung from the ceiling, illuminated by the fire-light. He gazed upon them in ecstasy, and felt as if the transport of his bosom, which invested them with splendour, was derived from those unmeaning forms, till Zelneth, again presenting herself, occupied his whole fancy, and seemed once more to be the fountain of all his glad sensations. (pp. 246–7)

Phantasmion uses multiple senses, more than just sight, in this moment of entrainment of affect. Phantasmion experiences feelings of pleasure through vapours and potions, and his affect has no physical boundaries or defined object. His entrainment begins with breath and ingestion when he inhales and drinks. Only then, after his senses are fully 'intoxicated', does Phantasmion move to sight. His visual sense, however, has been destabilized by the entrainment already in process. In this scene, sight does not work to reinforce boundaries and the 'othering' process. Instead, a 'thousand beauties' converge on the object of his vision, are 'mingled with new sensations', and then are veiled in 'dazzling mist'. Affect, notes Brennan, attaches itself with equal intensity to various phenomena: I may be as anxious about my mother's diabetes as I am about forgetting to take out the garbage. Phantasmion's affect exists in a gestalt of fluid sensations: the fantastic petrifactions, Zelneth's beauty, and the glowing liquid are all sites of powerful feeling and 'tended to no object' and were 'reflected and multiplied from all objects around'. As in scenes with the silver pitcher, the experience of drinking liquids from this crystal vessel overwhelms all rational thought with sensation. These sensations are emotionally charged and are detached from particular objects; everything is perceived in the 'supernatural light of beauty', a pleasure 'which sprang from no cause and tended to no object, yet was ever ready to be reflected and multiplied'. In S.T.C.'s 'Frost at Midnight', icicles are given meaning by the thought-projections of the viewer. With Sara Coleridge's stalactites, meaning is derived from sensations, the crossing of sensations, and a feedback loop of sensation building upon sensation. After drinking the ruby liquid, Phantasmion's bosom invests the scene with splendor, his deep love of Iarine mingles with new feelings for Zelneth. As Sara Coleridge describes it, pleasure comes from no object and tends to no object but is multiplied all around. The material world overflows with sensations.

Coleridge has reinterpreted a foundational allegory of Western civilization, Plato's allegory of the cave. In Sara Coleridge's version, Phantasmion is in a cave, illuminated by firelight and influenced by infusions that open him up, mentally and physically, to the process of entrainment. Coleridge describes the fantastic petrifactions as things that are 'unmeaning forms' until they are given meaning through the fluid interchanging of sensations. Coleridge does not separate shadow from form; rather, she infuses 'unmeaning forms' with a dizzying interplay of texture, smell, and sight.[30]

In the conclusion of the allegory of the cave scene, Phantasmion and Zelneth (now in a bower-of-bliss sort of garden) are themselves turned into fixed and unmoving forms by Oloola, the spirit of the wind:

> his tongue was arrested and the blood appeared to stagnate in his veins; the air had become piercing cold, and filled with white vapour; the brook ceased to murmur, and the birds to sing; the waters were congealed, the leaves and flowers wan and drooping, the branches encrusted with hoary rime. But the eyes of Phantasmion were fixed on Zelneth; motionless she stood, one arm raising aloft the urn, from whose lip an icicle depended, the other holding the empty crystal goblet. (p. 252)

Like the stalactites in the cavern that are 'unmeaning forms', Phantasmion is now himself not only an 'unmeaning form', but an unfeeling one as well. Phantasmion's tongue, blood, and body are frozen. He is no longer the man perusing the icicle. He has once again metamorphosed from one material form to another: from liquid to solid, warm blood to frozen object. In this frozen state, the wind literally picks him up and blows him away from the garden. Instead of the fantasy of control over the material world, Phantasmion is acted upon. The wind is the actant, and it frees him from the garden's spell.

This cavern scene is the most extreme and extended performance of Coleridge's opium involute. Coleridge challenges basic Romantic-era imagery in which the disembodied imagination is a vital force giving life to passive nature. In other words, she challenges aesthetic positions that insist that the mind can transcend the material world through the imagination. Such positions, she suggests, are denials of how the material environment and the body are inextricably connected to the mind and the imagination.

[30] For discussion of how Romantic-era women writers use sensory language to challenge masculine philosophical traditions, see Isobel Armstrong, 'The Gush of the Feminine: How Can We Read Women's Poetry of the Romantic Period?', in *Romantic Women Writers: Voices and Countervoices*, eds. Paula R. Feldman and Theresa M. Kelley (Lebanon, NH: University Press of New England, 1995), pp. 13–32.

Richard C. Sha suggests that the past century of Romanticism scholarship about the imagination has swung, like a pendulum, between considering the imagination as an evasion of materiality to the imagination as an embodiment of the very conditions of materiality.[31] By contrast, the Romantics themselves understood that 'corporeal materiality' was constantly evolving and included nerves, spirits, fibers, brain, mind, consciousness, and thought (p. 29). In a vitalist worldview, corporeal materiality is about the conditions of change and possibility. Hence, Coleridge's Phantasmion metamorphoses from human, to insect, to human, to icicle. The material world as liquids and vapors (or as Coleridge's poppy juice) breaches the boundaries between his body and the exterior world, and they take from him the ability to reject his own negative affects by projecting them onto his mother's body. Through entrainment, in this coming-of-age fairy tale, Phantasmion's material self aligns with the material world. And so he can no longer engage in the childish process of othering but must, instead, accept his connections and responsibilities to others and to himself.

Bibliography

Armstrong, Isobel. 'The Gush of the Feminine: How Can We Read Women's Poetry of the Romantic Period?' In *Romantic Women Writers: Voices and Countervoices*, eds. Paula R. Feldman and Theresa M. Kelley. Lebanon, NH: University Press of New England, 1995, pp. 13–32.

Barrell, John. *The Infection of Thomas De Quincey: A Psychopathology of Imperialism*. New Haven, CT: Yale University Press, 1991.

Bennett, Jane. *Vibrant Matter: A Political Ecology of Things*. Durham, NC: Duke University Press, 2010.

Berridge, Virginia. *Opium and the People: Opiate Use and Drug Control Policy in Nineteenth and Early Twentieth Century England*. New York: Free Association Books, 1999.

Brennan, Teresa. *The Transmission of Affect*. Ithaca, NY: Cornell University Press, 2004.

Brown, Eric. 'Introduction: Reading the Insect'. In *Insect Poetics*, ed. Eric C. Brown. Minneapolis: University of Minnesota Press, 2007, pp. ix–xxiii.

Castle, Terry. *The Female Thermometer: Eighteenth-Century Culture and the Invention of the Uncanny*. Oxford: Oxford University Press, 1995.

Coleridge, Derwent. 'Memoir of Hartley Coleridge'. In *Poems by Hartley Coleridge with a Memoir of his Life*, ed. Derwent Coleridge. 2 vols. London: Moxon, 1851, I: pp. xiii–ccvii.

Coleridge, Sara. *Collected Poems*, ed. Peter Swaab. Manchester: Carcanet, 2007.

[31] Richard C. Sha, 'Imagination', in *A Handbook of Romanticism Studies*, eds. Joel Faflak and Julia M. Wright (Malden, MA: Wiley-Blackwell, 2012), pp. 19–35.

——. *Memoir and Letters of Sara Coleridge*, ed. Edith Coleridge. New York: Harper, 1874.

——. *Phantasmion.* London: Pickering, 1837.

——. *Pretty Lessons in Verse for Good Children.* 1834. London: Matthews, 1927.

——. *The Regions of Sara Coleridge's Thought: Selected Literary Criticism*, ed. Peter Swaab. New York: Palgrave, 2012.

Dobrizhoffer, Martin. *Historia de Abiponibus*, 1784. Trans. by Sara Coleridge as *An Account of the Abipones, An Equestrian People of Paraguay.* London: J. Murray, 1822.

Doody, Margaret Anne. 'Sensuousness in the Poetry of Eighteenth-Century Women Poets'. In *Women's Poetry in the Enlightenment: The Making of a Canon, 1730–1820*, eds. Isobel Armstrong and Virginia Blain. New York: St. Martin's Press, 1999, pp. 3–32.

Enochs, Ross. 'Catholic Missions to the Native Americans'. In *American Indian Studies: An Interdisciplinary Approach to Contemporary Issues*, ed. Dane Morrison. New York: Peter Lang, 2000, pp. 195–216.

Freeman, Hannah Cowles. 'Opium Use and Romantic Women's Poetry'. *South Central Review*, 29: 1 (Spring/Summer 2012), pp. 1–20.

Hayter, Alethea. *Opium and the Romantic Imagination.* Berkeley: University of California Press, 1968.

Kerr, Richard. *Nature through Microscope & Camera.* London: Religious Tract Society, 1909.

Logan, Peter Melville. *Nerves and Narratives: A Cultural History of Hysteria in Nineteenth-Century British Prose.* Berkeley: University of California Press, 1997.

Low, Dennis. '"The Very Way to be *Not Read*": The Creative Significance of Literary Inconsequentiality in Sara Coleridge's *Phantasmion*'. *The Coleridge Bulletin*, 12 (Winter 1998), pp. 27–56.

Newman, Hilary. 'The Structure of Sara Coleridge's *Phantasmion, A Fairy Tale*'. *The Coleridge Bulletin*, 42 (Winter 2013), pp. 39–48.

Plotz, Judith. 'The Annus Mirabilis and the Lost Boy: Hartley's Case'. *Studies in Romanticism*, 33: 2 (Summer 1994), pp. 181–200.

——. *Romanticism and the Vocation of Childhood.* New York: Palgrave, 2001.

Ruwe, Donelle. *Children's Poetry in the Romantic Era: Verse, Riddle, and Rhyme.* Houndmills: Palgrave Macmillan, 2014.

——. 'Opium Addictions and Meta-Physicians: Sara Coleridge's *Biographia Literaria*'. In *Nervous Reactions: Victorian Recollections of Romanticism*, eds. Julia Wright and Joel Faflak. Albany, NY: SUNY Press, 2004, pp. 229–51.

Sha, Richard C. 'Imagination'. In *A Handbook of Romanticism Studies*, eds. Joel Faflak and Julia M. Wright. Malden, MA: Wiley-Blackwell, 2012. pp. 19–35.

Shteir, Ann B. *Cultivating Women, Cultivating Science: Flora's Daughters and Botany in England, 1760–1860.* Baltimore, MD: Johns Hopkins University Press, 1996.

Swaab, Peter. *The Regions of Sara Coleridge's Thought: Selected Literary Criticism*. New York: Palgrave Macmillan, 2012.

Taylor, Joanna E. '(Re-)Mapping the "Native Vale": Sara Coleridge's *Phantasmion*'. *Romanticism: The Journal of Romantic Culture and Criticism*, 21: 3 (October 2015), pp. 265–79.

Thomas, Joyce. 'Woods and Castles, Towers and Huts: Aspects of Setting in the Fairy Tale'. *Children's Literature in Education*, 17: 2 (June 1986), pp. 126–34.

Thomson, Heidi. 'Sara Coleridge's Annotation in *Pretty Lessons in Verse for Good Children*'. *Notes and Queries*, 58: 4 (2011), pp. 548–9.

Trotter, Thomas. *A View of the Nervous Temperament: Being a Practical Enquiry into the Increasing Prevalence, Prevention, and Treatment of Those Diseases Commonly Called Nervous, Bilious, Stomach and Liver Complaints*. New York: Arno, [1807] 1976.

Turner, Beatrice. *Romantic Childhood, Romantic Heirs: Reproduction and Retrospection, 1820–1850*. New York: Palgrave MacMillan, 2017.

Wright, Julia and Joel Faflak, eds. *Reactions: Victorian Recollections of Romanticism*. Albany: SUNY Press, 2004, pp. 229–51.

Chapter Thirteen

Voices against the Universe

Material Transgressions in the Blakean Multiverse

Mark Lussier

Semiotics can lead to a *historical typology of signifying practices* by the mere fact of recognizing the specific status within them of the speaking subject.

—Julia Kristeva, 'The System and the Speaking Subject', 1973

The Daughters of Albion hear her woes & eccho back her sighs.

—William Blake, *Visions of the Daughters of Albion*, 1793

I.

Female voices frequently function as transgressive vessels within the sexual/textual politics of William Blake's illuminated prophecies, from the hesitant and plaintive Thel, the defiant and lamenting Oothoon, the insightful and melancholic Ahania, the multitudinous Ololon, to all their sisters and daughters across the later epics (e.g., *Vala* or *Jerusalem*). The dimension of emanations—a politically oppressed and psychologically repressed space—nonetheless manifests a resilient and vibrant 'voice' at the semiotic foundation of Blake's evolving myth. Emanations function as 'a product and a process', providing a fluid poetic alternative 'that continues to resist symbolization' to the aggressive and rigid declarations of the Urizenic principle and patriarchal tendencies of the zoas.[1]

[1] Diana Hume George, *Blake and Freud* (Ithaca, NY: Cornell University Press, 1980), p. 153; Luce Irigaray, *This Sex Which Is Not One*, trans. Catherine Porter (Cornell, NY: Cornell University Press, 1985), p. 106.

Emanations offer a heterological semiotic presence, a *chora* placed under erasure yet constantly erupting forth through cracks and fissures in the symbolic to lay bare both the fruits and roots of patriarchal oppression and its structures.[2] This emanative choric presence operates at numerous textual and metatextual levels in the illuminated prophecies as aspects (i.e., products) of a composite textual state conceived in complementarity yet provides a turbulent counterflow beneath the symbolic sea of time and space (i.e., process).

These voices often unveil phallic dominion (as in Thel's poetic adventures beyond Har) or contest masculine authority (as in Enitharmon's power play to assert counter-dominion over sexuality itself to open *Europe*). Between these works, in *Visions of the Daughters of Albion*, Blake situates the individual voice of Oothoon against two forms of male tendencies (rapacity and projection) and traces her evolving forms of poetic resistance, creating from the lyrical maturation and visual flow a vibrant semiosis (formed from the fusion of all signifying fields operative in acts of narration and reception). Oothoon, from this paradigmatic location of discursive presence, generates rhetorical (verbal) strategies and aesthetic (visual) techniques of resistance and transmits them in two directions. Within the turbulent narrative, her visual and vocal presence flows towards the historical imaginary of the daughters (who function as chorus/*chor*a and reside at the outer boundaries of a textual echo chamber). Within the plateau of metatextual processes of reception, the reader registers 'a certain rhythm or order', experiencing at the margins of textuality Kristeva's 'the speaking subject' whose voice does not simply get absorbed by a patriarchal 'system' (in spite of masculine efforts to do so) and benefits, via affective modes of transference, the reading subject in the realm of the real.[3]

Beneath the composite textual complementarity undergirding *Visions*, Blake forges a dual rhythmic aesthetic process (visual modulation and visual sequential periodicity), whose coherence provides the product of semiosis across the planes of the historical (within and without the work). *Visions* registers its revolution through interactive signifying fields (thus pursuing more than a revolution in poetic language, more like revolution in semiosis), and Blake forces an immediate encounter with this effect as a reader enters the imaginary geographies and visionary temporalities implied in/on the title plate and frontispiece (more on this below). The third dimension analyzed—a coalescence of rhythmic functions—manifests at the event horizon where affective techniques generate effective outcomes. For this reason, like the editors of *The Early Illuminated Books*, I have

[2] Julia Kristeva, *Revolution in Poetic Language*, trans. Margaret Waller (New York: Columbia University Press, 1984), pp. 25–8.

[3] The phrase 'a certain rhythm or order' is from P. Shelley's 'A Defence of Poetry'. Percy Bysshe Shelley, *Shelley's Poetry and Prose*, eds. Donald H. Reiman and Neil Fraistat (New York: W.W. Norton, 2002), p. 512.

chosen Copy G for discussion, where 'frontispiece and title plate are [uniquely] placed sequentially … rather than facing each other'.[4] Equally important, the engraving hand displays techniques that reflect familiarity with 'colour printing' and 'deepen the tones', while 'all leaves … are foliated in pen and ink in a single sequence' (p. 226), suggesting the work arriving at a singular or exemplary state of production and representation. The sequential arrangement also eliminates the prospect of apprehending the plates through some form of 'simultaneity' most famously posited by Northrop Frye, since the negotiation of the 'gap' from the title plate to the frontispiece takes time (the hand must turn the page, and the eye does not see both juxtaposed) and the verbal and visual narratives pass from event to results in the process (into another dimension of temporality).[5]

As Blake moved physically to Lambeth, he shifted spiritually toward the visionary and its embodiment in illuminated prophecy, a confluence leading into his most productive decade (c. 1790s). In many ways, *The Marriage* and *Visions* open Blake's visionary campaign to weave from the turbulent wake of the French Revolution historical and psychological works into a semiotic sea of time and space.[6] And, like the nomadic I-persona of the former, Oothoon functions as exemplum, with the sequential (rather than simultaneous) apprehension of the title plate and frontispiece bringing receptive processes to bear on the reading subject via sequential movement, which must operate within symbolic/historical and semiotic/psychological zones of contact. The figural triangulation of bodies in the foreground of the frontispiece underwrites the trilateral enframement of the masculine—Bromion and Theotormon to left and right and the 'dark sun'/eye of Urizen in the background. By the closing design, however, Oothoon's soaring ascendency renders the masculine mute (literally both male characters fall silent) and cloaks the eye of ideology (by clouds created in her wake as she appears to the daughters—who lift their heads).

Oothoon's poetic passage from abject lamentations to transgressive, declarative lyric places in context both Enitharmon's strident intervention in history (in *Europe*) and the multitudinous voices led by Ololon (in *Milton*), providing a choral melding of the individual and the collective into a 'Vox Populi'.[7]

[4] William Blake, *Visions of the Daughters of Albion*, eds. Morris Eaves, Robert N. Essick, and Joseph Viscomi, in *Blake's Illuminated Books*, gen. ed. David Bindman, 6 vols. (Princeton, NJ: Princeton University Press, 1993), 3: p. 226 (hereafter cited as *VDA*).

[5] The specific phrase is used by Frye in *The Anatomy of Criticism: Four Essays* (Princeton, NJ: Princeton University Press, 1957), p. 77; Frye analyzes Blake in *Fearful Symmetry: A Study of William Blake* (Princeton, NJ: Princeton University Press, 1947).

[6] On the *Marriage*, see Lussier, 'Affective Textualities: Restructuring Subjectivity in Blake's *Marriage*', in *Romanticism and Affect Studies, A Romantic Circles Praxis Volume*, ed. Seth T. Reno, *Romantic Circles* (May 2018).

[7] William Blake, *The Complete Poetry and Prose of William Blake*, ed. David Erdman (Garden City, NY: Anchor/Doubleday, 1982), plate 32, line 15, p. 131. All citations from

Individually and collectively, women articulate a contrary vision that critiques clashing masculine forms of desire and derides the social inscription of these flawed forms, which are inscribed onto the female body and psyche by oppressive male scribes. Their vision renders more problematic the analysis of Blake's oft-discussed misogynistic tendencies. Such voices address the warring male members of Blake's 'sublime allegory' to make apparent the phallic pillars of support for masculine legal authority and patriarchal privilege (E, p. 730). Across the illuminated prophecies, female figures (e.g., Thel, Oothoon, Enitharmon, Ololon, Jerusalem) challenge 'the premises of oppressive dominant ideologies', and within the early canon Oothoon stands—to combine phrases from Jacques Lacan's and Judith Butler's critical discussions of Antigone—'at the center of [events in] her unbearable splendor', functioning in 'her exemplary political status as a feminine figure who defies the state through a powerful set of physical and linguistic acts'.[8]

II.

Oothoon, a nascent visionary form dramatized, communicates simultaneously as *figura* for and speech about the plight of woman. These are registered in visual and verbal fields, respectively, and challenge the monological control typically enjoyed in both Bromianesque or Theotormonic symbology of male codes and phallocratic laws. Blake's techniques methodize her process of appropriation and transmutation, conceptualizing infinite 'phenotypes' from finite 'genotypes' to achieve a 'revolution in poetic language' (Kristeva, *Revolution*, p. 87) that enfolds the semiosis that precedes feminine oppression and transmits those weaponized attributes to her daughters on the margins of

this volume will be cited hereafter as E, followed by plate, line number, and page, as (E, 32.15: p. 131).

8 Helen P. Bruder, 'Blake and Gender Studies', in *Palgrave Advances in William Blake Studies*, ed. Nicholas M. Williams (Houndsmill and New York: Palgrave Macmillan, 2006), p. 135; Jacques Lacan, *The Ethics of Psychoanalysis, 1959–1960, The Seminar of Jacques Lacan, Book VII*, ed. Jacques-Alain Miller, trans. Dennis Porter (New York: W.W. Norton, 1997), p. 247; Judith Butler, *Antigone's Claim: Kinship between Life and Death* (New York: Columbia University Press, 2000), p. 2. Oothoon vocalizes Antigone's elemental force, for example, when Antigone turns to her sister, saying: 'Don't fear for me. Set your own fate in order' (Sophocles, *Antigone*, trans. Ian Johnson [Arlington, VA: Richer Resources Publications, 2007], p. 9). Her voice appropriates the controlling rhetoric of patriarchal discourse, articulates a powerful poetry of consolation, and unleashes an inspiring cry for freedom articulated as fatalism. The relevant discussion of Antigone's exemplary status extends critically from Hegel's *Phenomenology* through Lacan's *Ethics* to Butler's *Antigone's Claim*. While what follows threads together elements unique to each 'voice' in this critical triumvirate, I reserve the full elaboration for a book-length discussion ('Blake's Affective Textualities: Dynamic Exchange in Illuminated Canon').

textuality and history. Thus, she personifies (and so shares with the daughters she addresses) 'woman's condition as one of enslavement by an imperial patriarchy which naturalizes its barbarities through ideologies of fixed sexual and racial difference' (Bruder, p. 142), with this state reinforced by the first word of the poem proper, 'Enslaved' (E, 1: p. 45).

Blake rather systemically establishes Oothoon as the literal, symbolic, and imaginary 'exemplification' of woman's disempowered condition, with her exemplary status (a given among Blake scholars) emanating from her poetic and social functions and conveying ethical and moral power that grants her escalating agency across the poem. Brian Massumi's concept of affect helps clarify Oothoon's capacity to promulgate cultural, political, sexual, and social forms of revolution (an imperative for the field of reception), while she remains bound within a poetic narrative in which she moves no one and goes virtually disregarded.[9] Thus, as argued by Nelson Hilton, she historically embodies, as person and text, Mary Wollstonecraft, whom Blake directly encountered.[10] She serves as the nominal sign of woman's historical condition and provides a powerful poetic voice that appropriates the linguistic resources of her male tormentors to unveil the facts of ex/sistence when caught in the vice of masculine desire and control.

Women, as Lacan noted, are barred from discourse and thus denied discursive presence by symbolic forms and processes reflecting masculine priority: 'The woman, therefore, is *not*, because she is defined purely against the man', which Lacan and his female others (i.e., Irigaray and Kristeva) identify as the *objet a* of male desire and cultural structuration.[11] Nonetheless, woman—in her alterity and prioritized function as originary other beyond the split cultural process enacts for subjectivity—gains 'access to an archaic form of expressivity outside the circuit of linguistic exchange' (Rose, p. 54). This is not 'the hysteric's discourse' but a semiotic flow whose currents, being 'of the body', open onto 'a jouissance beyond the phallus' and expressive of alternative existential and spiritual dimensions.[12] Women remain primal agents of jouissance capable of accessing within the choric miasma of semiosis (in

[9] Brian Massumi, *Parables for the Virtual* (Durham, NC: Duke University Press, 2002), pp. 15–16.

[10] Nelson Hilton, 'An Original Story', in *Unnam'd Forms: Blake and Textuality*, eds. Nelson Hilton and Thomas A. Vogler (Berkeley: University of California Press, 1986), pp. 69–104.

[11] Jacqueline Rose, 'Introduction—II', in *Feminine Sexuality: Jacques Lacan and the école freudienne*, eds. Juliet Mitchell and Jacqueline Rose, trans. Jacqueline Rose (New York: W.W. Norton, 1982), p. 49.

[12] Lacan, *On Feminine Sexuality: The Limits of Love and Knowledge, 1972–3, Encore: The Seminar of Jacques Lacan, Book XX*, ed. Jacques-Alain, trans. Bruce Fink (New York: W.W. Norton, 1998), pp. 41, 74.

Kristeva's iteration) a subversive poetics—in the current case, excoriating the trans-cultural and trans-historical suppression of all women. Through this exemplary status, Oothoon literally, within the horizon of the poem, must serve, in Luce Irigaray's well-known phrases, as 'the locus of a more or less competitive exchange between two men' (pp. 31–2), rendering her 'man's business' (p. 188).[13]

Poetic events and pictorial images make this horrifically clear, with social dynamics displayed within distinct patriarchal and structural hierarchies equally familiar in forms of gothic art and literature or from documents addressing slavery and the rights of women. The entwined verbal and visual narratives represent a 'theatre of cruelty' as the scene of instruction and encrypt phallic energies within the mind as symbolic structures (i.e., 'mind-forg'd manacles' breeding 'reptiles of the mind' in perpetuity [E, pp. 27, 42]). While the focus remains primarily on Oothoon, the male members as well—Bromion and Theotormon—writhe in pain and self-enclosure, although, unlike their victim, born of their own acts and decisions forged in obeisance to phallic forces mustered in service to patriarchal authority (woman as commodity for use and exchange). Lacan's conceptual terms, 'Name of the Father' and 'Symbolic Order', encapsulate a wide range of inner and outer controlling ideological elements that write the tragic plot of the feminine into the force field of culture, which are reflected as verbal and visual textual layers subtly entangled by Blake's mode of production. In contradistinction, Oothoon alone undergoes an evolution in consciousness (manifest vocally as 'a revolution in poetic language' [Kristeva, *Revolution*, pp. 205–6]) across the poem and grows in discursive power and vision by 'appropriating the voice of the other' (Butler, p. 11).[14]

Blake's work, which is 'operatic: passionate, hopeless, tragic, and simple' (George, p. 127), opens with a woman's acceptance of her sexuality, her immediate brutalization by a colonizing rapist (Bromion), and proceeds to her subsequent victimization by her beloved and betrothed (Theotormon),

[13] As Lacan discusses in his seminar, *Encore*, within the ambient linguistic environment, 'words' designate woman as 'signifier', but given her cloven being ('she is not-whole') the term 'woman can only be written with a bar through it. … [S]he is excluded by the nature of things [yet] she has a supplementary *jouissance* compared to what the phallic function designates by way of *jouissance*' (*Encore*, pp. 72, 73).

[14] The first parenthetical phrase depends upon Kristeva's definition of the semiotic *chora* and its revolutionary pulsations in *Revolution in Poetic Language* (pp. 25–30), while the second phrase, from Butler, is related to Michel De Certeau's analysis of the permutations involved in 'writing the voice', as Anna Gibbs has noted in 'Writing as Method: Attunement, Resonance, and Rhythm', in *Affective Methodologies: Developing Cultural Research Strategies for the Study of Affect*, eds. Britta Timm Knudsen and Carsten Stage (Houndmills and New York: Palgrave Macmillan, 2015), p. 223.

who becomes trapped in mental and spiritual torment related to the body (i.e., Oothoon's body) as conditioned by social suppression and theological repression, and who chains her back-to-back with her ravager. Oothoon moves beyond both males across the body of the poem, passing through self-degradation by lamentation to end in exultation, a story apparent in verbal and visual scenes and one rendered with poetic power founded upon linguistic and representational techniques predating Blake's poem. Of the triangular characters contesting for discursive authority, only Oothoon has an audience through the daughters of Albion, who sit on the margins of the poem—between the imaginary clime of the poem and the real of historical and material conditions—and hear 'her lamentations and echo back her sighs' (*VDA*, 3.5: p. 250). Though liminal and even minimal, they exist in trans-temporal verbal and visual spaces—being situated in the 'Present, Past & Future' (E, p. 18)—and thereby function as the choral cypher of historical conditions. They lament, upon hearing Oothoon's woes, because they either already know them or intuit that they will. Oothoon's voice is propagated via the chords of the semiotic (i.e., something energized and rhythmic emitted from the Kristevan *chora* and transmitted to the Blakean chorus) and perpetuates a technique through which, as Tristanne Connolly observes, 'transformative power [is] found by transgressing the limits of the [patriarchal] system'.[15]

III.

The quotations from Lacan and Butler applied to Oothoon just above, while fitting her quite well, actually refer to Antigone, with both critical (Hegel's evocation of the play in the *Phenomenology*) and historical (the revival of the play in the 1790s) connection to Blake's dramatic poem, which cannot be fully integrated into the current discussion. To offer a quick sense of this critical dimension, Oothoon's techniques partake of poetic modes that, Hegel suggests, Antigone exemplifies—a voice capable of adaption/adoption of voice as *techne* (technique and technology) deployed against both the individual bearer of law (Creon) and the *polis* upon which authority rests (Thebes). Antigone's relentless voicing of opposition to gendered authority has led to 'a peculiar persistence' for Sophocles' play and its heroine, with one such resurgence taking hold in the final decade of the eighteenth century.[16] However, this persistence can be perceived, as well, in our current moment as a trans-cultural prominence that

[15] Tristanne J. Connolly, *William Blake and the Body* (Houndmills, Basingstoke and New York: Palgrave Macmillan, 2002), p. 4.

[16] Tara Beaney, 'Beautiful Death: The Nineteenth-Century Fascination with *Antigone*', *Opticon*, 1826: 7 (Autumn 2009), p. 1.

supplements the trans-historical presence of the transgressive voice echoing across time and space and reflects critical interest.

Blake via Oothoon articulates an analogous evolution in ethics, converting the semiosis of suffering (aesthetic, corporeal, linguistic) into a revolutionary, transgressive, and visionary vehicle energetically engaged 'in powerful and profound ways with [most] of the feminist debates of his day' (Bruder, *William Blake*, p. 180) and arrayed against political, social, and psychological forms of patriarchal authority and power draped across the feminine. Oothoon's vocal (poetic) performance (pictorial) slowly coalesces into a transformational rhetoric registered in the entangled interstices of method enabled by the enriched semiotic environment. The entwined elements of design provide an experience of her overcoming, as verbal and visual planes of signification 'hail' their observers, calling them to follow the poetic beyond the injustice and violence defining Oothoon's plight.[17] Blake's intensified textualities depend upon this 'interpellation', one of many affective elements encoded into the mode of production for the illuminated works.[18] The inverse 'mirroring' dynamic achieved between the title page and frontispiece of *Visions*, for example, 'brings to the surface concealed hierarchies and suppressed conflicts' and embodies '[at least] three affective processes' that activate the ability of readers to 'take the presence of others as a cue for their experience'.[19] As Bonnie Honig had hoped, the result does push forward 'beyond the mirror stage' but, in Blake's case, well before Lacan proposed it as a governing dynamic of psychological development and subject formation.[20]

Blake's *Visions* stands at the headwaters of the larger myth and follows immediately in the wake of *The Marriage* and the conjoined *Songs of Innocence and of Experience*, bringing to a close the early dyadic contraries model in favor of the complex dynamism of the emerging myth of mind, a sublime allegory. The triad of works, brought to fruition at the opening of the Lambeth period, affords the opportunity to stand within a distinct aesthetic and epistemic shift, with the fusion of standard linguistics signs and the creation of narrative micro/spaces within those words creating an activated semiotic space dependent

[17] Louis Althusser, *Lenin and Philosophy and Other Essays*, trans. Ben Brewster (New York: Monthly Review Press, 1971), pp. 174–6.

[18] Mark Bracher, 'Rouzing the Faculties: Lacanian Psychoanalysis and the Marriage of Heaven and Hell in the Reader', in *Critical Paths: Blake and the Argument of Method* (Durham, NC: Duke University Press, 1987), p. 177; Diane Piccitto, *Blake's Drama: Theatre, Performance, and Identity in the Illuminated Books* (London & New York: Palgrave Macmillan, 2014), p. 126.

[19] Cristina Albu, *Mirror Affect: Seeing Self, Observing Others in Contemporary Art* (Minneapolis: Minnesota University Press, 2016), pp. 8, 17.

[20] Bonnie Honig, *Antigone, Interrupted* (Cambridge: Cambridge University Press, 2013), p. xii.

on affective functions, a textual tendency that continues through *Jerusalem*. Indeed, the work introduces characters/tendencies who/that will persist as periodic presences to the end of the myth (which would include the unilluminated manuscript of *The Four Zoas*), since the problem of subject formation regarding women locked within patriarchal structures manifest as forms of male desire erected within and without continues without interruption to the end of the poetic oeuvres (and obviously persists in our own moment). Blake registers the tension between writing and speech, the visual and vocal, at the opening of *Visions* through the sequential encounter of its title page and frontispiece. The sequence dramatically re/presents, through liminal and subliminal designs, respectively, the boundary conditions and psychological dispositions that await individual women beyond cultural structuration of female subjectivity. The oppressed female voice erupts in opposition, providing an exemplary subject-position for a poetic critique of cultural process and articulating a counter-process capable of achieving mental evolution and political revolution simultaneously. The female voice itself, exemplified by Oothoon, is broadcast to all daughters of Albion (regardless of ethnicity, gender, nation, race, space, or time) for the language it engages and resists, a symbolic order under sway of the phallus, and requires semiotic strategies to thwart the symbolic law of social practices and its systems of control.

Diane Piccitto forcefully argues that the 'self-reflective technique' of the first two plates creates an inverse mirror effect with affective implications, for the voice of the text interpolates, and 'the spectator is called to act, to participate in the dilemmas encountered … and to create change in a socio-political context'. Rather than abandoning the engaged spectator in an imaginary web of unrealizable actions, the poem provokes through 'the spectator's individual entrance into the work' an opportunity for responsive acts of opposition capable of becoming 'imperative step[s] toward change on a larger scale' (pp. 87–9).[21] Such modes of co-optation and interpellation form what I have elsewhere described as 'the textual gaze' of the illuminated books made manifest within discrete textual operations that give rise to an affective textual effect, one that acts upon its readers/spectators.[22] Oothoon's assertive act establishes, at the beginning of the prophecies and its mythic participants, a model later emulated in varied ways by the most articulate and powerful female emanations, with the female voice of the plentitude of semiosis providing a counter expression to the relentless monological uni/verse of the symbolic and all that it bears/

[21] See also Piccitto, p. 87 and Connolly, p. 112.

[22] This is not a new idea in Blake Studies certainly but one somewhat more active than previously proposed. See my recent essays: 'Affective Textualities' and 'The Horrors of Subjectivity/The *Jouissance* of Immanence', in *Blake's Gothic Imagination: Bodies of Horror*, eds. Chris Bundock and Elizabeth Effinger (Manchester: Manchester University Press, 2018), pp. 213–34.

Figure 11: Title page and frontispiece to *Visions of the Daughters of Albion* (copy I, printed 1795). Yale Center for British Art.

bares and bars, with Ololon's (i.e., ululation's) multitudinous manifestation achieving the rhythmic apex in Book II of *Milton*.

The visual planes of the title page serve conjoined representational and titular functions, creating a horizontal dimensionality whose contours contain micro-worlds in the gaps between letters and terms and furthering future narrative lines of force, and the discrete acts unfolding in these varied spatial and temporal spaces recall medieval painting techniques, even incorporating a lack of depth in the visual field familiar to the mode (see Fig. 11). These

spatio-linguistic facets echo a similar use of space for narrative ends in the title plate of *The Marriage* (which immediately preceded *Visions*). The scale and size of the lettering, oriented head to foot, establishes a skeletal semiotic structure within which to place petite dramas, which abound around the title. The most important micronarrative—indeed one serving as the very foundation of all subsequent acts and events—occupies the lower center, where a female figure with her head turned backwards flees from the winged male figure pursuing her as she races toward the reader for succor. Blakean logic of design fashions the left side of the page as women's space, occupying the same titular space as hell (for the prior title page of *The Marriage*).

To Oothoon's right (i.e., the left side of the page) nymphs dance in a circle, celebrating the impending event when Oothoon embraces jouissance in an overt act of self-determination, one located in the following poetic argument (two plates in the reading future): 'I plucked Leutha's flower, / And I rose up from the vale' (E, p. 45). As Bruder notes, plucking the flower literally evokes deflowering, an affirmation associated with the assumption of sexual identity, yet Oothoon's encounters with real and symbolic forms of phallic power and privilege confirm a darkening of these desires. Immediately above the group, the play of power appears as a woman pictorially expressing 'woe and worse' (*VDA*, p. 234), with her hands bound behind her back, while the figure above completes the per(e)-version of the natural desire first conveyed by the dancing ballerinas (reading foot to head). Literally perched atop the 'Daughters' a hoary-haired male pours power down the masculine right side of the plate to feed the storm that breaks over Oothoon, which occurs in a single line of the poem: 'Bromion rent her with his thunders, on his stormy bed' (*VDA*, p. 248; E, p. 46).[23] The page, then, evinces a circular flow around and through the title and tells a complicated future tale unknowable to a new reader but all too apparent to those who passed through this portal in the past.

Turning the page to the frontispiece, the circular flows found on the title page collapse inward, generating one of Blake's best known and most disturbing images, one presented as a demonic scene of instruction appropriate for a theater of cruelty designed to unveil forms of love founded upon use and exchange values (the subject positions of Bromion and Theotormon respectively).[24] The foregrounded scene, literally created by Theotormon yet symbolically inspired by the Urizenic ideology 'eye' in the background, reflects in its torturous tableau something akin to the mode of Sade's narrative

[23] While most have noted the pictorial lineage of this figure of the Old Testament god and his intellectual/poetic offspring Urizen (a common figuration in Blake's pictorial references in all media), the leaning posture and pushing hand of the figure corresponds quite precisely (in both motivation [the constraint of female desire] and action [pushing the main character into a circular narrative of psychological and social imposition]) to the figure of fate in his illustrations for Thomas Gray's 'Ode on the Death of a Favorite Cat'.

[24] Given the nature of the lesson enacted on and through Oothoon, her situation seems more precisely theorized (relative to Blake's dramatic, dynamic, and re/presentational commitments) by Antonin Artaud, in chapters seven and eight of *The Theatre and Its Doubles*, who sought in the formalities of theatre a dramaturgy designed to address the dis/eases of 'civilization [which] had turned humans into sick and repressed creatures' and whose purpose would be 'to rid humankind of these repressions and liberate each individual's instinctual energy'. In his impulses, Artaud is quite close to the Blakean poetic idiom of the illuminated books and the use of the visual field in particular as a 'theatre of cruelty' performing the function of a scene of instruction. See 'Theatre of Cruelty', *Encyclopedia Britannica*, 6 March 2016, at https://www.britannica.com/topic/Theatre-of-Cruelty.

techniques, putting pornography in the service of political revolution.[25] The figural postures are static, although the design has the depth missing from the title page, and the drawing is now shorn of linguistic signs. The entangled figures strain against restraints and are positioned in a mediational space (between interiority and exteriority), the mouth of a cave, which opens onto a cloudy and watery background. Above the waves, a partial face (formed by the outlines of the cavern) broods around the characters, with its baleful solar 'eye' looking through the foreground to engage observers on the other side of the scene in the position of reception. Unlike Morris Eaves, Robert Essick, and Joseph Viscomi, who see 'the profile of a skull looking to the left, an image of the 'narrow circle' into which 'they inclos'd [Oothoon's] infinite brain' (*VDA*, p. 236; E p. 47), I argue that seeing the eye of the text as directly engaged with the I of the observer offers the stronger interpretation (i.e., more in line with the dimension of 'vision' evoked in the title and the motto on the title page), with the half-face looking directly out of the frame, an argument that embraces Piccitto's analysis of Blake's use of semiotic engagement (the intersection of verbal and visual fields) pursued for subjective purposes (representational and personal transformation).[26] Under this malevolent eye, the frontispiece establishes the most abject state of the feminine, yet Oothoon's perception inaugurates a movement away from the dismal state of subjectivity constructed by 'Religion, Morality, Law' (E, p. 47) which, while wholly 'always arbitrary', nonetheless proves 'unfailingly oppressive'.[27] In spite of the ideological modes of control at the core of culture, Oothoon nonetheless transforms this perception into a means for achieving an evolution in consciousness registered as a revolution in poetic language moving from self-abasement (the design at the foot of plate six) to self-assertion (the final half-page design at the foot of page eleven). Oothoon, enchained between rapist and egoist (primary and secondary narcissists), exists in a particularly singular scene of cruelty, with the image poised somewhere between philosophy and pornography (rendering

[25] Bruder, *William Blake*, pp. 59–79. In *Sade, Fourier, Loyola* (trans. Richard Miller. [New York: Hill & Wang, 1976]), Roland Barthes analyzes the entwined modes of complementary signification in Sade's work, where 'two codes, that of the sentence (oratorical) and that of the figure (erotic), continually relay each other, form one same line' (p. 32), a description that equally applies to the interplay of poetic line and visual figure in *Visions*.

[26] Given Oothoon's vocal assault on her oppressors, this visual mode functions as a subliminal figure, fearful and foreshadowing upon first encounter and confirming and confining upon repeated encounter. A different mode fashioned by necessity occurs on plates 20 and 21 of *The Four Zoas* manuscript, where Blake's scissoring of a page upon which is drawn a patriarchal figure and then writing over the design achieves similar ends. *The Four Zoas by William Blake: A Photographic Facsimile*, eds. Cettina Tramontano Magno and David Erdman (Lewisburg, PA: Bucknell University Press, 1987), pp. 36–7, 134–5.

[27] Julia Kristeva, *Powers of Horror: An Essay on Abjection* (New York: Columbia University Press, 1982), p. 16.

it appropriate for the age of Sade's contemporary works of demented carnality and perverse philosophy).

This reading of the 'textual gaze' intensifies the view of Oothoon's own hermeneutic powers, since she re/cognizes from her foregrounded enclosure the background ideological forces that dictate her own horrors: 'Instead of morn arises a bright shadow, like an eye / In the eastern cloud; instead of night a sickly charnel house (E, 2: p. 47). Oothoon directly denounces—and thereby announces and names—this political unconscious presence on the following page: 'Urizen! Creator of men! Mistaken Demon of heaven' (*VDA*, 8.3, p. 256). Her pronouncement marks the first titular appearance of Blake's complex Zoa of rational control, although the 'Starry King' in the 'Song of Liberty' that concludes *The Marriage* directly leads to this identification. Her denouncement of Urizen, still a future textual event, occurs relatively early in Oothoon's development, serving as a transitional moment from her initial act of self-abasement ('Rend away this defiled bosom that I may reflect / The image of Theotormon on my pure breast' [E, p. 46]) to the conclusion of this initial speech act of self-assertion ('Arise my Theotormon I am pure / Because the night is gone that clos'd me in its deadly black' [E, p. 47]).

Such integral methods and operations work within the entangled fields of semiosis that define the illuminated books. As transition to the 'voice' proper, consider three final images through which Blake registers in the visual field (images given for the eye) attributes of the verbal field (orality and sound given to the ear). For example, while the transition into the work proper on plate four virtually shouts the term 'Visions' in large swash lettering, the design again entangles figures in the letters, with the first image encountered (reading left to right and head to foot) being an imp sounding a vegetative horn. The image calls for an awakening to the abject state of female subjectivity aligned with the enlightened arguments proposed by Mary Wollstonecraft, an echoing sound that passes to the end of the poetic canon.[28] By plate seven, the visual narrative presents an enchained yet nonetheless ascendant Oothoon hovering over Theotormon and mounting her daily argument borne on a tongue-shaped wave almost flame-like in shape.[29]

By the final plate, Oothoon again moves toward the observer (i.e., towards the space of reception), emerging from clouds with arms outspread and having assumed in countenance and bodily position (*sans* beard) the posture of her abuser. Her arms part the clouds as she swims through a brightness that illuminates all in her wake, and she has awakened the daughters, who after

[28] On Oothoon's connection to Wollstonecraft, see Hilton, pp. 69–72.

[29] 'The wave is also a tongue of the sea and thus a visual pun on the human tongue to which Oothoon is confined, unable to take effective action outside of language' (*VDA*, p. 239), although I disagree (see below) with the last clause of this statement.

cowering in fright and night (on plate 10) have lifted up their heads. Oothoon in exultation, with gaze firmly fixed on anyone before the work, exudes a power gained through the appropriation of the strength of her opponents (hence her assumption of the *imago* of the title plate). Oothoon propagates her stolen strengths beyond the text in acts of reading (i.e., she seems now simply to disregard the daughters) that are equally speech acts enacted at the event of reception. Her voice emanates across trans-temporal and trans-cultural dimensions, articulating through shared narrative with the transgressive voice fully embodied as a vehicle of individual and social transformation.[30] The evocation of voice, through the visual field, returns focus to the power of Oothoon's voice, its ability to mimic masculine discourses and use them to destabilize the processes of subject formation promoted through those forms of containment and thereby to transmute them into vehicles of transgression and transformation.[31]

IV.

The title page, frontispiece, and subsequent illustrations tell in imaginary, literal, and symbolic ways Blake's sequential engagements with mental and social systems of oppression binding women and their modes of enforced sexual repression (Piccitto, pp. 84–5), which coincide with years 'pivotal in the history of thinking about the nature, rights, and role of women' (Bruder, *William Blake*, p. 181). Oothoon's explosive and revolutionary discourse systematically occupies similar linguistic layers—the real, symbolic, and imaginary topologies projected by Lacan. Her transgressive vocal assault and its mode of ex/pression (i.e., 'the unconscious desire given voice in the symptom' as an act of counter-repression) provides the vehicle to appropriate the metaphors and modes of the males that victimize her, with the first speech act after her rape being an alarmingly intra-poetic use of the *mise-en-abyme* trope:[32] 'I call with holy voice! King of the sounding air, / Rend away this defiled bosom that I may reflect / The image of Theotormon on my pure transparent breast' (E,

[30] She has, like her distant sister Antigone, performed her liberation against encompassing forms of power through speech acts that 'appropriate the stance and idiom of the one she opposes' (Butler, p. 23).

[31] As Susan Matthews notes, the inauguration of the action of the poem through sexual assault, even though horrific, establishes any 'sexual encounter' as an 'event which precipitates or allows the possibility of change' (p. 150). I disagree, however, that by the end of the poetic event, 'Oothoon's voice lacks a sense of self in its ability to reflect the feelings of others' (p. 147). Susan Matthews, *Blake, Sexuality, and Bourgeois Politeness* (Cambridge: Cambridge University Press, 2011).

[32] Matthew Sharpe, 'Jacques Lacan', in *Internet Encyclopedia of Philosophy*, eds. Bradley Dowden and James Feiser, at http://www.iep.utm.edu/lacweb/.

12.14–16: p. 46). The female voice of righteous indignation turns initially to the self but, once deflected, functions as a weapon arrayed against the *polis* and those masculinist and patriarchal mechanisms through which women are victimized within all political and social forms of subjection.[33] One can hear, here, those 'Tongues in thunderous majesty [who] converse in visionary forms dramatic' that close *Jerusalem* (E, 98: p. 257). Oothoon articulates a song of liberty related to that sung at the close of *The Marriage of Heaven and Hell* but now addressing the plight of 'the Eternal Female' whose groans '[were] heard over all the Earth' (E, p. 44), a (psycho)logical and 'natural' evolution leading from *Thel* through *The Marriage* to the convergent climax of concerns in *Visions*.

The first words attributable to Oothoon form 'The Argument' (plate 3) and are spoken in first-person past tense, establishing the priority of her voice for the work, although sadly expressing a retrospective tragic narrative emblematic of the Blakean state of 'experience'. To an experienced reader, the argument evokes the event imaged at the foot of the title page and its later narration, creating an intra-textual bridge and forcing an integration across reading spacetime. The first words she speaks within the poem, rather than its framing devices, articulate an innocent perspective, voicing the eternal spirit of the curious and searching subjectivity: 'I turn my face to where my whole soul seeks' (E, 4: p. 46). This excitement and optimism are crushed almost immediately with her rape and enchainment as imaged in the title plate and frontispiece, respectively. Bromion brags and blusters, and his comments of conquest, spoken to Theotormon in patriarchal terms of possession ('this harlot'), predictably objectify Oothoon as woman and slave:

> Thy soft American plains are mine, and mine thy north & south
> Stampt with my signet are the swarthy children of the sun: …
> Their daughters worship terrors and obey the violent.
> Now thou maist marry Bromions harlot, and protect the child
> Of Bromions rage, that Oothoon shall put forth in nine moons time[.]
> (E, 1.18–2.2: p. 46)

Blake's well-known passage touches upon virtually every prevailing mental and physical mind-forged shackle imaginable: Bromion pronounces Oothoon a 'harlot'; he associates her state with slavery (i.e., 'the swarthy children of the sun'); he take physical possession of her as a right ('Thy soft American plains

[33] I am indebted to the expansive sense of 'forms' (close to what Blake terms 'systems') and for the articulation of methods for assessing such formal operations broached by Caroline Levine in *Forms: Whole, Rhythm, Hierarchy, Network* (Princeton, NJ: Princeton University Press, 2015), p. xiii.

are mine'); he impregnates her, establishing the continuity of the father's seed; and he gives her to Theotormon ('Now thou maist marry' her).

The topological layers of subjugation provide a rather complete map for the cultural and psychological forces at work in Lacan's symbolic order, 'the primary order' (i.e., Name-of-the-Father, Law, Death, and The Phallus) that 'represents and structures both of the others', the imaginary and the real.[34] When Oothoon 'weeps not' but adopts the 'voice of slaves' and begins to 'howl incessant', she also appropriates the 'holy voice', which initially leads to her self-directed masochism, an unsurprising act given the ideologies of the perspective assumed (E, p. 46). She perfectly embodies her abject state as object, an other (small 'o') functioning as the mirror of male desire and patriarchal control as her 'snowy limbs' are torn by 'Theotormons Eagles' (E, p. 46) to reflect him 'on [her] pure transparent breast' (E, 2: p. 46). She embodies the literal mirror; her presence is doubled as she becomes the *imago* as well, which grants aspects of her agency as she absorbs Theotormon's gaze and, in reflecting back the *imago*, gains discursive control. The eagles obey her; she 'calls with holy voice'; she subjects herself to the pain and torture evocative of Prometheus; and her speech acts (whose impact can be perceived as much in Theotormon's 'severe smile' as in her 'defiled bosom') gain imaginative authority. She achieves, in Steven Goldsmith's fine phrase, 'agency under erasure', a state like Antigone's.[35] In the following line with its overt analogy to nature, Oothoon manifests the dynamic dimension of the physical process by which something 'muddied' by 'beasts grows pure'.

Oothoon has absorbed the language of abusers and written it onto her own body, a painful act of self-determination that wrests discursive control from her rapist and torturer. Thus inscribed, she utters speech acts, articulating a 'howl incessant' anchored in 'holy voice', and the elemental breath of the wind and storm breaks outward across the remainder of the poem. She commands her beloved to 'arise', she asserts her purity, and she proceeds to articulate an acute diagnosis of the primal constraints beneath the cultural and historical conditions of woman that remains relevant to our own moment:

> They told me that the night & day were all that I could see;
> They told me that I had five senses to inclose me up.
> And they inclos'd my infinite brain into a narrow circle.
> And sunk my heart into the Abyss, a red round globe hot burning
> Till all from life I was obliterated and erased. (E, 2.30–4: p. 47)

[34] Lacan, *Speech and Language in Psychoanalysis*, trans. Anthony Wilden (Baltimore, MD and London: Johns Hopkins University Press, 1968), p. 161.

[35] Steven Goldsmith, *Blake's Agitation: Criticism & the Emotions* (Baltimore, MD: Johns Hopkins University Press, 2013), p. 243.

This anaphoric sequence reinforces, in its repetition, the narrowing of female consciousness within language (given what 'They told me'). The third line ('they inclos'd my infinite brain') registers something more material not sounded in language *per se* but anchored in culture more broadly (i.e., education and social instruction). Initially ushered in by the first choral refrain of the daughters, Oothoon's voice builds in intensity like a powerful storm.

V.

Oothoon's evolving poetic revolution fuses the analogical and dialogical with the anagogical, forming a syncretic semiosis grounded in voice and body and aligned with all forms of the material world, building force through form by embracing what Caroline Levine calls 'the intricacies of overlapping literary patterns operating on different scales' (p. 4). The entangled rhetorical and metaphorical tropes operate across varied layers of the natural and achieve a biosemiotic effect, a form of the poetic deeply connected to bodies through the rhythmic core oscillating and vibrating within all material beings. The effects of the poem reflect the impression of a poet's rhythm, although impacted by hidden variables, such as the biorhythmic pulsations of an observer/reader engaged with the text during reception, creating variable patterns of interference not localized but activated across the circuit of initial transmission and subsequent reception.

After an impotent response by Bromion, who clings to the 'absolute certainties of patriarchal restriction', and an uncertain string of questions from Theotormon, 'which suggest he's lost the power of thought', Blake brings Oothoon into prominence with 'perhaps the longest [speech] ever given, by the usually dialogic Blake, to a single character (102 uninterrupted lines)', and as Bruder further observes, Oothoon's voice, once engaged, 'opens with an assault on Urizenic masculinity's demonic construction of identity through likeness ... blasts the masculine abstractions ... and rages against patriarchal limitation with unparalleled ferocity' (Bruder, 'Blake and Gender', p. 143). Her mimicry of Bromion's and Theotormon's anaphoric sequential queries—'And are there other' and 'Tell me what is' respectively—feels like an interrogative mode fused from the shared befuddlement of the masculine confronted with the failure of oppression and repression as effective methods to silence Oothoon's voice that, ironically, empower her.

Male methods provide Oothoon the skeletal discursive structure from which to articulate a countering, transgressive treatise designed to free rather than contain, woven from their own narrowing modes of expression (the question as form of unknowing). The language constantly erodes a singular vision of desire (phallic primacy), where imaginary and real operations are controlled by uniform symbolic mechanisms materialized as a 'uni/verse' (etymologically, 'all' brought under the sway of 'one bend' [or orientation]).[36] The movement from lamentation to assertion unleashes pleas promoting adherence to difference ('How different their eye and ear! how different the world to them!' [E, p. 49]), which provides the impetus for an astute and extended poetic analysis of entangled political, psychological, sexual, and social layers of constraint attributable to the agency of the phallus and its patriarchal materializations in the real:

> What are his nets & gins & traps. & how does he surround himself
> With cold floods of abstraction. And with forests of solitude
> To build him castles and high spires. Where kings and priests may dwell
> Till she who burns in youth. And knows no fixed lot: is bound
> In spells of law to one she loaths: and must she drag the chain
> Of life, in weary lust! Must chilling murderous thoughts. Obscure
> The clear heaven of eternal spring? To bear the wintry rage
> Of a harsh terror driv'n to madness. Bound to hold a rod
> Over her shrinking shoulders all the day: & all the night
> To turn the wheel of false desire: and longings that wake her womb
> To the abhorred birth of cherubs in the human form
> That live a pestilence & die a meteor & are no more.
>
> (E, 5.18–29: p. 49)

This stunning and extended indictment of the social structuration that binds by 'spells of law' a woman 'to one she loaths' and dooms her to 'turn the wheel of false desire' deconstructs the system from within its operations.

In a remarkable textual turn, the echoing of the lack of knowledge begins a figural shift in the interrogative mode toward animal analogies, anchoring the praise of plenitude pursued by Oothoon. Her linguistic shift in symbolic filiation to natural rather than cultural processes highlights analogically the 'unnaturalness' of patriarchal mechanisms of control, the single vision that masks as knowledge:

> Does the whale worship at thy footsteps as the hungry dog?
> Or does he scent the mountain prey, because his nostrils wide

[36] While I find Bruder's arguments definitive, one must recognize the strong counter case argued by Christopher Hobson relative to the need to conform, finally, within the 'poetiscape' to heterosexuality as the norm, making 'the autoerotic or homoerotic action … preparatory to heterosexual initiation' (*Blake and Homosexuality* [New York: Palgrave, 2000], p. 30). Given the echo chamber created by Oothoon's voice and the cave of the ear (the males forced to listen) and the caverns of history (the daughters who actually hear in whatever 'here' they occupy), however, this remains indeterminate relative to process, existing in a dynamic state like that of Schrödinger's cat prior to any act of observation.

Draw in the ocean? Does his eye discern the flying cloud
As the ravens eye? Or does he measure the expanse like the vulture?
(E, 5.33–36: p. 49)

The four-line query of the whale is the first of only three references across the canon (the next two appear in *America a Prophecy* [also 1793]), perhaps registering Blake's knowledge of the brutal industry being perfected in America, another form of colonialism, of the earth itself, reflected in Bromion's rapacity. Oothoon changes perspective, going from the largest creature to some of the smallest (spider and fly) to make the same point—a dynamic difference defines relations in a multitudinous world of interacting energies and entities experienced across the biosemiotic sphere as rhythmic pulsations.

The interrogative mode has limits, since the query expresses an epistemological lack and so limits its efficacy as a counter, yet the transformation of the mode is achieved with subtlety, the mere supplement of a single term ('not'):

Does not the eagle scorn the earth & despise the treasures beneath?
But the mole knoweth what is there, & the worm shall tell it thee.
Does not the worm erect a pillar in the mouldering church yard?
And a palace of eternity in the jaws of the hungry grave
Over his porch these words are written. Take thy bliss O Man!
And sweet shall be thy taste & sweet thy infant joys renew!
(E, 5.39–6.3: p. 49)

Blake/Oothoon achieves the transformation with simplicity, with one word turning the fable inside out, breaking the relentless repetition of anaphora (while creating another such sequence), yet achieving a shift from unknowing to knowledge while returning to animals with prominent symbolic roles in prior works. The addition of 'not' alters the speaking position and adopts a positive state/ment of knowledge through a negative dialectics, an apt formal modification to conclude the contrary mechanisms pursued in earlier works. The animals that fly, dig, and crawl through the closing lines (the eagle, the mole, and the worm) create intra-textual strings that connect Oothoon's poetics of difference to prior concerns for the state of feminine sexuality and subjectivity expressed in works extending back to *Thel*, and they auger other female transgressive discourses to come (e.g., Enitharmon in *Europe a Prophecy*). Here and elsewhere, the words of the worm rule: 'Take thy bliss O Man'.

Once Oothoon's discourse achieves its transgressive oracular power, she immediately directs it towards her primary auditor, Theotormon, exhibiting a growing discursive power that renders him silent through an acute diagnosis of the dis/ease from which masculine sexuality suffers. Although patriarchy objectifies woman, this seeming assertion of sexual potency and social power that reduces the feminine actually suffers from the adoption of constricted and rigid forms of sexual behavior governed by 'modesty' that mutate natural 'infant joys' and 'virgin bliss' into 'the name of whore' and then commodify that 'delight' to 'sell it in the night' (E, 6: p. 49)—literally in prostitution but, more troubling, symbolically in 'the Marriage hearse' that concludes 'London' (E, p. 27). Her indictment of him is direct, expressed with passion and without fear: 'And does my Theotormon seek this hypocrite modesty! / The knowing, artful, secret, fearful, cautious, trembling hypocrite / Then Oothoon is indeed a whore' (E, 6: pp. 49–50). She immediately denounces this position, fixing her eyes instead on 'happy copulation' born in (and by) 'the pleasure of this free born joy', asserting ownership over her beloved ('my Theotormon'). The critique of 'self-denial' fostered by 'religion' as the vehicle that embraces 'reflections of desire' (E, 11: p. 50), as Christopher Hobson and Bruder posit, promotes the self-pleasures of masturbation, and, respectively, since the rule of modesty that contains the feminine simultaneously restrains the masculine, leads to the second verbal assault on the political unconscious of this sexual system of oppression and repression (named Urizen two plates in the past):

> Father of Jealousy, be thou accursed from the earth!
> Why hast thou taught my Theotormon this accursed thing?
> Till beauty fades from off my shoulders darken'd and cast out
> A solitary shadow wailing on the margin of non-entity.
>
> (E, 7.12–15: p. 50)

Oothoon's existence on 'the margins of non-entity' aligns with the daughters she addresses, who occupy the spatio-temporal margins of the poem, and her diagnosis of the dis/ease at the core of cultural control of desire is shared by Lacan: 'Woman cannot be said (*se dire*). Nothing can be said of woman', since she functions as the object subjected within phallic structuration, embodying a 'double' aspect that points beyond the phallus (*Encore*, p. 81).

The following passage, the most discussed and most powerful in the poem and across the canon, shows Oothoon at the high-water mark (i.e., the tongue of ocean upon which she surges above Theotormon discussed previously), crying for a 'Love! Free as the mountain wind', asking 'Can that be Love, that drinks another as a sponge drinks water', and answering her own query: 'Such is self-love that envies all' (E, 7: p. 50). More troubling at a number of levels, Oothoon proposes to 'catch for thee girls', offering to 'lie beside [and] view their wanton play … bliss on bliss with Theotormon' and thereby embody (i.e., perform) a form of love unshaded by 'jealous cloud' (E, p. 50). Her assumption of the center of discourse is accompanied by agency and power akin to her male tormentors, here preparing another scene of instruction that heals one malady (jealousy) but hurts others (girls, probably the daughters of

Albion). She has 'become what [she] beheld' (E, p. 178), the process of identification beneath the Lacanian mirror stage and the Blakean illuminated text alike, assuming the discourse of the other and deploying it against her state of constraint—but with slippage that creates collateral damage.

Oothoon returns to natural analogy, in the closing lines, to contextualize her revolution in poetic language within a biosemiotic environment populated by a plenitude of fauna and flora, a heterological and sentient chorus that 'behold their eternal joy[s]' (E, 8.5: p. 51). Oothoon's final words—appropriately a closing anaphoric sequence—make a final plea to her tormentor (Theotormon): 'Arise you little glancing wings, and sing your infant joy! / Arise and drink your bliss, for every thing that lives is holy!' (E, 8.10–11: p. 51). Theotormon hears her not, since his self-enclosure leaves him 'conversing with shadows dire' (i.e., a dialogue between primary and secondary narcissism), yet Oothoon mounts this argument 'every morning' (E, 8.11–12, p. 51), exhibiting the perseverance of Prometheus but more emblematic, within the horizon of the poem, of the gritty courage of everyday life.

VI.

The sequence of early illuminated works leading to Oothoon's unleashed voice begins within the individual (Thel), expands to the most generic (Eternal Female), and then contracts again, returning to the individual (Oothoon). This process of contraction and expansion becomes the steady state for developing mythologies and textualities alike, as if taking an inward breath that gathers the semiotic exploration of the state of feminine subjectivity and bringing to full maturation the earlier illuminated works in preparation for the subsequent search for a system beyond system, one defined by dialogism and capable of ex/pressing a multiverse in opposition to the constraints of a Urizenic uni-verse. The outward breath of Blake's living canon inspires the critique of this universe in the historical (e.g., *America* and *Europe*) and psychological prophecies (e.g., *The Book of Urizen*) that shape the Lambeth prophecies. The sequential shape of this breathing, then, maps the contours of Blake's evolving model of expanding and contracting consciousness, establishing a rhythm not just in a line or a plate but among the production of discrete works entangled by intra-textual resonances pulsing backward and forward with a remarkable vibrancy. Rather than completely endorsing the view that *Visions* takes up the concerns raised in *Thel* (*VDA*, pp. 228–9), the work seemingly speaks to the broader issues of enslavement raised in Blake's *Marriage* (the work immediately preceding the poetic narrative of Oothoon's circumstances).

The speech act exchanges dialogically performed in the visual field reinforce the multidimensional functions of voice that grows within the verbal field in ways hinted at, but not made explicit, within the title page, until a reading subject completes the work, and it is 'experienced' in a typical Blakean way. The masculine acts and voices have corporeal and linguistic priority, with Bromion proclaiming his ownership through sexual victimization ('Now thou maist marry Bromions harlot, and protect the child / Of Bromions rage' [E, 2.1–2: p. 46]) and Theotormon performing through a secondary, symbolic act of violence control over both, when he 'folded his black jealous waters round the adulterate pair / Bound back to back in Bromion' caves' (E, 2.4–5: p. 46). Oothoon finally speaks after the men have had their way and says, 'howl[ing] incessant' and 'with holy voice, calling Theotormon's Eagles to prey upon her flesh'. In a textual gesture that would satisfy Hegel's sense of actualization, voice takes up residence in the semiotic field of the visual as well as driving the poetics of the verbal. The textuality of the works that follow Oothoon's oracular performance—a poetic event reproduced in Ololon's multidimensional descent to Felpham in *Milton*—finds its voice; its dynamic commitment to dialogism joins what I have elsewhere termed the illuminated textual and helps inform an affective textuality designed to entangle the material fields of creation and reception.

Given her means and methods, Oothoon is certainly a daughter of Antigone, but she equally deserves a seat at the dinner table shared among Ezekiel, Isaiah, and the I-persona in *The Marriage*, since her agency stems from a 'desire of raising other men into a perception of the infinite' and sharing with them an unwillingness to ignore 'genius, or conscience, only for the sake of present ease and gratification' (E, p. 39). Woman functions as the petite object within a masculine economy of desire (as its objects and thus its promise of jouissance), but only so long as ideological constraints enforce silence. Once Oothoon speaks, inaugurating her transformation, she supplants the use and exchange values in preference for an oracular and prophetic agency, something beyond her exchange- and use-oriented male tormentors—with her commitment to life and love (versus love and death) unveiling the primary difference from Antigone. While both women share methods (the assumption of discourse and power located originally with the males), their sought outcome marks their divergent psychological commitments to complementary yet opposed drives (*Eros* versus *Thanatos* in Freudian terms).

As Piccitto recently observed, 'Blake's verbal call' (the interpellation hyperactivated within the illuminated works) provides a mechanism to evoke an affective experience capable of crossing 'the threshold of the imagination [and] finds it pictorial equivalent in the many frontispieces and title pages of the illuminated books' (p. 84), as seen above. As well, the 'call' provides a vocal dimension that supplements the visual, with the dynamic elements performing multiversical speech acts as the semiotic confrontation with forms of symbolic power. In this way, one can say, Oothoon is a more than worthy daughter of Antigone. This dramatic dimension—the performative factor discussed by Hegel and cited periodically in subsequent critical references to Antigone—has long been a discernible aspect of the illuminated books. In the case of the dynamic and mirror image relationship of title page and frontispiece in *Visions of the Daughters of Albion*, Oothoon's analogous resistance has been equally experienced in trans-historical and trans-cultural circumstances and communicated to all daughters of Albion (although her plight is more allegorized yet more personalized given her dual victimization by mutually reinforcing mirrors of male desire and patriarchal authority, Bromion and Theotormon).

Voice as speech—entangled with and thus the embodiment of the mechanics of cognition and defined as a performed poetics of transgression—suggests that the prophetic mode perhaps best serves as the exemplar of the method and its implications for individuals and the collective alike. The diversified forms of speech in *Visions* are enacted through embodiment, performing an ethos of opposition in the face of remorseless opposition (apparent in related Hellenic and Hebraic contexts). At a fundamental level of technique, the poem provides its own exemplum to analyze the ways that Blake 'write[s] the voice', to evoke Michel De Certeau's phrase (and its redeployment by Anna Gibbs).[37] The writing of the voice suits Blake's technique in *Visions*, emerging as an organizing principle in subsequent prophetic books and most especially encompassing the self-annihilative rhetoric of both Ololon and Jerusalem in the final illuminated books. The dramatic deployment of voice against what will become, only a little later in the Lambeth period, the fixed solidity of the metallic books under Urizenic control anchors the primary vehicle of opposition in the Kristevan semiotic as the antidote to the Lacanian tyranny of the symbolic order.

When Oothoon finds her voice, she thereafter moves into a free-flowing form of lamentation that, across the span of its passage, articulates a transgressive poetics of self-assertion and self-determination and establishes the 'rhythm' (Gk. 'flow') of its perennial appeal as a vocalization against tyranny inscribed on the body and victimization etched in the mind. Something elemental and emotional—a powerful vocalization of a local situation yet expressive of

[37] Michel De Certeau, *The Practice of Everyday Life*, trans. S. Rendell (Berkeley: University of California Press, 1984), p. 159. At a primal level, Antigone and Oothoon operate within what De Certeau terms 'the heterological counter-tradition' in its secondary formation, where a discourse 'must critique [an empowered] epistemology from the outside' and which thereby 'runs the risk of relying upon the ethical and the figure of the other' (Godzich, pp. xviii–xix). However, one formal aspect of counter-tradition points to the degree of 'liberation' which 'poetry had achieved'. Gibbs points to a path through the hazardous use of voice configured within heterological discourse capable of avoiding 'naive, unreflective, and untutored' usage through a strategy of 'reversal of this process' that allows voice to function as the vehicle 'to interrogate' discourses of power (p. 223).

a collective trans-historical condition—comes through the voice that stands behind the presentation of speech acts that organize the poem. Oothoon propagates her emblematic and exemplary discursive arguments (hence grounded in exemplification) across time and space to provide instruction to the titular characters, the daughters of Albion, in a mutated process of subject formation that secures presence by penetrating the semi-impermeable membrane of semiosis separating history and myth in the forms of speech that organize the poem.

Visions manifests aspects of Blake's 'affective textuality' in *The Marriage* and *Milton*, works grounded in vibratory functions related to poetic rhythm, although extending to the very 'rhythm of thought' caught in the complementary dimensions of textuality and in the dynamic aspects of voice by which 'progress' is propagated in the work (Knudsen and Stage, p. 11). For this particular work, critical activity has created an especially enriched environment within which to analyze its entangled fields of semiosis, with the title plate and the frontispiece registering the split operations of what Lacan termed 'The eye and the gaze' (and actually delineating their split): 'this is for us the split in which the drive is manifested at the level of the scopic field' (Lacan, *Four Fundamental Concepts*, p. 73). Blake, in the motto to *Visions*, evokes this split as the portal through which any passage into Oothoon's passions must proceed: 'The Eye sees more than the Heart knows' (E, p. 45).[38] With the contestatory voice married in support to the gaze of the text, Blake establishes affect itself as a dimension of the dynamic textual conditions put in play.

Encoded into the semiotic skeletal design, affect assumes local and global functions, including propagation through poetic lamentation, a particular voice standing at the nexus of the historical and mythic later methodized through the fusion of discursive and structural elements that create a feedback loop for female discursive presence, a technique well on display in the works to follow.[39] Affect assumes both discursive and structural presence, becoming the very material conditions for an affective textuality designed to establish a field of force within which numerous forms of consciousness collide. The dynamic design (incorporating verbal, visual, and varied interlinear intrusions) encodes within the illuminated process a dialogic imperative that functions

[38] For an extended analysis, please see my 'The Horrors of Subjectivity'.

[39] The type of experiment referenced would be that described by Knudsen and Stage, quoting Noortje Marres: 'The inventive experiment *creat[es]* either a) *artificial environments (e.g., a laboratory) in which tests of various sorts are conducted to develop, falsify/verify or discuss hypotheses,* or b) *natural everyday environments (e.g., peoples' homes, classrooms or the street) that the researcher, designer, artist or social activist influences or modifies in order to investigate participants' emotional and affective responses to a particular stimulation* (Marres, 2012)' (p. 11, emphasis added).

through forms of emotive interpellation (both imagistic and narrativistic).[40] This path through (but not to) jouissance provides a passage for the passions engaged in a process of embodiment, with a periodic rupture of the poetic into the symbolic (via the semiotic) forcing a restructuration of subjectivity and, therein, a reconditioning of social praxis at the point of delivery, the rhythmic resonances within and without acts of articulation and reception.[41]

Bibliography

Albu, Cristina. *Mirror Affect: Seeing Self, Observing Others in Contemporary Art.* Minneapolis: Minnesota University Press, 2016.

Althusser, Louis. *Lenin and Philosophy and Other Essays*, trans. Ben Brewster. New York: Monthly Review Press, 1971.

Barthes, Roland. *Sade, Fourier, Loyola*, trans. Richard Miller. New York: Hill & Wang, 1976.

Beaney, Tara. 'Beautiful Death: The Nineteenth-Century Fascination with *Antigone*'. *Opticon*, 1826: 7 (Autumn 2009), pp. 1–8, at http://www.ucl.ac.uk/opticon1826/archive/issue7/Articles/Article_Tara_Antigone.pdf.

Blake, William. *The Complete Poetry and Prose of William Blake*, ed. David Erdman. Garden City, NJ: Anchor/Doubleday, 1982.

——. *Visions of the Daughters of Albion*, eds. Morris Eaves, Robert N. Essick, and Joseph Viscomi. In *Blake's Illuminated Books*, gen. ed. David Bindman. 6 vols. Princeton, NJ: Princeton University Press, 1993, 3: pp. 225–86.

Bracher, Mark. 'Rouzing the Faculties: Lacanian Psychoanalysis and the Marriage of Heaven and Hell in the Reader'. In *Critical Paths: Blake and the Argument of Method.* Durham, NC and London: Duke University Press, 1987, pp. 168–203.

Bruder, Helen P. 'Blake and Gender Studies'. In *Palgrave Advances in William Blake Studies*, ed. Nicholas M. Williams. Houndsmill and New York: Palgrave Macmillan, 2006, pp. 132–66.

——. *William Blake and the Daughters of Albion*. Houndsmill and New York: Macmillan Press and St. Martin's Press, 1997.

Butler, Judith. *Antigone's Claim: Kinship Between Life and Death.* New York: Columbia University Press, 2000.

Connolly, Tristanne J. *William Blake and the Body.* Houndsmill, Basingstoke, and New York: Palgrave Macmillan, 2002.

[40] The movement towards affective textualities is occasioned by the thinking emergent within neuroscience, which has begun to articulate an 'affective neuroscience' relative to the recognition that 'emotional processes, including subjectively experienced feelings, do, in fact, play a key role in the causal chain of events' (Jaak Panksepp, *Affective Neuroscience: The Foundations of Human and Animal Emotions* [Oxford: Oxford University Press, 1998], p. 14). This type of thinking provides methods by which to analyze the material operations of the Blakean text.

[41] See Lussier, 'Affective'.

De Certeau, Michel. *Heterologies; Discourse on the Other*, trans. Brian Massumi. *Theory and History of Literature*, vol. 17. Minneapolis: University of Minnesota Press, 1986.

——. *The Practice of Everyday Life*, trans. S. Rendell. Berkeley: University of California Press, 1984.

Editors of the Encyclopedia Britannica. 'Theatre of Cruelty'. *Encyclopedia Britannica.* 6 March 2016, at https://www.britannica.com/topic/Theatre-of-Cruelty.

Frye, Northrop. *The Anatomy of Criticism: Four Essays.* Princeton, NJ: Princeton University Press, 1957.

——. *Fearful Symmetry: A Study of William Blake.* Princeton, NJ: Princeton University Press, 1947.

George, Diana Hume. *Blake and Freud.* Ithaca, NY: Cornell University Press, 1980.

Gibbs, Anna. 'Writing as Method: Attunement, Resonance, and Rhythm'. In *Affective Methodologies: Developing Cultural Research Strategies for the Study of Affect*, eds. Britta Timm Knudsen and Carsten Stage. Houndsmill and New York: Palgrave Macmillan, 2015, pp. 222–36.

Godzich, Wlad. 'The Further Possibility of Knowledge'. In Michel De Certeau. *Heterologies: Discourse on the Other*, trans. Brian Massumi. *Theory and History of Literature*, vol. 17. Minneapolis: Minnesota University Press, 1986, pp. vii–xxi.

Goldsmith, Steven. *Blake's Agitation: Criticism & the Emotions.* Baltimore, MD: Johns Hopkins University Press, 2013.

Hegel, G.W.F. *Phenomenology of Spirit*, trans. A.V. Miller. Oxford: Oxford University Press, 1977.

Hilton, Nelson. 'An Original Story'. In *Unnam'd Forms: Blake and Textuality*, eds. Nelson Hilton and Thomas A. Vogler. Berkeley: University of California Press, 1986, pp. 69–104.

Hobson, Christopher Z. *Blake and Homosexuality.* New York: Palgrave, 2000.

Honig, Bonnie. *Antigone, Interrupted.* Cambridge: Cambridge University Press, 2013.

Irigaray, Luce. *This Sex Which Is Not One*, trans. Catherine Porter. Cornell, NY: Cornell University Press, 1985.

Knudsen, Britta Timm and Carsten Stage, eds. *Affective Methodologies: Developing Cultural Research Strategies for the Study of Affect.* New York: Palgrave Macmillan, 2015.

Kristeva, Julia. *Powers of Horror: An Essay on Abjection.* New York: Columbia University Press, 1982.

——. *Revolution in Poetic Language*, trans. Margaret Waller. New York: Columbia University Press, 1984.

——. 'The System and the Speaking Subject'. In *The Kristeva Reader*, ed. Toril Moi. New York: Columbia University Press, 1986, pp. 24–33.

Lacan, Jacques. *The Ethics of Psychoanalysis, 1959–1960. The Seminar of Jacques Lacan, Book VII*, ed. Jacques-Alain Miller, trans. Dennis Porter. New York: W.W. Norton, 1997.

——. *The Four Fundamental Concepts of Psychoanalysis*, ed. Jacques-Alain Miller, trans. Alan Sheridan. New York: W.W. Norton, 1981.

——. *On Feminine Sexuality: The Limits of Love and Knowledge, 1972–3. Encore: The Seminar of Jacques Lacan, Book XX*, ed. Jacques-Alain Miller, trans. Bruce Fink. New York: W.W. Norton, 1998.

——. *Speech and Language in Psychoanalysis*, trans. Anthony Wilden. Baltimore, MD: Johns Hopkins University Press, 1968.

Levine, Caroline. *Forms: Whole, Rhythm, Hierarchy, Network*. Princeton, NJ: Princeton University Press, 2015.

Lussier, Mark. 'Affective Textualities: Restructuring Subjectivity in Blake's *Marriage*'. In *Romanticism and Affect Studies. A Romantic Circles Praxis Volume*, ed. Seth T. Reno. *Romantic Circles* (May 2018), at https://www.rc.umd.edu/praxis/affect/praxis.2018.affect.lussier.html.

——. 'The Horrors of Subjectivity/The *Jouissance* of Immanence'. In *Blake's Gothic Imagination: Bodies of Horror*, eds. Chris Bundock and Elizabeth Effinger. Manchester: Manchester University Press, 2018, pp. 213–34.

Magno, Cettina Tramontano and David Erdman, eds. *The Four Zoas by William Blake: A Photographic Facsimile*. Lewisburg, PA: Bucknell University Press, 1987.

Massumi, Brian. *Parables for the Virtual: Movement, Affect, Sensation*. Durham, NC: Duke University Press, 2002.

Matthews, Susan. *Blake, Sexuality, and Bourgeois Politeness*. Cambridge: Cambridge University Press, 2011.

Panksepp, Jaak. *Affective Neuroscience: The Foundations of Human and Animal Emotions*. Oxford: Oxford University Press, 1998.

Piccitto, Diane. *Blake's Drama: Theatre, Performance, and Identity in the Illuminated Books*. London & New York: Palgrave Macmillan, 2014.

Rose, Jacqueline. 'Introduction – II'. In *Feminine Sexuality: Jacques Lacan and the école freudienne*, eds. Juliet Mitchell and Jacqueline Rose, trans. Jacqueline Rose. New York: W.W. Norton, 1982, pp. 27–57.

Sharpe, Matthew. 'Jacques Lacan'. In *Internet Encyclopedia of Philosophy*, eds. Bradley Dowden and James Feiser, at http://www.iep.utm.edu/lacweb/, accessed November 2017.

Shelley, Percy Bysshe. *Shelley's Poetry and Prose*, eds. Donald H. Reiman and Neil Fraistat. New York: W.W. Norton, 2002.

Sophocles. *Antigone*, trans. Ian Johnson. Arlington, VA. Richer Resources Publications, 2007.

Index

Printed and bound by CPI Group (UK) Ltd, Croydon, CR0 4YY

02/03/2023

03196679-0002